Studies on Islam

Studies on Islam

Translated and Edited by
MERLIN L. SWARTZ

New York Oxford
OXFORD UNIVERSITY PRESS
1981

Library of Congress Cataloging in Publication Data
Main entry under title:
Studies on Islam.
Includes index.
Contents: Henninger, J. Pre-Islamic Bedouin religion—
Rodinson, M. A critical survey of modern studies on Muhammad.—
Fueck, J. The originality of the Arabian prophet. [etc.]
1. Islam—History—Addresses, essays, lectures.
I. Swartz, Merlin L., 1933–
BP55.S87 297'.09 80-12573
ISBN 0-19-502716-7 ISBN 0-19-502717-5 (pbk.)

Printed in the United States of America

TO MY PARENTS

Preface

The studies that constitute this volume are presented here for the first time in English translation. They were published originally in French and German, and represent the work of scholars whose contributions to the field of Islamic studies have received international recognition. These studies, confined for the most part to early and medieval Islam, treat a wide range of topics and problems. They deal with the history and culture of pre-Islamic Arabia; the life and teaching of Muhammad; Islamic Law; Tradition; Sufism; Hanbalism; and Islamic Orthodoxy in various of its aspects. Although no neat scheme of classification is possible, in general these studies fall into two rather broad categories. The first group constitutes what might be characterized as studies of a secondary nature. They trace the development of the modern, critical study of Islam in its various branches, summarize the present state of our knowledge, and isolate problematic areas for further investigation and reflection. The studies by Henninger (I), Rodinson (II), and Caspar (VII) fall into this category. The second group consists of what might be described as primary studies. That is, they focus on Islam directly (as opposed to the first group of studies which are more properly studies of the study of Islam) and are concerned with particular problems and issues in Islamic history. The studies of the second group quite naturally reflect the methods, orientations, and views of their authors. The contributions by Fueck (III and IV), Goldziher (V and VIII), Massignon (VI), and Makdisi (IX) belong to the second category. In contrast to the studies of the first group, all of which were written during the last decade and a half, those of the second group appeared over a period of some sixty years. Though the earlier studies of this latter group should be read in the light of more recent research, they may still be regarded as important contributions to the field of Islamic studies and therefore read with considerable profit. It should also be pointed out that apart from Goldziher (VIII), all of the studies contained in this volume were translated in full. Unfortunately, the difficulty and cost of printing Arabic made it necessary to delete the Arabic texts quoted by Goldziher. In any case, the substance of the study was not affected.

The translation and publication of this volume would certainly not have been possible without the assistance and encouragement of many persons, and I should like to express my deep gratitude to each of them. The imperfections and inadequacies of the work, however, are entirely my own. I owe a special word of thanks to Maxime Rodinson who not only checked the whole of my translation of his study, but also revised portions of the text and substantially expanded the notes at a number of points. I should like to thank Herbert Mason who generously made available to me his translation of chapter XIII of Massignon's *La Passion de Husayn Ibn Mansūr Hallāj* (Paris, 1975). I am also grateful to George Makdisi who kindly consented to the translation of his lectures on Hanbalism and who reviewed my translation of them in its entirety.

To those who gave generously of their time to check my translations I am in special debt: to Ilse Lichtenstadter, Robert Dankoff, Marianna Forde, and Gisela Lincoln. For their painstaking effort I am most grateful. I wish to express my special thanks to Rebecca Low and James Dutton for their meticulous care in the typing of a very difficult manuscript.

Finally, I should like to express my appreciation to The University Professors Program of Boston University whose generous financial support made this undertaking possible.

Bedford, Massachusetts M. S.
July 18, 1979

Sources and Acknowledgments

I am grateful to the publishers and editors of the following publications for permission to translate and publish the studies that constitute this volume:

I "Pre-Islamic Bedouin Religion" by Joseph Henninger, translated from "La Religion bedouine préislamique," *L'antica società beduina,* ed. F. Gabrieli (Rome: Instituto di Studi Orientali, 1959), pp. 115–40.

II "A Critical Survey of Modern Studies on Muhammad" by Maxime Rodinson, translated from "Bilan des études mohammediennes," *Revue Historique,* 229 (1963), pp. 169–220.

III "The Originality of the Arabian Prophet" by J. Fueck, translated from "Die Originalität des arabischen Propheten," *Zeitschrift der Deutschen Morgenländischen Gesellschaft,* 90(1936), pp. 509–25.

IV "The Role of Traditionalism in Islam" by J. Fueck, translated from "Die Rolle des Traditionalismus in Islam,' *Zeitschrift der Deutschen Morgenländischen Gesellschaft,* 93(1939), pp. 1–32.

V "Catholic Tendencies and Particularism in Islam" by Ignaz Goldziher, translated from "Katholische Tendenz und Partikularismus im Islam" *Beiträge zur Religionswissenschaft,* *I (Jahrgang 1913/1914), Heft 2 (Stockholm-Leipzig), pp. 115–42.

VI "The Juridical Consequences of the Doctrines of Al-Ḥallāj" by Louis Massignon, translated from "Les Conséquences juridiques; et les objections adressées à cette doctrine," chapter XIII of *La Passion de Husayn Ibn Manṣūr Ḥallāj* (Paris, 1975), volume III, pp. 235–58.

VII "Muslim Mysticism: Tendencies in Recent Research" by R. Caspar, translated from "La Mystique musulmane: recherches et tendences," *Revue de l'Institut des Belles Lettres Arabes (Tunis),* 25(1962), pp. 271–89.

VIII "The Attitude of Orthodox Islam Toward the 'Ancient Sciences,' " by Ignaz Goldziher, translated from "Stellung der alten islamischen Orthodoxie zu den antiken Wissenschaften," *Abhandlungen der Königlich Preussischen Akademie der Wissenschaft,* Jahrgang 1915, no. 8(Berlin, 1916), pp. 3–46.

IX "Hanbalite Islam" by George Makdisi, translated from "L'Islam Hanbalisant," originally delivered as lectures at the Collège de France in December 1969, and subsequently published in the *Revue des Études Islamiques,* 42(1974), pp. 211–44; 43(1975), pp. 45–76.

Abbreviations Used in Notes

AION	*Annali dell' Institute Orientali di Napoli*
AJSL	*American Journal of Semitic Languages and Literatures*
BASOR	*Bulletin of the American School of Oriental Research*
BEO	*Bulletin des Études Orientales*
BO	*Bibliotheca Orientalis*
BSOAS	*Bulletin of the School of Oriental and African Studies*
EI	*Encyclopaedia of Islam* (first edition).
EI^2	*Encyclopaedia of Islam* (second edition).
GAL	*Geschichte des arabischen Litteratur*
GAS	*Geschichte des arabischen Schrifttums*
IBLA	*Revue de l'Institut des Belles Lettres Arabes à Tunis*
JAOS	*Journal of the American Oriental Society*
JRAS	*Journal of the Royal Asiatic Society*
MIDEO	*Mélanges de l'Institut Dominicain d'Études Orientales du Caire*
OLZ	*Orientalistische Literaturzeitung*
RB	*Revue Biblique*
REI	*Revue des Études Islamiques*
REJ	*Revue des Études Juives*
RHR	*Revue de l'histoire des religions*
SWBA	*Sitzungsberichte der Akademie der Wissenschaften*
WZKM	*Wiener Zeitschrift für die Kunde des Morgenlandes*
ZDMG	*Zeitschrift der Deutschen morgenländischen Gesellschaft*

Contents

Studies on Islam

I

Pre-Islamic Bedouin Religion

JOSEPH HENNINGER

Introduction

To describe the religion of pre-Islamic Arabia, and especially the pre-Islamic *Bedouin* religion, is no less difficult a task than portraying ancient Bedouin society, and that precisely because of serious lacunae in our documentation. It was with good reason that J. Wellhausen entitled his book on the subject, *Reste arabischen Heidentums* (*Remnants of Arab Heathendom*).[1] Cuneiform literature, the Old Testament, and the classical authors (Greek as well as Latin) throw very little light on religious phenomena in ancient Arabia. It is only the Byzantine, Syriac, and especially the Arab writers (all from a somewhat later period) who furnish more detailed information, although it is hardly systematic or complete.[2] It is not surprising, therefore, that no attempt appears to have been made in Europe before the seventeenth century to publish monograph-length studies on pre-Islamic religion, because of this lack of relevant documents. Since the classical and biblical references were too few and the cuneiform inscriptions still unknown, it was impossible to consider undertaking such a project before the Arabic sources became at least partially accessible in the West. It is true that as early as the tenth century, Arabic works were translated into Latin or into other European languages in Spain. First to be translated were treatises on philosophy, astronomy, mathematics, medicine, etc. Works on the Quran as well as books dealing with the religion of Islam followed. Information on pre-Islamic Arabia is to be found for the most part in works by Muslim historians, traditionists, and jurists. These are works that did not come to the attention of Christian Europe until the Renaissance, and then only gradually.[3]

The first to describe pre-Islamic religion *ex professo* was Edward Pococke, in his *Specimen historiae Arabum* (Oxford, 1649).[4] After an interval of almost two centuries, G. Bergmann published his dissertation (1834) on pre-Islamic Arabic religion,[5] certainly a work of merit for its time, but soon made obsolete by the works of E. Osiander (1853),[6] L. Krehl (1863),[7] and especially those of J. Wellhausen, the most important of which has already been mentioned, the *Reste arabischen Ḥeidentums*, published for the first time in 1887.[8] In it Wellhausen drew primarily on the *Kitāb al-Asnām* (*The Book of Idols*) of Ibn al-Kalbī, a work known at that time only through quotations in Yāqūt's geographical dictionary.[8a] In his *Lectures on the Religion of the Semites*, first published in 1889, W. R. Smith contributed to our understanding of pre-Islamic religion through explanations that were largely speculative. For his factual data he relied on Wellhausen's work.[9] Much the same may be said of the work of M.-J. Lagrange[10] who, like W. R. Smith, made a number of valuable contributions to an understanding of the religions of other Semitic peoples. Th. Nöldeke, on the other hand, advanced our knowledge in the field by his critical scholarship[11] and also by an important article in which he summarized the results of research up to that point.[12]

Toward the end of the nineteenth century and on into the twentieth, South-Arabic and proto-Arabic epigraphy (entirely absent from the works of Wellhausen) was taken more and more into consideration. Although not particularly relevant to the study of the nomadic peoples, D. Nielsen from 1904 onwards made use of epigraphic evidence as a basis for reconstructing an astral religion common to proto-Semitic peoples and thus also attributable to Arab Bedouin. This much too speculative theory met with strong opposition.[13] More reliable studies followed the discovery of Ibn al-Kalbī's *Kitāb al-Aṣnām,* published in 1913 in Cairo by Ahmad Zakī Pacha,[14] later translated into German and English,[15] and referred to in numerous articles.[16]

Credit must be given to G. Ryckmans for producing an important survey in his monograph, *Les Religions arabes préislamiques*, first published in 1947.[17] He made extensive use of the expanding corpus of epigraphic material while carefully avoiding Nielsen's dubious theories. More recently, in his works on the religions and social organization of pre-Islamic Arabia,[18] J. Chelhod attempted to present an overall picture of pre-Islmaic religion. Though debatable in some respects, his work is essentially sound. Finally one will find discussions of varying lengths dealing with the religious situation of pre-Islamic Arabia in introductions to biographies of Muhammad[19] and to monographs on Islam.[20]

Arab and Bedouin Religion

The sheer volume of this literature would seem to contradict the remark made earlier that the documentation is meager and that it is thus difficult to paint a complete picture of pre-Islamic Bedouin religion. The difficulty, however, is real. Works dealing with this subject contain a large number of inferences (more or less justifiable) by which the authors have attempted to compensate for the lacunae in the existing data. On the other hand, scholars frequently speak of Arabs or even Semites without always distinguishing between nomads and sedentary peoples.[21] In general, however, most of the authors do differentiate clearly between the more developed civilizations of South Arabia and those in other parts of the peninsula.[22] More precisely than his predecessors, G. Ryckmans makes a tripartite distinction between central Arabia (where there are no inscriptions), northern Arabia (important for its Lihyānite, Thamūdic, and Safaitic inscriptions), and southern Arabia (known primarily through its inscriptions).[23] But even considering central Arabia by itself, we often have great difficulty distinguishing clearly between the religious practices of the nomads and those of the settled peoples.

One might be tempted to think that it is possible to make progress in this area by giving careful attention to the information provided, for example, by Ibn al-Kalbī. He often says, "Such and such a tribe worshipped such and such a god." One might suppose therefore that one need only divide the tribes into nomadic and settled. But these indications are often of little value in solving the question at hand, for many of the tribes were partly nomadic, partly settled, and the nomads often maintained a close symbiotic relationship with one or more oases, which also served as their religious centers. It has been shown that the priests or guardians of the sanctuary frequently belonged to another tribe which had emigrated and that "priestly" families tended to remain fixed.[24] What we know of the religious practices of pre-Islamic Arabia has to do primarily with the cultic centers located at oases, to which the Bedouins came as pilgrims, associating themselves with the religious practices of the settled groups.[25] (There were also, however, portable sanctuaries, and to H. Lammens goes the credit for having drawn attention to this very important fact.)[26]

Theories concerning the relationship between the religion of the settled peoples and that of the Bedouin reflect two tendencies which are not, however, always mutually exclusive. One group of scholars begins with the assumption that the nomads were more or less indifferent[27] and unoriginal in matters of religion, and that their gods were *borrowed from more advanced civilizations*.[28] The other school of thought holds that the nomads represent *a more primitive form of Semitic religion*. The most extreme form of the first tendency was found in the pan-Babylonian school at the beginning of this century, [29] though its veiws have since been generally abandoned. If C. E. Dubler has somewhat more recently gone back to H. Winckler[30] it is only to draw on a few details of the latter's ideas. In any case, the Babylonian influence, whether strong or weak, was felt primarily among the settled Arabs and reached the Bedouin only indirectly. In certain respects, therefore, one is brought back to W. Caskel's view regarding influences within Arabia.[31]

We turn now to a consideration of the other tendency which considers the Bedouin religion to be *older* than that of the settled peoples. It assumes an evolution from the less developed to the more developed. What the starting point was differs considerably from theory to theory.

1. According to some, it was an elementary form of *fetishism*, the worship of stones and similar objects; already certain Greek writers had pointed out that Arabs worshipped stones.[32]

2. Another view which originated in the field of Semitic studies under the influence of E. B. Tylor and gained recognition was that of *animism*. According to this theory, in the most primitive phases of the development of religion there were no gods bearing distinct personalities, but only spirits, that is, collective and anonymous beings. The *jinn* are interpreted as representing this primitive phase, and the origin of a belief in them is often attributed to the Bedouin, whereas the settled people are credited with the creation of individual gods. Wellhausen became the champion of this theory[33] which flourished most vigorously at the end of the nineteenth century. Indeed, in spite of criticism[34] it still has a loyal following today.[35]

3. A third though less important theory, *manism,* proposed that ancestors, not nature spirits, were the predecessors of the gods; and certainly ancestor-worship existed among pre-Islamic Bedouin.[36]

4. Recently another theory has been advanced, suggesting that religion

began with *le sacré impersonnel*, a force not yet personified. According to J. Chelhod, this impersonal force was still too diffused to constitute a true object of worship.[37]

5. We will not repeat here the details of W. R. Smith's *totemic* theory which attempts to explain both religious and social phenomena in terms of totemism.[38]

6. According to D. Nielsen, the starting point of the religion of the Semitic nomads was marked by the *astral triad*, Sun-Moon-Venus, the moon being more important for the nomads and the sun more important for the settled tribes.[39]

7. Finally, some have considered the oldest form of the Semitic religion to be a fairly pure *monotheism*. M.-J. Lagrange's claim: "El, the common, original, and probably only god of the Semites" is well known.[40] W. Schmidt adopted this view on the basis of a much more extensive documentation dealing with other pastoral nomadic peoples.[41] He held that the same belief also existed among the ancient Semitic nomads in addition to the pre-Islamic Bedouin Arabs.[42] C. Brockelmann has published a short but important study on this question.[43]

In order to assess these theories, it will first be necessary to give a purely descriptive account of pre-Islamic Bedouin religion as we are able to observe it immediately prior to the rise of Islam. This can be done only on a provisional basis, however. Other aspects of pre-Islamic Arabia remain to be studied in greater depth, and these may later oblige me to revise some of my conclusions.

Pre-Islamic Bedouin Religion[44]

We will not take into consideration here the influences of foreign religions such as Christianity which had won many followers in Arabia, even among the nomads.[45] Judaism,[46] Parseeism, and Manichaeism[47] on the other hand do not seem to have won many converts outside the sedentary communities.

Attempting now to describe what one may safely call *autochthonous* Bedouin religion, I will first discuss the superior beings they worshipped and then go on to describe their practices and cultic personnel. But first, one more general remark: it has become quite common to speak of the *religious indifference of the Bedouins*.[48] This view is not entirely without justification. In comparison with South Arabia where a very large body of data bears directly on the religious life, Bedouin Arabia seems to furnish very little evidence in this area. However, I think that certain qualifications are in order. First one must recognize that the Bedouin were never particularly zealous in the practice of Islam, which is not surprising in view of the fact that Islam is markedly urban in character.[49] As for the pre-Islamic Bedouin, one must also take into account the fact that their moral ideal of *muruwwa* ("virility") had no religious character.[50] Nevertheless, to conclude from this a total absence of religious sentiment is to go too far. When scholars use pre-Islamic poetry as a basis for this judgment, they make rather generous use of the argument from silence. One must not forget the rigid and conventional character of pre-Islamic poetry in the centuries immediately preceding the birth of Islam, narrowly limited as it was in its choice of subjects. It is for this reason, very probably, that pre-Islamic poetry does not reflect all aspects of contemporary life.[51]

In order to form a judgment on this point, let us observe some of the more concrete expressions of Bedouin religion.

1. One detail which already impressed the Greek authors was the role played by *sacred stones,*[52] a phenomenon that they interpreted as a worship of raw and unpolished stones, that is to say, fetishism, regarded as the oldest and crudest form of religion. However, the scientific study of religion has long since rejected the theory that accorded to fetishism such a place of honor. In fact what is customarily called fetishism is not an independent phenomenon. The material object is not venerated for itself but rather as the dwelling of either a personal being (god, spirit) or a force.[53] Especially in the area of Semitic beliefs, more recent research has led to a conclusion which R. Dussaud summarizes in his latest book: "One must realize that it is not to the stone itself that the worshipper gives his adoration, but to the god which it contains. . . . The term 'litholatry' therefore expresses a false idea and is based on a total lack of understanding of the rites."[54] In addition one must ask whether the religious significance of sacred rocks and stones arose among nomads who, we now know, possessed portable sanctuaries,[55] rather than among settled peoples who tended to worship concrete and stationary objects existing within a particular locality.[56] In my view it would therefore not be justifiable to consider this "stone worship" as a characteristic of Bedouin religion except in the sense defined by Dussaud, in which case it applies equally to the sedentary peoples.

2. One might perhaps object that the Bedouin were not yet capable of conceiving a personal god, that they were at an earlier stage which had

not yet moved beyond the *sacré impersonnel,* or at least the collective and anonymous phenomenon of the *jinn.*

This compels us to consider the role of these spirits in the religion of the pre-Islamic Bedouin. The persistence in the Quran of a belief in the *jinn* and the testimony of pre-Islamic as well as Islamic literature adequately demonstrate its importance at the beginning of the seventh century. But it will be necessary to define the role of this belief more precisely.

Wellhausen has rightly observed that these spirits which were thought to haunt desolate, dingy, and especially dark places in the desert were feared, that it was thought necessary to protect oneself against them, but that they were hardly the object of a true cult.[57] From this he drew the conclusion that these spirits had first to be elevated to the level of divinities in order to become objects of worship. Though there may be some truth in this assumption, the view that polydemonism everywhere preceded belief in divinities and that all gods are only spirits elevated to a higher rank, has been increasingly called into question by the science of comparative religion.[58]

It is often assumed that belief in the *jinn* who were thought to dwell in the desert originated with the Bedouin and was passed from them to the settled tribes. This assumption does not seem to me to be well founded. The Bedouin who are familiar with the desert feel much less fear there than do village or city dwellers who regard this unknown region as terrifying and who imagine that all sorts of monsters and demons dwell there. This tendency existed already in the Ancient East.[59] And there is another fact that deserves attention: among Arab peoples today, belief in spirits is much more intense among the agricultural population than among the Bedouin.[60] It is further worth noting that, according to W. F. Albright who bases his ideas on certain facts already established by Th. Nöldeke and M. Lidzbarski, the word *jinn* is not Arabic but derived from Aramaic. Aramaic-speaking Christians used the term to designate pagan gods reduced to the status of demons. He concludes from this that the *jinn* themselves were introduced into Arabic folklore only late in the pre-Islamic period.[61] However that may be,[62] one must reckon seriously with this possibility, for it is supported by other observations of detail.[63] Even if one accepts an *autochthonous* pre-Christian animism among the Bedouin (which seems reasonable to me), this animism could have been reinforced by contributions from sedentary Arabs, and one should not see in it either the core or the root of the pre-Islamic Bedouin religion. The possibility of the secondary diffusion even of beliefs and practices which one would prefer to designate as very primitive is not purely theoretical. We have a clear example of it in the spread of *Zār* ceremonies (with their ideology) into Egypt and Arabia. This diffusion which occurred only since the nineteenth century was effected by African slaves.[64] We now know that what is "primitive" in the sense of a value judgment is not necessarily so in the chronological sense.

3. There are more numerous indications of the existence of a cult of ancestors. Here we are undoubtedly dealing with an indigenous phenomenon. Proof of this is to be seen in the extensive diffusion of this cult even among Bedouin in more recent times, a fact that cannot be attributed to Islam whose principles are opposed to it. (In border areas this cult more nearly approximates Islam through the fact that the ancestor has been elevated to the rank of *walī* or Muslim saint.)[65] For pre-Islamic Arabia, explicit evidence is not lacking. It has not been sufficiently established that the dead generally were regarded as powerful, superhuman beings. They appear rather as beings deprived of protection, needing the charity of the living. This is why sacrifices for the dead in general do not seem to signify a cult of the dead but rather a continuation of social obligations beyond the grave. On the other hand ancestors, that is to say, especially the eponymous heroes of the tribe (as well as certain other celebrated heroes, chiefs, and warriors), were an object of real veneration. People not only slew animals and made libations by their tombs but also erected stone structures as they did at the sanctuaries of the local gods. Like the santuaries these graves were places of refuge.[66] These are instances of a real cult; moreover, this veneration of the ancestor reflects a social organization which assigned a great deal of importance to genealogy. It is difficult to understand J. Chelhod's remark that the sacred remained too diffused to coalesce into a clearly defined cultic object.[67] For the Bedouin the hero was (in my view) a rather concrete figure. If it does not appear so to us, it is because we know very little about the ancestor traditions within each tribe. Furthermore, the transition from tribal ancestor to *tribal god* does not seem to me too difficult. Although it would be going too far to see this as the origin of all individual divinities, one may admit that some of them were originally only ancestors and heroes, wrapped in legends, and slowly elevated to the status of deity.

4. Let us now examine these *local divinities,* which Muslim authors call "idols" (*aṣnām*) or "companions" (*shurakā'*)—supposedly companions mistakenly associated with Allāh—local divinities because their cult was restricted to a certain place or to a particular tribe. In most cases we have

very little information about them. We scarcely know their names or the places where they were worshipped (and often not even the real name but a surname meaning, for example, "lord of such and such a place"). The myths which might have been able to illuminate the character of these gods are almost entirely lost.[68] In view of this one can see why it is difficult to decide in each case whether the god in question owes its origin to the Bedouin or to sedentary peoples. It is undeniable that the Bedouin often borrowed gods from the latter but, on the other hand, one cannot exclude the possibility that the Bedouin also had their own gods, as in the case of a god called after the name of a mountain.

The mass of these gods presents a chaotic picture (it does not seem justifiable to me to speak of a pantheon).[69] In trying to substantiate certain data regarding their origin, one is hardly able to go beyond hypotheses. Those which I have already mentioned all seem to me to contain some element of truth. Among these gods there may be some that were originally *jinn,* mythical ancestors or legendary heroes, elevated little by little to the rank of god. On the other hand, some of the gods developed directly from the personification of natural forces (in Quzaḥ, for example, one may still discern the features of a storm god).[70] It should not be thought, however, that these gods must first have passed through a spirit or demon stage, and that celestial beings are posterior to earth spirits.[71] Pre-Islamic Arabic stellar myths (which are, at least in part, Bedouin in origin)[72] prove that the sky was studied and that stars also were personified. To what degree were the stars the object of real worship? That is a separate question, which we will look at now.

5. The importance of *astral divinities* in central Arabia has been exaggerated by pan-Babylonian theories and those of D. Nielsen. Certainly they dominated the religion of South Arabia, but not of central Arabia. The information given by several later Muslim authors on the worship of certain planets and fixed stars is not very well founded except for the cult of the Pleiades which arose through north Semitic influences.[73] The three great goddesses venerated at Mecca by the Quraish (and by several other tribes), mentioned in the Quran as "daughters of Allāh" (in the opinion of inhabitants of Mecca), al-Lāt, al-'Uzzā and Manāt, were not exempt either from such influences and cannot be considered as divinities of purely Bedouin origin.[74] Manāt was a goddess of destiny, without an astral character. Al-Lāt and al-'Uzzā probably represented two phases of the planet Venus (evening and morning), but it is possible that their identification with this planet represented a secondary development.[75] In

Bedouin Arabia (as in South Arabia) there was probably first a masculine divinity of the planet Venus which only later became feminine under a north Semitic influence.[76] The existence of a *sun* goddess (which some had attempted to recover in al-Lāt) is less certain, and it is impossible to prove the existence of an *earth* goddess among the nomadic Semites.[77]

6. The final divinity to be considered is Allāh who was recognized before Islam as god, and if not as the only god at least as a supreme god. The Quran makes it quite clear that he was recognized at Mecca, though belief in him was certainly more widespread.[78] How is this to be explained? Earlier scholars attributed the diffusion of this belief solely to Christian and Judaic influences. But now a growing number of authors maintain that this idea had older roots in Arabia. Wellhausen's view that Allāh (al-ilāh, "the god") is a sort of abstraction which (originating in the local gods) gave rise first to a common word, then a common concept that merged the various gods into one single god has rightly been judged inadequate. One must rather see in this pre-Islamic Allāh one of those great supreme gods who created the world but who plays a minor role in the actual cult.[79] If, therefore, Allāh is indigenous to Arabia, one must ask further: Are there indications of a nomadic origin? I think there are, based on a comparison of the beliefs of the nomads in central and northern Asia with those of northeastern Africa. Like the supreme being of many other nomads, Allāh is a god of the sky and *dispenser of rain*.[80] These indications might not seem sufficiently peculiar to Bedouin, for the notion of such a god might just as well have been formed by settled farming people. But one must not forget that rain is even more important for nomads. Whereas agriculture is possible with artificial systems of irrigation which lessen the direct dependence on rain, for the nomads the condition of the pasture lands, vitally important for both animals and people, is much more directly dependent on the rain. I am certainly not advocating that one should conclude simply on the basis of the monotheism of other nomadic peoples that the Semites, including the pre-Islamic Bedouin, were also monotheists. Nevertheless, a comparison with these other nomads might help us to better understand the fragmentary data for pre-Islamic religion. This is especially true for certain cultic practices which we shall discuss now.

In the *practices* of the pre-Islamic cult, *prayer* does not seem to have been very important. In any case, we know very little about it. More frequently mentioned are the sacrifices, bloody sacrifices as well as those that did not involve the shedding of blood. The animals which were immolated were the camel, the sheep, and the ox; fowl are never mentioned.[81] There seems to have been a certain preference for white animals. As for other types of sacrifice, libations of milk are indigenous, whereas libations of wine and oil are of foreign origin. Human sacrifices, on the whole rather rare among the Bedouin, may be attributed to the influence of the northern Semites.[82] The offering of human hair was not a true sacrifice but a rite of passage, involving a transition from the profane to sacred or in the reverse direction.[83] If the preference for white in the sacrificial animal recalls the customs of central and northern Asia, this is even more true for the *non-bloody consecration* of animals, a rite which expressed gratitude for the fertility of cattle. Camels and other domesticated animals dedicated to a god were exempt from work. In the case of camels, their milk was reserved for visitors and the poor. Sometimes after these animals were marked, they remained with the herd, but very often as the special property of the god they were kept in a sacred enclosure (*ḥimā*) near a sanctuary until their natural death.[84] The sacrificial rites were simple; each man had the right to sacrifice his own victim. Owing to the scarcity of fuel in the desert, victims were not burned. Usually the sacrifices ended in a common meal. Sometimes too the slaughtered animals were abandoned to wild animals and birds of prey. If the ceremonies of pouring and sprinkling the blood are not in any way peculiar to a nomadic civilization, the *interdiction against breaking the bones,*[85] on the other hand, can only be explained by an ideological complex which is still very much alive among hunters and stock farmers of northern Asia. This custom is based on the belief that the animal can be regenerated if the bones remain intact. In the very fragmentary Arabic documentation, this custom is barely comprehensible and has given rise to very different and sometimes rather arbitrary interpretations; but it appears in a new light when compared with the customs and beliefs of the above-mentioned peoples. The same is true for the *festivals of springtime*[86] as far as the sacrifice of the firstborn is concerned. There are solid reasons for believing that the Arabic feast of the month of Rajab, for which originally the firstborn of the herd were sacrificed, and the Jewish Passover have a common origin. Both are derived from a spring festival common to nomadic Semites (although after the exodus from Egypt, the Passover was given a new significance). These spring observances have numerous analogies among other shepherd groups.

The question of *pilgrimage* which was an element foreign to nomadic civilization and of a late date among Semitic peoples will not be dealt with in detail here.[87] It is precisely through pilgrimage that certain cultic practices of the settled tribes found their way into nomadic culture. Nor is there sufficient space here to discuss in detail the various practices of *divination, magic,* and *sorcery,*[88] which certainly receive ample attention from Muslim authors in their descriptions of pre-Islamic religion, but which must be studied much more thoroughly. As in the case of the belief in the *jinn,* we must try to discover what share the nomads and the sedentaries had respectively in these practices. By the inherent (perhaps magical) force of his utterances, the *shāʿir* (poet)[89] resembles the *kāhin* (soothsayer);[90] both were said to be inspired by the *jinn.*

This leads us to mention briefly the individuals who played a special role in the religion. Can one speak of *cultic officials?* The priests (*sādin,* pl. *sadana*) mentioned in the Arabic sources[91] were not sacrificers but rather guardians of the sanctuaries, for each man was allowed to slaughter his own victim. The absence of a special class of priests recalls the primitive situation of the Semites and other shepherd nomads.[92] It is not our intention here to deal with the typology of the priesthood and related phenomena in the history of religions.[93] However, within the Semitic domain, we must at least touch briefly on a problem which is suggested by the linguistic identity of the words *kāhin* (soothsayer) in Arabic and *kōhēn* (priest) in Hebrew. Scholars since Wellhausen have seen in this fact proof of a development from the sorcerer through the soothsayer to the priest.[94] This view, however, is contradicted by W. F. Albright who on the basis of Ugaritic documents writes: "Unfortunately, however, the word (*kāhin*) is isolated in Arabic and may, therefore, like thousands of other cultural words in that language, be considered equally well as a loanword from older Canaanite *kāhin* or from Aramaic *kāhnā,* both meaning 'priest'; should this be true, we have an indication of a specialization in function among the Arabs and not of a supposed magical background of the Israelite priesthood."[95] I cannot resolve this problem here. May I simply point out that in this case also, an explanation by uniform evolution from the less developed to the more developed is not at all clear. Moreover, the portable sanctuaries were also accompanied by soothsayers and other persons playing a religious or magical role, among whom there were also women.[96] I would not venture to identify such institutions with shamanism, a phenomenon which has been vigorously debated in recent years as to its nature and origin and which is probably no more indigenous to nomadic pastoral civilization than the institution of the priesthood.[97]

Conclusion

To conclude, let us attempt briefly to characterize the pre-Islamic Bedouin religion. In 1958 A. Brelich, in analyzing the results of studies on ancient Semitic divinities, came to the following conclusion: one cannot speak of polytheism in proto-Semitic civilization, but one does find the belief in a *supreme being,* coupled with *animism.*[98] I am inclined to accept this formula, with a few slight modifications, for pre-Islamic Bedouin religion. It seems to me that one must attribute a little less importance to animism (belief in nature spirits), and emphasize ancestor worship a little more.

Here then are the elements of this religion: Allāh, creator of the world, supreme and undisputed lord, but relegated to the background in the cultic and practical life of the people; next, manifesting the rudiments of a polytheism, several *astral divinities* (at least that of the planet Venus) and *atmospheric divinities* (perhaps the attributes of a creator god which have been hypostatized);[99] finally, ancestors and *jinn,* these last having more importance in the belief system than in the cult. All of this, moreover, is somewhat vague and far from being organized into a real pantheon or hierarchical system. The cultic practices as well were characterized by very little ritual and in turn reflected the individualism of the Bedouin and the lack of rigidity in their entire social system.

Islam which followed this religion did not grow out of a void, nor was it of purely foreign origin. It was not a Bedouin religion, for its principal roots are to be found in the biblical religions; however, in Arabia it found not only human values[100] but also religious values it could and did incorporate.

NOTES

(See page xi for list of abbreviations of journal titles)

1. J. Wellhausen, *Reste arabischen Heidentums* (Berlin, 1887; 2nd ed. 1897, reprinted 1927).
2. On these sources see: "La société bédouine ancienne" [in *L'antica societa beduina* (ed. F. Gabrieli; Rome, 1959)], pp. 71–76.
3. See J. Fueck, *Die arabischen Studien in Europe bis in den Anfang des 20. Jahrhunderts* (Leipzig, 1955), especially pp. 1–166 *passim;* cf. also: F. Wüstenfeld, *Die Übersetzungen arabischer Werke in das Lateinische seit dem 11. Jahrhundert* (*Abhandl. der Ges. der Wiss. zu Göttingen, Hist.-phil. Classe 22,* 1877, no. 2); U. Monneret de Villard, *Lo studio dell' Islām in Europa nel XII e nel XIII secolo* (Città del Vaticano, 1944); other references in J. Henninger, "Sur la contribution des missionnaires à la connaissance de

l'Islam, surtout pendant le moyen âge," *Neue Zeitschrift für Missionswiss.*, 9 (1953), pp. 161–85.

4. Pococke's account was used extensively by G. Sale in the introduction to his translation of the Quran (London, 1734), and by many authors who relied on one or the other of these; see G. Pfannmüller, *Handbuch der Islam-Literature* (Berlin and Leipzig, 1923), pp. 91, 96, 164, 171–72, 209, 216.
5. G. Bergmann, *De religione Arabum anteislamica dissertatio historico-theologica* (Strasbourg, 1834).
6. E. Osiander, "Studien über die vorislâmische Religion der Araber," *ZDMG*, 7 (1853), pp. 463–505.
7. L. Krehl, *Über die Religion der vorislamischen Araber* (Leipzig, 1863).
8. See above, note 1.

8a. [*Mu'jam al-Buldān,* edited by F. Wüstenfeld and published in 6 vols. (Leipzig, 1866/73). See *GAL,* I, 480, Suppl. I, 880.]

9. W. R. Smith, *Lectures on the Religion of the Semites: The Fundamental Institutions* (London, 1889; 3rd ed., 1927). See *ibid.*, pp. XVI–XVII: "For Arabia I have been able to refer throughout to my friend Wellhausen's excellent volume, *Reste arabischen Heidentums* (Berlin, 1887), in which the extant material for this branch of Semitic heathenism is fully brought together, and criticized with the author's well-known acumen."
10. M.-J. Lagrange, *Etudes sur les religions sémitiques* (2nd ed., Paris, 1905).
11. Th. Nöldeke, review of W. R. Smith, *Kinship and Marriage in Early Arabia* (London, 1885), in *ZDMG,* 40 (1886), pp. 148–87; *idem,* review of J. Wellhausen, *Reste arabischen Heidentums* (Berlin, 1887) in *ZDMG,* 41 (1887), pp. 707–26.
12. Th. Nöldeke, article: "Arabs (Ancient)," in Hastings, *Encyclopaedia of Religion and Ethics* I (Edinburgh, 1908), pp. 659a–73a.
13. D. Nielsen, *Die altarabische Mondreligion und die mosaische Überlieferung* (Strassburg, 1904); *idem, Der dreienige Gott in religionshistorischer Beleuchtung,* I (Copenhagen, 1922), II (1942); *idem, Handbuch der altarabischen Altertumskunde,* I (Paris-Copenhagen-Leipzig, 1927), and other publications. For a critique of these theories see: G. Furlani, "Triadi semitiche e Trinità cristiana," *Bulletin de l'Institut d'Egypte,* 6 (1924), pp. 115–33; E. Dhorme, "La religion primitive des Sémites. A propos d'un ouvrage récent," *RHR,* 128 (1944), pp. 5–27; A. Jamme, "Le panthéon sudarabe préislamique d'après les sources épigraphiques," *Le Muséon,* 60 (1947), pp. 57–147; *idem,* "D. Nielsen et le Panthéon sud-arabe préislamique." *RB,* 55 (1948), pp. 227–44;; other references in J. Henninger, *Anthropos,* pp. 37–40 (1942–45), pp. 802–5; cf. also Henninger, *Zeitschr. für Ethnol.*, 79 (1954), pp. 107–10; *idem, Anthropos* 53 (1958), p. 743.
14. First edition: Cairo, 1913, 2nd edition, Cairo, 1924 (text reprinted in R. Klinke-Rosenberger, see note 15).
15. See R. Klinke-Rosenberger, *Das Götzenbuch* (*Kitāb al-Aṣnām*) of Ibn al-Kalbī (Leipzig, 1941); N. A. Faris, *The Book of Idols, Being a Translation from the Arabic of the Kitāb al-Aṣnām by Hishām Ibn al-Kalbī* (Princeton, New Jersey, 1952).
16. See, for example: M. S. Marmadji, "Les dieux du paganisme arabe d'après Ibn al-Kalbī," *RB,* 35 (1926), pp. 397–420; H. S. Nyberg, *Bemerkungen Zum "Buch der Götzenbilder" von Ibn al-Kalbī,* in ΔΡΑΓΜΑ, *Martino P. Nilsson A.D. IV Id. Jul. Anno MCMXXXIX dedicatum* (Lund, 1939), pp. 346–66; F. Stummer, "Bemerkungen zum Götzenbuch des Ibn al-Kalbī," *ZDMG,* 98 (N.F. 23) (1944), pp. 377–94; A. Jepsen, "Ibn al-Kalbīs *Buch der Götzenbilder.* Aufbau und Bedeutung," *Theol. Literatur-Zeitung,* 72 (1947), Col. 139–44.
17. G. Ryckmans, *Les Religions arabes préislamiques,* in M. Gorce and R. Mortier, *Histoire*

générale des religions, IV (Paris, 1947), pp. 307–22, 526–34; 2nd ed. (*Bibliothèque du Muséon,* vol. 26) Louvain, 1951; cf. E. Dhorme, "Les Religions arabes préislamiques d'après une publication récente," *RHR,* 133 (1947–48), pp. 34–48.

18. J. Chelhod, *Le Sacrifice chez les Arabes* (Paris, 1955); *idem, Introduction à la sociologie de l'Islam. De l'animisme à l'universalisme* (Paris, 1958), as well as several articles, mostly in the *RHR.* For a critique of some of the details see: Henninger, *Anthropos,* 50 (1955), pp. 106 with note 135; *idem, Anthropos,* 53 (1958), pp. 748–57, *passim,* 786, 795, note 339. A general criticism has yet to be written.
19. See, for example: F. Buhl, *Das Leben Mohammeds* (German translation by H. H. Schaeder: Leipzig, 1930; 2nd ed. Heidelberg 1955); T. Andrae, *Mohammed, Sein Leben und sein Glaube* (Göttingen, 1932; French translation: *Mahomet, sa vie et sa doctrine,* Paris, 1945 [English translation: *Mohammed, The Man and His Faith,* New York, 1936]); W. M. Watt, *Muhammad at Mecca* (Oxford, 1953; French translation: *Mahomet à la Mecque.* Paris, 1958); *idem, Muhammad at Medina* (Oxford, 1956); M. Gaudefroy-Demombynes, *Mahomet* (Paris, 1957); R. Paret, *Mohammed und der Koran* (Stuttgart, 1957).
20. See, for example, F. M. Pareja, *Islamologia* (Roma, 1951) [translated into French under the title of *Islamologie* (Beirut, 1964)]; cf. also M. Guidi, *Storia e cultura degli Arabi fino alla morte di Maometto* (Firenze, 1951), especially pp. 122–43.
21. W. R. Smith assumes a primitive religion common to all Semites, as is expressed in the title of his work: *Lectures on the Religion of the Semites.* M.-J. Lagrange writes more cautiously in his *Etudes sur les religion sémitiques.*
22. Cf. J. Henninger, "Das Opfer in den altsüdarabischen Hochkulturen," *Anthropos,* 37–40 (1942–45), pp. 779–810, especially pp. 787–93, 805–10.
23. See G. Ryckmans, *op. cit.*, pp. 7–18: central Arabia; pp. 19–24: northern Arabia; pp. 25–48: southern Arabia.
24. See Buhl, *op. cit.*, pp. 73–74, 81–82; other references in J. Henninger, *Anthropos,* 50 (1955), pp. 119–20.
25. See Smith, *Religion,* pp. 111–13; cf. also G. Levi Della Vida, *Les Sémites et leur rôle dans l'histoire religieuse* (Paris, 1938), pp. 81–91 *passim,* especially pp. 89–91, and 116–17, note 40; Gaudefroy-Demombynes, *op. cit.*, pp. 34–39.
26. See H. Lammens, "Le Culte des bétyles et les processions religieuses chez les Arabes préislamites," *Bulletin de l'Institut français d'archaéologie orientale, Le Caire,* 18 (1919), reprinted in H. Lammens, *L'Arabie Occidentale avant l'Hégire* (Beyrouth, 1928), pp. 101–79; J. Morgenstern, *The Ark, the Ephod and the "Tent of Meeting"* (Cincinnati, 1945), *passim,* especially pp. 1–77; cf. also Henninger, *Internat. Archiv für Ethnogr.*, 42 (1943), pp. 23–26, especially p. 26, note 116; *idem, Anthropos,* 50 (1955), p. 121, note 189; K. Dussaud, *La Pénétration des Arabes en Syrie avant l'Islam* (Paris, 1955), pp. 113–17.
27. See Smith, *Religion,* p. 47; Wellhausen, *Reste,* 2nd ed., pp. 224–28; Nöldeke, in Hastings, I (1908), p. 659b. One could also cite many more references.
28. See W. Caskel, in *Le Antiche divinità semitiche* (Roma, 1958), pp. 104–5 (cf. S. Moscati, *ibid.*, pp. 120–21); W. Caskel, *ZDMG,* 103 (1953), p. 31 [English translation: "The Bedouinization of Arabia," in *Studies in Islamic Cultural History,* edited by G. E. von Grunebaum (*The American Anthropological Association. Memoir No. 76,* April 1954, Menasha, Wisconsin), p. 39]; *idem, Die Bedeutung der Beduinen in der Geschichte der Araber* (Köln and Opladen, 1953), p. 6.
29. See, for example, H. Winckler, *Arabisch-Semitisch-Orientalisch. Mitteilungen der Vorderasiatischen Gesellschaft,* 6 (1901), pp. 151–373, *passim.* Merely as a curiosity one might also mention Ahmad-Bey Kamal, *Les idoles arabes et les divinités égyptiennes.*

(*Recueil de travaux relatifs à la philologie et à l'archéologie égyptiennes et assyriennes, 24*[e] année, Nouvelle série, tome 8[e][Paris, 1902], pp. 11–24.) This author compiles a list of gods which supposedly had been identical in ancient Egypt and in Arabia. According to the Egyptologist Werner Vycichl, that is entirely inadmissible (Letter of 26 May 1959). Besides, this risky theory does not seem to have gained any supporters.

30. See C. E Dubler, "Survivances de l'ancien Orient dans l'Islam (Considérations générales)," *Studia Islamica,* 7 (1957), pp. 47–75, especially 53–54; *idem, Das Weiterleben des Alten Orients im Islam* (Antrittsvorlesung, Zürich, 1958), pp. 5–6.
31. See Caskel, above note 28.
32. The earliest testimony seems to be that of Maximus of Tyre and Clement of Alexandria; see references in G. E. von Grunebaum, *Medieval Islam* (2nd ed., Chicago, 1953), p. 131, n. 89; cf. also A. Bertholet, "Über kultische Motivvershiebungen," *Sitzungsberichte der Preussischen Akademie der Wissenschaften, Phil. hist. Klasse,* 18 (Berlin, 1938), pp. 164–84, especially pp. 165–69; E. G. Gobert, "Essai sur la Litholâtrie," *Revue africaine,* 92 (1948), pp. 24–110, *passim;* other references in Henninger, *Zeitschr. für Ethnol.*, 79 (1954), pp. 103–6; *idem, Anthropos,* 50 (1955), pp. 107–9; Dussaud, *op. cit.*, pp. 41–42; cf. also Lammens, *op. cit.*, *passim;* Krehl, *op. cit.*, pp. 69–73.
33. See Wellhausen, *Reste,* 2nd ed., pp. 211–14.
34. See Lagrange, *op cit.*, pp. 16–28, especially pp. 16–18; cf. also W. Schmidt, *Der Ursprung der Gottesidee,* I (2nd ed., Münster i. W. 1926), pp. 20–55, 69–133, *passim.*
35. I will mention only some of the most recent ones: Chelhod, *Sociologie,* pp. 15, 42–62, *passim,* 77–83, 88–90, 180–81; Gaudefroy-Demombynes, *op. cit.*, pp. 25, 26, 29, 32–33.
36. This theory is found already in Ibn *al-Kalbī* for some of the gods of pre-Islamic Arabia; see Klinke-Rosenberger, *op cit.*, pp. 56–61. Cf. also Krehl, *op. cit.*, pp. 54–69, *passim;* A. Lods, *La croyance à la vie future et le culte des morts dans l'antiquité israélite* (Paris, 1906), especially I, pp. 8–17, 29–31; II, pp. 101–3, 112–13.
37. Chelhod, *Sacrifice,* p. 125; *idem, Sociologie,* pp. 42–43, 180–81.
38. See "La société bédouine ancienne" [*L'antica società beduina* (Rome, 1959), p. 85, n. 68].
39. See above, note 13.
40. Lagrange, *op. cit.*, p. 70, cf. Moscati, *loc. cit.* (above, note 28), p. 122.
41. See W. Schmidt, *Der Ursprung der Gottesidee VII–XII: Die Religionen der Hirtenvölker* (Münster, 1940–1955; vol. XII, posthumous, edited by F. Bornemann).
42. W. Schmidt, *op. cit.* I, pp. 670–74.
43. C. Brockelmann, "Allah und die Götzen, der Ursprung des islamischen Monotheismus," *Archiv für Religionswiss.*, 21 (1922), pp. 99–121.
44. For this brief survey, the references cannot always be given in detail. It is based on the materials used in the publication mentioned above, notes 1–20, and on a study by the author entitled: *Das Opfer bei den Arabern. Eine religionsgeschichtliche Studie,* and composed of about 450 pages of manuscript. As of the present moment only a summary has been published in French ("Le sacrifice chez les Arabes," *Ethnos,* 13 (1948) pp. 1–16), and certain parts dealing with specific problems (see the list: *Anthropos,* 50 (1955), p. 99, n. 113; in addition, see below, notes 81–86).
45. See H. Charles, *Le Christianisme des Arabes nomades sur le Limes et dans le désert syro-mésopotamien aux alentours de l'Hégire* (Paris, 1936).
46. See W. M. Watt, *EI,* new ed. [French edition] I, p. 919a (English edition, p. 892b), "Bdw."
47. One must perhaps admit a certain diffusion of Manichaeism, which had a center at Hira, among the Bedouin of the Syrian desert. See U. Monneret de Villard, *Annali*

Lateranensi, 12 (1948), pp. 169–74, and references cited there. For Parseeism, see Buhl, *op. cit.*, pp. 71–72.

48. See above, note 27.
49. See X. de Planhol, *Le Monde islamique* (Paris, 1957), pp. 5–45, and the bibliography, *ibid.*, pp. 132–35; Dussaud, *op. cit.*, p. 140.
50. See I. Goldziher, "Muruwwa und Din" in *Muhammedanische studien,* I (Halle, 1889), pp. 1–39 [translated into English under the title *Muslim Studies,* I (London, 1967), pp. 11–44]. Watt, *Muhammad at Mecca,* pp. 20–33 (French translation, pp. 43–46).
51. See the discerning comments of Levi Della Vida, *op. cit.*, pp. 89–90. It would be easy to list a great number of references emphasizing the strictly limited content of this poetry.
52. See above, note 32.
53. See M. Eliade, *Traité d'histoire des religions* (Paris, 1949), pp. 191–210, *passim* [translated into English under the title *Patterns in Comparative Religion* (New York, 1963), pp. 216–38]; A. Bertholet, *Wörterbuch der Religionen* (Stuttgart, 1952), see under "Fetischismus"; P. Schebesta, "Fetischismus" in F. König, *Religionswissenschaftliches Wörterbuch* (Freiburg i. Br., 1956), col. 252–53.
54. Dussaud, *op. cit.*, p. 41, and note 3; cf. also Lagrange, *op. cit.*, pp. 187–216, *passim.*
55. See above, note 26.
56. See A. Musil, *Österr. Monatsschrift für den Orient,* 43 (1917), p. 164; the same text in English: A. Musil, *Northern Neǧd* (New York, 1928), p. 257.
57. Wellhausen, *Reste,* 2nd ed., p. 213; cf. *ibid.*, pp. 148–60, *passim.*
58. See Bertholet, Wörterbuch, see under "Animismus"; P. Schebesta, "Animismus," in F. König, *op. cit.*, col. 52–54; J. Goetz, "Dämonen," *ibid.*, col. 154–56.
59. See A. Haldar, *The Notion of the Desert in Sumero-Accadian and West-Semitic Religions* (Uppsala-Leipzig, 1950; summary in *Anthropos,* 46[1951], p. 624); cf. also Ebeling, "Dämonen" in *Reallexikon der Assyriologie,* II (Berlin und Leipzig, 1938), pp. 107a–13a; E. Zbinden, *Die Djinn des Islam und der altorientalische Geisterglaube* (Bern und Stuttgart, 1953), especially pp. 101–10.
60. For the Bedouin, see A. Musil, *The Manners and Customs of the Rwala Bedouins* (New York, 1928), pp. 411–17; for the *Fellāhīn:* T. Canaan, *Aberglaube und Volksmedizin im Lande der Bibel* (Hamburg, 1914), *passim; idem,* "Haunted Springs and Water Demons in Palestine," *Journal of the Palestine Oriental Society,* I (1920–1921), pp. 153–70; *idem, Dämonenglaube im Lande der Bibel* (Leipzig, 1929); W. S. Blackman, *The Fellāhīn of Upper Egypt* (London, 1927; French translation: *Les Fellahs de la Haute-Egypte,* Paris, 1948); cf. also Henninger, *Anthropos,* 41–44 (1946–1949), pp. 337–46, especially pp. 343–46, on the diffusion of certain animist beliefs and practices with the introduction of chicken breeding.
61. See W. F. Albright, *Journal of the American Oriental Society,* 57 (1937), pp. 319–20; 60 (1940), pp. 292–93, with the references cited there.
62. D. Schlumberger, *La Palmyrène du Nord-Ouest* (Paris, 1951), pp. 121–22, 135–37, maintains the priority of the Arabic word *jinn* and considers that the Palmyran form *jny'* derives from the former.
63. According to A. Haldar, *Associations of Cult Prophets Among the Ancient Semites* (Uppsala, 1945), p. 180, the demoting of gods to the level of demons had already begun before Islam.
64. See the references in Henninger, *Anthropos,* 50 (1955), pp. 130–36; cf. also *Bulletin des études arabes,* 3 (1943), pp. 104–6; M. Rodinson, *Journal Asiatique,* 240 (1952), pp. 129–32; *idem, Comptes rendus sommaires des séances de l'Institut Français d'Anthropologie,* fasc. 7 (1953), pp. 21–24.

65. See the details in my essay on Arab sacrifice, mentioned above, note 44; cf. also Chelhod, *Sacrifice,* pp. 118–19; *idem, Sociologie,* pp. 50–52.
66. See I. Goldziher, "Le culte des ancêtres et le culte des morts chez les Arabes," *RHR,* 10 (1884), pp. 332–59; *idem,* "Über Todtenverehrung im Heidentum und im Islam," in *Muhammedanische Studien,* I, pp. 229–63; [translated into English under the title *Muslim Studies,* I (London, 1967), pp. 209–38 ("The Veneration of the Dead in Paganism and Islam")]; Wellhausen, *Reste,* 2nd ed., pp. 183–85; Lammens, *L'Arabie Occidentale,* pp. 163–79, *passim;* Buhl, *op. cit.*, pp. 78–79; Chelhod, *Sacrifice,* pp. 101, 106, 118–19; *idem, Sociologie,* pp. 15, 180–81. On the question of human sacrifice (rather doubtful) in the cult of the dead, see Henninger, *Anthropos,* 53 (1958), pp. 749–52.
67. In *Sociologie,* pp. 42–43, Chelhod does not speak of the cult of ancestors; but *ibid.*, pp. 15, 180–81, he places this cult on the same level (palier) with the notion of a diffused and impersonal sacred. This kind of systematization does not appear justified to me.
68. See Buhl, *op. cit.*, pp. 76–77. J. Chelhod's attempt to reconstruct a myth concerning the origins of civilization ("Le monde mythique arabe," *Journal de la Société des Africanistes,* 24 (1954), pp. 49–61) is not convincing.
69. See Ryckmans, *op. cit.*, pp. 14–18, and the works mentioned above, note 16. According to Chelhod, *Sociologie,* pp. 118–25, in the course of the formation of an Arab national religion, a kind of pantheon developed at Mecca. However that may be, even Chelhod admits that the formation of an Arab national religion followed the adoption of a sedentary mode of life and does therefore not concern Bedouin religion as such.
70. See Wellhausen, *Reste,* 2nd ed., pp. 67, 209; Buhl, *op. cit.* pp. 76–77; Albright, *Journal of the American Oriental Society,* 60 (1940), pp. 295–96.
71. Wellhausen, *Reste,* 2nd ed., pp. 211–14.
72. See J. Henninger, "Über Sternkunde und Sternkult in Nord und Zentral-arabien," *Zeitschr. für Ethnol.*, 79 (1954), pp. 82–117, especially pp. 88–93, 110–15.
73. See Henninger, *loc. cit.*, pp. 93–110, *passim,* 115–17.
74. See W. Caskel, in *Le antiche devinità semitiche,* p. 105.
75. See Henninger, *Zeitschr. für Ethnol.*, 79 (1954), pp. 97–110.
76. See Henninger, *loc. cit.*, pp. 107–10.
77. See Henninger, *loc. cit.*, pp. 99–100, 110. The question of solar and lunar cults in central Arabia still remains to be examined in a special study.
78. The fact is too well known to need detailed references. For a succinct account, see Wellhausen, *Reste,* 2nd ed., pp. 217–24, and the article of C. Brockelmann, mentioned above, note 43; cf. also Paret, *op. cit.*, pp. 15–17, and the references cited, *ibid.*, p. 156.
79. See Wellhausen, *Reste,* 2nd ed., pp. 218–19; opposed to this opinion: Brockelmann, *loc. cit.*, pp. 103–5; Buhl, *op. cit.*, p. 94; Andrae, *op. cit.*, pp. 20–21; Paret, *op. cit.*, p. 17. Cf. also Levi Della Vida, *op. cit.*, pp. 85–92 *passim,* 116, n. 37; and below, notes 98 and 99.
80. See Brockelmann, *loc. cit.*, pp. 107–8; Smith, *Religion,* p. 111; Wellhausen, *Reste,* 2nd ed., p. 222.
81. See J. Henninger, "Über Huhnopfer und Verwandtes in Arabien und seinen Randgebieten," *Anthropos,* 41–44 (1946–1949), pp. 337–46.
82. See J. Henninger, "Menschenopfer bei den Arabern," *Anthropos,* 53 (1958), pp. 721–805.
83. See J. Henninger, "Zur Frage des Haaropfers bei den Semiten," in *Die Wiener Schule*

der Völkerkunde. Festschrift anlässlich des 25 jährigen Bestandes des Instituts für Völkerkunde der Universität Wien (1929–1954) (Horn-Wien, 1956), pp. 349–68.

84. See J. Henninger, "Die unblutige Tierweihe der vorislamischen Araber in ethnologischer Sicht," *Paideuma,* 4 (1950), pp. 179–90.
85. See J. Henninger, "Zum Verbot des Knochenzerbrechens bei den Semiten" in *Studi Orientalistici in onore di Giorgio Levi Della Vida* (Roma, 1956), I, pp. 448–58.
86. See J. Henninger, "Les fêtes de printemps chez les Arabes et leurs implications historiques," *Revista do Museu Paulista,* n.s. 4 (1950), pp. 389–432.
87. See Smith, *Religion,* p. 80; cf. also *ibid.*, pp. 109–10; Wellhausen, *Reste,* 2nd ed., pp. 121–22, with note 3; Buhl, *op. cit.*, p. 86.
88. See Wellhausen, *Reste,* 2nd ed., pp. 159–77, *passim;* Gaudefroy-Demombynes, *op. cit.*, pp. 39–44.
89. Cf. above: "La société bédouine ancienne," n. 62.
90. Cf. above: "La société bédouine ancienne," n. 61.
91. See the references in Henninger, *Anthropos,* 50 (1955), pp. 119–21; Chelhod, *Sacrifice,* p. 169, writes: "He (i.e. the pre-Islamic priest) was the guardian of the temple as well as the sacrificer, as one may easily determine from the root *sadana* which gives *sādin,* priest, and *sadīne,* grease, blood, wool." In this context he refers to my article in *Ethnos,* 13 (1948), p. 12 (see above, note 44), where I say quite clearly that the *sādin* was not a sacrificer. The etymological argument does not seem to prove the contrary. On Chelhod's linguistic method in general, see the references in Henninger, *Anthropos,* 53 (1958), p. 795, n. 339.
92. See Smith, *Religion,* p. 143; A. J. Wensinck, *Some Semitic Rites of Mourning and Religion* (Amsterdam, 1917), p. 74; Levi Della Vida, *op. cit.*, p. 116, n. 39.
93. See E. O. James, *The Nature and Function of Priesthood* (London, 1955; German translation: *Das Priestertum, Wesen und Funktion* [Wiesbaden, 1951]).
94. See Levi Della Vida, *op. cit.*, pp. 87–89, 96, 116, n. 39; W. F. Albright, *From the Stone Age to Christianity* (Baltimore, 1940), pp. 18–19 (according to Morgenstern, *op. cit.*, p. 58, n. 82; German translation: *Von der Steinzeit zum Christentum* (Bern, 1949), p. 32; French translation: *De l'âge de la pierre à la chrétienté* [Paris 1951] p. 26).
95. Albright, *op. cit.* (English translation), p. 47; cf. the German translation pp. 32, 409, n. 34; cf. also Lagrange, *op. cit.*, p. 218. Morgenstern, *op. cit.*, p. 58, n. 82, would be disposed to concede the borrowing of this word, but on the other hand, he maintains that among all the Semites the soothsayer preceded the priest as we understand him today.
96. See Lammens, *L'Arabie Occidentale,* pp. 103–4, 106–10, 112–25, 132–41; Morgenstern, *op. cit.*, pp. 58–61, 64; Haldar, *Associations of Cult Prophets,* pp. 161–98 *passim,* especially pp. 190–93, 195–97; Henninger, *Anthropos,* 50 (1955), p. 121, n. 189.
97. See W. Schmidt, *Der Ursprung der Gottesidee,* XII (1955), pp. 615–759; M. Eliade, *Le Chamanisme et les techniques archaiques de l'extase* (Paris, 1951) [translated into English under the title *Shamanism* (Bollingen Series LXXVI, New York, 1964)]; D. Schröder, "Zur Struktur des Schamanismus," *Anthropos,* 50 (1955), pp. 848–81; H. Findeisen, *Schamanentum* (Zurich-Wien, 1957); J. P. Roux, "Le nom du chaman dans les textes turco-mongols," *Anthropos,* 53 (1958), pp. 133–42; *idem,* "Eléments Chamaniques dans les textes pré-mongols," *Anthropos,* 53 (1958), pp. 441–56; *idem,* "Le Chaman gengiskhanide," *Anthropos,* 54 (1959), pp. 49–80, and the literature mentioned in these articles.
98. See A. Brelich, in *Le Antiche divinità semitiche,* pp. 135–40, especially pp. 136, 139, 140.

99. On this process in general, see H. Ringgren, *Word and Wisdom. Studies in the Hypostatization of Divine Qualities and Functions in the Ancient Near East* (Lund, 1947); cf. the recensions of O. Eissfeldt, *Theol. Literatur-Zeitung,* 76 (1951), col. 154–55 and of J. Henninger, *Anthropos,* 46 (1951), pp. 646–47.

100. See Watt, *Muhammad at Mecca,* pp. 24–25, on "tribal humanism" (cf. also p. 23). Although the decadence of the archaic religion (*ibid.*, pp. 23–24) is an incontestable fact, this author (like others) perhaps goes too far in the separation of this ethic from religion; see Th. Nöldeke, " 'Gottesfurcht' bei den alten Arabern," *Archiv für Religionswiss.*, 1 (1898), pp. 361–63; Wellhausen, *Reste,* 2nd ed., p. 224; Brockelmann, *Archiv für Religionswiss.*, 21 (1922), pp. 113–14; Lammens, *L'Arabie Occidentale,* p. 229; Buhl, *op. cit.*, pp. 90–91; cf. also above, note 51.

II

A Critical Survey of Modern Studies on Muhammad[1]

MAXIME RODINSON

It is a constant temptation for the nonspecialist (and also for the specialist whose expertise lies in another field) to imagine that everything has been said on a particular subject. We are all deplorably lacking in imagination in the face of discoveries that remain to be made. However, the perpetual revolution in historic ideas (even when the documentation increases only modestly) constantly defies this weakness of mind.

When the massive study on the life of the Prophet (and also on the subsequent period) by Leone Caetani appeared in Milan beginning in 1905[2] the researcher could rightfully feel a sense of discouragement. And yet, in the years following the publication of Caetani's study, a number of works appeared which have profoundly altered our perspective. Indeed, in recent years a number of interesting biographical studies have been published, and at least some of them are of such a nature as to overturn ideas previously held.

This current interest in the Prophet has causes which are in good measure fortuitous. The political situation of recent years has attracted the attention of the general public to the peoples of Islam and especially to those who, one may say, created this religion, *viz.*, the Arabs. A French book club involved in publishing a series of biographies recently conducted a kind of poll among its readership for the purpose of determining which of the great men they wished to appear in this biographical series and in what order of preference. Muhammad was at the head of the list and by a large margin. If this interest has facilitated the publication of some good works, one ought perhaps to be satisfied and to overlook the tares that are mixed in with the good grain.

The *Annali dell' Islam* of Caetani, to which reference has already been made, marks both the culmination and the end of a period of scholarly investigation. Following the early efforts of R. P. Ludovico Marracci[2a] who prefaced his translation of the Quran with a biographical study of Muhammad, two centuries ensued during which scholarly investigation made significant progress.[3] European scholars collected Arabic manuscripts, began to edit, translate, and write commentaries upon them. Scholarly studies thus gradually accumulated. The historical outlook of the nineteenth century coupled with a critical attitude which had first been applied in studies on Homer and the Bible made possible the first really scientific works based on the material which untiring philological investigation had produced.[4]

Following a lengthy introduction on pre-Islamic Arabia, Caetani, assisted by his collaborators, compiled and arranged (year by year, and event by event) all the material which the sources, the Arab historians, offered. The resultant conclusions based on the facts, which took into account the variant forms in which they were found in the sources, were accompanied by a critical analysis that reflected the methodological skepticism which Langlois and Seignobos had just set forth as absolutely indispensible for the historian.[5] Later generations, freed from the positivist ascendancy, have regarded this attitude as hypercritical. In other areas too they were able to show that it had been excessive. However, in the field under consideration here, there are unfortunately numerous examples which point up the value of this critical approach. Numerous works in Arabic appear each year evidencing blind confidence in sources that are several centuries later than the events which they report.[6] The accounts found in our Muslim sources of events which occurred at the beginning of Islam do indeed require special methodological study, for the process of oral transmission constitutes a problem whose implications have not yet been fully explored.

Be that as it may, it might have seemed difficult to go beyond the quasi-exhaustive compilation of Caetani. Nevertheless while this monumental production was coming out, a serious lacuna in his work became evident precisely in the area of the compilation of material from the sources. During the same period, another team, composed of the most qualified Orientalists, published the *Ṭabaqāt* of Ibn Sa'd[7] in fifteen volumes, a source of capital importance which contained some of the most valuable and varied documents that have come down to us, but which Caetani utilized only partially.[8]

However, above and beyond the matter of this documentary lacuna, certain scholars were able to show that it was possible to make progress in the field more by shifting the focus of one's examination of texts already known than by utilizing new documents. Thus the Swedish scholar Tor Andrae attempted to explore in greater depth the personality of the Prophet in the light of the work of the early part of this century on the psychology of religion.[9] From another vantage point, his thorough knowledge of the Syriac Church permitted him to shed entirely new light on the Christian environment in which Islam developed.[10] These investigations were continued by K. Aherns who asserted (accurate only up to a certain point) that the attitude of Muhammad toward Christianity was essentially Christian.[11] The scholars of the period were interested in the investigation of influences. Those works which insisted on Christian influence were counterbalanced by those which emphasized Jewish influence, this latter having been studied as early as 1833 by Rabbi Abraham Geiger in a carefully balanced study.[12] The same tendency was subsequently continued by C. C. Torrey and others.[13] Somewhat more broadly, serious studies were devoted to Judeo-Christian sources of Quranic narratives and concepts.[14] Studies of this genre are assuredly very necessary. Islam was not born in a sealed container in an environment sterilized against the germs of other ideologies as contemporary Muslim authors and certain others frequently imagine. It is highly presumptuous to believe that one can study the development of nascent Islam by ignoring the great world religions whose influence, we now know, penetrated all parts of Arabia at the beginning of the seventh century. This kind of investigation, however, had its excesses. It ran the risk of forgetting the definite originality of Islam[15] and the evident fact that a study of influence cannot fully explain the origin of a new ideological phenomenon or its own particular dynamism. One must never under any circumstances or in any area shun a structural analysis which takes into account the functional necessity of the new ideology. After all, Muhammad became neither a Jew nor a Christian. And if that had happened, it would have been necessary not only to determine the influences that had brought about his conversion but also to explain why it was that he had allowed himself to be influenced.

While not having devoted a complete work to the life of Muhammad in its entirety, one man dominated European studies on Muhammad during the first third of this century. He was Henri Lammens. This Belgian Jesuit, French at heart, a good Arabist though not without his weaknesses in this regard, was endowed with the power of indefatigable work and with a combative temperament which his priestly profession channeled in the direction of scholarship. He also possessed a remarkable ability to lay hold of those living qualities communicated by the ancient texts along with a literary talent which enabled him to convey these to his readers. His scholarly and historical expositions (which were always a little oratorical) did not disdain the use of rhetorical devices; and often in their blazing crescendo he made use of Arabic quotations or resorted to his favorite French poets such as Victor Hugo and Henri de Bornier. In addition, he was filled with a holy contempt for Islam, for its "delusive glory" and its works, for its "dissembling" and "lascivious" Prophet, for the Arabs of the desert who in his judgment were cowards and swaggerers, plunderers and destroyers. Associated with the Université Saint-Joseph of Beirut, an active center of Arabic studies, he bitterly attacked (in the same spirit) the Sharifian troops led by the Meccan Faisal (and supported by the Protestant Lawrence) against the French who were represented by the pious general Gouraud. Turning toward the past he lashed out against the caliph 'Alī, Faisal's distant ancestor, whom he characterized as obese, ugly, timid, immoral, given to the tyrannizing of his wife, the "dull" and "complaining" Fāṭima. Taking a position opposed to Muslim tradition, he rehabilitated the Umayyad dynasty whose relative indifference toward Islam delighted him, a dynasty which (to their credit as he saw it) called upon Syrian Christians to administer the cultivated lands conquered by the Arabs, and which attempted to subdue the chronic anarchism of the "savage" Bedouin. Taking up the investigations begun by Ignaz Goldziher and the ideas which he had set forth, Lammens pushed to the extreme the critical analysis of Muslim tradition, unmasked without mercy the later political tendencies behind the narratives which recounted the deeds and sayings of the Prophet and those of his Companions. In this relentless and desperate pursuit of the apocryphal, he utilized without discretion the critical tools which the nineteenth century had used against his own faith.[16] The only accounts acceptable to him were those that reflected unfavorably on Muhammad and his family. His excessive prejudice, his violation of the texts a little too often, and his errors have justly called forth severe judgments. However, one must recognize that his colossal efforts at demolishing also had constructive results. They have forced us to be much more highly demanding of our sources. With the traditional edifice of history definitively brought down, one could now proceed to the reconstsruction.[17]

Serious attempts at rebuilding, however, were rare. We must mention in this connection the careful study by the Danish scholar Frants Buhl, which represents a comprehensive summary of European Scholarship of the period prior to World War II. This work which appeared in German in 1930 is an enlargement of an earlier Danish edition published in 1903, and contains a considerable mass of information taken from all of the available sources, studied and analyzed critically in the light of the discussions of European Islamists, of whom he had an almost exhaustive knowledge. With the robust good sense of a careful researcher, he rejected both the hypercriticism of certain Arabists and the blind confidence of Muslims in their sources. Within the area of its concern, the work has not been excelled and remains an indispensable tool.[18]

Apart from this monumental summary and the very perceptive and original biography of Tor Andrae cited above as well as certain other special works, this period produced only biographical sketches which perpetuated rather unimaginatively the ideas of the great Islamists whom we have mentioned, and numerous specialized investigations in progress.[19] Though a little apart, we must call attention to the biography of Muhammad by Émile Dermenghem,[20] a well-informed work, though without the trappings of scholarship. It is essentially a literary work as seen by the artistic care taken in its composition, the frequent use of dialogue, the absence of any argumentation for, or justification of, its views. This highly colorful work succeeds in giving a substantially correct impression of the milieu in which the life of the Prophet unfolded. It has received a warm reception in the Arab world.

Generally outside the main stream of European scientific studies, Russian Islamists during the period of Stalin were encouraged by their ideological environment to undertake studies and promote viewpoints which were often more interesting for the light they threw on this ideology than for their scientific value. This is especially true (and functions as a kind of law in those states built upon an official ideology) since the quasi-scholar often had the advantage over conscientious researchers. However, the Marxist method did lead them to pose more clearly (though under a somewhat more schematic form) the crucial questions connected with the social coordinates of the early Muslim movement. These scholars were, moreover, of different opinions with the result that there were (around

1930) a number of heated exchanges on this subject. Curiously enough, the polemical methods employed in the struggle against Christianity and frequently based on the thesis of the "myth of Jesus" developed by A. Drews (whose book is occasionally referred to by Lenin), J. P. Couchoud, and others, were applied to Islam. Several scholars, for example, attempted to show that Muhammad and his associates were mythical personages.[21] It is difficult to understand why this reduction of the founders of religions to mythical figures should be considered the only properly Marxist attitude, in much the same way that a small group of Frenchmen had considered it to be the only properly rationalist view of Jesus.

It was also an ideological environment (this time religious) that prevented Arab scholars (who were much better equipped in general than their European colleagues by their superior knowledge of the language and the sources) from doing valuable work in this area. From the point of view of method, many had recovered the ground which once separated them from Europeans. However, the storm which Taha Husain aroused by his critical analysis of pre-Islamic Arabic poetry is very well known.[22] It was very difficult to make progress under such conditions. Consequently Arab scholars have produced works that are mainly apologetic, though some concessions have been made to the modern mode of presenting facts. The educated public in the Muslim East, having received an education based upon the European model or at least bathed in the atmosphere of the modern world by the press, the radio, and so on, found studies patterned after the traditional mode and produced by shaikhs cut off from contemporary life unacceptable. However, for complex sociological reasons, the larger part of this educated bourgeois public rejected the scientific enthusiasm of the preceding generation and returned to the faith of the ancestors. This explains the immense popularity of the biography of the Prophet published in 1935 by the writer and politician, Muhammad Husain Haykal, to which a rather good parallel might be the work of M. Daniel-Rops on Christian origins. In an easy and modern style, Haykal retraces the life of the Prophet, writing a "scientific study according to the modern western method" (5th ed., p. 18). But if this "scientific method" leads him to reject a certain number of miracles attributed (at a rather late date) to the Prophet and to interpret some of them in a "natural" fashion, it leads him also to affirm the foundations of the Muslim faith. He undertakes a critical study of the sources but only for the purpose of attacking certain narratives preserved by Muslim tradition which appear offensive to the modern conception of the Prophet. It is a skillful reconstruction of the life of Muhammad suited to the needs of a modern apologetic, but it is far from being scientific in its viewpoint.[23] At about the same time, the Egyptian savant Ahmad Amin, in a book entitled *Fajr al-Islām* (the Dawn of Islam),[24] commenced an extensive history of Arab and Muslim civilization. However, he carefully avoided the difficult and dangerous area of the biography of the founder. Taha Husain quickly came around to a less threatening approach; following the literary style of Jules Lemaître, he wrote delightful narratives in the margin of the *sīra* (the traditional life of Muhammad).[25] The talented essayist 'Abbās Maḥmūd al-'Aqqād, a man of fascist sympathies, assumed the apologetic stance in a more virulent, "up-dated" manner, but also with less caution.[26] From the scientific point of view one may disregard such works. We must, however, take note of a striking exception, *viz.*, the work of the Arab Marxist, Bandalī Jawzī, who had previously been professor in Soviet Russia. This work was published in Jerusalem during the British Mandate, and, apart from a few attacks, did not become a source of serious controversy. Though in a somewhat cursory fashion, he did raise the question of the historical forces at work in the rise of Islam, and he did so without recourse to the principle of divine intervention.[27]

Such in summary fashion was the state of studies on Muhammad some twenty-five years ago. Since that time the study of Muhammad has undergone profound change, as we shall attempt to show in what follows. We shall focus our attention on the most recent works, and shall not attempt to establish an exhaustive list of the lesser important works devoted to the Prophet.[28]

The Milieu: Pre-Islamic Arabia

We obviously cannot discuss here the state of all the problems relative to pre-Islamic Arabia. It will be important, however, to indicate in a summary fashion how recent works have affected our understanding of the milieu in which Islam developed.

South Arabia

On pre-Islamic South Arabia our knowledge has progressed dramatically. This ancient and highly civilized region which consisted of a group of developed states based upon an advanced agricultural system and which maintained important ties with both the Indian and Mediterranean world might not be considered as constituting part of the immediate environment in which Islam arose. However, between the caravan cities of the Hijaz (which was the immediate environment of Islam) and the great states of the South on which they depended in many respects, relations were numerous and frequent, and the contribution of these states to the creation of the new ideology is beyond question. A bibliographical article by Father Y. Moubarac,[29] which also contains discussions on certain particular points, attempts an assessment of the present state of our knowledge as a whole. The recent reports of J. Pirenne give an account of current work in a more detailed fashion.[30] Let us merely take note of certain facts. Only a very small number of specialists carried forward the work on the mass of inscriptions known in South Arabic.[31] These very often enigmatic inscriptions are, together with some Greek and Latin texts, our principal source of information. On the philological level, they have been supplemented by the publication of the South Arabic grammar of Maria Höfner,[32] a student of the great South Arabist of Vienna, Nikolaus Rhodokanakis, and more recently by the up-dated and very convenient grammar of A. F. L. Beeston.[32a] Among these specialists, mention must be made especially of the following: the indefatigable Louvanian editor of the South Arabic *Corpus* and of the *Répertoire d'épigraphie sémitique,* Canon Gonzague Ryckmans, without whose untiring labors we would be seriously handicapped in this area;[33] Maria Höfner who has already been mentioned;[34] and the Oxonian A. F. L. Beeston whose penetrating insight and wisdom led to the revising of many philological and historical problems.[35] We must also add here William Foxwell Albright to whom nothing that touches the ancient Near East is foreign and who made several vigorous attempts at solving the problem of chronology.[36] Since the war or thereabouts, new names have appeared, especially A. Jamme of the White Fathers, at first a student of G. Ryckmans, later his opponent,[37] and the nephew of the latter, Jacques Ryckmans, who from the beginning distinguished himself by a massive, general work, rich in new conclusions based upon a simple, fresh examination of the texts.[38] We must also add here the German travelers, Carl Rathjens and H. von Wissmann,[39] long familiar with this area, who little by little published their notebooks filled with geographical, ethnographical, and archeological observations. In connection with her studies on the centuries preceding Islam, the well-known Russian specialist of Leningrad, N. V. Pigulevskaia, published an important study on South Arabia and the international commerce of the period.[40] We must point out with satisfaction the fact that Arab scholars, equipped with the necessary scientific tools along with a knowledge of the classical Arabic sources much superior to the majority of European South Arabists, have recently joined the ranks. We ought to mention especially M. A. Ghul.[41]

This scholarly effort received a shot of fresh blood through an effort to uncover new documents and documents of another order than those already known. The political, social, and cultural conditions of South Arabia had long prevented excavations.[42] At best, travelers had been able to make rough sketches of existing monuments, copy inscriptions, and collect antiquities found fortuitously by the inhabitants. The first extensive excavation was made in the Hadramawt in 1937 by three English women, G. Caton-Thompson, Freya Stark, and Elinor Gardner.[43] The small temple of the moon which was the object of their investigation proved interesting; however, no definite conclusions on any large scale may be drawn from their discoveries. Of greater importance were the archeological expeditions led more recently and with much superior means by the American Foundation for the Study of Man, a well-endowed organization under the administrative direction of Wendell Phillips. In 1950–51 one of these expeditions excavated the site of the ancient capital of the kingdom of Qataban, *viz.* Tamna‘ and its environs, which were located in a region then under English protection. In 1951–52, excavations were carried out at Māreb, the ancient capital of the kingdom of Saba, and its oval temple located in present day Yemen [now the Yemen Arab Republic]. Finally, in 1952, the Americans excavated at Salālah in Oman, an ancient port on the spice route. Taken as a whole, these excavations (unfortunately interrupted at Māreb by political difficulties and in such a way that the expedition had to abandon a part of its equipment) provided a very rich epigraphical and archeological documentation (with a stratigraphy finally established) which is only beginning to be published and discussed. Excavators were able to make visits to Dhofār in 1960 with interesting results.[44]

These efforts provided a body of new material (still apparently not decisive) relating to the chronological discussions which Jacquiline Pirenne had just initiated. Bearing an illustrious name, she took up in a highly commendable fashion a complete paleographic examination of all the South Arabic inscriptions from which some reproductions had been published. This very large work, accomplished with an impressive knowledge of paleographic method as well as that of the history of art, involved systematic comparison with Greek paleography and led to some revolutionary conclusions regarding chronology. Whereas the date of the most ancient inscriptions (placed by certain scholars in the thirteenth century B.C.) was generally situated in the eighth century by Mlaker, J. Pirenne placed it in the fifth century.[45] This was of considerable consequence from the historical point of view. She no longer saw the ancient South Arabian civilization as an ancient Oriental civilization briefly exposed to Hellenistic influences, but rather as a civilization closely tied to Greece (whose epigraphic forms, for example, had appeared almost immediately in South Arabia), and maintaining itself through its connections with the Hellenistic and Roman world.[46]

These efforts have aroused some critical responses which are only in the beginning stage,[47] for few even of the specialists are sufficiently equipped to take part in the debate on chronology. However that may be, the conclusions of J. Pirenne will certainly inspire new investigations and studies, which can now be undertaken without having to reckon with the dead weight of past theories. Continuing her investigations with great vigor, she was led by the logic of her position to re-examine the classical sources on South Arabia (in collaboration with the late André Maricq). Very recently she has questioned the dating accepted by *The Periplus of the Erythraean Sea.* That in turn has led to some unexpected consequences for the chronology of the dynasties of India.[48]

These discussions deal with distant periods whose influence on the history of the beginning of Islam may appear remote. That influence, however, is a fact. Recent investigations into periods closer to Muhammad have provided much new material. The study of monotheistic inscriptions has permitted us to follow more precisely the introduction of this current of ideas into South Arabia. In particular J. M. Solá Solé has published the text of the earliest monotheistic inscription[49] (it dates from 493 of the Sabaean era, or around A.D. 380). He has very skillfully shown the stages of transition from polytheism to monotheism in Saba. It is remarkable that the data of the inscriptions confirm essentially what later Arab tradition tells us about the conversion of Abū Karib As'ad, the king of Saba, to monotheism. It is interesting that the first names of the monotheistic deity in the inscriptions are *'l* ('Il, 'El), *'lh* ('Ilāh, which is in 'Allāh) and only later (from 574 of the Sabaean era, ca. A.D. 464) *Rḥmnn* (Raḥmānān = ar-Raḥmān, "the merciful" of the Quran, a name for God peculiar to certain Judeo-Christian milieux, while Allāh was the name of a god of the Hijaz).[50]

But it is especially the expedition to Saudi Arabia of Canon G. Ryckmans, H. St. J. B. Philby, J. Ryckmans, and Ph. Lippens in 1951–1952 which was to bring to light texts of particular interest.[51] Inscriptions from the first quarter of the fifth century, found in Wādī Māsil, about 200 kilometers to the east of Riyad, attest Sabaean expeditions very far to the north, entirely in accord with Arab tradition. In the inscription Ry. 510 (dated ca. A.D. 526) we meet a king of Hira who was well known in Arabic and Byzantine sources as al-Mundhir III. Further to the south, at Kawkab, the same expedition discovered an inscription engraved on the side of a rock, dated 633 of the Sabaean era (ca. A.D. 520). It was the work, like that of Himā found not far from there (Ry. 507), of the general of a king who was celebrated in Arab tradition, the Jewish king of Yemen, persecutor of Christians, and known by the Arabs under the nickname of Dhū Nuwās ("the man with the dangling locks of hair"). We now know his true name, Yūsuf (Joseph) As'ar, and we can follow in more detail the history of his persecution of Christians, of the expedition against him by the Axumites who were allied with Byzantium, and of the vicissitudes of the war which ended in 525(?) with the defeat and death of Joseph.[52] These events which made a profound impression on the thinking of the Arabs of Muhammad's time, and to which an allusion is evidently found in the Quran, are thus much better known and we can understand much better the intertwining of South Arabian, Sassanid Persian, Byzantine, and Axumite politics in Arabia. This more accurate information ought to enable us to better comprehend the political situation in the Peninsula at the time of the Prophet.

One account places the birth of Muhammad at the time of the expedition against Mecca led by Abraha, a Christian viceroy of South Arabia for Ethiopia. We have no explicit confirmation of this raid which tradition embellished with legends (perhaps already in the Quran) and certainly postdated. However, the above mentioned archeological expedition discovered at Muraygh̄an, between Najrān and Mecca, an inscription dated 662 of the Sabaean era (ca.A.D. 550) marked by a cross and engraved by this same Abraha in the course of a razzia to the north.

Besides these works and discoveries which enrich, modify, and define more precisely our knowledge, especially from the historical and political point of view, we ought to give some attention to the studies that have appeared on South Arabian religion. Though these have not brought about radical changes in perspective analogous to those to which we have just made reference, the revision and the bringing to light of materials, very much enriched when compared with the earlier studies, permits a much better utilization of South Arabian data for a great variety of purposes such as internal analysis, the establishment of connections and influences, etc. Here we must cite the small but very detailed and valuable fascicule by G. Ryckmans on pre-Islamic Arabian religion,[53] in which South Arabian religion occupies an important place, as well as the copious article by A. Jamme[54] which contains abundant references and which he has subsequently resumed and completed (without references) in a larger collective work on the history of religions.[55] One ought to mention the useful critical exposé of earlier theories found in this latter work, especially those of D. Nielsen on the essentially astral character of South Arabian religion, theories which had their vogue but which still continue to exert a great influence. Among more specialized works, but still covering a wide area, we must mention the fine article by J. Henninger on sacrifice in South Arabia.[56] The systematic comparison with facts from Muslim sources is only just beginning; one will read with interest the remarks of Y. Moubarac on this question.[57]

An important attempt at analyzing the social structure of a South Arabian city belonging to the seventh century has been undertaken by N. V. Pigulevskaia.[58] The city in question is Najrān, regarding which we have information from Greek and Syriac hagiographic sources because of the religious persecution initiated by Dhū Nuwās. [She was mistaken, however, in regarding as a genuine source the Byzantine forgery called *The Laws of the Homerites!*]

North and Central Arabia

The remainder of the peninsula is known to us through sources that are very diverse in nature. Unfortunately, however, knowledge of these requires expertise in a number of different disciplines. Scholars who are conversant with the various categories of sources are unfortunately rare, even though these latter are very evidently complementary. Some scholars manage to remain in touch with investigations outside their own special field, though not without some difficulty. It is certainly unfortunate that some writers believe themselves qualified to offer generalizations while at the same time cheerfully ignoring whatever does not have to do with their own particular field.[59]

Our sources for this region are first of all ancient Oriental texts, above all Assyro-Babylonian[60] and Hebrew (the Old Testament).[61] For a later period there are Greek and Latin texts on which J. Ryckmans has written a work which remains unpublished.[62]

Next come the inscriptions in systems of writing related to the South Arabic monumental script and which one finds scattered over the whole of the peninsula. They are written in dialects very near, it would appear, to the Arabic which we know.[63] The study of these has moved forward in important respects over the last twenty years. In the light of a new examination, F. V. Winnett[64] proposed in 1937 a chronological classification of Thamūdic and Liḥyānite inscriptions based upon paleographic considerations. In 1950 A. Van den Branden published a veritable corpus of Thamūdic inscriptions, at the same time reclassifying all information available on the language, the social condition, history, and religion of the authors of these inscriptions.[65] Following classical doctrine, he attributed these inscriptions to the people of Thamūd who figure in certain Akkadian, Greek, and Latin texts and whose memory, embroidered by legendary details, is found immortalized in the Quran. By qualifying them further, he modified the theses of Winnett on the graphic evolution and the chronology of the texts. He subsequently completed his work with an edition (prefaced by a general introduction) of the Thamūdic texts collected by H. St. J. B. Philby in the course of his lengthy stay in Arabia along with those which the latter copied in North Arabia during a visit there in 1950–51.[66] However, the expedition of Ryckmans, Philby, and Lippens in central Arabia (which we mentioned above in connection with the material which they provided on South Arabia) also yielded some Thamūdic texts. J. Ryckmans[67] who demonstrated the great diffusion of these texts challenged the view that they derived exclusively from the "people" of Thamūd. Moreover, instead of regarding the authors of these graffiti as sedentary people exercising the profession of caravaneers when the occasion presented itself, he gave a number of reasons for thinking that they were pastoral nomads or semi-nomadic clans of different Arab tribes. It is perhaps suitable then to return to the term "proto-Arabs," used formerly to designate these inscriptions rather than to continue using the too restrictive term "Thamūdic."[68] A. Van den Branden[69] has argued against the conclusion of J. Ryckmans by maintaining his earlier theses. Thus the debate has begun. In the light of what these inscriptions (despite their laconic and often enigmatic character) tell us about their authors who were pre-Islamic Arabs in any case, one can not overestimate their value for a knowledge of the milieu in which Islam was born.

The Liḥyānite inscriptions which emanated from an organized state, the kingdom of Liḥyān in the northern Hijaz, are of the same order of importance. They have been studied paleographically by Winnett in the work cited above and were published in 1937. All the Liḥyānite materials have been re-examined by Werner Caskel who has published an important study of the problems posed by this epigraphy and the Liḥyānite state.[70] His views on this subject are both interesting and original. The chronology which he proposed (the first Liḥyānite kingdom from 115 to ca. 25 B.C., the Nabatean domination from 25 B.C. to 64 A.D., a second Liḥyānite kingdom from 64 to 150 A.D.), reversing that of Winnett (fifth–fourth century B.C.) who had already been criticized by W. W. Tarn (Lagid period), has in its turn been criticized by A. Van den Branden (the end of ca. fifth century of our era).[71] The institutions of the kingdom of Liḥyān, a state living off caravan traffic and one in which "the assembly of the people" played an important role, should be called to mind when one studies the Meccan state in the period of Muhammad.

Also of great interest are the Safaitic inscriptions which were recovered from the basalt plain that lies to the southeast of Damascus. These inscriptions go back to pastoral nomads speaking a proto-Arabic dialect. They were written in a script very similar to Liḥyānite and Thamūdic. The epigraphic material has been considerably augmented, first by E. Littmann who in 1943 published some 1,300 texts copied in the course of the celebrated Princeton University expedition in Syria in 1904.[72] On the other hand, G. Ryckmans undertook to publish periodically in the *Corpus inscriptionum semiticarum*[73] all the texts known, including 1,413 unedited texts recovered in 1929 by M. and Mme. Dunand. Among the less important collections, one must mention the 1,009 texts published recently by Winnett[74] and the 208 texts published by G. Lankester Harding, [75] all from Jordan. Those of Harding, in addition to their intrinsic interest, are important because they were collected by systematically clearing away (the only time that this has been done) a *rajm*, *viz.*, a *tumulus* or "cairn" formed of stones, many of them with inscriptions, that had accumulated over the tomb of a saint. Among these stones was found one written in Latin (deciphered by H. Seyrig),[76] thrown there by an African(?) soldier by the name of Extricatus. The customs, the religion, the social condition of the Safaites who were contemporaries roughly with the pagan Roman Empire,[77] should prove to be interesting to study more closely. Regarding these people, we possess the work by E. Littmann which appeared in 1940,[78] a copious introduction by the same author at the beginning of his edition of texts, [79] a number of very valuable articles by G. Ryckmans in which he brings together the data of the texts which he gathered for his

Corpus,[80] and an article by M. Rodinson (in Arabic) in which he brings together the external data relating to the Safaitic region.[81]

In addition, we possess for Central Arabia, the testimony of Arabic literature which directly concerns only the last century before Muhammad. The controversy that has raged over the authenticity of this literature is well known. A first-rate study of the subject is to be found in the first volume of R. Blachère's *Historie de la littérature arabe*. This is a very careful examination based on a flawless documentation and one which, it would seem, can hardly be surpassed short of some sensational discovery.[82] For the moment, if the mass of Arabic texts which we possess has been further enriched by the publication of new texts and by improved re-editions of previously edited texts (it may be useful to mention in this connection the very great contribution made by young Arab scholars in the technique of critical editions), nothing of major importance has emerged to invalidate the information that we possess from literary works, information long available in works such as those by Georg Jacob[83] on the material culture and by Julius Wellhausen on the religion.[84] However, it is clear that these works ought to be rewritten on the basis of a larger and more systematic examination including also newly published texts.

General works on pre-Islamic Arabia as a whole are rare. The most complete and the most extensive has been the history (in Arabic) written by Jawād 'Ali, an Iraqi student of the German Islamist R. Strothmann, and one which makes full use of the works of European Orientalists.[85] The very well informed and admirable work of Michelangelo Guidi is beginning to become a little dated.[86] The interesting historical essay of H. St. J. B. Philby[87] has been quickly surpassed by the progress of discoveries and scholarly publications. One could say as much of my modest, more recent summary expostion.[88] W. Caskel, who is one of the leading experts on the question, has attempted to put forward a general theory of the history of this period.[89] He regards the Bedouin culture of pre-Islamic Arabia described by Arab authors as a late phenomenon. According to him, the Greek and Latin authors who speak of Arabian kingdoms and cities were describing a pre-Bedouin state in Arabia which continued until about the year 100 of our era. The "bedouinization" (undoubtedly in this case a "re-bedouinization") which began in the North following the annexation of the Nabatean kingdom by Rome in A.D. 106 slowly moved southward. This is a very learned reconstruction, but not entirely convincing. There certainly had always been sedentary peoples and cities in

Arabia; however, the Bedouin mode of life is attested by texts which come from a very ancient period and, to begin with, by very early Egyptian texts. Dictated by nature, Bedouin life could scarcely have undergone a general eclipse and could have been abandoned only in a very technically advanced period such as our own. The term "kingdom" in the writings of the classical authors is without doubt to be taken with some reservation as designating a state with a strong authority. One will welcome with less reticence the recent ideas conveniently summarized in the article "Badw" by H. von Wissmann and F. Kusmaul in the new edition of the *Encyclopedia of Islam*.[90] From a world or, at least, pan-Asiatic perspective, and taking as a basis recent investigation in paleo-botany, paleo-zoology, and ethnology, they trace the history of the appearance and development of nomadism which extended itself into Arabia from the agricultural lands of the Fertile Crescent. But this happened at a very early period and involved displacing a culture of collectors and hunters, not of sedentary and urbanized people. There is a very valuable collection of studies which deals with these problems.[91]

General works on religion have been relatively numerous. We have already cited the excellent précis by G. Ryckmans,[92] which sticks to the facts and does not hazard dubious hypotheses. The important rite of sacrifice was the object of a massive work by J. Henninger which unfortunately remains unpublished, though summarized in a lengthy article.[93] J. Chelhod has devoted to this question a large work, but one that is confused, not sufficiently conversant with current scholarly discussions of the matters in question, and based on dubious perspectives.[94] Finally, in the collection of studies which we mentioned above, J. Henninger surveys pre-Islamic religion.[95] This study aims not so much at summarizing the factual data as at sketching the larger outline of this religion in a sober, well documented fashion. Despite the fact that it is inspired by ideas of the historico-cultural school, this study does not reflect a narrow horizon.[96]

In the period immediately preceding Islam, Northwest and Northeast Arabia, which were under Byzantine and Sassanian influences respectively, played an important role in international politics. The implications of the political events of this area for understanding the origins of Islam are far from having been fully identified and examined. We must also welcome with interest the works on this period based upon recently published Greek, Syriac, and other sources. We shall have to be satisfied here with mentioning the following studies: those of Irfan Kawar (who later changed his name to Irfan Shahīd),[97] who occasionally offers interesting general considerations regarding the historical situation which prepared the way for Islam; the important article of Sidney Smith which attempts to reclassify all the information on the events of the sixth century in Arabia;[98] and the article by Roger Paret which deals with the Arab phylarchs in the service of the Byzantine Empire.[99] The same author wrote a dissertation on Syria in the sixth century. He has given us a sketch of part of his conclusions in a communication delivered to a congress on Byzantine studies.[100] In this latter he presents new indications of a process of extensive and profound Arabization preceding the conquest. It is regrettable that the dissertation of the American, W. Smeaton, on the Ghassānid state has appeared only in the form of a very brief extract.[101] On the rival state of the Lakhmids, a vassal of Persia, there is a good, well-informed study (in Arabic) by Yūsuf R. Ghanīma.[102] In a rather imprudent effort to fix the date of the birth of Muhammad, F. Altheim and R. Stiehl have given an interesting sketch dealing with the extension of Persian power in Arabia during this period.[103]

Sources for the Life of Muhammad

Among the sources for the life of Muhammad, the only one that is almost entirely reliable, but also the most difficult to use, is the Quran. More than a century of Western scholarly investigation into the extremely difficult problems posed by this document has been summarized in the second edition of Theodore Nöldeke's masterful study published originally in 1860 by this patriarch of Near Eastern Studies.[104] This important work was itself eventually to be superseded in certain respects. One of those who contributed most to our understanding of the Quran was certainly the Scotsman, Richard Bell. Possessing one of the keenest critical minds, he took up an examination of the question of the date of the various parts of the Quran which had been debated since the Muslim middle ages. For purposes of this study he developed certain new principles or, perhaps better, applied more rigorously principles already established along with all of their corollaries. The results of the considerable work which he carried out on the basis of these principles was a new translation of the Quran[105] in which the surahs were separated into constituent parts (frequently quite short) and dated separately. One of the principles taken over by R. Bell and carried to its logical conclusion was that the unit of "revelation" was not the surah but rather the short passage. According to him, Muhammad himself joined these "revealed" fragments of varying dates into surahs and then later revised them. After the death of Bell, a short but very substantial and original work of his was published[106] in which he set forth the principles and conclusions which emerged from his long study on the Quran. It is most regrettable that the lengthy and numerous notes which originally accompanied his translation were never published, apparently for financial reasons.

The other great work on the Quran was the French translation of Regis Blachère. This translation was preceded by a volume containing a valuable and substantial introduction.[107] This latter deals primarily with the history of the "received text" of the Quran and with the problem of canonical and noncanonical "readings" of this text. In these very important studies, R. Blachère brought to bear his very considerable knowledge of Arabic literature. He devoted less space to the critical analysis of the Quranic text itself. His two-volume translation of the Quran[108] took into account (in the notes and in the introduction to each surah) the various issues raised in earlier discussions. Breaking with tradition, R. Blachère reclassified the surahs into a chronological order based upon the critical studies of Nöldeke and his successors. He accorded only limited credence to Bell's efforts to break up the surahs into numerous short passages of varying dates. Although R. Blachère accepted many of the statements of Bell, he felt that the latter had taken his views too far. It is important to assess Blachère's introduction and notes cautiously and not to take too literally his chronological classification of surahs according to the date of the dominant section of each.

With regard to the Quran, mention ought to be made of the recent French translation by Muhammad Hamidullah. It is of interest in that it was carried out by a Muslim whose faith is clearly evident in the apologetic exegesis of the introduction and the notes.[109] Other translations, more important from the scientific point of view (or, in a less absolute sense, from the point of view of understanding the text situated historically in the period in which it was formulated), unfortunately remain uncompleted or unpublished. Setting aside the Muslim commentaries on the Quran and utilizing only the text itself to interpret the text, E. Beck has produced a remarkable commentary on selected portions of the Quran.[110] Rudy Paret proposed to follow the same method when he published his plan for a "new scientific translation of the Quran with brief commentary" in 1935. In 1950 he published a specimen of his exegesis along with an interesting translation.[111] This commentary was not intended for the layman as is at least partially the case with those of R.

Blachère and R. Bell, but rather for the specialist. It consists of a "translation that is as literal as possible," with more comprehensible paraphrases (in parentheses) and with additions (in italics) necessary for an understanding of the sense. At the bottom of the page, one finds references to parallel passages along with a detailed and thorough commentary. [This very important work which calls for a careful perusal to be fully appreciated is now published in two large volumes, the second being a copious but sober commentary containing numerous cross-references for every verse to all more or less parallel passages.] The plan for an edition of the Quranic text along with a critical apparatus, though elaborated already by G. Bergsträsser (who died prematurely), has never been completed; the plan was adopted by the Bavarian Academy of Science and was worked on by O. Pretzl.[112] Important materials have been collected by the Academy in question while, in a parallel effort, A. Jeffery published a volume of textual materials which will contribute toward the realization of this project.[113]

However, the most important work of recent years having to do with the analysis of the Quran (though its importance has not been fully appreciated in general) is the work of Harris Birkeland[114]—a work that is rather difficult to read and concerned only with five surahs. These surahs, according to Birkeland, represent the earliest stratum of the Quran and express the early ideas of Muhammad, which may have been rather different than what Orientalists have supposed. We shall return to this point a little later. The real value of the work, however, seems to us to lie in its methodology, which the author develops in certain other of his works that are rather difficult of access.[115] H. Birkeland has studied Muslim exegetical literature very carefully. Traditional Muslim interpretation appeared to depend so heavily on dogmatic, political, and other tendencies much later than the Prophet's death, that the attempt to extract historically valuable material had generally been abandoned. By a very meticulous study of the text of traditions (upon which the traditional interpretation was based) and a careful analysis of their chains of guarantors (*isnād*), Birkeland shows that this literature in places has preserved information of a very early date, going back to the first century of the *hijra* (622–719), and some of it having a real historical value. One can at times reconstruct first-century interpretations of certain passages, even when the tradition which represented this opinion has disappeared. The method is one which is very difficult to control, but one which may well furnish interesting results.[116]

This investigation reflects a methodological issue of the greatest importance which is being debated by Arabists, though in a somewhat muted fashion. We have already alluded above to the critique of the sources which has been the principal contribution of contemporary Orientalism in this field of study. In addition to the Quran, our most important source is the *ḥadīth* or tradition which is not only exegetical in nature. The term *ḥadīth* is a collective noun referring to the entire corpus of tradition which is composed of thousands of individual *ḥadīths* or narratives that claim to provide information pertaining to the sayings and deeds of the Prophet. The authenticity of each is "guaranteed" by a chain (*isnād*) which goes back from the latest reporter to the eye witness, normally a contemporary of the Prophet. The pattern of a typical *ḥadīth* may be illustrated as follows: X heard from Y who took it from Z, etc., that the Prophet said or did such and such a thing. A critical analysis of thousands of these traditions had already been carried out by medieval Muslim scholars. Moreover, a great number of these were rejected as false by Muslim scholars of very great authority. However, the criteria which they used to arrive at their judgments can hardly satisfy us today; the traditions which they accepted appear to us to be as suspect as those which they rejected. I. Goldziher, one of the first Western scholars to take up the problem, has shown systematically how traditions were forged in the Middle Ages in terms of the interest of a clan, a doctrine, or a party, in support of an ideological opinion or practice.[117] H. Lammens, as we have already seen, extended his radical critique particularly into the area of biographical traditions on the Prophet.[118] More recently, J. Schacht has completed a very important work on law by studying more closely still the late formation of traditions and the rather late date at which tradition was accepted (not without resistance) as authoritative.[119] Biographical studies of the Prophet, however, were confronted by a rather serious dilemma. If the Quran is the only definitely authentic source for his life, one ought to draw only from it. Unfortunately, however, this supposedly divine text refers to historical events only in very vague terms. Thus, if one is limited to it, one is condemned to a state of perpetual ignorance. Tradition, on the other hand, offers us clear, detailed explanations of obscure phrases in the sacred text and, even though there are differences on a myriad of details, it provides us with a coherent thread of events which best explains the text of the Quran. It is perhaps worth noting that no scholar has limited himself to the text of the Quran;[120] even the most critical have taken over from tradition the thread to which we have made reference.

This approach, however, is fraught with some danger. Under normal conditions one must build upon the facts provided by tradition, place these in their proper context, and elucidate them. When traditions are found that agree with the viewpoint of the scholar as to the causes, consequences, and conditions of a particular event (even though there are other traditions which contradict it), Orientalists are tempted to do as the Orientals have tended to do without any great sense of shame, that is, to accept as authentic those traditions that suit their own interpretation of an event and to reject others.

J. Schacht who himself had an extensive knowledge of these traditional materials took a firm stand against this very powerful tendency. He shows how even in matters of historical details this material reflects the influence of legal discussions. Some traditions assert that the Prophet had married a certain Maymūna during his pilgrimage to Mecca in the year 7 of the *Hijra* (629); others, however, indicate that he waited until his return to Medina. Is this a simple matter of history? Hardly, for the discussion raises the problem of whether marriage could be legally contracted when one is in the sacred state of the pilgrim. The schools of law discussed the matter and produced these contradictory traditions to support their positons.[121] One might well reply, of course, that none of these traditions puts in doubt the fact itself of the marriage of Muhammad to Maymūna in the year 7. Schacht based his critique on a very careful study of the fragments of the earliest extant biography of the Prophet, *viz.*, that of Mūsā b. ʻUqba who died in 758. While rejecting a number of traditions as lacking in authenticity, he shows that the remaining core of materials represents the historical memory of the generation which preceded Mūsā in the first quarter of the second century of the *Hijra* (718–742). This core consists of dates of certain events and lists of names (of individuals who had participated in a particular battle or event). The names listed might have been influenced by the interests of families.[122] Schacht did not declare himself formally against the historicity of these dates or of portions of these lists, though he obviously remained dubious. This attitude is certainly justified. Only after a very thorough examination can anything be admitted and even then only with serious reservation. However, in the final analysis, the thread of which I spoke and around which all the traditions are woven in itself reflects no partisan interest. It seems to have been the uncontested basis to which many flourishes were eventually added. The significant events of the Prophet's life, their approximate sequence (especially after the *Hijra*), the names of the principal actors in this vast historical drama, their relationship to each other, and their general attitudes—these remain essentially beyond question. As is often the case (notably in the life of Jesus), the facts that are embarrassing for later piety, explained in ways that are often confused and scarcely convincing, seem difficult to contest. The great Muslim general, Khālid b. al-Walīd, who died rather early without having participated in the great partisan struggles, had definitely, before his conversion, employed his talent for strategy in the struggle against Islam. He had played an important role in the defeat of the Muslims at Uḥud. His supporters may have attempted to minimize his role in this battle and to exaggerate the contributions which he later made to Islam; they may even have succeeded in advancing the date of his conversion. His adversaries, on the other hand, may have exerted pressure in the opposite direction. However, no one denies that he was on the side of the Quraish at Uḥud and on that of the Muslims at Mu'ta, and thus that he was converted between the two battles; no one denies the victory of the former when he directed their cavalry, etc. These are matters of fact which cannot be doubted, guaranteed as they are by family traditions and undoubtedly by documents that have since disappeared. An interval of a hundred years is not excessive for the collective memory of a society such as that formed by early Arab Islam. An Arab tribe of the Sudan transmits orally (even today) historical traditions and poetry, the oldest of which are attributed to an important tribal ancestor who lived in the second half of the sixteenth century and whose existence is attested by texts.[123] It ought to be pointed out here that in ideological movements the question of origins is a matter of great interest during times of expansion. In my childhood and adolescence I personally knew Charles Rappoport who in his own youth had visited Friedrich Engels. Both of us had a considerable number of books on the biography of this latter (born, it should be noted, in 1820); otherwise I would undoubtedly have questioned my informer avidly on the life of one of the founders of Marxism. If I had done so I would now be in the position of informing those younger than myself regarding events going back to 1840.[124]

Those traditions having to do with the life of the Prophet were collected rather early and grouped into special works. These are the *sīra*, i.e., traditional biographies of Muhammad written by Muslim authors. The constitution of the *sīra* has been the object of numerous studies which need to be expanded and deepened.[125] It is, in any case, gratifying to have at our disposal the English translation[126] (there is a German translation, though it is quite old) of the most classic production of this literature, the biography of Ibn Isḥāq written around A.D. 750 which has come down to us in a recension edited by Ibn Hishām around A.D. 800. The educated public and the non-Arabist historian thus have easy access to one of our principal sources. The translation by Professor A. Guillaume has been the object of minor criticism, but it is on the whole deserving of confidence.[127] Guillaume, who directed a team of scholars concerned with the publication of documents on the life of the Prophet[128] at the School of Oriental and African Studies at the University of London, has recently published a translation of extracts from a manuscript in the Qarawiyīn Library in Fez, which provides us with a different version (transmitted via another route) of the lectures of Ibn Isḥāq which were arranged and classified by Ibn Hishām. The differences from the former version are in general secondary but occasionally interesting.[129]

Important and detailed studies have been made along the same line by J. M. B. Jones who also published a critical edition of the text of Wāqidī.[130] This latter, a Medinan author who died in 823, collected numerous traditions on the life of the Prophet and arranged a certain number of them in the form of a *kitāb al-maghāzī*, "a book of the campaigns (of Muhammad)." Only a small fragment of this important source had previously been edited. It was done by Von Kremer in 1856, and published in a defective edition in Cairo in 1948. This work was known primarily in the abridged translation made by J. Wellhausen in 1882. In several preliminary studies, J. M. B. Jones has shown that one cannot consider Wāqidī as having plagerized Ibn Isḥāq. A comparative examination of the texts shows that both authors, in reality, produced parallel works from traditional material which had already taken shape, by adding the results of their own investigations.[131] In a series of critical studies, W. Arafat endeavored to demonstrate the mechanism of successive additions which, in the *sīra*, developed and gradually transformed an original theme.[132]

New Biographies

The patient work of scholars on the details of the Prophet's life and the progress of the studies on both the Arab and non-Arab milieu of this period have led (along with the influence of more recent conceptions of history) to a series of new biographical studies. Setting aside those that are not scientifically based, each of these studies has its own particular interest and point of view which afford some contribution to an overall comprehension of the personality and work of Muhammad. They are the point of departure for new investigations. It is appropriate, therefore, that we look a little more closely at these works.

The short study by R. Blachère which appeared in 1952[133] is the first of this new wave of biographies. It is clear, precise, and well thought out. Taking a mediating position between an uncritical view of the sources and a hyper-critical stance, and thoroughly steeped in the literature on the subject, Blachère underscores very clearly the serious problem presented by the sources viewed from a critical perspective. He regards the Quran as the only fully reliable source and utilizes biographical tradition with great caution. His reconstruction of the sequence of events is highly probable; but it is also accompanied by certain necessary qualifications. It is regrettable that the exigencies of publication forced Blachère to abridge and mutilate his original text. One might ask whether he does not assign too much importance to comparative mystical psychology in his reconstruction and whether he has not neglected the potential contribution of a sociological analysis of the Arab world and in particular of the Meccan world contemporary with the Prophet.

The following year, in 1953, the first of two books by W. Montgomery Watt on Muhammad appeared.[134] I have spoken elsewhere of what I regard as the methodological importance of these works so that here I will limit myself to a few brief remarks. Let me say first of all that W. M. Watt has undertaken a re-examination of a number of unresolved questions from a new vantage point. He has taken the sources seriously, analyzed them, and formulated his conclusions with great sharpness and clarity. Taking as his point of departure the great Muslim biographies, he drew up (with the purpose, for example, of determining the age and the tribal affiliation of the first converts) a catalogue of information regarding the "Companions" and the enemies of the Prophet. The clear and direct way in which he formulates his conclusions on the various events of the Prophet's life, the confident fashion in which he employs his conclusions, has appeared to some to indicate an exaggerated confidence in the reliability of these latter. But above all, he is the first one in a very long time to pose the problem of the success of Muhammad's preaching by going beyond the history of religions' viewpoint to which Orientalists, since the trenchent response of Snouck Hurgronje to the simplistic theses of Grimme regarding the purely "socialist" character of this preaching, have clung.[135] W. M. Watt attempted to understand earliest Islam in relation to the total (and not only the religious) situation of the society in which it was born. In this total situation, the economic upheaval and the resultant social reorganization played a role of capital importance. This interpretation led G. H. Bousquet to "accuse" W. M. Watt, an Episcopalian clergyman, of Marxism. One may designate this type of approach as one wishes, and it is certain that its diffusion owes much to Marx, but from the point of view of the investigator it is sufficient recommendation to point out that it rests on an analysis which seems to be essentially correct as regards the springs of social action and appears to offer rich possibilities for further investigation.

In 1956 W. Montgomery Watt published the second part of his biography of the Prophet, [136] this time concerning himself with the Medinan period. Though less original than the first, this volume offers much that is new, for example, on the evolution of relations between Muhammad and the Jews of Medina, on the position of the tribes of Medina, and especially on the social legislation of the Prophet in Medina. However, the reasons why the majority of the Arab tribes quickly rallied to the side of the Medinan state and its official ideology, Islam, appears to us to have been insufficiently clarified. In any case, Watt's work as a whole appears to constitute an important step forward in the study of the origins of Islam. One may no longer write on this subject as one would have before its appearance.

Published in the same year, the work of R. P. Charles -J. Ledit,[137] whose essential purpose is not biographical, ought to be mentioned. Indeed, its primary concern is to integrate Islam into a new Christian theological perspective which regards an alliance among those who adhere to monotheistic convictions in opposition to "atheistic materialism" as a matter of some importance (a view presently very widespread in Catholic circles). The author goes very far in this direction, having taken over from St. Thomas the definition of a type of prophecy which he calls "directive" and which enables a group or *cité* to progress beyond a given stage, but which does not require inerrancy. In a certain sense, therefore, Muhammad could become a divine messenger and Islam the culminating point of an extra-scriptural revelation. This, as the author says, is only a hypothesis. It is rather doubtful that it will meet with acceptance by Christian theologians, and Muslims certainly will not be satisfied with the secondary role assigned to their prophet. But beyond this point which is scarcely relevant to us, R. P. Ledit has devoted a large part of his work to the biography of Muhammad. He very usefully places the birth of Islam in the context of both the internal and external history of the Byzantine Empire. His ideas on the psychology of Muhammad, influenced by the school of Jung (L. Massignon had already made use of the theory of archetypes)[138] are interesting and ought to be taken into consideration. His views on Islam are perceptive and symphathetic. The author has brought to bear an impressive erudition, great ingenuity, and above all a very large humanity in this well-informed book which deserves to be read with care.

In the following year a biography of the Prophet which had long been awaited made its appearance, written by a highly respected Islamist and Arabist, Maurice Gaudefroy-Demombynes, who had distinguished himself through a series of works which have become classics.[139] The work which was begun some decades ago appeared when the author was on the verge of death, at the age of ninety-four. Despite his physical condition, however, he retained his lucidity, clarity, and finesses of judgment. His book is a veritable *summa* calling to mind the work of Buhl by its copious and comprehensive character. The first part (following a substantial introduction on pre-Islamic Arabia) is devoted to the life of the Prophet, and embraces a wealth of detail, analyzed with a subtlety and human sympathy that are essential if one is to understand and assess a man as distant from us as the time, place, and milieu in which he lived. The second part of the work, which is more complete than the biographies examined up to this point, treats the message of Muhammad, including his conception of God, universal history (creation, the prophets, the end of the world and the last judgement, death, paradise, and hell), the faith and duty of believers, social ethics, and economic and family life. All of this is based upon a profound and almost exhaustive knowledge of the sources and of earlier works. It evidences a sensitive and careful reflection based on the texts whose value and deficiencies the author assesses in an objective fashion. The final preparation of the work for publication unfortunately suffered as a result of the state of the author's health: numerous errors in printing, especially in connection with transcriptions, but also including references that are insufficiently precise. He does acknowledge that he had not been able to give adequate attention to more recent studies. On pre-Islamic Arabia his discussion is largely outdated. The spirit which animates the work is that of rationalism, of an *Aufklärung* that is open and receptive. On the whole, it is an important manual which will not be easily surpassed.

In 1957, a small book appeared in Germany (in a widely read though scholarly series) from the pen of a scholar who had not previously presented his views on the Prophet's life as a whole, but who was nonetheless one of the most competent authorities on the subject.[140] I am referring to Rudi Paret whose succinct exposition deserves careful attention. His views are well grounded and secure, as is seen, for example, in his assessment of the controversy raised by R. Bell and H. Brikeland regarding the content of the earliest revelation. Contrary to these authors, he holds that there is no valid reason for thinking that Muhammad's preaching on the Last Judgment was later than his statements on gratitude for divine benefits. Against W. M. Watt, he believes (rightly in our view) that, in the somewhat scandalous matter of Muhammad's marriage to Zainab (wife of his adopted son), the desire to establish a juridical precedent played no role in his mind. He also correctly insists on the largely improvised character of the political behavior of the Prophet, which contradicts Watt's understanding of his plans for expansion. On the other hand, though R. Paret's opposition to Grimme's thesis of the socialist Muhammad" is correct in itself, it leads him to minimize unduly the role of economic and social factors in the origin of Islam.

In 1959 a lengthy though quite different biography of the Prophet, also claiming to be exhaustive, was published in Paris. I am referring here to a rather new phenomenon, *viz.*, a work by a Muslim, Muhammad Hamidullah.[141] This latter, originally from Haidarabad, sent into exile following the destruction by India of the Muslim state of the *niẓām*, has been known for some time to Orientalists through his numerous works on Islam. In his work on the Prophet one meets those characteristics that have become consistent features of his works: an extensive knowledge of the Muslim sources, a considerable knowledge of the relevant European literature [141a] which he makes little of because he finds it to be generally irrelevant, and finally an unshakable faith in Islam and in all of its teachings. One can only admire this quiet faith. But that gives to all of his works and, in particular, to the one just mentioned (given its subject and also the present state of Muslim dogmatics on the question of divine revelation), an apologetic flavor supported by an absolute, uncritical confidence in the sources. The traditions (*ḥadīths*) on the deeds and sayings of the Prophet are invoked as unimpeachable historical documents despite the fact that many of them obviously reflect conditions and conflicts of a period very much posterior to the death of the Prophet.[142] All the deeds of the Prophet, even the most questionable, are justified and admired. In a kind of transhistorical perspective, all Muslim institutions are ardently defended, often with great naiveté, as definitive and eternally valid (since they are divinely inspired) for the whole of human existence, both social and individual. Having said this, the work is extremely interesting, not as an elaborate scientific exposition of what one can know regarding the life and work of Muhammad, but as a compendium of what Muslim authors have said on the subject and as an accurate reflection of the traditional view. It is also important for the historian who makes critical use of it in that it provides him with material drawn from little known sources, and he should not hesitate to take the views of M. Hamidullah into consideration on a number of questions. And, finally, even for those who do not share the faith of the author it is an attractive work because of the fact that it is inspired by an ardent sincerity.

In 1961 W. Montgomery Watt summarized the substance of his two earlier volumes; this time, however, he arranged the contents chronologically[143] and omitted the scholarly apparatus. His ideas have sometimes gained in clarity for having been stated in a more concise fashion. They are shaped by his more recent reflections on some of the larger sociological problems posed by the Arabic sources. He gives particular attention to role of ideas in human action, especially in the area of political action. These reflections led in the same year to the publication of a more ambitious book, [144] but one on which we cannot comment here. From the strictly historical point of view, he has seen more clearly the importance of the Persian defeat of 627–628 in explaining the later successes of Muhammad.

In the same year the author of these lines published his own biography of the Prophet in a series designed for popular consumption.[145] Drawing on the achievements of his predecessors, he attempted to develop certain points of view which he regarded as not having been sufficiently treated by these latter. He attempted somewhat cautiously to show the relationship between the eschatological visions of the early preaching of Muhammad and the international political situation of that period. Taking the sociological correlations of his preaching as established (notably by Watt), the author attempted to show how a personal, psychological evolution shaped Muhammad into an instrument capable of formulating and communicating an ideology that corresponded to the needs of the time and the milieu. At various points he noted how this ideology exhibited characteristics which seem to be persistent features of movements of this type.[146] He attempted to delineate the successive sociological forms which the community that formed around Muhammad took, and to underline the factors behind its evolution in the direction of a new state as well as the causes for the massive rallying of Arabia to this state and its ideology.

Under the influence of this massive European scholarly activity, an evolution also began to take place in Arab historiography. In this connection mention must be made of the work by Salih Ahmad al- Ali (an Iraqi professor and a graduate of Oxford) on pre-Islamic Arabia and the life of Muhammad.[147] The author, it is true, did not have access to classical sources or to epigraphy; he traces facts of Arab history known only by these sources at second hand. In addition, the force of Muslim religious opinion prevented him from "explaining" the birth of Islam as an ideological movement reflecting the state of the milieu. But he does make wise use of the work of Orientalists (unfortunately, he knew only what had been published or translated into English or French) in the hope of influencing the views of Muslims on certain questions. He skillfully protected himself behind a wall of medieval Muslim views. However, the history of revelation which he traces is no longer presented as a unique and monolithic given. The stages in the evolution of the thought of Muhammad as set forth by certain non-Muslims (the author utilizes especially W. M. Watt) are transposed into successive waves of revelations. This interpretation is a first step in the direction of an historiography freed from the chains of theology, and as such corresponds precisely to the stage represented by Richard Simon in the seventeenth century in his treatment of the Old Testament.[147a] We must hope that in Islam the evolution will be more rapid than in the Catholic Church where the views of Simon were not adopted by the Magistracy until 1943 in the encyclical *Divino afflante spiritu*.[148]

Special Problems

Without entering into the details, it is now time to review the principal problems which the biography of the Prophet poses for the historian, sociologist, and psychologist and to indicate the important works which deal with these. It seems to us rather clear that the interrelationship and order of these problems have often been misunderstood.

The principal problem which strikes the general historian immediately is that of the factors behind the astounding wave of Muslim conquests of the seventh century. They might be divided into two classes: those factors that led to the launching of the conquest and those that contributed to its success. These latter, in large measure, fall under the jursidiction of specialists in Byzantine and Persian history. Why did these great empires collapse at the first blow? There was obviously the great war from 602 to 628 which weakened both participants. However, there must have been deeper causes which prevented them from recovering in time. We shall leave the answer to this question to the experts.[149] As for the causes of the Arab conquest, they are only in part related to the campaigns begun at the end of the Prophet's life. The encroachment of the Arabs on the Fertile Crescent had been a fact for a very long time before Islam. Some see the cause of this expansion in the supposed progressive desiccation of Arabia (Caetani), others in an irresistible psychological penchant for raiding (Lammens), still others in a spontaneous tendency toward aggression (J. Schumpeter).[150] But the evolution of the climate was much more complex than had been imagined at the time of Caetani, so that if a period of drought had begun at the time of Muhammad it could in no way explain the earlier tendency toward expansion.[151] As for those explanations based on the notion of collective psychology and the idea of the soul or spirit of a people, one can only hope that they will no longer impress historians in view of the many demonstrations of their futility. As early as 1910, C. H. Becker[152] saw clearly the economic factors behind the expansive tendencies that appear when people who are at a lower level of material existence than those around them come to possess a military superiority over these latter. Conditions such as these are encountered particularly when cattle-breeding nomads are situated on the borders of an agricultural population which can no longer be protected by a strong state. One of the reasons for the Arab successes of the eighth century was the religious ideology which inspired them. This ideology prevented them from being assimilated by the surrounding civilzation, as had occurred repeatedly in the earlier waves of encroachment from the desert.

In order to stand up against Byzantium and Persia, however, the Arabs had first of all to form themselves into a state with an ideology of its own, *viz.*, Islam. This in turn raises the question of the factors behind the success of Islam in Arabia. It is important moreover to see that these factors are different from those of the success of the larger conquest. It is also essential to distinguish the causes of the success at Mecca (in our judgment very well elucidated by Watt) from those of the success at Medina (more complex) and those of the general conversion of Arabia. The authors of the more recent biographies cited above have discussed them extensively without the problem having been brought any closer to a solution.[153]

Besides the explanation of these successes which appear to us to be essentially linked to the political and the social situation (this latter having been profoundly disturbed by a major economic transformation of certain sectors of Arabia), it is necessary to understand why this situation led to this particular result when several others were possible. This question is clearly connected with the personality of Muhammad. It is essential, therefore, to study the development of Muhammad's personality in order to understand how he was able to offer the answer that he did in that particular situation, having forged it in his consciousness as a variable of the mode by which he apprehended it.

Here, it is also essential to raise the question of the psychology of Muhammad. The type of mysticism represented by this man who was in other respects so much a realist is not easy to unravel. The Finnish scholar, H. Holma, an expert in Nordic works on mystical psychology, has written a biography whose primary value lies in the fact that it raises these problems with special clarity.[154] As Blachère has rightly suggested, one should not minimize the value of psychoanalysis as a resource.[155] On the other hand, the introduction of this discipline into the field of historical studies has often given rise to skepticism.[156] Naturally, here again one should go beyond the purely religious sphere and give a total explanation to this exceptional personality. Here the Quran offers us a very valuable source which has not yet been fully explored.

In addition to his predisposition and the interior structure of his psyche, some attention ought to be given to his cultural formation. Here we encounter the question of "influences" debated so extensively. We must pause a moment in connection with the work of Geo Widengren, a scholar whose vast learning extends far beyond Arabia and Islam. He is especially well known for his investigations into Iranian religions. However, he always conceived his work within the framework of the comparative history of religion, contributing to this field of study through his considerable knowledge of the literature dealing with (among other things) Semitic religions and Islam. Of particular interest is a series of works which he published under the general title of *King and Savior*, devoted to the study of sacred kinship in the ancient Orient. Somewhat surprisingly perhaps, his involved and very learned work, entitled *Muhammad, the Apostle of God and His Ascension*, [157] appeared in this series (number 5). This book is full of comparative suggestions, some of which had already been advanced by other authors, but enriched and defined more precisely by him. Here I can only refer the reader to this work and present a brief sketch of his general conclusions. Widengren attempts to situate Muhammad in the framework of a typology of the celestial messenger. In Islam (and not only early Islam, but also later forms of Islam such as that of Shīʿism where the personality of the *imām* plays such a considerable role) two types of religion come together: *the institutional type* in which revelation is communicated once and for all by a divine savior or by a prophet, and *the charismatic type* in which the inspiration is communicated in divine visions through the intermediary of a divine incarnation, from the Light or Spirit of God or celestial messenger to a series of new terrestial representatives forming a long chain of successive "descendents" of the same divine being, *viz.*, the celestial messenger. This latter type is reflected in the details of the ancient Oriental myth and ritual scheme having to do with the divine king. It can be seen, for example, in the early narrative of the *miʿrāj*, the ascension of Muhammad to heaven. The ideas of G. Widengren deserve to be discussed in detail. In any case, one point underscored by him needs to be kept in mind, *viz.*, the chain of fundamental ideas which linked early Islam with those of the great Eastern religious movements that issued from gnosticism, or in conjunction with this latter, in which the role of Iran was so extensive.

Less remote and diffused, and more easily accessible are the ideas of Jewish and Christian origin which influenced the Prophet. The question of influence which had been discussed extensively in an earlier period, as we have seen, has been taken up again notably under the influence of new tendencies in Catholic circles which aim at a rapprochement between Islam and Christianity. It is clearly out of doctrinal concerns that Father Jomier, a Dominican, published a valuable little book on the relationship of the Bible and the Quran.[158] With this concern in mind, Jomier turns to the question: what use was made of the biblical elements which the Quran contains, or of the belief in the prophets and in Jesus found in the sacred book of Islam? Though Jomier's exposition is of interest to those concerned with this question and treats the Quranic and biblical materials each within their own framework, he does nonetheless succeed in preserving an historical perspective. One finds in the work a series of precise and clear discussions (well researched, though without the visible trappings of scholarship) on the relation of the different parts of the Bible and the Quran, on what the Quran knows of the great biblical personalities such as Jesus, on what the Quran teaches concerning such issues as the brotherhood of man, the philosophy of history, the doctrine of salvation, underscoring similarities and differences with balance and wisdom.

The much more voluminous work of D. Masson[159] is of less value for the historian, despite the fact that it does represent a considerable effort on the author's part. The perspective of this work which is concerned with relations between Islam and the Jewish and Christian religions is, in effect, a comparative one, and as such devoid of any real historical interest. Masson provides a minimum of scholarly discussion, limiting herself to a classification of the texts (Jewish, Christian, and Muslim) within a theological framework which focuses on such themes as God and his unity, creation, revelation, the role of the Quran, and the future life. She draws on the Old and New Testaments and the Quran, each of which she quotes at length. The apocrypha, the Jewish and Muslim books of tradition, and the Fathers of the Church are also cited at some length, most often, however, from existing translations or (where Christian theological literature is concerned) from the very convenient *Enchiridia* put out by the Catholic (German) press. This collection of texts brought together by Masson is certainly very useful and offers interesting material for study thanks to the mass of documents which it contains. The historian however, will be disappointed and sometimes irritated by the almost complete absence of an historical framework.

There is little new to point to on the question of purely Christian influence. One ought to take note however of the convenient collection of Muslim texts on Jesus made by Michel Hayek which is of concern to us here only for the Quranic part.[160] By contrast, the matter of Jewish influence has been the object of several works, one of which is very poorly done, though it is scholarly in appearance and does contain some useful material.[161] Muhammad's knowledge of haggadic materials has been emphasized by certain scholars with the result that exaggerated conclusions have been drawn.[162] The discovery of manuscripts from the Judean desert has made it possible for C. Rabin to develop some very important views on the type of Judaism represented in Arabia in the seventh century. According to him it is a question of anti-rabbinic Jews standing in the tradition of the Qumrān community among which Rabin sees Pharisee rigorists. Though one may not always be convinced by his arguments (this definition of the Qumrān sectaries, as is well known, can no longer be maintained), we do have here an interesting lead which deserves to be pursued.[163]

The discussion of influence has recently led to the outbreak of a polemic that has very little scientific merit. It is appropriate that we draw attention to it here, for the nonspecialist might easily be misled. A clergyman writing under the pseudonym of Hanna Zakarias (died January 1959) took up and promoted an "hypothesis" already advanced in different forms by G. Weil in 1843 and A. Sprenger in 1858.[164] An anti-Muslim fanatic, opposed to those Catholics who call for a rapprochement with Islam, Zakarias sets forth the view (influenced also in part by the politics of the Algerian war) that Muhammad was merely an uncultured Arab, the puppet of a Machiavellian rabbi who disguised himself as an Arab in order to spread Judaism around the world in disguise. The Quran, according to him, is the work of this rabbi and what are presented as the words of God addressed directly to his Prophet ("Say . . . ," "O you who . . .") are in reality the orders of this rabbi to his *golem*. This obviously absurd[165] hypothesis is set forth in a virulent and brazen fashion, and is based upon disciplines obviously unknown to the author. But it continues to receive support from partisans of the same political and religious persuasion and has had an impact on a large sector of French opinion despite its unscientific character and its defiance of simple good sense.[166]

The content of Muhammad's preaching has given rise to numerous short studies which we cannot consider here. In connection with the works of Rudi Paret and H. Birkeland, we have referred to the controversy over the content of his earliest preaching, *viz.*, whether the theme of divine judgment is prior in time to the emphasis on God's goodness and mercy, and man's duty to show gratitude to God for his blessings. Here in connection with the evolution of his preachings we must raise the important point of Muhammad's adoption of Abraham as a model and precursor. Father Y. Moubarac devoted an entire work to this subject.[167] This author espouses a point of view very different from that represented by the majority of the works mentioned above. His approach places great emphasis on the coherence and internal logic of Quranic teaching and the thought of Muhammad. He insists on the specifically religious character of Muhammad's action rather than on its extra-religious motivations, *viz.*, political, social, etc. Father Moubarac thus follows the thought of the late Louis Massignon whose lectures and statements (scattered throughout his works) on the problem of the Prophet and his message[168] have had an impact and an influence well beyond what our brief treatment here might suggest. Following Massignon, Moubarac is particularly interested in Abraham as the recognized ancestor of the three monotheistic religions. The Quran regards him, in effect, as the first Muslim, the one who first built the Ka'ba at Mecca, the prototype of the later prophets including Moses,

Jesus, and Muhammad, and the one who (following a divine revelation) first established monotheistic teaching. We know of course that biblical genealogies recognize him as both the ancestor of the Jews (by Isaac) and the Arabs (by Ishmael).[169] Beyond his scholarly objective, Moubarac aims at a religious and perhaps even political rapprochement. His conscientious and exhaustive work includes a critique of the viewpoint of certain Orientalists, particularly Snouck Hurgronje and Wensinck who present the evolution of the personality of Abraham in the Quran as a consequence of the political "reorientation" of Muhammad at Medina. According to Moubarac, the figure of Abraham is anterior to the *Hijra*. The evolution of Abraham is therefore independent of the aforementioned event and is to be explained as the autonomous maturation of a religious idea. A large part of the book is moreover devoted to a study of the meaning of the life of Abraham for the Quran, and of his role in religious history. There is an interesting comparison between the role of a "model" and the notion of "type" in the Judeo-Christian tradition. The book of Y. Moubarac, written with great learning and skill, though not without a certain lack of order in the exposition, presents serious arguments (always deserving to be studied and to be carefully pondered) in favor of views often at variance with those that have become classic among Orientalists. The perspective of L. Massignon, Y. Moubarac, and others undoubtedly represents a necessary reaction against an understanding of a text in terms that were too often foreign to the text, and a tendency to isolate themes from the religious context to which they belong—tendencies which were characteristic of the nineteenth century. However, the historian must occasionally ask himself if the reaction has not gone too far. Some of the methods of this school of thought must be a matter of concern to historians. To study the internal logic of a faith and to show respect are very legitimate objectives. The scholar has a perfect right to attempt to re-experience within himself the "fire" and the exigencies of the religious consciousness under study. However, the elements that comprise a coherent system could indeed have derived from a variety of very different sources and might well have played an entirely different role in other systems. Respect for the faith of sincere believers cannot be allowed either to block or deflect the investigation of the historian. The results derived from examining a particular faith on a personal "mental testing bench" ought to be made the object of a very severe critical examination. One must defend the rights of elementary historical methodology, in other words, to brandish Langlois and Seignobos. Passing directly from the plane of the coherence of religious ideas or of respect for the religious life to the plane of objective reconstruction of past religious consciousness is inadmissible.[170]

The most interesting contributions to the study of the content of the Quran have come from the analysis of concepts and words. There is some controversy on this subject, for the concepts of the Quran are particularly fluid and each conceals an evolution that is difficult to trace. Here we can only mention in passing the important article by H. Ringgren on *islam* and the words connected with it;[171] the very original study of M. M. Bravmann on the same word and also on others, notably on *Imān* "faith";[172] the response of Ringgren on the question of "faith";[173] and the article by the same author on the fear of God in the Quran.[174] In a very careful and searching study of Quranic vocabulary, he shows that the attribution of a positive value to the idea of fear in Arabia is of Judeo-Christian origin. However, the word *taqwā* (often translated by "fear [of God]") which has given rise to the view that fear plays a greater role in Islam than love has in reality a much larger meaning. The study of Al-verny on prayer provides some light on the psychological evolution of Muhammad and his conception of God.[175]

We must refer here to studies on the divine names, the hypostases and the action of God in the Quran,[176] and to studies on Quranic language, style, and vocabulary.[177] Mention must be made of the use of computerized methods to carry out a conceptual analysis of the Quran.[178]

Studies on the social meaning of the laws enacted in Medina will be of as much interest to the historian as discussions on the various events of the life of the Prophet. There are serious differences of opinion in this area particularly as it relates to the Meccan period (that is the period before 622). However, discussion of these matters will be found (or at least referred to) in the biographies cited above.[179]

The On-Going Influence of Muhammad

The founders of triumphant ideologies are in general greater in death than in life. The figure of Muhammad continued to grow in importance in the consciousness of the adherents of the religion which he established. He never concealed his weakness, never ceased to consider himself as human (often all too human), as an unworthy instrument in the hands of the Almighty, a megaphone for the dissemination of messages from on high. But he went on to become the Holy Prophet whose intercession had sovereign authority before God, "the best of creatures," endowed with charisma, with supernatural powers. How this evolution came about and under what influences is a subject of great importance for historians and sociologists. Fortunately we possess an excellent work on this subject. The wealth of detail which it contains renders it an important tool and one that will be indispensible for years to come, though one that ought to be expanded and supplemented at certain points.[180] Among studies of this latter type we shall mention only the perceptive sketch of A. Abel;[181] the very detailed and learned study of A. Fischer on the reverence and the taboo of the name of Muhammad;[182] and the text (in the colloquial Arabic of Egypt) collected in 1938 and published by Enno Littmann in 1950.[183] The latter text is indeed a "popular epic" (*Volksepos*) in which the events related by the traditional biography of the Prophet are reflected in great detail, in a kind of sonorous verse recited before a fervent public, in an atmosphere of adoration, inspired both by popular religion and by stories of chivalry familiar to the professional Muslim narrators. It would be well worthwhile to collect as many of the texts of this type as possible while there is still time.

Not less interesting is the study of the evolution of conceptions of Muhammad which were formed in the Christian West. The latter in some cases borrowed genuine data and themes previously adopted in the East. The Christian West integrated these Eastern facts, reinterpreted and reconstituted them in the light of its own needs and ideas.[184] One of the great events in this connection was the discovery by E. Cerulli and J. Muñoz Sendino (independently of each other, according to information provided by U. Monneret de Villard) of the Latin and Medieval French translations of the *Kitāb al-Miʿrāj*. This was an Arabic work which recounted the legendary ascension of the Prophet to heaven, mounted on the mare Burāq and accompanied by the angel Gabriel. It is now clear that these translations were known between 1350 and 1360 by the poet Fazio degli Uberti and in the century following by Roberto Caracciolo of Lecce. It is entirely possible, therefore, that they influenced Dante. E. Cerulli has collected and grouped around these texts a number of documents relating to the knowledge of Islam in the Middle Ages in Europe. In particular one should take note of the very precise study of the life of the Prophet written in the twelfth century by Godfrey of Viterbe, secretary of the German emperors.[185]

It is very interesting to trace the evolution of the conceptions which were formed of the Prophet of Islam in more recent times. This is a question that pertains to studies of an entirely different sort, *viz.*, those having to do with the history of ideas in modern Europe. For example, as M. Petrocchi[186] has emphasized, the period of the *Aufklärung* also had its myth of the wise, tolerant sovereign and legislator. It took its place beside the myth of the good savage and that of China and, as such, expressed the ideals of the period. The theme was taken up especially by the Count Henry de Boulainvilliers (1658–1722) in a work that still continues to be influential in certain (though somewhat unexpected) quarters. It would be interesting and worthwhile to carry this study of Western conceptions of Muhammad further.

NOTES

(See page xi for list of abbreviations of journal titles)

1. [The English translation of this study has been examined and revised by the author. We regret that it has not been possible to bring the study up to date in every respect. However, we have added in brackets [ ] the more important new references, information regarding new editions, translations, etc. We have been particularly concerned to note references to English translations of texts and scholarly treatises.]
2. L. Caetani, *Annali dell'Islam* (Milan, 1905–1926) 10 vols. Only the first two volumes (vol. I [1905], vol. II, part 1 [1907]) have to do with the life of the Prophet. On the author, cf. J. Fueck, *Die arabischen Studien in Europa* (Leipzig, 1955), p. 297f., and also L. Bouvat, "Le Prince Caetani et son oeuvre," *Revue du monde musulman,* 27 (1914), p. 53–89.

2a. Marracci was a dedicated Christian driven not only by a deep antipathy for one he believed to be an archimposter, but also by a desire to educate the masses; an apologist but at the same time a learned Arabist who sought to base his arguments on reliable sources.

3. On Ludovico Marracci (1612–1700) and his work, see the communication by G. Levi Della Vida reprinted in his *Anedotti e Svaghi arabi e non arabi* (Milan—Naples, 1959), pp. 193–210. On the image of Muhammad in the Middle Ages, see pp. 00–00.
4. On the history of these studies, see especially J. Fueck, *Die arabischen Studien in Europa* (Leipzig, 1955) which considers them primarily from the philological point of view. D. G. Pfannmüller, *Handbuch der Islam Literatur* (Berlin and Leipzig, 1923), pp. 115–206, gives a substantial history of the conceptions which were formed of the Prophet and of studies on him in the West. For more details, there is the bibliographical volume of V. Chauvin, *Bibliographie des ouvrages arabes ou relatifs aux Arabes publiés dans l'Europe chrétienne de 1810 à 1885* (Liège, 1892 ff. [vol. X: *Le Coran et la tradition,* 1907; vol. XI: *Mahomet,* 1909]). For a bibliography on the whole of Islam which mentions the important works that are still valuable, cf. J. Sauvaget, *Introduction to the History of the Muslim East: A Bibliographical Guide* [a translation of the second French edition recast by C. Cahen; published by the University of California, Berkeley and Los Angeles, 1965]; and B. Spuler and L. Forrer, *Der vordere Orient in islamischer Zeit* (Bern, 1954 [*Orientalistik,* III Teil]).
5. [The reference here is to the bible of the positive-minded historians, in France at least,

viz., the work by Ch. V. Langlois and Ch. Seignobos, *Introduction aux études historiques* (Paris, 1898), English trans., *Introduction to the Study of History* (London, 1898; 5th ed. New York, 1932)].

6. I believe it is very necessary in the present atmosphere to indicate clearly that it is in no way a question of an incapacity congenital to the "Arab spirit." Many contemporary Arab authors have given us excellent historical studies and remarkable critical editions which in all points conform to the rules of historical and philological method. However, in the present state of affairs and for precise sociological reasons, the biography of Muhammad is a subject that is taboo and is permitted only when written as apologetic and edifying literature. For more details regarding this judgment, see pp. 00–00.
7. Ibn Saad, *Biographien Muhammeds, seiner Gefährten und der späteren Träger des Islams bis zum Jahre 230 der Flucht* (edited by Eduard Sachau; Leiden, 1905–1940), 9 vols., some of which are in several parts. The first two volumes (in four parts) which appeared from 1905 to 1917 are concerned with the life of the Prophet.
8. See the restrained and competent judgment of R. Blachère, *Le problème de Mahomet* (Paris 1952), pp. 8f. (see the present study, note 133).
9. Tor Andrae, *Muhammed, hans liv och hans tro* (Stockholm, 1930), 243 pages [translated into English under the title of *Muhammed: The Man and His Faith* (New York, 1936) from the German translation of the Swedish edition]; translated into French under the title: *Mahomet, sa vie et sa doctrine* by J. Gaudefroy-Demombynes (Paris, 1945), 193 pages. I have not seen the new Swedish edition, edited and reworked by Geo Widengren (Stockholm, 1950), 269 pages.
10. Tor Andrae, "Der Ursprung des Islams und das Christentum," *Kyrkohistorik Arsskrift* (1923), pp. 149–206; (1924), pp. 213–92; (1925), pp. 45–112. Later the study appeared in book form (Uppsala-Stockholm, 1926); a French translation (not especially good) under the title, *Les Origines de l'Islam et le Christianisme* (Paris, 1955), 215 pages. Cf. M. Gaudefroy-Demombynes, "Les Origines de l'Islam d'après M. Tor Andrea," *Revue d'histoire des religions,* 96 (1927), pp. 340–46.
11. K. Ahrens, "Christliches im Qoran," *ZDMG,* 84 (1930), pp. 15–68, 148–90; also by the same author, *Muhammed als Religionsstifter* (Leipzig, 1935). One of the best assessments of this work is that by M. Guidi, *Rivista degli studi orientali,* 17 (1938), pp. 123–27. The scrupulous thesis of Wilhelm Rudolph (*Die Abhängigkeit des Qorans von Judentum und Christentum* [Stuttgart, 1922]) while recognizing the extensive nature of Jewish influence, came to the conclusion that it was Christianity that was the decisive factor in the rise of Islam.
12. Abraham Geiger, *Was hat Mohammed aus dem Judenthume aufgenommen?* (Bonn, 1833; republished in Leipzig, 1902), 215 pages.
13. C. C. Torrey, *The Jewish Foundation of Islam* (New York, 1933). [The work was published again in 1967 with a new introduction by Franz Rosenthal (New York).] G. Vajda ("Juifs et musulmans selon le ḥadīth," *Journal Asiatique,* 229 [1937], pp. 57–127) has given a very careful analysis of information from Tradition on Jews during the time of the Prophet, information that is clearly open to criticism, but it is almost the only information we possess.
14. In addition to the admirably concise work of J. Horovitz, *Koranische Untersuchungen* (Berlin and Leipzig, 1926), one has a more developed exposition with lengthy citations of texts in D. Sidersky, *Les Origines des légendes musulmanes dans le Coran et dans les vies des prophetes* (Paris, 1933). This work, however, has certain serious weaknesses; the basic work on this subject is the remarkable study by a student of Horovitz, H. Speyer, *Die biblischen Erzählungen im Qoran* (Gräfenhainischen, 1931). This excel-

lent work which, as Rudi Paret has observed, is known and used very little outside Germany (however, the reason was the destruction of the majority of the copies of the work in the course of anti-Semitic developments of the period), has just been republished photomechanically (Hildesheim, G. Olms, 1961).

15. A point which two remarkable articles have emphasized *viz.*, one by J. Fueck, "Die Originalität des arabischen Propheten," *ZDMG,* 90 (1936), pp. 509–25, and another by G. von Grunebaum, "Von Muhammads Wirkung and Originalität," *WZKM,* 44 (1937), pp. 29–50.
16. Many (including myself) have felt the same way that I. Goldziher once expressed himself (reported to me by the late Louis Massignon in a letter dated August 7, 1961): "What would remain of the Gospels if he applied to them the same methods he applies to the Quran?"
17. Among his principal works, we may mention the following: *Fâṭima et les filles de Mahomet, notes critiques pour l'étude de la Sîra* (Rome, 1912); *Le Berceau de l'Islam, l'Arabie occidentale à la veille de l'hégire* (Rome, 1914); *La Mecque à la veille de l'hégire* (Beirut, 1924); *L'Arabie occidentale avant l'hégire* (Beirut, 1928: a collection of articles); *Études sur le siècle des Omayyades* (Beirut, 1930: also a collection of articles).
18. F. Buhl, *Das Leben Muhammeds* (German translation by H. H. Schaeder; Leipzig, 1930; reprinted, Heideberg, 1955). In an abridged form one finds his ideas set forth in his lengthy article, "Muḥammad" in the *Encyclopedia of Islam* (first edition) and also his article "Ḳur'ān" in the same work [see also the *Shorter Encyclopedia of Islam,* pp. 390–405 and pp. 273–86 respectively].
19. For example the good, but succinct article by O. Pretzl intended for historians ("Mohammed als geschichtliche Persönlichkeit," *Historiche Zeitschrift,* 161 [1939–1940], pp. 457–76), a balanced study whose analysis of the relation between the Prophet and the Jews (virtually ignored) suffers from having been published in Germany during this period. We can only cite here in passing the following: a militant Catholic work which attempts—without success—to be fair (M. D'Herbigny, *L'Islam naissant, notes psychologiques* [Rome, 1929, in the series *Orientalia Christiana,* vol. XIV, part 2 no. 51]); a rather admiring, though nonapologetic biography by a German Jew writing under the assumed name of Essed Bey, but lacking any critical study of the sources and, therefore, without scientific value (Mohammed Essed Bey, *Mahomet,* French translation, Paris, 1934; there is also an English translation entitled *Mohammad: A Biography,* New York, 1936); a highly apologetic biography (E. Dinet et el-Hadj Sliman ben Ibrahim, *La Vie de Mohammed, prophète d'Allah* [Paris, 1937; translated into Arabic, Cairo, 1959]); a poorly informed, though well-intentioned work by a French admirer of Islam from North Africa (R. Lerouge, *Vie de Mahomet* [Paris, 1939]); an uncritical compilation that is sympathetic to its hero (P. Achard, *L'Historie de la Méditerranée, Mahomet* [Paris, 1942]); and a romanticized biography, full of errors and fabrication (Jean Barois, *Mahomet, le Napoléon du Ciel* [Paris, 1943]). I have not been able to see the biography by D. Von Mikusch, with the perceptive title *Muhammed, Tragödie des Erfolges* (Leipzig, 1932). We must also mention the very wise pages written by G. Vajda "L'état actuel des recherches sur les origines de l'Islam," *Revue de synthèse,* 9 (1935), pp. 185–95.
20. E. Dermenghem, *La Vie de Mahomet* (Paris, 1929; second edition, Paris, 1950). [This work was translated into English under the title, *The Life of Mahomet* (New York, 1930).] More recently the same author has written a very small, condensed work, a little too "spiritualistic" for my taste, but delightfully illustrated, under the title, *Mahomet et la tradition islamique* (Paris, 1955).
21. We have a critical discussion of these positions in a substantial analysis which N.

Ellisséeff has given in "L'Islamologie en U.R.S.S. d'après un ouvrage recent" (*Mélanges Louis Massignon,* II, pp. 23–76) of the work by the Russian N. A. Smirnov. One will also find expositions of the general lines of Soviet policy by W. Z. Laqueur, *The Soviet Union and the Middle East* (London, 1959), pp. 56–60 and *passim.*

22. *Fī'sh-Shi'r al-Jāhilī* (Cairo, 1926); also *Fī'l-Adab al-Jāhilī* (Cairo, 1927). On the heart of the matter, cf. R. Blachère, *Histoire de la littérature arabe,* I (Paris, 1952), p. 171ff. On political developments associated with the publication of these works, cf. M. Colombe, *L'évolution de l'Egypte 1924–1950* (Paris, 1951), pp. 123ff.
23. One might mention (using as reference the 5th edition, Cairo, 1952) as typical passages, the attack on the narrative of the "satanic verses" inspired in Muhammad by the devil (pp. 160–67), and the reconstruction of the history of the "revolt" of the wives of the Prophet (pp. 447 ff.). The work is interspersed with discussions that are purely apologetic and with attacks against "the Orientalists" of whom he mentions only the popular work of Dermenghem and espcially the work of the American author, Washington Irving, written in 1849. Occasionally, there are opportune silences, as for example, the murder of Ka'b b. al-Ashraf (pp. 278ff.); he passes over in silence the incitement to murder by Muhammad (Ibn Hishām, p. 550); there are even some falsifications (according to him [p. 339] the Jews of Quraiẓa chose "as though they were blinded by fate" the arbiter Sa'd b. Mu'ādh who was going to decide in favor of their massacre; however, according to the early sources it was Muhammad who made that decision [cf. Ibn Hishām, p. 688; Wāqidī, trans. by Wellhausen, p. 215]). On the work and its conservative critics, cf. Brockelmann, *Geschichte der arabischen Literatur,* Supplement, vol. III, pp. 208ff.
24. Cairo, 1929.
25. *'Alā Hāmish as-Sīra* (Cairo, 1933).
26. *'Abqarīyat Muḥammd* (The Genius of Muhammad [Cairo, 1940]). Later the author took up the study of the life of Muhammad together with the lives of the successors of the Prophet in *al-'Abqarīyāt al-Islāmīya* (The Genius of Muslims) (Cairo, 1376/1957), with an introduction in which the author claims to find the name of Muhammad in the Vedas and elsewhere. He also indulges in chronological calculations supposedly demonstrating that the coming of Muhammad was predicted in the Book of Daniel. Other biographical works by Muslims of this period which I have seen are purely apologetic; they are of the traditional type and without any value. It is nonetheless significant to find one of them ('Umar Abū'n-Naṣr, *al-Muḥammadīyāt,* Beirut, 1353/1934) declaring on the title page that the work "is drawn from the books of the *Sīra,* from historical works, and the studies of orientalists." Of the latter, only some very early ones are mentioned and merely in order to support certain views favorable to Islam. I have not been able to see either the biography of the Prophet by the learned author, M. A. Jād al-Mawlā, *Muḥammad al-Mathal al-Kāmil* (Muhammad, the Ideal Model) (Cairo, 1932), or the biography by the Lebanese poet, Labīb ar-Riyāshī *as-Subērmān al-Awwal al-'Ālamī* (*The First Global "Superman,"* Beirut, 1934) with its title taken from Nietzche or Shaw.
27. *Min Tārīkh al-Ḥarakāt al-Fikrīya fī'l-Islām* (On the History of Intellectual Movements in Islam); vol. I: *Min Tārīkh al-Ḥarakāt al-Ijtimā'īya* (On the History of Social Movements) Jerusalem, without date (preface dated 1928), especially pp. 12–39.
28. In addition to the bibliographies mentioned in note 4, one will want to consult the bibliographical surveys of current scholarly journals (in particular, the *Abstracta Islamica* in the *Revue des études islamiques,* the survey of *Arabica* and that of the *Middle East Journal*), and the extremely valuable (though sometimes inadequate) collection of titles of articles published in periodicals and in collected studies found in J. D. Pearson's

Index Islamicus 1906–1955 (Cambridge, 1958): pp. 356–57 on Muhammad and his time; pp. 52–56 on Muhammad; pp. 56–63 on the Quran; *Index Islamicus Supplement 1956–1960* (by the same author) (Cambridge, 1962); [*Index Islamicus 1961–1965* (Cambridge, 1967); *Index Islamicus, Third Supplement,* 1966–1970, by J. D. Pearson and Ann Walsh (London, 1972); *Fourth Supplement,* part 1, 1971–1972 (London, 1973) and part 2, 1972–1973 (*ibid.*, by the same authors)]. Some shorter and less detailed reviews than those that we have given here have been published by A. Guillaume, "The Biography of the Prophet in Recent Research," *Islamic Quarterly,* I (1954), pp. 5–11; and by Rudi Paret, "Recent European Research on the Life and Work of Prophet Muḥammad," *Journal of the Pakistan Historical Society,* 6 (1958), 81–96.

29. "Les études d'épigraphie sud-sémitiques et la naissance de l'Islam, éléments de bibliographie et lignes de recherches" (*Revue des études islamiques* (1955), pp. 121–76 and (1957), pp. 13–68; reprinted with a new pagination, Paris, 1957, 118 pages). This valuable collection would have benefited from being re-edited in a more uniform fashion in accordance with the norms generally used for bibliographical materials. The numerous errors and lack of precision in details could easily be remedied by a more careful revision.
30. J. Pirenne, "Chronique d'archéologie sud arabe 1955–1956," *Annales d'Ethiopie,* 2 (1957), pp. 37–73. [Among recent short essays on South Arabia, one might cite the popular but illuminating paper by G. W. Van Beek, "The Rise and Fall of Felix Arabia," *Scientific American* (Dec. 1969), pp. 36–46, and the chapter by A. K. Irvine in D. J. Wiseman, ed., *Peoples of Old Testament Times* (Oxford, 1973)].
31. The most important collection of inscriptions is the *Corpus inscriptionum semiticarum,* pars quarta *Inscriptiones ḥimyariticas et sabaeas continens* (Paris, Impr. nationale; three volumes appeared between 1887 and 1932). It contains 985 carefully published inscriptions. Unfortunately, it has been impossible to continue it, and G. Ryckmans has published or republished with less delay 2,482 inscriptions in the *Répertoire d'épigraphie sémitique,* vols. V–VII (Paris, 1928–1950). Since the time of this latter effort, the publications [of inscriptions] have been scattered about and not published systematically in a general collection. Nevertheless, G. Ryckmans enumerates in *Muséon* all the epigraphic publications and treats some unedited inscriptions (or those that appear to him to merit attention) in a series of articles entitled, "Inscriptions sud-arabes" (the first series published in vol. XL, 1927, pp. 161–200). Cf. also his article, "L'épigraphie arabe préislamique au cours de ces dix dernières années," *Muséon,* 61 (1948), pp. 197–213. [Mlle. J. Pirenne is now planning a new systematic collection of all recently discovered inscriptions in a more up-to-date fashion.] A selection of inscriptions accompanied by a glossary, which is for the moment practically our only dictionary of South Arabic epigraphy, was published by C. Conti-Rossini, *Chrestomathia arabica meridionalis epigraphica* (Rome, 1931; subsequently reprinted). This collection contains also the principal Greek (translated into Latin) and Latin texts relating to South Arabia. [There is now also a more complete dictionary of those words derived from a special class of roots, *viz.*, the thesis of W. W. Müller, *Die Wurzeln Mediae und Tertiae Y/W im Altsüdarabischen, eine etymologische und lexikographische Studie* (Tübingen, 1962).]
32. M. Höfner, *Altsüdarabische Grammatik* (Leipzig, 1943).

32a. A. F. L. Beeston, *A Descriptive Grammar of Epigraphic South Arabian* (London, 1962). [Cf. also the recent Russian work by G. M. Bauér, *Iazyk Iuzhnoarabiĭskoĭ pis' mennosti* (Moscow, 1966).]

33. We owe to him almost all our scholarly tools. Cf. in particular his rich list of proper names, *Les noms propres sud-sémitique* (Louvain, 1934–1935; 3 vols.) which now

needs to be substantially supplemented. The last volume is a very useful concordance of the diverse numberings of the inscriptions. Cf. also note 43. [This work has been partially superseded by G. Lankester Harding's work, *An Index and Concordance of pre-Islamic Arabian Names and Inscriptions* (Toronto, 1971), a very valuable tool in spite of certain defects which compel the reader to verify the data furnished and frequently to supplement them.]

34. We ought to mention here her summary articles: "Der Stand und die Aufgaben der südarabischen Forschung" (*Beiträge zur Arabistik, Semitik und Islamwissenschaft* (Leipzig, 1944), p. 42–66; "Die Kultur der vorislamischen Südarabien" (*ZDMG,* 99 [1945–1949], pp. 15–28); and the valuable research tool represented by the work which she edited in collaboration with H. von Wissmann, *Beiträge zur historischen Geographie des vorislamischen Südarabien* (Wiesbaden, 1953).

35. In addition to his numerous articles, he published a volume of *Sabaean Studies* (Oxford, 1937).

36. Cf. his notes in *BASOR,* 119 (1950), pp. 5–15; 129 (1953), pp. 20–24; 143 (1956), pp. 9–10; his communication, "Zur Chronologie des vorislamischen Arabien," in *Akten des 24sten Internationalen-Orientalisten-Kongresses, München . . . 1957* (Wiesbaden, 1959), pp. 153–55.

37. His essays on the religion constitute a serious effort to trace a view of the whole (cf. below, notes 54 and 55). Also his *Classification descriptive générale des inscriptions sud-arabes* (Tunis, 1948 [a supplement to *IBLA,* 11, 1948]), p. 401–76, is a very useful work. [He published numerous inscriptions and discussed those already known. In addition to his book mentioned below (note 44), see his important publication, *Sabaean and Hasaean Inscriptions from Saudi Arabia* (Rome, 1966).]

38. *L'Institution monarchique en Arabie méridionale avant l'Islam* (*Ma'în et Saba*) (Louvain, 1951). [See also his very valuable article, "Petits royaumes sud-arabes," *Muséon,* 70 (1957), pp. 75–96.]

39. We must especially mention their massive report on the *Rathjens-V. Wissmannsche Südarabienreise;* vol. II: *Vorislamische Altertümer* (Hamburg, 1932); vol. III: *Landeskundliche Ergebnisse* (Hamburg, 1934). Vol. I (*Sabäische Inschriften*) had been published in 1931 by J. H. Mordtmann and E. Mittwoch. On his later travels, C. Rathjens published his *Sabaeica, Bericht über die archäologischen Ergebnisse seiner zweiten, dritten und vierten Reise nach Südarabien;* Part I: *Der Reisebericht* (Hamburg, 1953); Part II: *Die unlokalisierten Funde* (Hamburg, 1955) (*Mitteilungen aus dem Museum f. Völkerkunde in Hamburg,* XXIV). H. von Wissmann especially has studied the geographical factors in his articles on physical geography and historical geography in a book published in collaboration with Maria Höfner (see above, note 34), and in his valuable "De Mari Erythraeo" (*Lautensach-Festschrift* in *Stuttgarter Geographische Studien,* vol. 69, Stuttgart, 1957, pp. 289–324). He has also studied the ethnological materials relating to the settlement of Arabia ("Badw" on Bedouin civilization in the *Encyclopaedia of Islam,* 2nd ed., vol. I, 827 ff, partly in collaboration with F. Kussmaul). [In addition to numerous articles, he has now published a very important work in which he attempts to give a general sketch of the history of South Arabia, together with discussions concerning problems of regional history and the geography of this part of Arabia: *Zur Geschichte und Landeskunde von Alt-Südarabien* (Vienna, 1964). Another, shorter work, following a partial revision of the historical sketch, contains studies on areas known least: *Zur Archäologie und antiken Geographie von Südarabien, Ḥaḍramaut, Qatabān und das 'Aden-Gebiet in der Antike* (Istanbul, 1968). He has announced a forthcoming work entitled: *Arabien nach Ptolemäus und anderen antiken Schriftstellern,* to be published by the Academy of Mainz.]

40. "Efiopiia i Khym'iar v ikh vzaimootnosheniiakh s vostotshnorimskoĭ imperiei" (*Vestnik drevnei istorii,* no. 23, 1948, no. 1, pp. 87–97).
41. M. A. Ghul, "New Qatabani Inscriptions," *BSOAS,* 22 (1959) pp. 1–22. [Among the latest works of Yemenite scholars, sometimes publishing new inscriptions, sometimes commenting on those already known, I shall limit myself to the following: A. H. Sharafaddin, *Yemen, Arabia Felix* (Taiz, 1961) (in English); by the same author, *Tārīkh al-Yaman ath-Thaqāfī,* I (Cairo, 1967); M.'A. Bāfaqīh, *Āthār wa-Nuqūsh al-'Uqla* (Cairo, 1967); by the same author, *Tākīkh al-Yāmān al-Qadīm* (Beirut, 1973), a survey in Arabic exhibiting a very good knowledge of the works of European Orientalists; Muṭahhar 'Alī al-Iryānī, *Min Tārīkh al-Yaman* (English title: M. A. al-Eryani, *On Yemen History, 34 New Inscriptions*) (Ṣana'ā and Cairo, 1973).]
42. The only exception was the excavation of a small temple in Ḥuqqa (Yemen) by Rathjens and von Wissmann in 1928.
43. G. Caton Thompson, *The Tombs and Moon Temple of Hureidha* (*Hadhramout*) (London, 1944).
44. Only the first volume of the American publication has appeared: R. Le Baron Bowen, Jr., and Frank P. Albright, *Archaeological Discoveries in South Arabia* (Baltimore, 1958). It is a collection of preliminary studies by several specialists on various points, based on material discovered by the expedition but not, properly speaking, a publication of excavations. See the important review by J. Ryckmans, *BO,* 17 (1960), pp. 204–7, which contains a very interesting discussion of the problem of the great dike of Mārib mentioned in the Quran. The director of the expedition, Wendell Phillips, has given a colorful and lively account of it in *Qataban and Sheba: Exploring Ancient Kingdoms on the Biblical Spice Route of Arabia* (London, 1955). On the expedition of 1960 at Dhofar, cf. Ray L. Cleveland, *BASOR,* 159 (October, 1960), pp. 14–26. [Volumes II and III have now been published in the same series: A. Jamme, *Sabaean Inscriptions from Maḥram Bilqīs* (*Mārib*) (Baltimore, 1962), in which a considerable number of inscriptions (new and known previously) are published, though unfortunately with questionable translations and commentary (see the reviews by A. F. L. Beeston in *BSOAS,* 35 [1972], pp. 350–53; by A. K. Irvine in the *Journal of Semitic Studies,* 10 [1965], pp. 128–32; by J. Ryckmans in *BO,* 21 [1964], pp. 90–94, and others), and R. L. Cleveland, *An Ancient South Arabian Necropolis, Objects from the Second Campaign (1951) in the Timna' Cemetery* (Baltimore, 1965).] One must be grateful for the recent expeditions of Egyptian scholars who, operating much more freely than their non-Muslim colleagues, have produced excellent photographs, and have drawn up some sketch-plans and made some good copies; cf. especially Kh. Y. Namī, *Les Monuments de Ma'īn* (*Yemen*), *étude épigraphique et philologique* (Cairo, 1952) in *Publications de l'Institut français d'archéologie orientale du Caire, Études sud-arabiques,* II (in Arabic), and A. Fakhry, *An Archaeological Journey to Yemen* (March–May, 1947) (Cairo, 1951–1952, 3 vols. [See the review by A. F. L. Beeston in *BSOAS,* 16 (1954), p. 395–97.] Works of this genre must become numerous in the future; see above note 41. [The book by Brian Doe (*Southern Arabia,* London, 1971), beautifully illustrated, is valuable especially for archeology and art. It is particularly detailed as regards archeological sites in what is now the People's Republic of Yemen. The author was the first and last director of the Department of Antiquities in British Southern Yemen. See also G. L. Harding, *Archaeology in the Protectorates* (London, 1964).

Much will be gained by a systematic study of ancient South Arabian coins. See G. F. Hill, *Catalogue of the Greek Coins of Arabia, Mesopotamia and Persia* (in the British Museum) (London, 1922, reprint in Bologna, 1965), and A. K. Irvine, "Some Notes

on Old South Arabian Monetary Terminology," *JRAS* (1964), pp. 18–36. My student, Christian Robin, is preparing a work on this subject.
Recently the Italian scholar G. Garbini, as well as a number of his students, has begun to work on South Arabian archeology and epigraphy. There now are a number of interesting papers from this school in *AION.*]

45. Already A. F. L. Beeston ("Problems of Sabaean Chronology," *BSOAS,* 16 [1954], pp. 37–56) had expressed some doubt on the value of the Assyrian synchronism as a basis for the chronology of Mlaker, and placed the beginning of the South Arabian states attested by epigraphy only in the sixth century (pp. 42ff).
46. J. Pirenne, *La Grèce et Saba, une nouvelle base pour la chronologie sud-arabe* (Paris, 1955) in *Mémories presentés par divers savants à l'Académie des Inscriptions et Belles-Lettres,* vol. XV, pp. 89–196; *Paléographie des inscriptions sud-arabes, contribution à la chronologie et à l'histoire de l'Arabie du Sud antique,* Vol. I: *Des origines jusqu'à l'époque himyarite* (Bruxelles, 1956) in *Verhandelingen van de Koninklijke Vlaamse Akademie voor Wetenschappen, Letteren en schone Kunsten van België, Klasse der Lettern,* 26. [See the interesting remarks on the beginnings of South Arabian history and its links with the economic development of Greece by G. Garbini, "Un nuovo documento per la storia dell' antico Yemen," *Oriens Antiquus,* Rome, 12 (1973), pp. 143–63.]
47. Cf. for example, the review of *Paleographie* by A. van den Branden in *Marchriq* (Beirut, 1959) pp. 378–91, and by A. F. L. Beeston in *BO,* 16 (1959), pp. 76–79; also the review of *La Grèce et Saba* by R. P. De Vaux in *Rev. biblique,* 64 (1957), p. 308–10, and the communication of W. F. Albright mentioned above, note 35.
48. *Le Royaume sud-arabe de Qatabân et sa datation d'après l'archéologie et les sources classiques jusqu'au Périple de la mer Erythrée* (with a contribution by A. Maricq) (Louvain, 1961) in *Bibliothèque de Muséon,* 48; cf. now his article, "La date du 'Périple de la mer Erythrée'," *Journal asiatique,* 249 (1961), pp. 441–60. [Mlle. Pirenne's conclusions on this subject have been criticized by some scholars. See especially the acute and systematic rejoinder by Albrecht Dihle, *Umstrittene Daten . . . ,* Köln and Opladen, 1965 (*Wissenschaftliche Abhandlungen der Arbeitsgemeinschaft für Forschung des Landes Nordheim—Westfalen,* vol. 32) and, on Indian history, D. C. MacDowall, "The Early Western Satraps and the Date of the Periplus," *The Numismatic Chronicle,* 7th series, 4 (1964), pp. 271–80, and D. C. Sircar, "Early Western Satraps and the Date of the Periplus," *ibid.*, 6 (1966), pp. 241–49. Both authors, though holding very different views on other points, agree on denying the possibility of placing the *Periplus* in the third century as Mlle. Pirenne wishes to do. On the other hand, the latter has been supported by F. Altheim and R. Stiehl, *Die Araber in der alter Welt,* vol. 1 (Berlin, 1966), pp. 40–45, vol. 4 (Berlin, 1967), pp. 492–502, and vol. 5/2 (Berlin, 1969), pp. 536–39, and after some reluctance, by H. von Wissmann. All of the very different dates given for the *Periplus* have been listed by W. Raunig ("Die Versuche einer Datierung des *Periplus maris Erythraei,*" *Mitteilungen der anthropologischen Gesellschaft in Wein,* 100 [1970], pp. 231–42). I have discussed the problem very recently in *Ecole Pratique des Hautes Etudes, IV ème section, Annuaire, 1974–1975* (now going to press). I recognize the difficulties of the problem, but I still think that the evidence for the end of the first or the beginning of the second century A.D. is stronger. On a limited and surer basis, there has been a great advance on the chronology of the first two centuries of our era, initiated, on the basis of inscriptions found at Mārib, by J. Ryckmans, *La Chronologie des rois de Saba et Dū Raydān* (Istanbul, 1964). This little book has given rise to numerous supplements (already by A. Lundin and J. Ryckmans in *Muséon,* 77 [1964], pp. 402–27) and discussions (reviewed by H.

von Wissmann, *BO,* 22 [1965], pp. 82–88; etc.; a very clear, conclusive statement by J. Ryckmans, *Muséon,* 80 [1967], pp. 269–300), all of which was recast by H. von Wissmann in the two books quoted above, note 39.]

49. J. M. Solá Solé, "La inscripcion Gl. 389 y los comienzos del monotéismo en Sudarabia," *Muséon,* 72 (1959), pp. 197–206. The study which brings together the information relative to the South Arabian monotheistic epigraphic texts is that by G. Ryckmans, "Les inscriptions monothéistes sabéennes," *Miscellanea historica in honorem Alberti de Meyer* (Louvain-Bruxelles, 1946), pp. 195–205. If one fixes the beginning of the Sabaean era at 110 B.C. with Beeston or in 109 with J. Ryckmans, it is necessary to lower all the dates given in accord with the early hypothesis which placed the origin in 115. But A. G. Lundin, "K voprosu o khronologii khum'jaritskikh nadpiseĭ," *Palestinskĭ Sbornik,* vol. 66 (1958), pp. 98–106, maintains the validity of the latter. [The fixing of the origin in 115 now seems to be proven by the new texts published by I. Shahīd, the *Martyrs of Najrān, New Documents* (Bruxelles, 1971) (*Studio Hagiographia,* no. 49).]

50. J. Jomier, "Le nom divin 'Al-Rahmān' dans le Coran," *Mélanges Louis Massignon,* vol. II (Damascus, 1957), pp. 361–81. [We now understand much better the penetration of the monotheisitc religions into pre-Islamic South Arabia. See especially the very valuable article by J. Ryckmans, "Le Christianisme en Arabie du Sud préislamique," *L'Oriente cristiano nella storia della civiltà* (Rome, 1964), pp. 413–53 which also deals with Judaism. Especially concerning Judaism, Hebrew inscriptions have recently been found in Yemen dating from pre-Islamic times; see G. Garbini, "Una bilinque sabeo-ebraica da Ẓafar," *AION,* 30 (1970), pp. 153–65; S. D. Goitein in *Tarbiz* (in Hebrew), 41 (1972), pp. 151–56; and G. Moscati Steindler, "Le mišmarōt in una inscrizione di Beit Ḥaḍir," *AION,* 34 (1974), p. 277–82.]

51. An account of Ph. Lippens, *Expédition en Arabie centrale* (Paris, 1956).

52. See especially G. Ryckmans, "Inscriptions sud-arabes, 10e série," (*Muséon,* 66 [1953]), pp. 267–317; J. Ryckmans, "Inscriptions historiques sabéennes de l'Arabie centrale," (*Ibid.*), pp. 319–42; by the same author, *La Persécution des chrétiens himyarites au VIe siècle* (Istanbul, 1956), II, 24 pages (in *Publications de l'Institut historique et archéologique néerlandais de Stanboul,* 1); A. F. L. Beeston, "Abraha," *Encyclopaedia of Islam* (new edition), I, 102–3; W. Caskel, *Entdeckungen in Arabien* (Köln, 1952) in *Arbeitsgemeinschaft für Forschung des Landes Nordrhein-Westfalen,* H. 30. A. G. Lundin, a very gifted student of N. B. Pigulevskaia, has devoted his dissertation as "candidate in the historical sciences" to a study of South Arabia in the sixth century. [It has been published under the title: *Yuzhnaia Araviia v VI vêke,* Moscow-Leningrad, 1961 (Palestinskiĭ Sbornik, fasc. 8/71).] It is necessary that the reports not very convincingly established at first sight, regarding a certain struggle of the classes, be more adequately demonstrated. [An important article by A. G. Lundin corresponds in part to the desire expressed here ("Sotsial' no-ekonomicheskie dannye sabeĭskikh posviatitel' nyh nadpiseĭ perioda mukarribou," *Vestnik drevneĭ istorii,* 3 (1962), pp. 96–120).] The same author published several interesting and careful articles of detail. [See his book in Russian with a copious summary in French: *Gosudartstvo mukarribov Saba'* (Moscow, 1971). However, some of the ideas of Lundin concerning the chronology of the earliest Sabaean times seem rather questionable. See his short paper: "The List of Sabaean Eponyms Again," *JAOS,* 89 (1969), pp. 533–54. Russian studies on ancient South Arabia are regularly analyzed by J. Ryckmans in *BO.*] For an attempt to coordinate chronologically the events of the century in the whole of Arabia, cf. the article of Sidney Smith cited below (note 98). [I have studied most of the historical inscriptions relating to the period of Dhū Nuwās in my early reports published in

Annuaire de l'Ecole Pratique des Hautes Etudes, 4ème Section, 1965–1966 (Paris, 1965), pp. 125–41; *1966–1967* (1966), pp. 121–39; *1968–1969* (1969), pp. 97–118; *1969–1970* (1970), pp. 161–83; *1970–1971* (1971), pp. 161–65; and in my article, "Sur une nouvelle inscription du règne de Dhoû Nowās," *BO,* 26 (1969), pp. 26–34. The problem has been to a large extent reopened by the publication of a very important Syriac text by I. Shahīd. See the reference above in note 49. The problem has been treated frequently and extensively, but with their usual over-confidence, by F. Altheim and R. Stiehl, *Die Araber in den alten Welt,* 5 vols., especially in vol. 5, the first part (Berlin, 1968).]

53. *Les Religions arabes préislamiques* (Louvain, 1951). It is a republication (with some additions, but stripped of a larger part of the illustration) of what was a chapter of the collaborative work edited by M. Gorce and R. Mortier, *Histoire générale des religions,* 5 vols. (Paris, 1947), vol. IV, pp. 307–32, 526–34.
54. "Le panthéon sud-arabe préislamique d'après les sources épigraphiques," *Muséon,* 60 (1947), pp. 57–147. We cannot share the confidence of the author in the possibility of utilizing etymologies, frequently very doubtful, of names and epithets of divinities in order to define the character of these latter or to identify them.
55. "La religion sud-arabe préislamique," in M. Brillant and R. Aigrain, *Histoire des religions,* 5 vols. (Paris, 1957), vol. 4, pp. 239–307; cf. also his article "D. Nielsen et le Panthéon sud-arabe préislamique," *RB,* 55 (1948), pp. 227–44. [There is now a very valuable synthesis on the religions of ancient Arabia, though primarily devoted to South Arabia, by M. Höfner, "Die vorislamischen Religionen Arabiens," in *Religionen Altsyriens, Altarabiens und der Mandäer* (Stuttgart, 1970), pp. 234–402. On this subject the observations by J. Ryckmans, "De quelques divinités sud-arabes," *Ephemrides theologicae Lovanienses,* 39 (1963), pp. 458–68, are especially valuable.]
56. "Das Opfer in der altsüdarabischen Hochkulturen," *Anthropos,* 37–40 (1942–1945), pp. 779–810.
57. "Les noms, titres et attributs de Dieu dans le Coran et leur correspondants en épigraphie sud-sémitique," *Muséon,* 68 (1955), pp. 93–135, 325–68. [I have found, I think, a stylistic parallelism; see my short paper: "Une phrase de style coranique dans une inscription sudarabique?", *Comptes rendus du GLECS,* 12–13 (1967–1969), pp. 102–5.]
58. "Les rapports sociaux à Nedjrân au début du VIe siècle de l'ère chrétienne," *Journal of the Economic and Social History of the Orient,* 3 (1960), pp. 113–30; 4 (1961) pp. 1–14. [On economic conditions see *inter alia* W. W. Müller, "Alt-Südarabien als Weihrauchland," *Theologische Quartalschrift,* 149 (1969), pp. 350–68, and A. F. L. Beeston, *Qahtan,* I, *The Mercantile Code of Qatabân* (London, 1959). On South Arabian art, see especially the short but valuable synthesis by J. Pirenne, "Arabie préislamique," *Encyclopédie de la Pléiade, Histoire de l'art,* I (Paris, 1961), pp. 901–29, with her "Notes d'archéologie sud-arabe," *Syria* from 1960 on.]
59. [At the time I wrote this paper, archeology in the peninsula, outside of the South, amounted to almost nothing. Occasional findings and visible ruins were listed by Henry Field, *Ancient and Modern Man in Southwestern Asia* (Coral Gables, Florida, 1956). Now, however, the discoveries of the Danish archeological expeditions after 1953 in the Persian Gulf region are known and have proved to be very interesting. Outside scientific reports, there is a popular, but very useful book summarizing all the findings up to 1969 by G. Bibby, *Looking for Dilmun* (New York, 1969; London, 1970).]
60. Texts collected by T. Weiss-Rosmarin, "Aribi und Arabien in den Babylonisch-Assyrischen Quellen," *Journal of the Society of Oriental Research* (1932), pp. 1–37.
61. See especially the book by J. A. Montgomery, *Arabia and the Bible* (Philadelphia,

1934). [The reprint of this book is the USA (Ktav Publishing House, Inc., 1969) is preceded by an introduction by G. W. van Beek bringing the information up to date.]

62. It is a matter of a dissertation which the author has not published. A convenient collection of all the classical texts relating to Arabia would be most desirable. The collection of C. Conti-Rossini, *Chrestomathia arabica meridionalis epigraphica* (Rome, 1931), pp. 1–37, concerns in particular South Arabia (the Greek texts are given only in Latin translation), although rather frequently going beyond it. Likewise the translations by A. Maricq in J. Pirenne, *Le Royaume sud-arabe de Qatabān* (Louvain, 1961) (see note 48). One finds *faute de mieux* some almost exhaustive references on classical texts (and others) along with scholarly discussions in copious articles in *Realencyclopädie* of Pauly-Wissowa-Kroll-Mittelhaus. The article "Arabia" (vol. II, 1896) by D. H. Müller is unfortunately out of date. The article of J. Tkač, "Saba," in the new series (*Neue Bearbeitung,* I A2 [1920], col 1297–2558), is a mine of information, though full of digressions, often going beyond Saba and even South Arabia. [The forthcoming book announced by H. von Wissmann will surely bring some progress on this matter; see above note 39.]

63. A judiciously selected bibliography in a very well informed article by C. Rabin "'Arabiyya," A, I, 2, *Encyclopaedia of Islam* (new edition) I, pp. 561–67. [Among the new collections of inscriptions of the various types described below, one may cite F. L. Winnett and W. L. Reed, *Ancient Records from North Arabia* (Toronto, 1979).]

64. *A Study of the Liḥyanite and Thamūdic Inscriptions* (Toronto, 1937).

65. *Les Inscriptions thamoudéennes* (Louvain-Heverlé, 1950).

66. *Les Textes thamoudéenns de Philby* (Louvain, 1956), 2 vols.

67. J. Ryckmans, "Aspects nouveaux de problème thamoudéen," *Studia Islamica,* 5 (1956), pp. 5–18.

68. E. Littmann (*Thamūd und Safā* [Leipzig, 1940], p. 1) rejected, following M. Lidzbarski, the term "protoarabisch" (proto-Arabic) as "unklar und irreführend" (unclear and misleading). He recognized moreover that Thamūdic (like Ṣafāitic) was only an expedient, but it was, according to him, significant and "would no longer give rise to misunderstanding." The result proved the contrary. The term "proto-Arabic" has been used by C. Rabin in the article cited above (note 63) to designate the dialects or languages written in the scripts close to the monumental South Arabic ("Thamūdic," Safaitic, Lihyanite, etc.). One might perhaps propose for this usage "Old Arabic" or "Old North-Arabic" (Altnordarabisch) as one says "Old Turkic," etc.—or, again "Saracen" adopted in Latin by the *Corpus inscriptionum semiticarum* to designate its fifth series (since 1950); cf. below, note 73.

69. "L'unité de l'alphabet thamoudéen," *Studia Islamica,* 7 (1957), pp. 5–28; "Essai de solution du problème thamoudéen," *BO,* 15 (1958), pp. 7–12.

70. *Lihyan und Lihyanisch* (Köln and Opladen, 1954).

71. Cf. his review in *BO,* 14 (1957), pp. 95–97, and especially his article "La chronologie de Dedan et de Lihyân," *BO,* 14 (1957), pp. 13–16.

72. *Safaitic Inscriptions* (Leiden, 1943) in *Publications of the Princeton University Archaeological Expeditions to Syria in 1904–1905 and 1909,* Division IV, *Semitic Inscriptions,* section C.

73. *Corpus inscriptionum semiticarum,* pars quinta *Inscriptiones saracenicas continens,* tomus I (Paris, 1950 [with a volume of plates, *Tabulae,* 1951]).

74. *Safaitic Inscriptions from Jordan* (Toronto, 1957) in *Near and Middle East Series,* 2. In 1958–1959 Winnett collected 4,500 other texts; 480 of them he gave to his student, W. Oxtoby, who made them the subject of a dissertation at Princeton University. [Now published under the title: *Some Inscriptions of the Safaitic Bedouin* (New Haven,

Conn., 1968, *American Oriental Society,* vol. 50). See the reviews by A. Van den Branden, *BO,* 27 (1970), pp. 261–63, and by myself in *Bulletin de la Societé de linguistique,* 66, fasc. 2 (1971), p. 204–6.]

75. G. Lankester Harding, "The Cairn of Hani'," *Annual of the Department of Antiquities of Jordan* (Amman), 2 (1953) pp. 8–56.
76. *Syria,* 31 (1954), 357–59.
77. The discussion on the chronology is complex, for very little of the data is certain; cf. my review of the book cited above (note 74) by Winnett in *Arabica,* 6 (1959), 214–20.
78. *Thamūd und Safā* (Leipzig, 1940) in *Abhandlungen für Kunde des Morgenlandes,* XXV, 1.
79. A work mentioned above (note 72).
80. "L'épigraphie safaitique" (*Académie des Inscriptions et Belle-Lettres. Compets rendus des séances,* 1941, pp. 27–32); "Les inscriptions safaitiques relevées par M. and Mme. Dumand" (*ibid.*, 1942, p. 127–36).
81. "Histoire de la region safaitique," *Sumer* (1946), pp. 137–54.
82. R. Blachère, *Histoire de la littérature arabe des origines à la fin du XVe siècle de J.-C.*, I (Paris, 1952), pp. 166–86. On the other hand, in the areas where the use of a documentation foreign to classical Arabic predominates, studies and discussions have progressed much since the appearance of this work. R. Blachère seems, on the other hand, to have moved gradually in the direction of a more and more radical skepticism regarding the possibility of drawing anything authentic from pre-Islamic poetry. Cf. his article "A propos de trois poètes arabes d'époque archaique," *Arabica,* 4 (1957), p. 231–49, and particularly p. 248.
83. One ought to refer to the second edition: G. Jacob, *Studien in arabischen Dichtern,* H. 3: *Altarabisches Beduinenleben nach den Quellen geschildert,* 2nd ed. (Berlin, 1897). The first edition bore the title: *Das Leben der vorislāmischen Beduine . . .* (1895). [Among recent Arabic monographs on ancient Arab culture according to Arab literary sources, see e.g., 'Ali al-Hashimi, *al-Mar'a fī sh-Shi'r al-Jāhilī* (Baghdad, 1960).]
84. J. Wellhausen, *Reste Arabischen Heidentums* (2nd ed., Berlin, 1897; reprinted by W. de Gruyter, Berlin, 1927). One ought to mention the re-edition (with a German translation and a copious annotation) of the *Kitāb al-Aṣnām* of Ibn al-Kalbī by Rosa Klinke-Rosenberger, *Das Götzenbuch, Kitāb al-Aṣnām des Ibn al-Kalbī* (Leipzig, 1941) in *Sammlung orientalistischer Arbeiten,* H. 8. There is also an English translation with scanty annotation (*The Book of Idols by Hishām Ibn al-Kalbī,* translated by N. A. Faris, Princeton, 1952). [See also the new French translation with critical edition of the text and copious introduction by W. Atallah, *Les Idoles de Hicham Ibn al-Kalbi* (Paris, 1969.] It is a valuable source (but to be used with some caution) on Arab paganism through the image of an educated Kufan at the end of the eighth and the beginning of the ninth century.
85. Jawad 'Ali, *Tārīkh al-'Arab Qabl al-Islām* (Baghdad, 1369–1378/1950–1959), 8 vols. The shorter work of his compatriot, Salih Ahmad al-'Ali, *Muḥāḍarāt fī Tārīkh al-'Arab,* I (Baghdad, 1955), is especially interesting for the part devoted to Muhammad; cf. below, note 147.
86. M. Guidi, *Storia e cultura degli Arabi fino alla morte di Maometto* (Firenze, 1951). This is a posthumous work of the great Orientalist who died in 1946.
87. *The Background of Islam, Being a Sketch of Arabian History in Pre-Islamic Times* (Alexandria, 1947).
88. M. Rodinson, "L'Arabie avant l'Islam," *Encyclopédie de la Pléiade, Histoire universelle,* II (Paris, 1957), pp. 3–36. [There is now a voluminous work with a most promising title by F. Altheim and R. Stiehl, *Die Araber in der alten Welt,* 6 vols. (Berlin,

1964–1969). This is a rather strange collection of numerous papers (often by other authors) on very different points (some connected with the ancient Arabs only in a very tenuous fashion), displaying a tremendously varied level of scholarship. The authors (chiefly F. Altheim) seem to think that progress in History is brought about by advancing conjectures as much as possible; their only criteria seem to be their ability to mobilize erudition and ingenuity, without too much regard for probabilities. See my review of vol. I in *Annales E.S.C.*, 21 (1966), pp. 1082–86. A. Grohmann has published a handbook which, it was hoped, would be a standard guide to ancient Arabia (*Arabien,* Munich, 1963). Though there is much valuable and useful information in it, the author, at the time of the final writing, was no longer in direct contact with all of the more recent discussions. Consequently, one must always be cautious and verify what one finds in this work. See the severe and detailed criticism by J. Pirenne in *BO,* 23 (1966), pp. 3–15.]

89. *ZDMG,* 103 (1959), pp. 28–36 (the English translation, "The Bedouinization of Arabia," in *Studies in Islamic Cultural History,* ed. by G. E. von Grunebaum [Menasha, Wisconsin, 1954] in *The American Anthropologist,* vol. 56, no. 2, pt. 2) pp. 36–46. Cf. W. Dostal, "The Evolution of Bedouin Life," *L'antica società beduina,* ed. F. Gabrieli (Rome, 1959), pp. 11–34, dubious on certain points but rather precise on the question here under discussion. [We are indebted to W. Caskel for a most important tool for all studies on pre-Islamic Arabia and early Islam, *viz.*, a dictionary of a great number of men and women with genealogical trees (compiled with the help of A. Strenziok), *Ǧamharat an-Nasab, das genealogische Werk des Hišām ibn Muḥammad al-Kalbī* (Leiden, 1966), 2 vols.]
90. Vol. I, pp. 872–92.
91. *L'antica società beduina* (ed. Gabrieli [Rome, 1959], a collection of studies which are in general of a high quality; cf. my review in *RHR* (1961), pp. 100–102.
92. Cf. above note 53 [and note 55 for the article by Höfner. It may be useful to recall here that the best account of the religion of pre-Islamic Arabia, though concise, is the article by Th. Nöldeke, "Arabs (Ancient)," in Hasting's *Encyclopedia of Religion,* vol. I (Edinburgh, 1908), pp. 659–73].
93. "Le sacrifice chez les Arabes," *Ethnos,* 13 (1948), pp. 1–16.
94. *Le Sacrifice chez les Arabes, recherches sur l'évolution, la nature et la fonction des rites sacrificiels en Arabie occidentale* (Paris, 1955, *Bibliothèque de sociologie contemporaine*); cf. the long review where I attempt to trace a more sure methodological framework, *RHR,* 150 (1956), pp. 232–41.
95. *Introduction à la sociologie de l'Islam, de l'animisme à l'universalisme* (Paris, 1958), *Islam d'hier et d'aujourd'hui*, XII; cf. my review in *Journal of Economic and Social History of the Orient*, 2 (1959), p. 219–24.
96. "La religion bédouine préislamique," in *L'antica società beduina* (mentioned above, notes 89 and 91), pp. 115–40. [Two large books by T. Fahd, *La Divination arabe* (Paris, 1966) and *Le Panthéon de l'Arabic centrale à la veille de l'hégire* (Paris, 1968) have some defects, but add valuable material. See the reviews by J. Henninger (*Anthropos*, 63/64 [1968–69], pp. 291–96, and 65 [1970], p. 309–15), and M. Rodinson (*RHR*, 181 [1972], pp. 79–83).]
97. "Arethas, son of Jabalah," *JAOS*, 75 (1955), p. 205–16; "The Arabs in the Peace Treaty of A. D. 561," *Arabica*, 3 (1956), pp. 181–213; "Procopius and Arethas," *Byzantinische Zeitschrift*, 50 (1957), 39–67, 362–82; "Procopius on the Ghassânids," *JAOS*, 77 (1957), pp. 79–87; "The Last Days of Salih," *Arabica*, 5 (1958), pp. 145–58.
98. "Events in Arabia in the 6th century A.D.," *BSOAS*, 16 (1954), pp. 425–68.

99. "Note sur un passage de Malalas concernant les phylarques arabes," *Arabica*, 5 (1958), pp. 251–62.
100. "Les villes de Syrie du Sud et les routes commerciales d'Arabie à la fin du VIe siècle," in *Akten des 11. internationalen Byzantinisten-Kongress*, 1958 (München, 1960), pp. 438–44.
101. "The Beginnings of Ghassān," part of a dissertation at the University of Chicago, 1943, pp. 5–16. Cf. also P. Goubert, "Le problème ghassanide à la veille de l'Islam," *Actes du VIe* Congrès international d'études byzantines, Paris, 1948, I (Paris, 1950), pp. 103–18.
102. *Al-Hīra, al-Madīna wa'l'Mamlaka al-'Arabīya* (Baghdad, 1936).
103. "Mohammeds Geburtsjahr," *La Nouvelle Clio*, 7–9 (1955–1957), pp. 113–22. [See also their large work cited above, note 88. On this period there is now an important work by N. V. Pigulevskaia, *Araby u granits Vizantii i Irana v IV - VI vv* (Moscow and Leningrad, 1964).]
104. *Geschichte des Qorāns* by Theodor Nöldeke, second edition prepared by Friedrich Schwally. Vol. I: *Über den Ursprung des Qorāns*, completely revised by F. Schwally (Leipzig, 1909); vol. II: *Die Sammlung des Qorāns (Leipzig, 1919); vol. III: Geschichte des Korantexts* by G. Bergsträsser and O. Pretzl (Leipzig, 1938). These three volumes have been reprinted recently in a single volume at Hildesheim, 1961.
103. *The Qur'ān, Translated with a Critical Rearrangement of the Surahs* by Richard Bell (Edinburgh, 1937–1939), 2 vols.
106. *Introduction to the Qur'ān* (Edinburgh, 1953) [this work has been completely rewritten by W. M. Watt and published by the Edinburgh University Press (1970) under the title: *Bell's Introduction to the Qur'ān*]; cf. W. M. Watt, "The Dating of the Qur'ān, a Review of Richard Bell's Theories," *JRAS* (1957), pp. 46–56. The latter contains a list of important articles by R. Bell and an excellent critical evaluation of his contribution. One will be able to assess the effect produced by these studies on traditionalist Muslim intellectuals in the very apologetic critical review by a reader in philosophy at Haidarabad, S. Vahiduddin, "R. Bell's Study of the Qur'ān," *Islamic Culture*, 30 (1956), pp. 263–72.
107. Le Coran . . . , vol. I: *Introduction au Coran* (Paris, 1947), *Islam d'hier et d'aujourd'hui*, III, republished with minor modifications in an independent work: *Introduction au Coran* (Paris, 1959) (the choice of titles given at the beginning of the work on Muhammad is now and then open to question).
108. *Le Coran . . .* , vols. II and III: *Le Coran, traduction nouvelle* (Paris, 1949–1950), 2 vols., with a continuous pagination. An edition with many of the notes removed was published in an elegant volume under the title: *Le Coran (al-Qur'ān)* in 1957. In this volume the surahs are arranged in their traditional order. The excellent and very valuable index has been retained and adapted. Because of the scholarship which it incorporates, the translation of Blachère renders obsolete the earlier French translations. However from the stylistic point of view, the old translation of Kazimirski which goes back to 1840 (and which is still frequently reprinted, the last time as Mahomet, *Le Coran* [Paris 1952], in 2 vols. with an introduction by G. H. Bousquet) does not deserve to be completely set aside. [A new edition of Kazimirski's translation will soon be published (without the attribution of authorship to Muhammad, which is very repulsive to Muslims), and preceded by two short essays from my pen on Muhammad and the Quran, plus the life of Muhammad by the historian Abū'l-Fidā' (1273–1331). On the edition with an introduction by M. Arkoun, see below, note 176.] For particularly good stylistic judgments, see G. C. Anawati (*Revue du Caire*, no. 237 [1960], pp. 411, 417). The

English translation of J. M. Rodwell of 1861 (published a number of times in *Everyman's Library* since 1909) already had the surahs arranged chronologically.

109. *Le Coran*, A translation with notes by Muhammad Hamidullah, in collaboration with Michel Léturmy and a preface by Louis Massignon (Paris, 1959). [The new French translation by D. Masson (Paris, 1967) is interesting chiefly from the literary side and the comparative notes along the lines of her book mentioned below in note 159. However, she is a stranger to all critical problems and is acquainted with scholarly discussions, for the most part, only at second hand. Her concern not to shock faithful Muslims and her disdain for human factors result in silence on delicate points.]

110. "Die Sure ar-Rūm (30)," *Orientalia*, n.s. 13 (1944), pp. 334–35; 14 (1945), pp. 118–42; cf. E. Beck, *Das christliche Mönchtum im Koran* (Helsinki, 1946).

111. "Plan einer neuen, leicht kommentierten wissenschaftlichen Koran-übersetzung," *Orientalistische Studien Enno Littmenn . . . überreicht* (Leiden, 1935), pp. 121–30; *Grenzen der Koranforschung* (Stuttgart, 1950) in *Bonner orientalistische Studien*, H. 27.

112. *Plan eines Apparatus criticus zum Koran* (München, 1930) in *Sitzungsberichte der Bayerischen Akademie der Wissenschaften, philos.-Histor. Abteilung, Jahrgang 1930*, H. 7; "Über Notwendigkeit und Möglichkeit einer kritischen Koranausgabe," *ZDMG*, 84 (1930), pp. 82–83; cf. O. Pretzl, "Die Fortführung des Apparatus Criticus zum Koran" (in Sitzungsb. d. Bayer. Ak.d.Wiss., Phil. - Hist. Abt., 1934, H. 5).

113. A. Jeffrey, *Materials for the History of the Text of the Qur'ān* (Leiden, 1937), with an index published in 1951, and various articles. One will find a more complete bibliographical review of the recent studies of the textual criticism of the Quran in the valuable article by Jeffery, "The Present Status of Qur'anic Studies," *Report on Current Research on the Middle East* (Washington, the Middle East Institute, 1957), pp. 1–16. The scholar devoting most attention to this area now is E. Beck for whom we will cite here only the valuable article, "Die b. Mas'ūdvarianten bei al-Farrā'," *Orientalia*, n.s. 25 (1956), pp. 353–83; 28 (1959), pp. 186–205, 230–56. [Among the early Arabic books on Quranic sciences published after the Jeffery report, let me cite the edition of the *Muḥkam* of ad-Dānī (d. 1053) by 'Izza Hassan, Damascus, 1960.]

114 *The Lord Guideth, Studies on Primitive Islam* (Oslo, 1956) in *Skrifter utgitt av Det Norske Videnskaps - Akademi i Oslo*, II: *Historisk-Filosofisk Klasse*, 1956, no. 2. A more recent article ("The Interpretation of Surah, 107," *Studia Islamica*, 9 [1958], pp. 13–30) continues this work by a study of a surah which, according to him, marked the stage immediately following in the evolution of the thought of Muhammad.

115. Cf. in particular his small work on *tafsīr* (the science of Quranic interpretation) and its development in his *Old Muslim Opposition Against Interpretation of the Koran* (Oslo, 1955) in *Avhandlinger utgitt av det Norske Videnskaps - Akademi i Oslo*, II: *Historisk - Filosofisk Klasse*, 1955, 1, and his essay on the development of a legendary theme on the infancy of the Prophet, *The Legend of the Opening of Muhammad's Breast* (Oslo, 1955) in the same collection, 1955, 3. The theses of the first have been conveniently summarized by R. Paret, *OLZ*, 52 (1957), pp. 56–58.

116. One will find a very complete critical bibliography of Quranic studies in the article by A. Jeffery cited above (note 113). The problems of Quranic studies are introduced in the little work by A. Abel, *Le Coran* (Brussels, 1951) in *Collections Lebègue et nationale*, 103. It is better to be on one's guard against Muslim apologetic expositions such as that by Shaikh M. A. Draz, *Initiation au Koran, exposé historique analytique et comparatif* (Paris, 1951), unless one wishes to analyze the mechanism of this apologetic approach. Among the recent translations, one should mention (among others) that of A. J. Arberry, *The Koran Interpreted* (London, 1955, 2 vols.) which aims at providing

an esthetic impression parallel to that of the Arabic text and succeeds, producing a text of great poetic beauty (he explains the basis for his translation in an earlier work, *The Holy Koran, An Introduction with Selections* [London, 1953]); that of the illustrious Islamist, J. H. Kramers in Dutch, *De Koran uit het Arabisch vertaald* (Amsterdam, 1956) with an excellent and copious index; that of A. Bausani in Italian (a scholarly and literarily successful work), *Il Corano* (Firenze, 1955) in *Classici della Religione*; cf. his "Postille a Cor. II 248, XXXIX 23, XX, 15," *Studi orientalistici in onore di Giorgio Levi della Vida* (Rome, 1956), I, pp. 32–51; that of the great Russian Arabist, I. Iu. Kratchkowskĭ [published in Moscow in 1963 by the Institute of the Peoples of Asia (*Koran*, translation and commentary of I. Iu. Krachkovskiĭ, 715 p.) together with valuable notes and commentary left by the learned scholar]. The recent English translation of N. J. Dawood, like that of R. Blachère, follows a chronological arrangement of the surahs (*The Koran*, Penguin Books, 1956). Henri Mercier published (with the Arabic text and transcription on the opposite page, following the "reading" in use in Morocco) a translation of the Quran in which the material is classified according to content (*Le Coran*, Rabat and Tangier, 1956). I will not mention the translations which have come out of the Ahmadiya propaganda effort and which are highly suspect because of their apologetic and modernist distortion (cf. A. Bausani, "On Some Recent Translations of the Qur'ān," *Numen*, 4 (1957), pp. 75–81). One will find in the translation of Hamidullah, pp. xxxv ff., a complete list of translations in European languages as well as in Turkish. [On the Muslim discussions, see the work of J. M. S. Baljon, *Modern Muslim Koran Interpretation (1880–1960)* (Leiden, 1961).]

117. Especially in his classical *Muhammedanische Studien* (Halle, 1889–1890), 2 vols. [translated into English under the title, *Muslim Studies* (London, 1967–1971), 2 vols.]. The important part of volume II devoted to tradition has been translated into French: *Etudes sur la tradition musulmane*, by L. Bercher (Paris, 1952). The two original volumes have been reproduced photo-mechanically (Hildesheim, 1961). [For the English speaking reader there is a very clear and simple introductory work by A. Guillaume, *The Traditions of Islam: An Introduction to the Study of the Hadith Literature* (Oxford, 1924).]

118. Cf. above pp. 173f. [On the attempts to criticize the *ḥadith* among modern Muslims, see the careful book by G. H. A. Juynboll, *the Authenticity of the Tradition Literature, Discussions in Modern Egypt* (Leiden, 1968).]

119. *the Origins of Muhammedan Jurisprudence* (Oxford, 1950). I have given a general sketch of the method and conclusions of J. Schacht in *L'Année sociologique*, 3e série (1952), pp. 447–49.

120. Except for some hypercritical Soviet scholars for whom the Quran itself is a composite work and not very reliable.

121. J. Schacht, "A Revaluation of Islamic Traditions," *JRAS*(1949), pp. 143–54; cf. his *Origins*, p. 153. The method of Schacht on this particular point has itself been questioned by J. Fueck, *BO*, 10 (1953), p. 198.

122. J. Schacht, "On Mūṣā b. 'Uqba's *Kitāb al-Maghāzī*, " *Acta Orientalia* (Copenhagen), 21 (1953), pp. 288–300. The fragments are translated by A. Guillaume, *The Life of Muhammad* (London, 1955), pp. xliii–xlvii. As a more recent example of a reconstitution of an early source, cf. A. A. Duri, "Al-Zuhri, A Study on the Beginnings of History Writing in Islam," *BSOAS*, 19 (1957), pp. 1–12.

123. S. Hillelson, "Historical Poems and Traditions of the Shukriya," *Sudan Notes and Records*, 3 (1920), pp. 33–75. On the facts which could not have been fabricated, cf. Th. Nöldeke, *WZKM*, 21 (1906), pp. 297–312 (a vigorous review of Caetani, abounding in notations in which his exceptional knowledge and soundness of judgment are

evident); *Der Islam*, 4 (1913), pp. 205–12; 5 (1914), pp. 160–70. Similar conclusions on the fundamental authenticity of the historical framework of the *sīra* (see below) are developed by R. Paret, "Die Lücke in der Überlieferung über den Urislam," *Westöstliche Abhandlungen Rudolf Tschudi . . . überreicht* (Wiesbaden, 1954), pp. 147–53. J. W. Fueck goes further in his rejection of the theses of Schacht, criticizing even his conception of the development of juridical tradition; however, his argumentation still rests, above all, on the early historians (*BO*, 10 [1953], pp. 196–99).

124. The Institute of Marxism-Leninism in Moscow just published a volume with a French edition (*Souvenirs sur Marx et Engles*, Moscow n.d., the Russian edition dated 1956) where one finds, for example (pp. 344–53), some recollections of Engels published in 1927 by Alexe Voden who died only in 1939. Engels had related to him some details of the period from 1840 to 1848 of his life and that of Marx. Cf. also (p. 290 ff.) the recollections of Franzisca Kugelmann, put into writing only in 1928, on Marx based on the latter's reminiscing about his childhood and the accounts of his parents. We might call that a family *isnād* . . . highly suspect according to Schacht. Moreover, many of the directors of the École Pratique des Hautes-Études (4e section) have been the colleagues of Bracke (A. M. Desrousseaux) (1861–1955) who had also known Engels.

125. Clear expositions have been given by G. Levi della Vida in his excellent article "Sīra" in the *Encyclopedia of Islam* (first edition), and by R. Blachère, *Le Problème de Mahomet* (Paris, 1952), pp. 2ff.

126. *The Life of Muhammad: A Translation of Ishāq's Sīrat Rasūl Allāh*, with introduction and notes by A. Guillaume (London, 1955).

127. Cf. in particular R. B. Serjeant, "Professor A. Guillaume's translation of Sīrah," *BSOAS*, 21 (1958), pp. 1–14, which contains some interesting notations and corrections.

128. Cf. A. Guillaume, "The Biography of the Prophet in Recent Research," *Islamic Quarterly*, I (1954), pp. 5–11.

129. A. Guillaume, *New Light on the Life of Muhammad* (Manchester, 1960), *Journal of Semitic Studies*, Monograph, no. 1. On a less important recension, cf. the article by the same author, "A Note on the *Sīra* of Ibn Ishāq," *BSOAS*, 18 (1956), pp. 1–4.

130. [*The Kitāb al-Maghāzī of al-Wāqidī* (London, 1966), three vol.]

131. J. M. B. Jones, "Ibn Isḥāq and al-Wāqidī, the Dream of 'Ātika and the Raid to Nakhla in Relation to the Charge of Plagiarism," *BSOAS*, 22 (1959), pp. 41–51.

132. "A Controversial Incident and the Related Poem in the Life of Ḥassān b. Thābit," *BSOAS*, 17 (1955), pp. 197–205; "An Interpretation of the Different Accounts of the Visit of the Tamim Delegation to the Prophet in A. H. 9," *BSOAS*, 17 (1955), pp. 416–25; "The Development of a Dramatic Theme in the Story of Khubaib b. 'Adiyy and the Related Poems," *BSOAS*, 21 (1958), pp. 15–30. "Early Critics of the Authenticity of the Poetry of the *Sīra*," *BSOAS*, 21 (1958), pp. 453–63; a more general sketch in his communication: "Some Aspects of the Art of the Forger in the Poetry of the *Sīra*" (*Akten des 24. Internationalen Orientalisten-Kongresses, München . . . 1957*, Wiesbaden, 1959), pp. 310–11.

133. *Le Problème de Mahomet, essai de biographie critique du fondateur de l'Islam* (Paris, 1952). Cf. also the excellent album of photographs in *Dans les pas de Mahomet*, with an introduction by R. Blachère and photography by Frederique Duran, notices by H. Delattre (Paris, 1956). The "idoles préislamiques" of the Museum of Jedda (figs. 24 and 35) are spurious. Cf. G. Ryckmans, *Muséon*, 71 (1958, p. 121, n. 9).

134. *Muhammad at Mecca* (Oxford, 1953); cf. my preface to the French translation which represents a rather poor job and lacks several of the original's valuable appendices (*Mahomet à la Mecque*, Paris, 1958); the article by G. H. Bousquet, "Une explication marxiste de l'Islam par un ecclésiastique épiscopalien," *Hesperis*, 41 (1954), pp. 231–

47; and my own, "La vie de Mahomet et le problème sociologique des origines de l'Islam," *Diogène*, 20 (1957), pp. 37–64. [This article appeared in an English translation by James J. Labadie under the title: "The Life of Muhammad and the Sociological Problem of the Beginnings of Islam," *Diogenes*, 20 (1957), p. 28–51.]

135. H. Grimme, *Muhammad*, 1st part: *Das Leben* (Münster, 1892), p. 14; C. Snouck, Hurgronje, "Une nouvelle biographie de Mohammed, *RHR*, 30 (1894), pp. 48–70, 149–78, reprinted in his *Verspreide Geschriften*, I (Bonn and Leipzig, 1923), pp. 319–62 [and also in *Selected Works of C. Snouck Hurgronje* (Leiden, 1957), pp. 109–49].
136. *Muhammad at Medina* (Oxford, 1956); French translation (better than that of the first volume but with some omissions and curious inconsistencies), *Mahomet à Médine* (Paris, 1959).
137. Charles J. Ledit, *Mahomet, Israël et le Christ* (Paris, 1956). Cf. the critical remarks of the Moroccan Muslim philosopher (and one of the most open), M. A. Lahbabi, *Revue de synthèse*, 3e série, nos.11–12 (1958), p. 305, and the notes of L. Massignon and Y. Moubarac, *REI*, 26 (1958) cahier, II, p. 127, who refer to the reaction aroused in the church by this publication.
138. [See, e.g., his "Thèmes archétypiques en onirocritique musulmane," *Eranos*, XII (1945), pp. 241–51. See also *Opera Minora*, II, pp. 554–61.]
139. *Mahomet* (Paris, 1957). [There is now a new edition (1969) of this book with the transcriptions corrected by Popovic, a more convenient system of reference in the footnotes, the bibliography corrected and brought up to date by myself.]
140. R. Paret, *Mohammed und der Koran, Geschichte und Verkündigung des arabischen Propheten* (Stuttgart, 1957). Cf. the review of J. Sedláková, *BO*, 17 (1960), pp. 207–8. His discussion of the ideas of Bell and Birkeland are also found in his article, "Leitgedanken in Mohammads frühesten Verkündigungen," *OLZ*, 52 (1957), pp. 389–92, and in part in the work mentioned above (note 28).
141. *Le Prophète de l'Islam*; I: *Sa Vie*; II: *Son oeuvre* (Paris, 1378/1959), 2 vols.
141a. He has a doctorate from the University of Bonn and also from the University of Paris.
142. With somewhat detached treatment of the texts (in the same sense as Haykal; cf. above note 22) where it is a question as embarrassing for the modern moral conscience as the massacre of the Banū Quraiẓa (pp. 388 ff). The attitude of an author regarding this massacre is a rather good test. [This remark has nothing to do with crypto-Zionism as is alleged by some of my Muslim critics.] It is moreover a rather painful irony to see the German, R. Paret, admit in 1957 that one ought not judge this act in the light of our moral conceptions, for "the customs of that time in the conduct of war were, in many respects, more brutal than we are accustomed to in the age of the convention of Geneva" (*Mohammed und der Koran*, p. 112). Without explanation!
143. *Muhammad, Prophet and Statesman* (London, 1961); French translation *Mahomet, prophète homme d'Etat* (Paris, 1962).
144. *Islam and the Integration of Society* (London, 1961).
145. Maxime Rodinson, *Mahomet* (Paris, 1961). [The work was revised and added to by the author in a second edition published in Paris in 1968. Since then the work has been translated into English under the title: *Mohammad* (New York and London, 1971) with the references omitted in the French edition.] On p. 280 (French edition; p. 245 of the English translation) I maintain, cognizant of the issue and despite the conclusions of E. Beck (*Orientalia Christiana Periodica*, 14 [1948], pp. 398–405; translated in French in *MIDEO*, 6 [1959–1961], pp. 405–8) which are accepted by J. Jomier (Études, Jan. 1961, pp. 82–92), that the text of St. Ephrem cited by Tor Andrae has indeed a veiled sexual connotation, evoking the welcoming femininity of the celestial "vine" which will compensate for chastity, just as a little earlier in the text (strophy 15)

the solitary virgin is seen being surrounded by male beings: angels, prophets, and apostles. Cf. the carefully formulated opinion of M. Guidi, *Rivista degli studi orientali*, 17 (1938), pp. 126–27. [Among the Muslim critics of my book, the Turkish pamphlet Kasim Küfrevi, *Hazreti Peygambere dil uzatanlar* (Istanbul, 1969) is especially curious. See below note 184.]

146. See my communication in the colloquium in Brussels (September, 1961) on the sociology of Islam: "Problématique de l'étude des rapports entre Islam et communisme (in *Colloque sur la Sociologie muslmane*, *Actes* [Brussels, 1962], pp. 119–49 [reprinted with a long introduction in my book, *Marxisme et monde musulmane* (Paris, 1973), pp. 130–80]), and my article: "Nature et fonction des mythes dans les mouvements socio-politiques d'après deux examples comparés," *Cahiers internationaux de sociologie*, 33 (1962), pp. 97–113 [reprinted in the same book, pp. 245–65].

147. *Muḥāḍarāt fī Tārīkh al-ʿArab,* I (in Arabic and also with an English title: Saleh A. El-Ali, *Lectures on the History of the Arabes*; vol. I: *Pre-Islamic States, Bedouin Life and Institutions, The Life of Muhammed and Islamic Preaching in Mecca*) (Baghdad, 1955). I have not seen the second volume.

147a. [His most important work, *Historie critique de Vieux Testament* (published in 1678) immediately aroused the indignation of the Catholic authorities in France, as a result of which the entire first edition of 1200 to 1500 copies was destroyed. A little later the work was published in Holland, and in 1682 an English translation appeared in London. See my "Richard Simon et la dédogmatisation," *Les Temps modernes*, no. 202 (March 1963), pp. 1700–1709; also the excellent account by Fr. Jean Steinmann, *Richard Simon et les Origines de l'exégèse biblique* (Paris, 1960).]

148. A very cautiously formulated dissertation on the Quran involving textual criticism still aroused violent reactions in Cairo in 1947. Among the biographies since the war, we shall mention the following: the posthumous edition of the great Italian Arabist, C. A. Nallino, *Vita di Maometto* (Rome, 1948) a very concise and eminently sound work; the study by H. Holma which we discussed above (p. 53); the short work of Dermenghem of which we have spoken (note 20); the imaginative and well-written partial biography by a distinguished Persian in which the Shīʿite spirit is reflected (Zain al Abedine Rahnema, *Le Prophète* [Paris, 1957]). The Muslim biographies in Arabic, with the exception of the one just cited, remain on this side of Haykal (e.g., Muhammad Khalid, *Khātam an-Nabīyīn* [Cairo, 1375/1955]). I have not seen the biography of al-Ghamrawi nor the *Sīrat ar-Rasūl* of the respectable Lebanese scholar ʿIzza Darwaza which I know only through the review of M. B. al-Bitar in the *Revue de l'Académie arabe de Damas*, 29 (1954), pp. 604–8. As in his work on pre-Islamic Arabia, he regards the Quran as the only reliable source, the only sure witness. Despite his fideism, this approach has the merit of encouraging the Arab world in the direction of a critical attitude toward the biographical tradition. I have not been able to consult the biographical work by Fathi Radwan, former Egyptian minister of the new regime whose rather unorthodox view consisted of seeing in Islam the manifestation of revolutionary genius of Muhammad (*Muḥammad ath-Thāʾir al-Aʿẓam,* 1954). Regarding this effort by Muslims to modernize the expressions of their faith without renouncing it, we ought to mention a curious but significant example in the slender booklet written in 1950 for the Muslim Scouts of Algeria by Mahmoud Bouzouzou (*Le dernier Messager*, Algiers, n.d., 32 pages, *Les cahiers S.M.A. au service de jeunes*, no. 1). Drawing on Essad Bey, Dinet, etc., as its source, it is a very intelligent and clear apologetic in which a modern vocabulary is used: "clandestinité," "le Prophète et les intellectuals," etc. One of its sources is the short apologetic biography included in the book by Muhammad Ali, *The Living Thoughts of the Prophet Muhammad* (London, 1947);

French translation, *La Pensée de Mahomet* (Paris, 1949). For example, this latter work passes over the massacre of the Banū Quraiẓa in complete silence. The author holds that the Prophet had married a number of women out of compassion. M. Hamidullah mentions (*Battlefields*, p. 36) a biography of the Prophet in four volumes by the Saudi parliamentarian Ba Salama (died in 1946). The latter conducted some travels and investigations on certain places relating to the life of Muhammad and was able thereby to provide some new information. We must note yet a recent Aḥmadīya biography, that is, one coming from a sect which one can characterize in a sense as somewhat modernist (despite Bausani), though reactionary: Mirza Bashir ud-Din Mahmud Ahamd, *The Life of Muhammad* (Rabwa [Pakistan], n.d.), 221 pages, examined by P. Masnou in *Arabica*, 8 (1961), pp. 324–25. [Among the later biographies, mention ought to be made of the careful Czech work, an attempt to introduce modern methods and a collection of views on the Prophet, by J. Hrbek, and K. Petzáček, *Muhammad* (Prague, 1967); the short portrait with translation of Arab biographical texts by F. Gabrieli (*Mahomet*, Paris, 1965); the sketch, from a religious point of view, along with a selection of texts, by R. Arnaldez (*Mahomet ou la Prédication prophetique*, Paris, 1970). Among Arab biographies, that by the talented leftist Egyptian novelist, ʻAbd ar-Rahman ash-Sharqawi, *Muḥammad Rasūl al-Ḥurriȳa* (Cairo, 1967), also intended for non-Muslim readers. See also the book by ʻAbd al-ʻAziz Kamil, *Durūz fī Ghazwat Uḥud* (Cairo, 1968), which attempts to analyze the attitude of the Prophet after his defeat at Uḥud as a model for the Arabs defeated by the Israelis in 1967.]

149. Cf. G. H. Bousquet, "Observations sur la nature et les causes de la conquête arabe," *Studia Islamica*, 6 (1956), pp. 37–52, an article which I criticized in my article in *Diogène*, 20 (1957), pp. 56f. Cf. A. Sharf, "Heraclius and Mahomet," *Past and Present*, 9 (1956), 1–16.

150. L. Caetani, *Studi di storia orientale*, vol. I (Milan, 1911), especially pp. 21f., 279, 366–68 and *passim* in his *Annali dell' Islam* (Milan, 1905ff.), vols. I and II; H. Lammens *Le berceau de l'Islam*, vol. I: *Le Climat, les Bédouins* (Rome, 1914); J. Schumpeter, "Zur Soziologie der Imperialismen," *Archiv für Sozialwissenschaft und Sozialpolitik* (Tübingen [46], 1918–1919), pp. 1–39, 275–310, partially translated into French by Bousquet, under the title "Les conquêtes de l'imperialisme arabe," in *Revue africaine*, 94 (1950), pp. 283–97. On the facts, the earlier synthesis of R. Dussaud, *Les Arabes en Syrie avant l'Islam* (Paris, 1907), revised and published by the author under the title: *La Pénétration des Arabes en Syrie avant l'Islam* (Paris, 1955) in *Institut français d'Archéologie de Beyrouth. Bibliothèque archéologique et historique*, 59. The indications given go beyond Syria.

151. K. W. Butzer, "Late Glacial and Postglacial Climatic Variations in the Near East," *Erdkunde*, 11 (1957), pp. 21–35. There had been, according to him, a period of drought in the Middle East from 590 to 645; we do not deny that it could have accentuated existing tendencies. Cf. by the same author, "Der Umweltfaktor in der grossen arabischen Expansion," *Saeculum*, 8 (1957), pp. 359–71.

152. *Der Islam*, I (1910), pp. 1–21, reprinted by C. H. Becker in *Vom Werden und Wesen der islamischen Welt, Islamstudien*, I (Leipzig, 1924), pp. 1–23. G. H. Bosquet ("Quelques remarques critiques et sociologiques sur la conquête arabe et les théories émises à ce sujet," in *Studi orientalistici in onore di Giorgio Levi della Vida* [Rome, 1956], I, pp. 52–60) rejects these conclusions. I have attempted to respond to him in *Diogène*, 20 (1957), pp. 56ff.

153. The exposé of E. A. Beliaev, "Formation of the Arab State and the Origin of Islam in the VIIth Century," *Obrazonvanie arabskogo gosudartsva i vozniknovenie Islama v VII veke* (Moscow, 1954) in *Papers Presented by the Soviet Delegation at the XXIII*

International Congress of Orientalists, Islamic Studies [in Russian and English], appears as a too highly schematized Marxism.

154. H. Holma, *Mahomet, prophète de l'Islam* (Paris, 1947). The original Finnish edition appeared in 1943. Cf. especially pp. 149–62.
155. *Le Problème de Mahomet*, p. 34.
156. Cf. on Muhammad, Owen Berkeley-Hill, "A Short Study of the Life and Character of Mohammed," *International Journal of Psycho-Analysis*, 2 (1921), pp. 31–53. The author believed too naively that "there was nothing shadowy or mysterious in the records of the life of the great Arabian prophet" (p. 31). However, certain of his suggestions are perhaps to be retained (cf. p. 45, regarding Khadīja as a substitute for his mother, like her, a widow). [Cf. also Einar Berg, "Muhammad: A Tentative Psychological Interpretation," *Temenos*, II (1966), pp. 22–39.]
157. *Muhammad, the Apostle of God, and His Ascension* (*King and Savior*, V) (Uppsala and Wiesbaden, 1955), In the same sense, more modestly, cf. I. Lichtenstadter, "Origin and Interpretation of some Qur'ānic Symbols," *Studi orientalistici in onore di G. Levi della Vida* (Rome, 1956), II, pp. 58–80.
158. J. Jomier, *Bible et Coran* (Paris, 1959). [Translated into English under the title: *The Bible and the Koran* by E. P. Arbez (Chicago, 1967); some of the chapters were rewritten for the English edition.]
159. D. Masson, *Le Coran et la révélation judéo-chrétienne, études comparées* (Paris, 1958), 2 vols.
160. Michel Hayek, *Le Christ de l'Islam, textes presentés, traduits et annotés* (Paris, 1959). Cf. also the valuable little work by J. M. Abd el-Jalil, *Marie et l'Islam* (Paris, 1950), and J. Henninger, *Spuren christ-licher Glaubenwahrheiten im Koran* (Beckenried, 1951) (a collection of articles which appeared in *Neue Zeitschrift für Missionswissenschaft*, vols. 1–5, [1945–1950]). We ought to mention the recent, remarkable, and very well informed little study by the late H. Michaud, *Jesus selon le Coran* (Neuchâtel, 1960). [Recently G. Lüling has tried to show that a large part of the Quran is nothing but the remodeling of a Christian "Ur-Qur'ān" with Judeo-Christian tendencies. His dissertation (*Über den Ur-Qur'ān, Ansätze zur Rekonstruktion vorislamischer christlicher Strophenlieder im Qur'ān*, Erlangen, 1974) has already created some problems for him; I intend to examine his arguments in a review for *Der Islam*.] A new approach which appears to be fruitful is the investigation of the relations of Islam with the Judeo-Christian tradition; it is set forth in the dense remarks of H. J. Schoeps on Ebionite elements in Islam in his *Theologie und Geschichte des Juden-Christentums* (Tübingen, 1949), pp. 334–42. [Now see, on a special point, the interesting paper by M. Philonenko, "Le décret apostolique et les interdits alimentaires du Coran," *Revue d'histoire et de philosophie religieuses*, 47 (1967), pp. 165–72, who suggests a probable Judeo-Christian source.]
161. A. I. Katsh, *Judaism and Islam: Biblical and Talmudic Backgrounds of the Koran and Its Commentaries, Surahs II and III* (New York, 1954); cf. the review of G. Vajda, *Revue des études juives*, 113 (1954), pp. 72–73.
162. Cf. J. Obermann, "Koran and Agada, the Events at Mount Sinai," *AJSL*, 58 (1941), pp. 23–48; by the same author, "Islamic Origins: A Study in Background and Foundation," in *The Arab Heritage*, ed. N. A. Faris (Princeton, 1944), pp. 58–120. Cf. Y. Moubarac, "Moise dans le Coran," in *Moise, l'homme de l'alliance* (Paris, 1954) pp. 373–91; J. Macdonald, "Joseph in the Qur'ān and Muslim commentary," *The Muslim World, 46 (1956), pp. 113–31, 207–24.*
163. C. Rabin, *Qumran Studies* (London, 1957); cf. also E. F. F. Bishop, "The Qumran Scrolls and the Qur'ān," *Muslim World*, 48 (1958), pp. 223–36. [See also the very

interesting papers of M. Philonenko, "Un tradition essénienne dans le Coran," *RHR*, 170 (1966), pp. 143–57, and "Une expression quomranienne dans le Coran," *Atti del III Congresso di Studi Arabici e Islamici* (Naples, 1967), pp. 553–56.]

164. Cf. Th. Nöldeke, *Geschichte des Qorāns*, 2nd ed. (by F. Schwally), vol. I (Leipzig, 1909), p. 27 ff.

165. Which does not mean that Muhammad had no Jewish informants who were reasonably well informed and orthodox. The Quran says clearly that he was accused of borrowing his knowledge from strangers. During a short period, at the time when his ideas were being formed, he could have investigated one such bit of information with one or several "masters." Cf. Goitein, "Who were Mohammad's Chief Teachers" (in Hebrew), *Tarbiz*, 23 (1952), pp. 146–59 (cf. G. Vajda, *REI*, 21 [1953], p. 113); by the same author, "Muhammad's Inspiration by Judaism," *Journal of Jewish Studies*, 9 (1958), pp. 149–162; *Jews and Arabs: Their Contacts Through the Ages* (New York, 1955) pp. 46–61, which sees there some uneducated, heterodox Jews, influenced by Christian monastic piety and inclined toward proselytism. But whatever the case, Muhammad vigorously recast all this information to create an original synthesis. He was in no way an instrument. Cf. still on this problem the remarks of S. W. Baron, *A Social and Religious History of the Jews*, III (New York, 1957), pp. 75–119 (with a very rich bibliography, but of unequal interest and confused), pp. 262–87.

166. H. Zakarias, *L'Islam, entreprise juive de Moise à Mohammed* (Cahors, 1955); *L'Islam et la critique historique, la fin du mythe musulman et accueil fait aux ouvrages de Hanna Zakarias* (Cahors, 1960). Cf. the review by A. Jeffery, *Middle East Journal*, 12 (1958), pp. 473–74 and the article by Father Jomier in *Études* (1961), pp. 82–92. We are informed by L. Massignon (*REI*, 26 [1958] cah. II, pp. 127–29) that H.Z. is the pseudonym of the Dominican G. Thery, well known by specialists on medieval Latin philosophy and the introduction of Muslim philosophy into the West. His order had refused the imprimatur, thus the pseudonym.

167. *Abraham dans le Coran* (Paris, 1958); cf. in the same vein the article by E. Beck, "Die Gestalt des Abraham am Wendepunkt der Entwicklung Mohammeds," *Muséon*, 65 (1952), pp. 73–94.

168. Cf. his bibliography by Y. Moubarac at the beginning of the *Mélanges Louis Massignon* (Damascus, 1956–1957), 3 vols.

169. [This Ishmaelite and Abrahamite filiation of the Arabs has brought on much theological speculation (with political inferences) on the place of the Arabs in God's plans and consequently the place of Islam; see especially Father M. Hayek in his recent books *Le Mystère d'Ismaël* (Tours, 1964) and *Les Arabes ou le baptême des larmes* (Paris, 1972). In these works, based on sound scholarship but lacking in a sense of reality, Ishmael is the "type" of Muhammad in the theological sense. Against this school of thought, Father R. Dagorn has written a book (*La Geste d'Ismaël d'après l'onomastique et la tradition arabes* to be published soon) in which he shows, following a painstaking inquiry into the texts, that the alleged Ishmaelite filiation of the Arabs was unknown to them before the Prophet (except for some marignal tribes) and that this idea, despite the Quran, did not impregnate the mind of Islamized Arabs for centuries after the *Hijra*].

170. Regarding the existence of parallels between texts, which is a sign of influences, Y. Moubarac tells us that "beyond the textual parallels, it is necessary to ascertain the connections (*apparentements*) between intentions and doctrines," and to give careful attention, beyond verbal parallels, to the "intentions which impregnate these words," to the "doctrines of which they are the vehicles" and which are much more variable. The denial of the actual crucifixion of Jesus by the Quran corresponds at first glance to

the Docetic point of view. However, one cannot "conclude a real connection since, quite evidently, the Quran is rather a stranger to the disembodied principles of Docetism. Even if the Quranic denial [of the crucifixion] could have issued from Docetic texts, it expresses something very different, and it is this that ought to be underscored" (p. 168 and note 2). What ought to be emphasized here is the inadmissibility of the methodology which this passage reveals. It contains a veritable play on the word "connection" (*apparentement*). The idea of the apparent punishment of Jesus is evidently of Docetic origin, and the fact that Muhammad integrated it into an entirely different context than that of the Docetics is certainly an interesting fact; it is permissible for Y. Moubarac to find it more important than the fact of the borrowing, but that can never destroy the fact of this latter. And this is what the thought of the author tends to do. Thus on pp. 108–10 he denies the connection between the Quranic text and the text of Josephus on the conversion of Abraham to monotheism, since Abraham's approach in the Quran is intuitive, while in the writing of the Jewish historian his approach is rational and deductive. That in no way proves that Muhammad had not drawn his intuitive conception of the event from the knowledge of a Jewish tradition which Josephus reflected (and from other texts cited by Speyer, pp. 124ff.) under a rational and deductive form. Thus one begins by declaring that a borrowing without the existence of a veritable "connection" is of no interest in order to later end up denying the borrowing because it does not involve a veritable connection. Y. Moubarac has the right to think that "objective reality (in the Christian cult of relics) is after all secondary in relation to the devotion of the believer who (beyond the object) attains the spiritual reality" (p. 78). But the historian is interested in this objective reality. And we take the liberty of believing that the problem of the sources of Quranic narratives, even if the ideas borrowed have been transposed and integrated into an entirely different framework of meaning, is a fact of capital importance. L. Massignon himself found in the end that it was useful to make a counter-balance from time to time to these approaches which he had supported (*REI*, 24 [1956], pp. 15–16). In the same sense, it is astonishing to see R. Blachère (*Introduction au Coran*, 2nd ed., 1959, p. 197) contest the value of a critical edition of the Quran on the ground that it is the received text, the vulgate, on which the doctrines of Islam are established. Has the thought of Muhammad himself no value beyond what subsequent centuries have discovered in it?

171. *Islam, 'Aslama and Muslim* (Lund, 1949). [See now the study by D. Z. H. Baneth, "What did Muḥammad mean when he called his religion 'Islam'? The Original Meaning of *aslama* and Its Derivatives," *Israel Oriental Studies*, I (1971), pp. 183–90.]
172. "On the Spiritual Background of Early Islam and the History of Its Principal Concepts," *Muséon* 64 (1951), pp. 317–56. [This paper has now been republished together with some others, already published or original, in a book by M. M. Bravmann entitled: *The Spiritual Background of Islam: Studies in Ancient Arab Concepts* (Leiden, 1972). Very interestingly and with a considerable knowledge of archaic poetry, Bravmann traces many early Islamic concepts back to the ancient Arab way of thinking.]
173. "The Concept of Faith in the Koran," *Oriens*, 4 (1951), pp. 1–20.
174. "Die Göttesfurcht im Koran," *Donum natalicium H. S. Nyberg oblatum* (Uppsala, 1954), pp. 118–34.
175. *Proche-Orient chrétien*, 10 (1950), pp. 212–26, 303–17; 11 (1961), pp. 3–16.
176. Let us mention (with no attempt to arrange them in a particular order) J. M. S. Baljon, "To Seek the Face of God in Koran and Hadith," *Acta Orientalia* (Copenhagen), 21 (1953), pp. 254–66; by the same author, "The *'Amr* of God in the Koran,"

Acta Orientalia, 23 (1959), pp. 7–18; Th. O'Shaughnessy, *The Koranic Concept of the Word of God* (Rome, 1948); by the same author, *The Development of the Meaning of Spirit in the Qor'ān* (Rome, 1953); R. Blachère, "Note sur le substantif nofs . . . dans le Coran," *Semitica*, I (1948), pp. 69–77; R. Brunschvig, "Simples remarkques negatives sur le vocabulaire du Coran," *Studia Islamica*, 5(1956), pp. 19–32; M. Gaudefroy-Demombynes, "Le sens du substantif *ghayb* dans le Coran," *Mélanges L. Massignon*, II (Beirut, 1957), pp. 245–50; J. Jomier, "Le nom divin *'al-Raḥman'*dans le Coran," *ibid.*, pp. 361–81; J. Chelhod, "Note sur l'emploi du mot *rabb* dans le Coran," *Arabica*, 5 (1958), pp. 159–67; J. Corbon, "Notes sur le vocabulaire de prédication des premières sourates mekkoises," *Mélanges de l'Université Saint-Joseph*, 36 (1959), pp. 149–95. One will find other references in the article by A. Jeffery mentioned above (note 113). [We must now emphasize especially the importance of two books by a Japanese Arabist, Toshihika Izutsu, who introduces a new way of studying these problems by the method of semantic analysis: *The Structure of the Ethical Terms in the Koran* (Tokyo, 1959), and *God and Man in the Koran: Semantics of the Koranic Weltanschauung* (Tokyo, 1964). M. Arkoun attempted a structural analysis of Quranic concepts in his introduction to one of the latest reprints of Kazimirski's translation (*Le Coran*, Paris, 1970). Among other studies relating to special points, see also O'Shaughnessy, *Muhammad's Thoughts on Death* (Leiden, 1969); K. Wagtendonk, *Fasting in the Koran* (Leiden, 1968); J. Nowoski, "The Pretensions—Activity of Muhammad in the Light of the Qur'ān and the most ancient Muslim traditions" (*Collectanea Theologica* [Warsaw, 32, 1961], pp. 5–84, in Polish with an English summary [English title as translated by the author]where the author attempts to examine the external factors that influenced Muhammad's relgious views); M. Causse, "Théologie de rupture et théologie de la communauté, étude sur la vocation prophétique de Moise d'après le Coran," *Revue d'histoire et de philosophie religieuses*, 44 (1964), pp. 60–82, a very clever analysis.]

177. Cf. T. Sabbagh, *La Métaphore dans le Coran* (Paris, 1943); G. H. Bousquet has very usefully translated into French Nöldeke's "Zur Sprache des Korāns" (in his *Neue Beiträge zur semitischen Sprachwissenschaft*, Strasbourg, 1910, pp. 5–23) under the title, *Remarques critiques sur le style et la syntaxe du Coran* (Paris, 1954). A dictionary of Quranic vocabulary has begun to be published in Cairo under the auspices of the Arabic Academy of Cairo.
178. *Analyse conceptuelle du Coran* on perforated cards by M. Allard, M. Elzière, J. C. Gardin, and F. Hours (Paris and the Hague, 1963). M. Allard in his "Une méthode nouvelle pour l'étude du Coran," *Studia Islamica*, 15 (1961), pp. 15–21, has given a sketch of the method and two examples of the kind of service that it can provide.
179. We may mention, however, the booklet of M. Hamidullah, *The Battlefields of the Prophet Muhammad* (Woking, 1953) where one will find useful maps and photographs of sites which few Europeans have visited, as well as a reconstruction of the strategic movements based upon this rare knowledge of the area. For a larger view, see the work of a high Egyptian officer, Muhammad Faraj, *Muḥammad al-Muḥārib* (Cairo, n.d. [about 1950]) which attempts to understand the military skill of the Prophet within the framework of our modern categories. M. Hamidullah claims even to have found graffiti by the Prophet's own hand and by the first caliphs on the rocks of Mount Sal' at the entrance to Medina ("Some Arabic Inscriptions of Medinah," *Islamic Culture*, 13 [1939], pp. 427–39). One should mention the important article by G. H. Stern which is a model of detailed research, "The First Women Converts in Early Islam," *Islamic Culture*, 13 (1939), pp. 290–305. This kind of work shows very clearly that it is impossible to reject tradition out of hand. There is an historical base to all the bio-

graphical details on the Companions of the Prophet. J. M. B. Jones made a very careful investigation into the chronology of the "campaigns" of Muhammad according to Wāqidī and the parallel sources ("The Chronology of the *Maghāzī*—A Textual Survey," *BSOAS*, 19 [1957], pp. 245–80) Cf. also the critical investigations of Blachère on the various versions of a speech by Muhammad ("L'allocution de Mahomet lors du pèlerinage d'adieu," *Mélanges L. Massignon*, I [Beirut, 1956], pp. 223–49). An adventurous thesis put forward by A. Guillaume (*Al-Andalus*, 18 [1953], pp. 323–36) on the primary (and according to him, "natural" and prosaic) sense of Surah 17:1 on which is based the account of Muhammad's ascension to heaven, has been refuted by M. Plessner (*Rivista degli studi orientali*, 32 [1957], pp. 525–30) and by R. Paret (*Der Islam*, 34 [1959], pp. 150–52).

180. Tor Andrae, *Die Person Mohammeds in Lehre und Glauben seiner Gemeinde* (Stockholm, 1918).

181. "Le caractère sociologique des origines du 'culte' de Mahomet dans l'Islam tardif," *Mélanges Georges Smets* (Brussels, 1952) pp. 43–55.

182. "Vergöttlichung und Tabuisierung der Namen Muhammad's bei den Muslimen," in *Beiträge zur Arabistik, Semitistik und Islamwissenschaft* (Leipzig, 1944), pp. 307–39.

183. *Mohammed im Volksepos, ein neuarabisches Heiligenlied* (Copenhagen, 1950). One ought to call to mind here equally all the medieval and modern Muslim literature which attempts, in its own way, to understand the Quran by reinterpreting it constantly according to the conceptions of the period. In the measure in which the Quranic text itself, despite all these reinterpretations, exercises a direct influence on these interpreters and on the thinking of people in general, it is necessary to speak of a posthumous influence by Muhammad who, for non-Muslims, is the real author of the Quran. However, Muslim faith clearly separates the two themes. For them it is a question of the work of God. We will not treat here this very vast subject, one that lies very far from our principal purpose.

184. Cf. the important work by Normal Daniel, *Islam and the West: The Making of an Image* (Edinburgh, 1960) where one will find much on the medieval western image of Muhammad. The author treats especially the formation of ideas on Islam in the Christian West between 1100 and 1340. However, he goes beyond these limits and pursues the matter, though in a less detailed fashion, up to our own time. [N. Daniel has continued his study of European views on Islam beyond the Middle Ages in his *Islam, Europe and Empire* (Edinburgh, 1966), a valuable book with a number of interesting texts cited or referred to. From the explanatory side, however, it has shortcomings to which A. Hourani has rightly pointed in his review (*Middle Eastern Studies,* 4 [1968], pp. 325f). More generally authorities like N. Daniel are to be criticized, to my mind, for the exclusiveness they grant to the theological point of view. No more in the Middle Ages than now were people *exclusively* interested in the status of Islam as a religion vis-à-vis Christianity, and consequently in the status of Muhammad as a false prophet, an impostor, etc., more or less assimilated to a Christian heretic. Many were also interested in Islam as a political grouping of enemy countries (at times, however, allied), as a field for profitable commercial ventures, as an exotic world of strange customs and many wonders. Consequently, "the image of Islam" cannot be identified purely and simply with the image of the Islamic religion. On another side, with their sympathetic concern to right the old wrongs done to Islam, these authors (N. Daniel especially) have gone so far as to place in the category of those conceptions permeated by medievalism and imperialism any criticisms of the Prophet's moral attitudes and to accuse of like tendencies any exposition of Islam and its characteristics by means of the normal mechanism of human history. Understanding has given way to apologetics pure

and simple. Along these lines, I, for example, have been accused by L. P. Elwell-Sutton (*New York Review of Books,* January 1972) of looking for my descriptions of Muhammad's private life and love affairs in the Christian, anti-Islamic books of the Middle Ages, even though all of these details ("lewd" as they may seem to a Puritan mind) are found in detail in Ṭabarī, Ibn Hishām, Ibn Sa'd, etc., as well as in the collections of *ḥadith,* let alone the allusions in the Quran itself. Some Muslim ideologists see, of course, in the sin of relating now what their predecessors have related, a sure sign of the imperialist mind or the Zionist allegiance of the author (see e.g., Muhammad al-'Īlāwī, *al-Hidāya* [Tunis], Rabī' al-Awwal, 1394/April 1974, pp. 89–92). The claim that historians should not treat the biography of Muhammad as that of a man is tantamount to asking them to practice hypocrisy or convert to Islam (see also note 145). Among the new works written on the image of Islam in Europe, including the image of the Prophet, the following are particularly interesting: R. W. Southern, *Western Views of Islam in the Middle Ages* (Cambridge, Mass., 1962), a very good study; and R. Schwoebel, *The Shadow of the Crescent: The Renaissance Image of the Turk* (Niewkoop, 1967). I have tried to draw a general picture of "The Western Image and Western Studies of Islam" in an essay that was published (in an abridged form) under this title in the new edition of *The Legacy of Islam* (Oxford, 1974).]

185. E. Cerulli, *Il 'Libro della Scala' e la questione delle fonti arabospagnole della Divina Commedia* (Vatican City, 1949); J. Muñoz Sendino, *La escala de Mahoma* (Madrid, 1949). Numerous reviews and articles have discussed the questions posed by the discovery and the theses of these authors. We shall be content to mention here G. Levi della Vida, "Nouva luce sulle fonti islamiche della Divina Commedia," *Al-Andalus,* 14 (1949), pp. 377–407 (without doubt the most important); L. Olschki, "Mohammedan Eschatology and Dante's Other World," *Comparative Literature,* III (1951), pp. 1–17; the review of E. Littmann, *Orientalia,* 20 (1951), pp. 508–12; J. Monfrin, "Les sources arabes de la 'Divine Comedie' et la traduction française du Livre de l'Ascension de Mahomet," *Bibliothèque de l'Ecole des chartes,* 109 (1951), pp. 279–90 (from the point of view of French philology); M. Rodinson, "Dante et l'Islam d'après des travaux récents" (*RHR,* 140 [1951], pp. 203–36). More recently, cf. E. Cerulli, "Dante e l'Islam," *Al-Andalus,* 21 (1956), pp. 229–53.

186. "Il mito di Maometto in Boulainvilliers," *Revista storica italiana,* 60 (1948), pp. 367–77. The study has already been undertaken on a larger base, but also more anecdotal, without underlining the ideological character of the ideas analysed, by P. Martino, "Mahomet en France au XVIIe siècle," *Actes du XIVe Congrès international des orientalistes, Alger, 1905* (Paris, 1906–1908), part 3, vol. I, pp. 206–41. Cf. also J. J. Saunders, "Mohammed in Europe: A Note on Western Interpretations of the Life of the Prophet," *History,* 39 (1954), pp. 14–25, perceptive, though slightly superficial.

III

The Originality of the Arabian Prophet[1]

J. FUECK

Muhammad continues to be regarded as one of the most controversial figures of world history down to our own time. Recognized by some already during his lifetime as God's messenger (though scoffed at by others as a demon-possessed individual) he was elevated after his death into a superhuman figure by his followers. The anti-Islamic polemic, on the other hand, painted him in the blackest of colors. Since then, however, even though observers free of religious fanaticism have given him a somewhat fairer assessment, their judgments extend over an entire spectrum, ranging from that of the highest recognition to a shoulder-shrugging sympathy for an epileptic, to a caustic rejection of him as an unprincipled imposter. The historicism of the nineteenth century brought a new note into this chorus with its emphasis on the dependence of the Prophet upon older religions of revelation, a trend which a Geiger initiated over somewhat more than one hundred years ago in his now famous prize essay.[2] However, the more investigation into questions of dependence became the vogue, the more scholarly study lost contact with the significant unifying themes of the Quran and eventually came to be satisfied with repeated investigation into each and every Quranic detail no matter whether it was a religious concept, an expression, a legal maxim, a narrative, or a motif. Individual words of a variety of patterns were traced back to prior models, as though it were possible to separate the living essence of the Prophet into a thousand bits and pieces. Already some years ago Tor Andrae[3] vigorously protested against this approach and defined the task of the scholarly study of Muhammad as an attempt to understand how the Prophet, as a result of the spiritual stimulation provided by his environment, forged numerous elements of the most varied sort into one living whole, original in the way in which the various components were combined. However, two subsequent studies of Muhammad, those by C. C. Torrey[4] and W. Ahrens,[5] represent a return to the older approach as can be seen by their concern to restrict the originality of the Prophet as much as possible through every conceivable counter-demonstration and conclusion, and to derive his doctrines essentially from the earlier monotheistic religions. Whether to Judaism or Christianity should be given the honor of being the model followed by Muhammad was a question answered in diametrically opposed ways by these two scholars. Just as definitely as Torrey saw Muhammad as a disciple of the synagogue, Ahrens was convinced that Christian influences were decisive for him. It would be idle to attempt to demonstrate the questionable character of such explanations by pointing to the obviously contradictory character of their results. It is perhaps not superfluous, however, to look briefly at both accounts of Muhammad in order to arrive at a fairer assessment of the value of the method employed through a comparison of their results.

For Torrey it is an established fact that since there were Jewish communities at each of the main points along the trade route from Palestine to South Arabia, established as a result of a migration dating back to pre-Christian times, there must have been one at Mecca which cherished and cultivated the religious and literary traditions of its forefathers. It is this Jewish community of Mecca (which cannot be proved to exist but which Torrey thinks can be necessarily inferred from the Quran) which, with its Jewish life, tradition, literature, and propaganda, aroused the Prophet and provided him with a model. His relationship with several Jews was allegedly so close that he was supposed to have entertained the idea of converting to Judaism. If he disappointed the hopes of his Jewish advisor, it was his secretive character that was responsible. It was supposedly this element in his character that made it possible for him to conceal his real intentions until he had profited sufficiently from his instructors in doctrine so as to make himself independent. If Torrey's thesis at this point flies directly in the face of the widely accepted, traditional recognition of the Prophet's uprightness and moral integrity, it leads in other areas to consequences that are completely untenable. Since the Quran reflects a rather naive confusion regarding several facets of biblical history (it is perhaps sufficient here to point out that it confuses Miriam, the mother of Jesus, with the sister of Aaron [Surah 19:29, 66:12] and identifies Haman as Pharaoh's vizier [Surah 28:5, 7, 38; 40:38]), and since it further mentions none of the writing prophets, Torrey comes to the conclusion that the Prophet's understanding was still quite limited and that the lofty doctrines of the writing prophets of the Old Testament were beyond his ability to comprehend. And yet the indisputable fact that Muhammad regarded Jesus as a prophet of the highest rank, that he accepted the virgin birth (though admittedly not the belief that Jesus was God's son), and that his statements, even where they are directed against Christianity, never give evidence of animosity or malice, clearly contradicts the position of Torrey. For Torrey would have us believe that the Jewish mentor of the Prophet, out of fear lest he be lost to the Christian church, communicated to him only so much about Jesus as was necessary to prevent him from enquiring amongst Christians regarding Jesus. This embarrassing information, therefore, required no detailed refutation. Torrey's arbitrary construction founders on both internal and external contradictions. There is no evidence for the existence of a strong Jewish colony with a living tradition at Mecca, nor does the Quran give evidence of that intimate knowledge of Jewish matters which we would expect if Muhammad had actually been heavily dependent on Judaism.

Inspired by the same motive, *viz.*, to understand the personality of the Prophet as the product of influences exerted on him, but with a completely different point of view and equipped with a more impressive set of scholarly credentials, Ahrens attempted to show that from the beginning of his public life the Prophet was influenced by Christianity and that during the greater part of the Meccan period he was predominantly dependent upon Christians in the formulation of his doctrines. In contrast to Torrey, who rejected the rather widely accepted chronology of the surahs of the Quran, and who attempted to replace it with his own arrangement, Ahrens emphatically accepts the chronology established by Nöldeke on the basis of content and linguistic considerations and, accordingly, works out a picture of Muhammad as prophet, teacher, and lawgiver. For each feature of this picture, he produces a mass of Christian parallels (in this case doing perhaps too much of a good thing) and not only assumes dependence where, at most, it is merely a question of an external contact, but here and there even brings together heterogeneous materials. Quite plainly, he does not strike a balance, and, above all, in the section on Muhammad as lawgiver,

Ahrens comes forward clearly as a Christian apologist who reacts sometimes with anger and sometimes with sorrow at how little the teaching of Muhammad in Medina conforms to the expectations which the early Meccan period appeared to foreshadow. If in Torrey's view it was selfishness and an inability to understand that kept Muhammad from adopting a clearly Jewish position, for Ahrens it was his political opportunism that allowed him to compromise (for the sake of worldly success) the best of those principles that had been drawn from Christianity. How, we ask, is it possible for a gang leader who supposedly had no scruples against using whatever means were available to achieve his goals, who carried out "general massacre," and who "took delight in enemies slain," to exert such influence on world history that 1300 years after his death over three hundred million[6] persons confess their faith in him? The witness of many centuries of history and the witness today of an Islam that is still vigorous refute more conclusively than any other argument the judgments that Ahrens expressed on the basis of a flawed interpretation.

If the efforts of Torrey and Ahrens are unsatisfactory, they are nonetheless highly instructive from a methodological point of view. They show that the undeniable contacts that Islam had with Judaism and Christianity (and which the Quran itself recognizes) cannot be used as proof of direct dependence. Every attempt to prove such leads inevitably to insoluble difficulties and contradictions. Now it might seem that the actual solution to this problem could be found if (putting aside all partiality) one explained the various contacts as just so many stimuli, so that the Quran could be represented as the product of Christian, Jewish, and numerous other impulses. In fact, such an attempt has been made. J. Horovitz in particular dealt with several special problems relating to the Quran in monograph-length studies in which he regarded the most varied influences as equal in importance.[7] Such investigations, however, tend to dissolve the Quran into a mosaic of countless individual stones of various origins which have no inner connection linking them together. Behind the mass of detail the personality of the Prophet vanishes. The living power of his personality cannot be explained through source analysis no matter how well executed. Andrae's critique appears to be completely justified in the case of this work as well. It is not possible even by means of an analysis that takes into consideration all details down to the most minute to isolate what is fundamentally creative in the Prophet. Studies based on rational and scientific method will never completely succeed in lifting the veil of mystery that surrounds the personality of this man. We will never be able to establish scientifically what it was that enabled him to find his way through difficult experiences to the certainty that God had appointed him to be a warner and an apostle. Once this point is understood, the question of possible prototypes, influences, and stimuli loses that decisive significance that it holds for a mechanistic conception of history. What is significant and worth knowing is how the Prophet employed the material provided him, how he altered it, selected from it, and rendered it amenable to his own purposes. That he did so more vigorously than perhaps any other religious hero in no way detracts from his originality. It belongs to the essence of all great men of the spirit to make generous use of material transmitted to them while impregnating it with new life.

Was the Prophet, however, a genuinely creative figure? Does not the Quran everywhere bear witness to a remarkable contact (sometimes intimate, sometimes more distant) with the older monotheistic religions? Do not Muslims themselves accept the Torah and the Gospel as distinctly revealed scriptures and also declare that there is an inner correspondence between their faith and that of Jews and Christians, even though they may charge them with having falsified the Scripture? In order to answer this question, it will be necessary to examine the religious ideas present in the earliest preaching of Islam as they are represented in the surahs of the first Meccan period.

It has long been recognized that the central idea of early Islamic preaching was not monotheism, but rather the notion of the last judgment—a notion, of course, very intimately bound up with monotheistic thought. It is precisely the one God who sits in judgment over men on the last day. In the earliest surahs monotheism certainly plays no leading role.[8] On page 24 of his work Andrae points out that Muhammad's confession of faith that "there is no god but Allāh" in no way implies the introduction of a new God.[9] The Meccans did not deny the existence of Allāh, "Lord of the House." Indeed, He was for them the highest god. They did not have a living faith in a plurality of equally ranked divine beings and clung to the old traditional cultic practices only out of an attachment to the past. Beyond that, there was the driving force of self-interest and a desire for profit on the part of the leading aristocratic merchants who benefited considerably from the cultic practices with their festivals and fairs. Andrae is inclined to regard this belief in Allāh as a "primitive monotheism." I believe, however, that the earlier interpretation of this phenomenon which saw in it the influence of the monotheistic religions to be the valid one. Trade which constituted the link between Mecca and the outside world had brought a knowledge (even though superficial) of foreign religions into the Hijaz which, already before the appearance of Muhammad, had given rise to doubts among thinking Meccans regarding the validity of pagan religion. Tradition has preserved for us the names of such seekers after God (*ḥanīfs*), some of whom sought salvation in Judaism and Christianity[10] while others, who did not wish to give up their national identity, took over from the older religions what appeared meaningful to them, *viz.*, belief in one God, rejection of a plurality of gods, and the demand for conduct that was morally upright. One such *ḥanīf* was Zaid b. 'Amr b. Nufail, an uncle of 'Umar who was later to become caliph. In other cities also we find men of a similar religious attitude. At Ṭā'if there was the poet Umayya b. Abī'ṣ-Ṣalt; in Medina there were Abū 'Amir ar-Rāhib and Abū Qais b. al-Aslat,[11] both of whom were leaders of the Aws-Allāh and became vigorous opponents of the Prophet after his migration to Medina. These men, like Umayya, died as *ḥanīfs*. Now as is well known, the Quran uses the term *ḥanīf* to designate the primordial monotheistic religion. Muhammad was thus clearly aware that his own teaching agreed with that of the early *ḥanīfs*. It follows from this that we have to assume here a national Arabian monotheism which was a preparatory stage to Islam and which, in any examination of the possible stimuli that made themselves felt on Muhammad, cannot be ignored. Most probably this Arabian religion was responsible for much of what Muhammad believed in common with Jews and Christians. This harmonizes admirably with the fact that precisely in the first period of his public life Muhammad's preaching reflected a surprisingly Arabian coloring. Three of the earliest surahs (111, 106, and 105) are cases in point. Fischer has shown that in surah 111 we have an example of the old Arabian practice of *hijā'* or satire.[12] In surah 106 the Meccan trade caravans are seen as proof of God's blessing and the sacred area [of the Ka'ba] is quite ingeniously recognized. Finally, in surah 105 we have a punishment story which shows through the example of the (Christian!) Abyssinians the fate that awaits those who transgress against God, "the Lord of the House." This certainly does not suggest sympathy for Christians, to say nothing of influence by them. Even the punishment story of Thamūd mentioned shortly thereafter in surah 91:11 (and which is cited more often than any other) is of Arabian origin. Closely related to it are the stories of 'Ād, Hūd, Iram, and (in the second Meccan period) that of the *aṣḥāb al-aika* [dwellers in the wood; cf. 15:78; 50:14, etc.] including Shu'aib, and also that of the *aṣḥāb ar-rass* [the men of ar-Rass; cf. 50:12] and Tubba' [50:12]. In surah 108 which likewise is very early, the Prophet is commanded to "pray to your Lord and offer sacrifice." Then there is the *ghrānīq-* episode in surah 53. Finally, there is the Meccan charge (which is understandable only within the context of Arabia) that the Prophet was a *Majnūn,* a *kāhin,* a *shā'ir,* or a *sāḥir*—charges which he (and this is of decisive importance) took very seriously. One must add to this the brilliant evidence furnished by Fischer[13] that Muhammad in may ways called to mind the old Arabian *kuhhān* (sing. *kāhin*) in his public appearance, and that even in the first years of the Medinan period the forms in which he gave judgment and adjudicated disputes corresponded essentially to that of the pagan *kāhin* and *ḥakam.* The style of the Quran as has long been recognized, reflects this same correspondence with pre-Islamic forms—the use of *saj'* or alliteration, and the many oaths that appear at the beginning of surahs (though limited to those of the first Meccan period). Finally there is the earliest description of hell and paradise (surah 77) which clearly reflects Arabian features.

The conception of the last judgment—a doctrine that stands at the center of early Islamic preaching—is connected in the most intimate fashion with faith in one God, the belief in his unlimited power (with which no other power can compare), and the consciousness of his moral essence which men are to keep before them as a model. All of these ideas which appear already in the first Meccan period (though perhaps not always clearly expressed) are rooted in a grand cyclical conception of revelations, without which Muhammad's prophetic consciousness and his appearance as a warner and preacher remain completely incomprehensible. This doctrine affirms that God sends to every nation a special messenger with a divine revelation in their own tongue, that hitherto all peoples (misled by leaders who stubbornly held fast to tradition) witnessed falsely against God's messengers, abused them and held them up to ridicule, and that God then visited judgment upon the sinners.[14] The Prophet clearly thought of these peoples as city-states after the model of his own native Mecca and its inhabitants, the Quraish. Thus, in the beginning he felt himself sent to Mecca and only later did he extend his activities beyond Mecca. This cyclical theory of revelation cannot be derived either from Judaism or from Christianity. The idea as such has parallels in gnosticism and especially in the thought of Mani,[15] but with no evidence to date indicating any direct historical connection. However, the special form of this doctrine as it appears in the Quran, particularly the inclusion of early Arabian prophets, seems to be Muhammad's own creation. It reflects his philosophy of history and indicates how he understood his relationship to other peoples who had previously received a divine revelation. It is convincing evidence that Muhammad could not have received the decisive stimulus to prophetic action from either Jews or Christians. It has been suggested by some that before his call he had witnessed the reciting of Jewish or Christian scriptures and that on one such occasion he was aroused by the desire to proclaim God's word to his own people. If this were so, he would almost certainly have associated himself more closely with Judaism or Christianity in the beginning. Why he should have hit upon the notion that God must send a *new* prophet to his people in order to proclaim to them the ancient truths in their own language remains entirely inconceivable. A translation would surely rather have suggested itself. The interpretation put forward by Andrae has just as little to commend it. He is convinced that Muhammad once overheard a Christian missionary sermon, probably that of a Nestorian,[16] and "that the Prophet was not only acquainted with the main outlines of the Christian doctrines of judgment, retribution, and good works, but also that he reproduced in detail the interpretations of these doctrines which were prevalent in the churches of the Orient and that at times he even employed a style and expressions which must have had a Christian origin" (p. 91). How could Muhammad have been so deeply influenced by a Christian missionary sermon as to borrow from it in details of style while at the same time ignoring its central christological element so completely that in the first Meccan period he makes no reference to it at all? Should we not have expected at least a slight reference to the fact that he rejected the Christian doctrine of redemption? And most important of all, Christianity gives not the least support for his prophetology—the metaphysical background of Muhammad's effectiveness. The remarkable points of agreement between the Quran and Christian writings to which Andrae refers are not found in the earliest surahs. It is too easily forgotten that the individual surahs include materials extending over many years and that even in the first Meccan period there are passages covering a period of several years. Whatever accords with Christianity and Judaism in the earliest surahs (and these are decisive for an answer to the question of the original character of Islam) is so vague that it cannot be attributed either to one or the other with any degree of certainty. The *ḥanīfs* were already acquainted with monotheistic ideas and held to the belief in the resurrection and final judgment. The religious terms of non-Arabic origin come, for the most part, from Aramaic which at that time was the international language of culture in the Near East and was used equally by the various religious communities. Only in the case of certain expressions of Ethopian origin does it appear probable that they had been conveyed to the Prophet by Christian slaves or merchants from Abyssinia.[17] However, even here South Arabia is to be considered as an intermediary. Moreover, the *ḥanīfs* must already have possessed a number of religious terms of their own. The reference to the *ṣuḥuf Ibrāhīm wa Mūsā* (the scrolls of Abraham and Moses) in surah 87 is certainly not to be taken as indicating a knowledge of Jewish or Christian orthodoxy. This much is confirmed by surah 53:37–54 according to which the history of ʿĀd and Thamūd, among others, is found in these *ṣuḥuf.* From the standpoint of his own theory of revelation, Muhammad attributed his own doctrines to an earlier revealed scripture.[18] With the passing of time Muhammad more and more placed his own words into the mouths of the earlier prophets and attributed to their opponents the same objections which he himself met with from the unbelieving Meccans.[19] In order to demonstrate that his doctrines were revealed, he enumerated the recurring examples of God's judgment against peoples of earlier times, including a whole series of biblical stories. However, the Christian elements do not by any means dominate. Among this material rather one also finds references to Arabian stories of the prophets Ṣāliḥ, Shuʿaib, and Hūd. To be sure, these cannot be traced in pre-Islamic literature; they surely owe their existence, however, not to a whim of the Prophet but rather to early Arabian tradition. The material for these stories Muhammad in fact took over from all sides: we meet with some name-forms that bear a clear Aramaic stamp, and also some which are of Abyssinian origin. On one occasion he employed a Christian style, on another a Jewish one. It was not that he wished to amuse a novelty-hungry public. He wanted rather to convert his unbelieving compatriots to the true faith, to a morally transformed life, and to warn them of the day of judgment and the torments of hell. The practical nature of his objective explains the stylistic peculiarities of the punishment stories, their brevity (frequently satisfied with a simple allusion), the lack of vivid detail, and endless repetition. Thus within the framework of Quranic revelation the biblical stories play only a subordinate role as illustrative material and may in no way be used as proof that the Prophet was dependent on Jews or Christians for the essential points of his religious belief. How little that was actually the case and how modest was Muhammad's knowledge of the earlier religions of revelation is shown most clearly in his naive hope that he would be recognized as a prophet by Jews and Christians. Indeed, it appears to me that it was the discovery of a substantive correspondence between his own preaching and what Christians and Jews found in their sacred books that first motivated him to concern himself more directly with their tradition, for it is the second Meccan period that first reflects an extensive knowledge of biblical stories. Stylistic agreements with Christian forms of liturgy appear for the first time in this period—a matter that has been very carefully analyzed by A. Baumstark.[20] During this period he sent several of his followers over to Christian Abyssinia. In the thi'd Meccan period he begins to draw upon the model of the older religions in external, cultic matters (fasts, the *qibla,* forms of worship, etc.). In Medina he would soon realize that his hopes were vain; and the rejection that he experienced at the hand of the Jews was all the more painful, since he had no depth-knowledge of Judaism to prepare him for it. Their sharp criticism of him was the severest blow that his teaching had thus far encountered—a blow that he warded off instinctively by going back to the immovable Arabian foundations of his religion. The notion of the *millat Ibrāhīm* [the religion of Abraham][21] was only the external symbol of this self-consciousness. The Prophet again now turns his attention to the Ka'ba and makes it the center of the Islamic cult. The pilgrimage and practices associated with it were stripped of their pagan features and definitively integrated into the new religion.

Christian polemical writings represent the Medinan period as one of inward disintegration, a time during which the enthusiasm of the Meccan period is completely lost, with only a cold egotism and calculating cleverness allegedly left to dominate the scene. Such an interpretation overlooks the fact that all genuine religion seizes the whole person and demands the total dedication of all his powers. No sphere is permitted to fall outside of its influence. If Muhammad elaborated Islamic legislation for the first time in Medina, it was in consequence of the fact that only there did the growing size of his following create the necessity for such action and only there did the possibilities for such exist. The controversy over whether Muhammad had been active politically already in Mecca is idle, for in his mind there was no conflict between religious and political activity. Muhammad's earliest preaching already necessarily included the demand that life be conducted in accordance with moral principles as the only safeguard against divine wrath and the punishment of hell. Above all, the Quran repeatedly insists that believers ought to give alms and to accept responsibility for the poor and the orphans.[22] Already very early a fixed tax is mentioned.[23] These and similar requirements (such as that the possessions of widows and orphans should not be violated, that property held in trust should be returned, that full measure be given in commercial transactions, and that perjury not be committed)[24] are intimately linked to the "religious" (in the modern sense of the term) requirements of prayer, the night vigil, and similar acts of practical piety. Tor Andrae is certainly right when he points out that the roots of this social ethic are religious and not humanitarian. One should guard against a hasty rejection of such an outlook as one of crass egotism, for the decisive fact is that the Prophet did create a remedy for the crying social abuses of his time and proclaimed an ethic which involved difficult personal sacrifices for his followers—sacrifices that were even more significant since the earliest believers were for the most part poverty stricken. If these social demands are mentioned only occasionally in the surahs of the first Meccan period and nowhere especially emphasized, part of the answer is to be found in the frenzy of the early period in which anxiety in the face of impending judgment forced all other things into the background. Moreover, the early community of believers was so small and lived in such close contact with the Prophet that detailed legislation with exact prescriptions for moral action would have been superfluous. The sharp increase in the number of converts in Medina and the difficult economic situation of the Meccan emigrants made a regulation of charity and public responsibility an absolute necessity for the first time. One should not see in this development any fundamental revolution or break in the inner development of the Prophet. The factors which had prevented him from building a community in Mecca, as he subsequently did in Medina, resided not in him but in the external situation. In Mecca the bitter and stubborn opposition of the Quraishi aristocracy stood in his way—an opposition which felt quite rightly that the new religion meant the destruction of the old Meccan system. In Medina the situation was different. There the old Arab tribal system was in such a state of decay that it was in no position to offer serious opposition. It is not true that the occasion to act as a politician led Muhammad to give up his earlier efforts and to betray what had once been sacred to him. Rather in Medina he found a favorable milieu where he could carry out what he had preached and taught in Mecca. On the occasion of his farewell pilgrimage in the year 10 A.H., a few months before his death, he was able to recite surah 5:3(5) with pride: "Today I have perfected your religion for you and I have completed my blessing upon you."

The image that we have of the Prophet would not be complete, however, if we did not also bear in mind his personality, in whose charisma lay concealed the final secret of his success. Tor Andrae has pointed out that the power of his personality showed itself in the fact that he attracted men of the caliber of Abū Bakr and 'Umar to his cause. The Prophet himself was appparently conscious of this strength of his. He presented himself as a "good example" (surah 6:163, third Meccan period). We are easily tempted to underestimate this personal influence. The continuing impact of Muhammad lies in the uniqueness of his personal character. Like every literary text, the Quran has had to submit to interpretations and reinterpretations over the centuries. The model of the Prophet, however, has illuminated the way and provided direction for his followers throughout the centuries. If foreign influences constantly threatened to submerge the real essence of Islam, the restoration of the *sunna* (the tradition of the Prophet) was the battle cry under which the struggle against foreign influence was carried forward. Thus his influence is traceable over the centuries, and even today we see in genuine Islamic piety a reflection of that experience of God which compelled Muhammad, son of 'Abd Allāh, to appear in public and to preach of God and the final judgment some 1300 years ago in distant Arabia.

NOTES

(See page xi for list of abbreviations of journal titles)

1. This paper was originally given as a lecture before the Achten Deutschen Orientalistentag in Bonn on 4 September 1936. In the discussion that followed, Professor Michelangelo Guidi referred to his article "Les origines de l'Islam et sa place dans l'histoire de la civilisation" (in *Trois conférences sur quelques problèmes généraux de l'Orientalisme,* an extract from the yearbook of the Institut de Philologie et de l'Histoire Orientales, vol. III [1935]), as well as to his exposition in *Storia della Religione Islam* (vol. II of *Storia delle Religioni* [Torino, 1936]). I am pleased to be able to say that Professor Guidi, in both of these works which became accessible to me only later through his kindness, presents an interpretation that is largely in agreement with my own exposition.
2. [Geiger, A. *Was hat Mohammed aus dem Judentum aufgenommen?* (Bonn, 1833). Translated into English under the title, *Judaism and Islam* (Madras, 1898).]
3. *Mohammed: The Man and His Faith,* translated from the German by Th. Menzel (New York, 1936).
4. *The Jewish Foundation of Islam* (New York, 1933). [This work was reprinted in 1967 with a new and important introduction by Franz Rosenthal.]
5. *Muhammad als Religionsstifter* (Leipzig, 1935).
6. [The figure of "200 million" which appears in the original German text of 1936 is far too low. In Pareja's *Islamologie* (Beirut, 1964) the Muslim world population is given as 365 million. There are reasons, however (which cannot be given here) for believing

that even this figure is too conservative (cf. L. Massignon, *Annuaire du monde musulmane* [Paris, 1955], pp. 427–28).]

7. [For example, his *Koranische Untersuchung* (Berlin, 1926).]
8. According to Nöldeke-Schwally (*Geschichte des Qorans,* I, p. 105) this passage belongs to a later addition.
9. Of the verses cited [by Andrae], the oldest (still from the first Meccan period) is surah 89:14–16: "As for man, when his Lord tries him, and gives him honor and bestows bounty upon him, he says: 'My Lord has honored me.' But when He tries him and stints for him his provision, he says: 'My Lord has scorned me.' "
10. That is certainly credible in and of itself. Admittedly one should not refer in this connection to Waraqa B. Nawfal, the alleged cousin of Khadīja. All reports on him give evidence of such a one-sided eagerness to represent him as a Christian versed in the Bible, who prophesies the appearance of the Arabian Prophet on the basis of messianic predictions, that it appears impossible to isolate the historical kernel.
11. See Wellhausen, *Skizzen und Vorarbeiten* IV (Berlin, 1887), pp. 16f. Later accounts have Abū Qais b. al-Aslat converting to Islam on his deathbed ('Abd al-Qādir, *Khizānat al-Adab,* II, 533). Earlier sources report the opposite (Jumaḥī, *Ṭabaqāt,* 55; Jāḥiẓ, *Ḥayawān,* 7,59). That he was a *ḥanīf* is shown by verses in Ibn Hishām (293), even if they are probably not genuine, for no Muslim could have had an interest in characterizing this opponent of the Prophet as one of the *ḥanīfs.*
12. *Zeitschrift der Deutchen morganländischen Gesellschaft* (86), p. 10.
13. [See "Kāhin" in the *Encyclopaedia of Islam.*]
14. This theory is already clearly presented in surah 91.
15. See Andrae, *Mohammed: The Man and His Faith,* pp. 103ff.
16. Andrae is clearly inclined to give some weight to the tradition according to which Muhammad heard Quss b. Sā'ida, a Christian preacher ". . . who is said to have been bishop of Najran," deliver a sermon in the fair-market of 'Ukāẓ (see Andrae, p. 92). Quss was rather a *ḥanīf.* He is called a Christian only in the later sources. The oldest source available to us (a report in Ibn Sa'd's *Ṭabaqāt al-Kubrā,* I/2, p. 55, from Madā'inī mentions only that he lived as a *ḥanīf* in pre-Islamic times and that he came to 'Ukāẓ and delivered an address "which was preserved in peoples' memories."
17. Nöldeke, *Neue Beiträge zür semitischen Sprachwissenschaft* (Strassburg, 1910), pp. 46ff. The term *jahannam,* e.g., which occurs already in the first Meccan period, is of the same origin.
18. I might also mention incidentally the form of the name Ibrāhīm which does not agree with the Hebrew form of Abraham (Rhodokanakis, *Wiener Zeitschrift für die Kunde des Morgenlandes,* XVII, p. 283, sees in the name a word form that rhymes with Ismā'īl) and clearly marks a divergence from the older religions. The same also holds true for *Ṭūr Sīnīn* [Mt. Sinai] of surah 95:1 and [the sacred valley of] Ṭuwan in surah 79:16. Moreover, the term *'illiyyūn* ["the upper ones"] in surah 83:18 shows that Muhammad's informers were not learned men.
19. Similarly, in surah 51:36 in the story of Abraham's guests, he refers to Lot and his family as a "Muslim house." This passage belongs to the second Meccan period (cf. Nöldeke-Schwally, *Geschichte des Qorans,* I, 105).
20. *Der Islam,* XVI, p. 299.
21. [*Shorter Encyclopaedia of Islam,* p. 380 (art. "Milla").]
22. Surah 92:18; 90:13–16; 93:9–10; 89:17–20 (18–21); 69:34.
23. Surah 51:19; 70:24f.
24. See especially surah 89:14–21.

IV

The Role of Traditionalism in Islam

J. FUECK

The uniformity of Islamic culture represents one of the most fascinating problems associated with the development of Islam from its modest beginnings in Mecca into a world religion today numbering 250 million believers.[1] How did it come about that in the vast world of Islam a distinctive culture came into being, in spite of all the geographical and temporal variations that resulted from the continuing influences of the earlier cultures and religions, and from the on-going life of indigenous habits, practices, and attitudes? How did this homogeneous Islamic culture succeed in establishing itself in areas whose individual provinces first felt the impact of Islamicization at different times and in a variety of different forms: sometimes as a conquest by Muslim armies, sometimes as the result of peaceful contact, sometimes through the consciously directed propaganda of missionary orders, sometimes through the unplanned influences that Muslim merchants exerted in areas possessing lower cultures? These questions are not answered by pointing to a commonness of belief, for the uniformity of this culture was not confined to similarity of creed; it expressed itself much more in a common mental attitude, and in a common style of life which pervaded all levels of personal and official existence, thus reaching beyond the boundaries of the "religious" as understood in the West. Moreover, even the Quran cannot in the first instance be credited with this achievement, for the history of its exegesis shows how strongly the interpretation of the Word of God was conditioned by the prevailing *Zeitgeist* and the influence of the environment. It was rather the example *(Vorbild)* of the Prophet, the *sunna* which, with its constant impact on the life of believers over the centuries, was the primary factor responsible for the unity of Islamic culture. It stamped itself upon the face of Islam and gave to it those features which we see today throughout the Muslim world.

The exemplary character *(Vorbildlichkeit)* of the Prophet is rooted in the very essence of Islam. Muhammad did not claim to bring a new revelation. He was convinced that his message was the same as that of all of his predecessors. The essential kinship of his teaching with that of the older revealed religions was in fact so great that its continued existence as a separate religion must astonish those who focus attention only on the doctrinal content of the new religion. The unprecedented success of Islam can be explained only if one takes into account the uniqueness of Muhammad's personality, whose power derived not from doctrine but from the new life to which he summoned men. We need only consider the men who were his closest associates to realize that he was endowed with an unusual ability to lead. The distinctive character of the original community of Medina resided not so much in the new Word of God in which they believed as in the person of their Prophet. According to the Quran, they had in him "a good example" (surah 33:21). He was "the first of those who believe" (surah 6:163). Beyond *his* words there was no appeal. It was he who decided matters of law, established taxes, and answered questions relating to ceremony and liturgy, etc. Thus from the beginning there stood, beside the Word of God, the living example of the Prophet. Indeed, so great was the spell cast by his personality that it has continued to the very present to exercise power over men.

During the stormy period of the conquest which set in after the Prophet's death, his influence appeared gradually to weaken until finally during the civil war which saw the former Companions of the Prophet in opposing camps, it seemed to go under entirely. However, after the battle of the Ḥarra in 63 A.H.[2] when Medina was forced to withdraw from the political arena, and after the confusion of a half century, the ideal of the Prophet's example again emerged victorious. In Medina sons of the earliest believers now began to devote themselves, along with their clients, to the task of collecting reports having to do with the life and work of the Prophet in order to establish a standard for the regulation of their affairs. Historical investigation, Quranic exegesis, and the administration of law merely formed different aspects of an activity whose real focus was quite naturally the historical prophet who was not subjected to a metaphysical reinterpretation. The gatherings of these earliest authorities on tradition in the mosque of Medina where they gave their eager fellow believers from all parts of the empire information regarding the early history of Islam, explained difficult passages in the Quran, and discussed questions regarding ceremonies, were the beginnings of the earliest doctrinal activity in Islam. From Medina the spirit of prophetic tradition was taken to the farthest corners of the Islamic empire through pilgrims who each year streamed in great numbers to Mecca and Medina; and it thus became customary to draw upon the Companions of the Prophet or their Successors for information about Muhammad.

'Urwa b. as-Zubair (ca. 23–94 A.H.), the head of the school of Medina, came to be known as the most distinguished representative of this early type of authority on tradition. He came from a family which belonged to the earliest Islamic aristocracy: his father Zubair b. al'Awwām (fell in 30 A.H. during the battle of the Camel) was a cousin of the Prophet and one of his earliest followers; his mother Asmā' was the daughter of the caliph Abū Bakr. He enjoyed special favor with his aunt 'Ā'isha; and 'Abd Allāh b. Zubair, the anti-caliph, was his brother. 'Urwa himself remained aloof from politics and devoted himself to the study of tradition, where his relationships, especially with 'Ā'isha, became very useful. His letters to the caliph 'Abd al-Malik (reigned 65–86 A.H.) regarding events in early Islamic times (preserved for us in Ṭabarī's chronicle) mark the beginning of Islamic historical writing. However, he gave his account of the Prophet's life to his hearers entirely in an oral form. His foster son, Abū'l-Aswad Muḥammad b. 'Abd ar-Raḥmān b. Nawfal Yatīm 'Urwa (d. 131 A.H.), was the first to compile a book on the campaigns of the Prophet on the basis of these reports.[3] 'Urwa was acquainted with the *isnād,* that is, the chain of oral authorities, which connected each tradition with its source. His use of this most characteristic formal feature of the literature of Islamic tradition was, however, still very simple, undeveloped, and uneven. Nonetheless, as an expert in law, 'Urwa had a great reputation. He was regarded as one of the "seven *fuqahā'* " of the Prophet's city.

From Medina the study of tradition spread very rapidly to Syria which bordered directly on the Hijaz. There were extensive communication links between these two provinces. The Umayyads maintained very close contact with their homeland. From around the year 75 A.H. by which time their rule had been regarded as secure, much aspiring talent was attracted to their court, talent which could find no room for realization within the narrow economic and political confines of the Hijaz. Already in the year 81 or 82 A.H., 'Urwa's most distinguished student, Muḥammad b. Muslim b. Shihāb az-Zuhrī (ca. 51–124 A.H.), went to Damascus. He came from a distinguised clan of the Quraish (his grandfather had fought against the Prophet in the battles of Badr and Uḥud) and during his youth in Medina, 'Urwa had ardently collected and recorded traditions. Introduced to the caliph 'Abd al-Malik by the Keeper of the Seal, Qabīsa b. Dhu'aib, he soon achieved fame and influence through his considerable knowledge which he devoted to the service of the Umayyads. Under Yazīd II (reigned 101–105 A.H.) he became a judge, and under Hishām (reigned 105–125 A.H.) he became tutor to the princes. He frequently went to Mecca and Medina on pilgrimage. The last years of his life he spent on an estate in the northern Hijaz which the Umayyads had given him. Zuhrī was one of the greatest traditionists in Islam. Through his extensive activity as a teacher he exerted an unusually strong influence, which is evident in the whole of the literature of tradition.

The study of tradition soon took root in Iraq. Here already there was an indigenous tradition; however, it was closely connected to the political past of the province, and it lacked the careful documentation which was demanded by the school of Medina. Distinguished Basrans such as the theologian Ḥasan al-Baṣrī (d. 110 A.H.) and the famous Quranic exegate Qatāda (61–157 A.H.) were so careless in indicating their sources that subsequent critical study was not able to check the reliability of their authorities. In the Hijaz, therefore, the wisdom of the East (i.e., the province of Iraq) was not held in high regard. Ibn Isḥāq (d. 150 A.H.) and Wāqidī (d. 206 A.H.) made only reluctant use of the data in the possession of the Iraqīs. Among his contemporary Iraqīs, Mālik b. Anas regarded only Hushaim b. Bashīr (104–183 A.H.) as a genuine expert in the study of tradtion.[4] Even Zuhrī is reported to have altered his unflattering opinion of them only after he had learned of the traditions of the Kufan al-A'mash (60–148 A.H.), a client from Tabaristan.[5] Nevertheless, it was said of this latter that he (along with Abū Isḥāq as-Sabī'ī [d. 127 A.H.]) was responsible for the corruption of Kufan traditions. In fact, he (like most Kufans, an ardent admirer of 'Alī) transmitted to the Shī'ite extremist, Sayyid al-Ḥimyarī, materials eulogizing the 'Alids.[6] By the beginning of the second century, however, the principles of the Medinan school with its stronger requirements had gradually come to prevail even in Iraq. The influence of the latter grew, especially when, after the fall of the Umayyads, many scholars migrated from the Hijaz to Baghdad, the young flourishing capital of the 'Abbaāsids.

In Egypt the study of tradition was introduced by Yazīd b. Abī Ḥabīb (53–128 A.H.), son of a Nubian prisoner of war from Dongola.[7] Previously, according to the testimony of the well-educated Ibn Yūnus, Egyptians had concerned themselves only with edifying stories *(at-targhīb)* and prophecies of wars and rebellions of the end time *(al-malāḥim wa'l-fitan)*. In the troubled time of the civil wars there were eager listeners to such eschatological fantasies—a corpus of material including, in addition to biblical legends and legends of the saints, secular elements such as South Arabian sagas, tales of the Bedouin, and the popular literature of amusement of the early Umayyad period which neither instructed nor inspired, but brought pleasure. As the Meccans, during the lifetime of the Prophet, had listened to the stories of Rustam and Isfandiyār which Naḍr b. al-Ḥārith told them,[8] so their sons during the caliphate of 'Umar were entertained by narratives of the storyteller (*q*āṣṣ) 'Ubaid b. 'Umair.[9] At the court of Mu'āwiya we meet the South Arabian storytellers Daghfal (d. 65 A.H.) and 'Abīd b. Shariya. Somewhat later there was Wahb b. Munabbih (34–110 A.H.), a Yemenite of Persian origin who, according to the evidence of numerous excerpts from his *Qiṣaṣ al-Anbiyā'*, presented his material in an artistic manner and treated the life of the Prophet in a romanticised fashion. The Medinan school which stressed the importance of collecting attested units of oral tradition rejected as basically unreliable this literature of amusement, in which fact and fiction were woven together into an entertaining story.[10] The Medinans, however, were not able to completely push this material aside, especially in view of the fact that in many areas such as the history of pre-Islamic prophets, no reliable alternative sources were available. Thus the traditionists were forced to lower the strict standards which they had set up for traditions essential to Islamic conduct in those cases where the narratives clearly served the cause of exhortation. Yazīd b. Abī Ḥabīb himself once quoted a book which apparently was an Islamic counterpart of the Christian apocryphal *Acts of the Apostles.*[11]

While the lands bordering on Arabia were penetrated relatively quickly by traditionalism, it took much longer for it to be established in the far-flung lands of the East and West. Only after the study of tradition had long assumed a firm place in the central lands of Islam did the first great traditionist of the East, 'Abd Allāh b. al-Mubārak (118–181 A.H.), the son of a Turk and a Khwarismī mother, raise it to a similar position in

Marw. Coming from modest circumstances (his father was a slave of an Arab trader in Hamadan), he made his way to impressive wealth through his skill as a trader, combined rather strangely with a vigorous asceticism. He utilized the occasion of his travels, which from the year 141 A.H. took him to Iraq, the Hijaz, Yemen, Egypt, and Syria, to study tradition under the greatest experts of his time. He "heard" Mālik b. Anas in Medina, Ibn Juraij and Sufyān ath-Thawrī in Mecca, Ma'mar and Yūnus b. Yazīd (students of Zuhrī), Awzā'ī (the great Syrian expert in law), Laith b. Sa'd in Egypt, A'mash in Kufa, and Shu'ba in Basra. In addition, he generously supported those who devoted themselves to these studies. "Apart from prophecy," he said, "there is nothing higher than spreading the knowledge [of religion]."[12] Through this highly educated and gifted man, the study of tradition became popular in Khurasan. In the capital city of the province, Nisabur, one of his students, Ibrāhīm b. Naṣr as-Sūriyānī, who in the year 201 A.H. fell in battle against Bābak at Dinawar,[13] introduced the study of this discipline. The soil was thereby prepared so that in the course of the third century a series of the greatest scholars were able to establish the study of tradition in the East.

The West was the last to follow suit. Certainly there were men who had transmitted traditions earlier, men such as the judge Mu'āwiya b. Ṣāliḥ (d. 158 A.H.) from Homs who migrated to Spain in 125 A.H. and was later sent by 'Abd ar-Raḥmān I ad-Dākhil on a diplomatic mission to Syria.[14] The study of tradition properly speaking was first introduced by the versatile 'Abd al-Malik b. Ḥabīb (ca. 170–238 A.H.) whose influence was still felt in the third century.[15] Like him, many other Spanish authorities remained in the East for years, after completing the pilgrimage to Mecca. The Spanish tradition of scholarship in this field was the last one to be spawned by the school of Medina.

The more the spirit of traditionalism spread, the larger became the circle of men who spent lengthy periods of time traversing the Islamic empire to collect reports about the Prophet and to increase their knowledge of traditions by exchanging ideas with like-minded men. This travel activity by men of a similar character contributed substantially to the fact that in the vast world of Islam a homogeneous culture developed. These men formed no single party. We find them in all political camps. Many of them supported the government—men such as the distinguished Zuhrī or the court theologian Rajā' b. Ḥaiwa (d. 112 A.H.) who was responsible for the fact that the 'Umar b. 'Abd al-'Azīz, who was nurtured in the spirit of Medinan piety, became caliph.[16] Others such as

'Urwa b. az-Zubair attached little value to a correct relationship with the court. The number of traditionists who held judgeships was considerable. However, the vast majority refused to take an office which might lead them to succumb to temptation,[17] refusing to be dazzled by the attraction of service for a ruler. The personal independence which their professions as traders, merchants, or manufacturers gave them, prevented the holders of power from misusing the science of tradition for their own purposes. Even in matters of doctrine there were many different shades of opinion in their ranks: among the men whom 'Alī b. al-Madīnī mentions as pillars of sound traditions,[18] the orthodox such as Malīk and Thawrī were in the majority; in addition to them, however, we meet Qadarites such as Qatāda (61–117 A.H.), Ibn Isḥāq (d. 150 A.H.), and Ibn Abī 'Arūba (d. 156 A.H.), the Murji'ite Ibn Abī Zā'ida (d. 183 A.H.), Kufans such as Abū Isḥāq as-Sabī'ī and al-A'mash who were sympathetic to Shī'ism, and finally Ḥammād b. Salama[19] who came close to an anthropomorphist position. Among the Quranic exegetes from the school of Ibn 'Abbās, the Khārijites laid claim (not without reason) to three:[20] Mujāhid (d. 104 A.H.), Jābir b. Zaid (d. 103 A.H.) and Ibāḍī,[21] and 'Ikrima (d. 105 A.H.) who propagated the views *(ra'y)* of the Ṣufrīya in the West.[22] Just as little did they form a social unity. In addition to those who were members of the Arab aristorcracy, clients from non-Arab tribes joined in the study of tradition in increasing numbers. It was their belief in the exemplary character of the Prophet and the conviction that he had provided for his community the example of a normative life style that united them. Through them the *sunna* became a unifying bond which united all parts of the empire. Certainly it was not followed everywhere and without exception. However, at the very least, it became the generally recognized ideal.

The traditionists themselves were clear about the fact that the *sunna* constituted no closed system of regulations and doctrinal propositions, but that the ideal or norm had to be painstakingly extrapolated from often incomplete and contradictory traditions. This task required a careful examination of numerous reports and a cautious weighing of all circumstances which might affect their reliability. From this fact arose, at the beginning of the Abbasid period, the earliest attempts at a critical evaluation of traditions. It was necessary, given the nature of oral tradition, that this critical study should begin with an examination of the trustworthiness of the individual authorities. The question of their manner of life, therefore, played no small role in this investigation. How could the critic recognize an individual as a relaible witness who in his personal conduct violated the *sunna?* Since they lacked generally recognized criteria, they did not always escape the danger of premature judgments resulting from personal bias. Thus Shu'ba (83–160 A.H.), who was regarded as the founder of the critical analysis of authorities,[23] contested transmitters because he disliked the way they prayed.[24] Similar statements were reported[25] from another critic of this period, Wuhaib (108–165 A.H.).

The more the number of transmitters increased so that it was no longer possible for a single individual to form a judgment based on direct personal knowledge, the more evident the need became for a critical assessment based on facts. Scholars, therefore, began to collect reports regarding each individual transmitter, his name, his origins, his method of study, his biography, the scope of his traditions and his reputation. Out of this there developed, toward the end of the second century, a biographical literature on the traditionists, the founder of which was Wāqidī (130–207 A.H.), a literature which reached its high point in the classical works of Ibn Sa'd, his student and secretary, and Khalīfa b. Khayyāṭ. In addition to Wāqidī, his contemporary al-Haytham b. 'Adī contributed greatly to the chronology of the history of the science of tradition.[26]

If the absence of school and party unity, in spite of the agreement on basic principles, contributed to the spread of traditionalism, the lack of a strong organization on the other hand limited its spread to Islamic areas. It lacked the impetus to go beyond these areas in a missionary capacity. To be sure, many traditionists personally took part in the wars of faith or settled in frontier areas.[27] However, they saw their task not as that of mission but, as the example of Abū Isḥāq al-Fazārī reveals,[28] that of combatting "innovations" *(bid'a)* opposed to the *sunna,* which threatened to find their way into Islam through the new converts. Other circles took Islam further out into the world; however as soon as a new region was Islamized, traditionalism saw to it that the faith suffered no loss. It showed itself strong not in attack but in defense. It celebrated its greatest achievements when a foreign culture trend broke into the Muslim world and threatened to inundate the religion of the Prophet. The restoration [of the *sunna*] under Aḥmad b. Ḥanbal in the third century, the activity of Ibn Taymīya in the seventh century, and the Wahhābī movement in our own age offer us significant examples of this phenomenon.

The restoration of the *sunna* under the leadership of Aḥmad b. Ḥanbal was a defense against the penetration of foreign influences as the latter appeared in the Mu'tazilite movement—influences that were becoming an increasing threat to Islam after the fall of the Arab kingdom. The Mu'tazilite movement was one of the most important by-products of the spiritual struggle between Islam and Iranian dualism; as such it offers a classic example (and one that occurred frequently in the history of Islamic propaganda) of the fact that a movement, which wished to propagate Islam and presumed to represent it in a pure and authentic form, was unconsciously guided by its opponent in the method of attack and fell unconsciously under its influence. In the struggle of a monotheistic religion against dualism, the unity and justice of God had to be the focal point of the confrontation. However, in seeking to defeat the enemy by its own methods, the Mu'tazilites applied the same caustic criteria of this approach to the simple teachings of the Quran. Their rationalism which regarded reason as the source of religious knowledge gave the simple statements of faith in the Quran an entirely new meaning. Whether we consider the Mu'tazilite doctrine of free will with its counterpart of a Creator who imposes limits on Himself out of regard for the well-being of man, or their abstruse theories of God's attributes and the nature of God's speech, or whether we examine their nature philosophy or submerse ourelves in their theory of the state (a prototype of the Shī'ite doctrine of the *imām*), the fact remains that the Islam which they espoused had only very little in common with the religion of the Arabian Prophet. All of that could be overlooked, however, so long as the Mu'tazilites perceived their main task as the struggle against dualism and propaganda on behalf of Islam, and so long as they left the orthodox undisturbed. That changed, however, when in the last decade of the second century the dualistic peril was overcome. Now the Mu'tazilites entered into the sphere of internal politics and in 212 A.H. won recognition for their doctrine as the official religion of the state for a quarter of a century. The attempt to assist rationalism to achieve a dominant position by means of political power, and to enforce acceptance of their doctrines, especially the doctrine of the created Quran, aroused the opposition of all those who adhered to the *sunna*. Under the internal and external pressure of the Mu'tazilite peril, orthodox Muslims gathered around the banner of tradition. During this turbulent period the position of those who had been persecuted [for their adherence to the *sunna*] was consolidated and strengthened. They were forced to scrutinize the foundations of their own position in order to secure it against attack. This led to important formal and material results. The classical critical study of authorities which thus arose around the turn of the second century was connected with the names of three men who through their teaching exercised a significant influence: Yaḥyā b. Ma'īn (158–233 A.H.),[29] 'Alī b. al-Madīnī (161–234 A.H.), and Aḥmad b. Ḥanbal (164–241 A.H.). All three were examples of a life style that conformed to the *sunna,* but especially Aḥmad b. Ḥanbal who despite imprisonment and physical mistreatment remained unalterably faithful to the *sunna.* The posthumous reputation of Ibn al-Madīnī, it is true, was clouded by the fact that he appeared too willing to compromise with the chief judge, Aḥmad b. Abī Dūwād, in order to escape the inquisition. As a critical scholar, Yaḥyā b. Ma'īn achieved the highest reputation.

The principles on which this critical study was based were essentially formal in nature. They examined the chronological feasibility of a given *isnād* and looked into the biographical details of all those transmitters who appeared in it; they determined the way in which each one received the tradition, how he passed it on, whether he possessed a good memory or was getting somewhat feebleminded in old age, whether he made use of written reports or not. They compared the various chains of transmitters in order to establish the correct reading and to acquire more certain criteria regarding the reliability of individual witnesses. As to the basic acceptability of witnesses (only the Companions of the Prophet were regarded *eo ipso* as trustworthy), they limited themselves to those requirements which canonical jurisprudence demanded of a witness before a court of law and thereby removed any grounds for the defamation of a witness because of personal prejudice. Even heterodoxy was not yet regarded in itself as an adequate reason for the rejection of an authority unless he actively propagated it. Not even conduct which violated the *sunna,* such as the use of alcohol, rendered a witness unreliable.[30] Therewith the critical study of transmitters was elevated to the level of a science which objectively weighed the reliability of each witness, a science which rendered the critic a valuable service. The last word, however, was reserved for personal judgment, and here unanimity did not always prevail among the critics. If their final judgment was thus determined by "interior" considerations, they never allowed themselves to accept a tradition as authentic which was obviously false. The fact that no traditions reflecting an anti-Mu'tazilite point of view were accepted in the canonical collections is a splendid testimony to the honesty of the traditionists. As great as the temptation must have been for them to silence their detested opponents through a statement from the Prophet, the realization that the controversy over the nature of the Quran was unknown to Muhammad and his Companions was even greater.

Although the integrity of the critics of the third/tenth century is beyond doubt,[31] they were not in a position, despite internal and external grounds, to purge tradition of all spurious elements. With the aid of their formal criticism they were able to follow the texts of individual traditions in general back to the first half of the second century. However, they lacked positive data to trace them back to an earlier period. Thus, e.g., the date of birth of many transmitters of the second century was not known; often it was not possible to determine whether they had a personal relationship with the earlier authorities and had "heard" from them directly. Given the lack of reliable reports, it was easy to succumb to the temptation to place the dates of transmitters too early, and thus to connect them incorrectly with the Companions of the Prophet. The situation was worse still regarding information about dates of the Prophet's Companions. The belief that some of them had lived to an age far beyond the usual limits was widespread not only among the masses. Contradicting this there was a well-known saying of Muhammad's to the effect that in a hundred years none of his contemporaries would be alive.[32] Serious scholars such as Muslim took this literally and they had the last "Companion"[33] dying in the year 100 A.H., a still very liberal claim if one remembers that Muhammad died in the year 11 A.H. Tradition as it circulated at the beginning of the second century lacked those external features of correct *isnād* usage which the critics of the third century set forth as their primary demand. Frequently enough, they were obliged to admit that these early transmitters had been negligent as to the statements of their authorities. If the giants such as Ḥasan al-Baṣrī, Ibn Sīrīn, Qatāda, al-A'mash, and even Zuhrī did not escape censure for confused statements in *isnāds* (*tadlīs*), critics had (in view of existing conditions) to judge deficiencies of this sort with considerable leniency if they did not want to forego a positive decision from the outset. In other cases, the form of the collective *isnād* which continued in vogue from the time of Zuhrī placed an obstacle in the way of their critical activity. When the somewhat older Suddī (d. 127 A.H.) in his commentary on the Quran (utilized extensively by Ṭabarī) always provided his statements with the following indications of source: *'an Abī Mālik wa Abī Sālih 'an Ibn 'Abbās wa 'an Murra 'an Ibn Mas'ūd wa 'an nās min aṣḥāb rasūl Allāh,* any possibility for the critical analysis of *isnāds* was excluded; and, in fact, the critics diverged widely in their judgments of Suddī.[34]

There was another matter that proved even more troublesome. When the earliest traditionists a half century after the death of Muhammad made an effort to collect traditions, his older Companions who had fought along side of and worked for him had long since died. These collectors had to depend on the younger "Companions" who had remembered him in their childhood. That Abū Bakr, 'Umar, and others of the Prophet's comrades-in-arms rarely make statements in tradition is, on the one hand, additional proof of the integrity of the traditionists. On the other hand, the fact that sound traditions rest primarily on the testimony of the younger Companions of the Prophet is important for the determination of their reliability. Here Sunnī theologians on internal grounds voluntarily waived the right of criticism. They recognized that a fresh examination of all questions which in the first century had so aroused the believers and brought about the dissensions of the civil wars would have presented the gravest of threats to the unity of the Islamic community. For this reason they could permit no criticism of the men who had lived during that stormy period. While the Shī'ites abused the first three caliphs and other "Companions," Sunnī theologians restrained themselves by the words of the Prophet: "Do not slander my Companions,"[35] and through this they avoided all criticism.

The rigorous critical standards which the transmitters applied to the mass of material handed down to them reduced the number of traditions regarded as reliable very considerably. If statements such as that Bukhārī had investigated 600,000 traditions may be exaggerated, it is certain in any case that only some 7,000 and, if one sets aside repetitions, hardly 3,000 satisfied the highest demands of critical analysis. This significant reduction of the material held to be trustworthy had to be all the more important in view of the fact that the principles of traditionalism simultaneously emerged with ever greater clarity in the battle of minds. Now for the first time they took seriously and without reservation the doctrine of the Prophet's exemplariness; they demanded that the life of the believer conform to the *sunna* in the smallest details and that the *sunna* could only be established by a critical examination of tradition. The orthodoxy of the second century, as Mālik's *Muwaṭṭa'* shows, had made use of traditions with the greatest carelessness, traditions which the unrelenting severity of classical criticism rejected as formally deficient. In addition to tradition, Mālik and his contemporaries had drawn rather freely on Quranic passages, the legal decisions of the Companions of the Prophet, and their successors as well as the customary law of Medina and, if necessary, relied on their own opinion. For the orthodoxy of the third century, however, only tradition was decisive. Bukhārī gives extra-traditional materials at least in the chapter headings of his collection. Muslim permitted only the traditions to decide. However, the traditions accepted by them, among which much historical and exegetical material is to be found, were not adequate to regulate in detail that manner of life regarded by the *sunna* as normative for believers. A consideration of the practical needs of the community required (in addition to traditions regarded as first rate and fully authentic) the acceptance of less well attested second and third rate ones. Tirmidhī accepted into his collection every tradition which had ever been cited by a legal expert as proof for a decision, adding however his own judgment as to the level of its trustworthiness. Also in Abū Dāwūd's collection of traditions, critical remarks on individual traditions are rather frequent. Finally, the youngest of the canonical collectors, Nasā'ī (ca. 215–303 A.H.), who in his criticism of authorities went his own way, took note of the differences of opinion among the transmitters themselves. On individual legal questions he quoted a variety of opposing views and in most cases left the decision to the reader. He also carefully cites cases in which a tradition having to do with a decision by one of the Prophet's Companions or another authority was not unanimous.[36]

If the Islamic critique did not succeed on either internal or external grounds in excluding all the spurious elements of tradition, it would be an inaccurate generalization, however, if one were to deny to it all confidence on that account. *Islamic tradition does contain an authentic body of material.* The view of some Orientalists that it was a creation of the first two centuries and only shows how later generations conceived of the Prophet and his contemporaries, seriously underrates the profound impact of the personality of Muhammad on his followers. The attempt to reject all traces of the historical Muhammad in tradition arose from a materialistic conception of history similar to that which was not prepared to admit the experience of God (*Gotteserlebnis*) even in the Quran, but sought for thousands of prototypes, influences, stimuli, and contacts. In both cases the outcome was a mosaic of innumerable little stones of different origins with no inner coherence. The investigation which grew out of such an outlook and led to the demand that "as a matter of course every legal tradition[37] had to be considered as false until proved otherwise,"[38] fostered an unlimited skepticism which opened the flood gates to caprice. It was impossible to find generally admissible criteria of authenticity; no general agreement emerged among the investigators even regarding those traditions unfavorable to the Prophet. A feature so starkly opposed to the traditional view of Muhammad's character as the *gharānīq*-episode was regarded by some as certainly authentic, while other scholars just as decidedly banished it to the realm of fiction.[39] These and similar reports such as that Muhammad had offered a lamb to the goddess 'Uzzā',[40] or that his sons had borne the names 'Abd al-Manāf, 'Abd al-'Uzzā', and al-Qāsim,[41] or the instructions to 'Abd Allāh b. Jaḥsh on the expedition to Nakhla[42] only prove that tradition is not one-sided. If we encounter reports even in the canonical collections that are the source of distress to the Muslim collector as, for example, the stories of Muhammad's domestic troubles,[43] not even the greatest skeptic of these reports can raise objection to their authenticity. If it is to be granted then that tradition has preserved authentic material, it would be clearly arbitrary to recognize only the few unfavorable features in the traditionalist picture of the Prophet as sound and to reject all other features as falsified, even in those cases where proof can never be adduced to the contrary. The imposing uniformity of the Islamic life style in spite of its multiplicity of individual forms is the best proof of the fact that traditionalism which always looked on the *sunna* as an immutable ideal, did not arise out of the quicksands of the conflicting opinions of later generations, but reached back with its roots to the soil of the early Muslim community of Medina. Certainly in the course of time, tradition did undergo modification, expansion, and addition. Precanonical writings, however, offer us in many cases a means of establishing whether an authentic core lies at the center of the larger body of tradition. A few examples of this may be presented.

1. Yaḥyā b. Ādam (ca. 140–203 A.H.) has preserved a report (*mursal*)[44] which goes back not to a Companion of the Prophet but only to Abū Mijlaz, a Basran born around the year 100 A.H. As a result of the requirements which classical criticism established for sound traditions, this report was not accepted. According to Abū Mijlaz's report, the Prophet once met some Anṣār who were just about to fertilize their palm trees. Since the Prophet expressed doubt about the value of this, they discontinued it. However when the fruit failed to appear he told them to follow rather their usual customs in such matters since he had spoken on this matter without knowing the facts. This tradition is indeed most striking for its account of Muhammad's candor and the blind trust of his followers. However, for many a transmitter it was most distressing to admit openly that the Prophet lacked knowledge. Thus, e.g., 'Urwa b.

Zubair in his account of the incident (which he too received from Yaḥyā b. Ādam)[45] omitted that part of the tradition in which Muhammad admitted his error. 'Urwa's account which went back to 'Ā'isha in a formally correct chain of authorities was accepted by Muslim and was included in his collection.[46] An account which Simāk b. Ḥarb (d. 123 A.H.) cited, also on the authority of Yaḥyā b. Ādam,[47] went even further: on the basis of a report allegedly from an eyewitness he has Muhammad adding that in matters of religion he (the Prophet) cannot err. Only such watered-down versions were included in the canonical collections to tradition.[48]

2. From Malik[49] we learn that Muhammad, in contrast to Abū Bakr, did not dye his hair. In Ibn Sa'd[50] we find reports from Iraqī sources in which he is alleged to have recommended the coloring of the hair, in opposition to Jewish and Christian practice. Other traditions report that remnants of colored hair belonging to Muhammad had been found in the possessions of his widows. Bukhārī harmonizes[51] these conflicting reports by the theory that Muhammad did not color his hair, since he had very few grey hairs, but that he recommended it for those who did. Bukhārī explains the relics of colored hair as resulting from the use of perfume.

3. In the *Muwaṭṭa'* of Mālik b. Anas[52] we find the following report (also found in several canonical collections):[53] when Sa'd b. Alī Waqqāṣ died in the year 50 A.H. (or 55), 'Ā'isha had his body brought into the mosque so that she could be present at the funeral ceremony. Many people objected to this action; 'Ā'isha, however, justified herself by pointing out that the Prophet had also performed the prayer of the dead for Suhail b. al-Baiḍā' in the mosque. Some Orientalists have expressed doubts about the validity of this report and have maintained that it was a fabrication by Mālik's contemporaries who wanted thereby to sanction a practice that prevailed in the Hijaz at that time.[54] On the other hand, it is to be noted neither Mālik nor his source, the renowned Abū'n-Naḍr (d. 129 A.H.), could be considered as fabricators of this report, and it is inconceivable that either of them would have accepted a contemporary falsification as such. This and the fact that the tradition was transmitted by various "paths" proves that it goes back to the first century. Furthermore, the performance of prayers for the dead in a mosque was in no way a ritual practice that prevailed in the Hijaz during the second century. It is rather for Mālik a question of whether one could also perform it in a mosque. Mālik himself gave permission only reluctantly under pressure of the precedent cited on the authority of 'Ā'isha. He himself, however, wished to have the bier placed in front of the mosque.[55] Shāfi'ī who

answered the question with an unconditional affirmative rightly criticized the Mālikites for their violation of tradition.[56] The conflict which arose over this practice already in 'Ā'isha's time was later given expression in a statement attributed to the Prophet by Abū Huraira, to which Shaibānī (like all Ḥanafites, an opponent to performing prayers for the dead in a mosque) alludes in his recension of the *Muwaṭṭa'*[57] and which Abū Dāwūd included in his collection. However, Islamic critics had already recognized that this statement, to which the ill-famed Ṣāliḥ b. Nabhān was the only witness, was not valid.[58]

4. The well-known prophetic statement that one should saddle a camel only on the pilgrimage to the three mosques of Mecca, Medina, and Jerusalem, is found in all canonical collections of tradition. It is maintained by some that Zuhrī had falsified this tradition in order to raise the *ḥajj* to Jerusalem to a position of equality [with the *ḥajj* to Mecca],[59] and thereby provide support for 'Abd al-Malik in his struggle against 'Abd Allāh b. Zubair who controlled the Meccan sanctuary.[60] This suspicion of one of the most celebrated of traditionists is certainly not tenable on chronological grounds. 'Abd Allāh's opposition to the caliphate took place during the period from 64 to 73 A.H. Zuhrī who was born in the year 51 A.H. (or perhaps even later), was at that time a young man who was not yet known as a transmitter. Furthermore, the question of fabrication cannot be raised because Zuhrī's source, the famous Sa'īd b. al-Musayyib (d. 94 A.H.), was at that time still alive and certainly would not have condoned a misuse of his name. And finally Zuhrī was not the only one who transmitted this prophetic statement from Sa'īd.

5. Even spurious traditions, however, were forged earlier than is generally thought. Thus, e.g., the tradition of Barwa' bint Wāshiq[61] concerning the dowry of a woman whose husband had died before the consummation of their marriage was presumed to be the product of later theologians on the grounds that even Shāfi'ī still denied the right of a woman to dowry in cases of this sort altogether. Now from all that we know of the great collectors of tradition of the third century and of the principles of criticism employed by them it is completely impossible that such recent fabrication could have misled them. The occasionally expressed opinion that one could regard a tradition appearing in the canonical collections as a fabrication of the third century rests on an inadmissible confusion of the date of origin of the tradition with the date of its literary attestation. In the case before us, external evidence demonstrates the greater age of the tradition. Not only does the Mu'tazilite an-Naẓẓām (who died between

220 and 228 A.H.) mention it in his polemic against the traditionists,[62] but Shāfi'ī also knew of its existence.[63] Indeed, Shāfi'ī was right in doubting its authenticity as shown by the fact that neither Bukhārī nor Muslim has recognized it.

In the battle against the Mu'tazilites, traditionalism elaborated its principles more and more clearly, and stubbornly defended the normative character of the *sunna* for Muslims against all of its detractors. However, even at the high point of its triumph, traditionalism in no way denied the validity of those forms of life for which there was no authorization in the *sunna*. It did not encroach upon the wider field of formal education, the focal point of which was grammar and the closely related study of poetry. The Arabic sciences of language blossomed independently of the religious disciplines. To be sure, the study of the Quran was a field in which grammarians and traditionists encountered each other; however, their scope remained clearly separate. Most grammarians were indifferent to or even disdainful of traditionalism. According to the judgment of Ibrāhīm al-Ḥarbī (d. 285 A.H.), all Basran grammarians, except the following four who adhered to the *sunna,* championed heretical points of view:[64] Abū 'Amr b. al-'Alā', well known also as a Quran reader, and his student Yūnus b. Ḥabīb (ca. 97–183 A.H.); Khalīl b. Aḥmad (ca. 100–170 A.H.) who was first an Ibāḍī but who was won over to orthodoxy by Ayyūb as-Sakhtiyānī (68–131 A.H.);[65] and finally the excessively pious Aṣma'ī (125–213 A.H.), who had misgivings about explaining the Quran and *ḥadīth* philologically,[66] who quickly skipped over all pagan elements in the interpretation of pre-Islamic poetry[67] and who even once edited out the name of a pagan god.[68] On the other hand, only a few traditionists paid attention to grammatical questions. The earlier collectors were satisfied with a faithful reproduction of the substance of what they had heard. The practice (widely followed from Zuhrī's time) of putting traditions with identical contents under a group *isnād* could never have come into vogue if they had been concerned with establishing literal, verbal precision. Preoccupied with content, they were little concerned with phrasing and formal expression. In taking a position on the newly flourishing grammatical studies they were divided. Several, like al-A'mash, corrected all grammatical errors on the ground that it would have been impossible for the Prophet to make an error in speech.[69] Others, on the other hand, did not risk tampering with the transmitted text.[70] For most of them however, such questions were a matter of indifference. No less a figure than Bukhārī drew on material concerning biblical expressions found in the

Quran from the *Kitāb al-majāz* of the Basran grammarian Abū 'Ubaida (d. 210 A.H.) and here and there incorporated comments from this work into his commentary, without, however, mentioning the name of its author or the fact that he was a Khārijite.[71]

The material with which the philologists were concerned was not so clearly a matter of indifference to the traditionists as grammar was. The pagan spirit of the pre-Islamic Arabic poetry must have been deeply offensive to them. However, the Prophet himself, in spite of his occasional attacks on poets, tolerated poetry. Indeed, the poetry-hating attitude of some persons did not succeed in gaining the upper hand. A leading traditionist such as Shu'ba had a direct personal relationship with Ru'ba and other poets,[72] and found in poetry a relaxation from the study of tradition.[73] Even music had many admirers among the traditionists, especially in the Hijaz. In Iraq, on the other hand, the majority stood in opposition to it. When the Quranic exegete 'Ikrima (d. 107 A.H.) stated in Basra that he liked singing, many of his listeners deserted him,[74] and the leading scholar of Mecca, Ibn Juraij (ca. 80–150 A.H.), one day aroused the displeasure of his guests from the East when he invited a singer into his house.[75] On the other hand, the traditionists from the East did not oppose Persian education, so long as it did not run counter to the spirit of Islam. It was said of the Basran Ḥammād b. Zaid (98–179 A.H.), whose orthodoxy could hardly be questioned, that 'Umar had taught him religious law (*fiqh*) and that the Khosrau had trained him in *adab*.[76] This liberal and open attitude of traditionalism which was prepared to recognize the value of training in the secular arts (*adab*) and to accept the existing forms of life insofar as they were in harmony with the *sunna*, we meet in its clearest form in the works of Ibn Qutaiba (218–276 A.H.), who played an important role in the restoration which resulted from the victory of orthodoxy (the Mu'tazilite state doctrine, it should be noted, was abolished in 237 A.H.). His polemical writings, especially his *Ta'wīl Mukhtalif al-Ḥadīth*, reveal him to be a highly orthodox theologian who sought to refute the objections brought forward by the Mu'tazilites through a series of selected traditions, and that with the support of a clever harmonizing interpretation. In another group of his writings, he took into account the culture of "scribes" (*kuttāb*) from whose ranks the civil servants of the state were recruited and gave expression to an ideal of culture which reflected a very broad outlook. In the introduction to his main work, the *'Uyūn al-Akhbār,* he sets forth the principle that the believer is bound to and must rely upon authorities in matters of religion, in matters of the permitted and the forbidden, but that in other areas (that is, those indifferent to religion) he may appropriate knowledge wherever he finds it: *al-'ilm ḍāllat al-mu'min.* Ibn Qutaiba thus in no way limited himself to what was peculiar to Islamic tradition (in the ten volumes of his work he covered the entire range of secular learning); if he preferred to begin a new chapter with the words of the Prophet, he also drew upon the whole of Arabian tradition, and freely inserted verses from pagan and Muslim poets and even some material from Persian literature. He did not hesitate to utilize material from the writings of the arch-heretic, Ibn al-Muqaffa', which promoted the amoral wisdom of the Orient.[77] Ibn Qutaiba demonstrated a similar broad-mindedness in his *Kitāb al-Ma'ārif,* a concise survey of world history, and also in his book of poetry in which he presents the best known poets from Imra' al-Qais to his own day, together with a brief biography of each and a specimen of their finest poetry.

It was this openness, this opposition to scholastic narrowness that enabled the traditionalists after their victory over the Mu'tazilites to resume their role as the bearers of Islamic cultural unity. The process of canonization, which elevated "the six books" from among a mass of orthodox writings, was completed only after some centuries. Bukhārī, whose work was to be recognized a century and a half later as the definitive collection of unquestionably authentic sayings of the Prophet, was subjected in his own lifetime to severe attacks. He did not want to extend the uncreatedness of the Quran to include the recitations of individual believers. When he later settled in Nisabur he was so severely oppressed on that account by the orthodox leader Dhuhlī (d. 258 A.H.; and very well known for his *Zuhrīyāt,* a collection of all the traditions going back to Zuhrī)[78] that he finally left the city and moved to Bukhara. However, even there he found no rest. Since he refused to bend to the wishes of the governor, he was banned and spent the last years of his life in the village of Khartank in Samarqand where he died in 256 A.H., not quite 62 years of age.[79] Bukhārī and Muslim, not to mention the authors of the four *Sunan,* were only fellow disputants in the minds of their contemporaries, not leaders in the battle against heresy. Their judgments were in no way regarded as binding. As before, the independent collecting of traditions (gathered from considerable study and travel) was regarded as the main thing. Even in the sphere of law traditionists did not submit to the authority of a particular school, but followed their own interpretation of the traditions. Precisely for this reason Ṭabarī (d. 310 A.H.) could contest Ibn Ḥanbal's title as a jurist. The importance of the independent study of tradition diminished only after the fourth century. When the door of *ijtihād* was closed it was inevitable that in this area too there would be a growing conformity to the great masters of the third century who were regarded as exemplary. Literary activity shows an increasing refinement in the mastery of the technical apparatus, of which the catalogue of the writings of Ibn Ḥibbān (d. 354 A.H.)[80] provides instructive examples. A gradual decline then began. The study and collection of traditions sank progressively lower in the fifth and sixth centuries until they reached a point of meaningless formality; the teaching activity of the mosques which had provided the best training for the battle against heresy fell into decay. Traditionalism had performed its task. From the traditions of the first two centuries it made a selection of traditions which formed the image of Muhammad for all time and provided believers with an exemplary model after which they could pattern their lives.

On the other hand, it was impossible to transmit the traditionalism of a Bukhārī or a Muslim unchanged down through the centuries. Slowly it succumbed to all those forces that had grown to independence and had come to express themselves in canonical law, Quranic exegesis, scholasticism, and, above all, in Sufism. However, as soon as a serious external danger threatened Islam, as happened in the Mongol invasion of the Muslim world in the seventh century, the collapse of the caliphate of Baghdad, and the establishment of a pagan as ruler over the believers, Ibn Taymīya (661–728 A.H.) emphasized (as Ibn Ḥanbal had done earlier) that salvation and deliverance were possible only in following the exemplary model given by the Prophet. He ruthlessly applied to all facets of public and domestic life the infallible standard of the Quran and the *sunna.* His criticism brought him into sharp conflict with almost all of the holders of power of that time. He fell out with the doctors of the canonical schools of law because he unmasked their hairsplitting casuistry and scourged their petty partisan spirit which the leaders of the schools held up more highly than the Prophet. The orthodox scholastics were offended by his assertion that their rationalism, which sought to corroborate the truth of revelation by the principles of reason, was a foreign growth in the Garden of Islam. He aroused the wrath of the powerful Sufi orders by branding their pantheism as un-Islamic. Ibn Taymīya's outlook which was satisfied with a simple, unpretentious faith in the Quran and the example of the Prophet stood in fundamental opposition to al-Ghazzālī's theology of mediation. This theology put the religious attitude of the mystic in place of the early faith and with the help of Ash'arite dogmatics gave the simple teachings of the Quran a new meaning; moreover, without any critical feeling for historical tradition, it accepted legendary materials provided only they were of devotional value. With equal vigor Ibn Taymīya fought against the popular cult of the Prophet and saints. However, the principle of *ijmāʿ* (*consensus omnium doctorum*), which was deeply rooted in the collective consciousness of Sunnī's, proved to be too powerful. Ibn Taymīya did not succeed in overthrowing the authority of the four main orthodox schools of law which rested on *ijmāʿ* or in re-opening the door of *ijtihād*. Even "innovations" which were clearly against the Quran and the *sunna* were invulnerable to attack as soon as consensus had sanctioned them. Next to *ijmāʿ*, it was Ash'arite theology on which Ibn Taymīya's plan of reform ran aground. The attempt to harmonize the anthropomorphic expressions of the Quran such as God's hands, feet, eyes, etc., with a purely spiritual conception of God had spanned the entire spectrum from a crass anthropomorphism to the sublimest spiritualization. Already in the second century the leaders of orthodoxy had realized that one could only escape the danger of both extremes if one accepted the Quranic statements as true without asking how or in what sense they were true. From the consistent standpoint of orthodoxy this could not be satisfactory in the long run, since it did not resolve the difficulty but rather implied the renunciation of a solution. In vain did Ibn Taymīya explain that it was presumptuous for a Muslim to claim to be more intelligent than the ancestors who had refused to meddle in any kind of speculation regarding the nature of God. He was no longer able to reawaken the spiritual powers which had filled the first believers. His unbending adherence to the text of the Quran and decisive rejection of any kind of *ta'wīl* only brought him (though without justification) the reputation of anthropomorphism. The impossibility of resurrecting the long since weakened world of Islam was, in the final analysis, the most basic cause of the fact that Ibn Taymīya's efforts were without success during his lifetime.

Nevertheless, belief in the exemplary character of the Prophet did live on in the Islamic community. The task in respect of which Ibn Taymīya failed was taken up again in the twelfth/eighteenth century by Muḥammad b. 'Abd al-Wahhāb. Like the former, he fought against all innovation and on most questions took a position similar to his great predecessor. However, this time traditionalism was to achieve greater results. The Wahhābī movement succeeded in establishing itself among the Bedouin who since the days of the Prophet had been only very superficially Islamized. Through the centuries traditionalism held fast unrelentingly to the *sunna* and prevented foreign influences from destroying the distinctive character of Islam. It now put the crowning touches on its achievement by establishing on the original, native soil of Islam direct contact with those religious forces which had once disclosed themselves in the figure of the Arabian Prophet.

NOTES

(See page xi for list of abbreviations of journal titles)

1. [See R. V. Weekes, *Muslim Peoples: A World Ethnographic Survey* (Westport, Conn.; London, England) where the total number of Muslims today is placed at slightly more than 700 million.]
2. [On this battle, see L. Veccia Vaglieri's article in *EI*², III, pp. 226–27.]
3. I have given references in *Muḥammad b. Isḥāq*, p. 11, n. 43.
4. Khaṭīb, *Tārīkh Baghdād,* XIV, p. 9. Hushaim regarded *tadlīs* as permissible; see Dhahabī, *Mīzān al-I'tidāl,* III, p. 257.
5. Ibn Sa'd, VI, p. 238.
6. *Kitāb al-Aghānī,* VII, p. 15.
7. Ibn Ḥajar, *Tahdhīb at-Tahdhīb,* XI, pp. 318f.
8. Ibn Hishām, pp. 191, 235.
9. Ibn Sa'd, V, p. 341.
10. The opinion of Ibn Ḥanbal *thalāthatu kutubin lā aṣla lahā al-maghāzī wa'l-malāḥimu wa't-tafsīr* (Suyūṭī, *Itqān,* p. 888) refers to the legendary biographies of the Prophet, prophecies of the end of time and popular interpretation of the Quran.
11. Ibn Hishām, p. 972.
12. Khaṭīb, *Tārīkh Baghdād,* X, p. 160.
13. Yāqūt, *Geographisches Wörterbuch,* III, p. 187; Dhahabī, *Tadhkirat al- Ḥuffāẓ,* II, p. 3.
14. Ibn Ḥajar, *Tahdhīb at-Tahdhīb,* X, p. 209.
15. Dhahabī, *Tadhkirat al-Ḥuffaẓ,* II, p. 107; Dhahabī, *Mīzān al-I'tidāl,* II, p. 148; Ibn Ḥajar, *Lisān al-Mīzān,* IV, p. 59; Ibn Farḥūn, *Dībāj* (Cairo, 1351 A.H.), 154; Yāqūt, *Geographisches Wörterbuch,* I, p. 349.
16. Wellhausen, *Das Arabische Reich,* p. 165 [English trans. by M. G. Weir, *The Arab Kingdom and Its Fall* (Beirut, 1963), p. 264–65].
17. Mez, *Die Renaissance des Islams,* pp. 209f. [English trans. by S. K. Bakhsh and D. S. Margoliouth, *The Renaissance of Islam* (Patna, 1937), p. 218f.]
18. Dhahabī, *Tadhkirat al-Ḥuffāẓ,* I, p. 328 and elsewhere.
19. See *Festschrift P. Kahle,* p. 98f.
20. Ash'arī, *Maqālāt al-Islāmīyīn,* I, pp. 109, 120.
21. Ibn Sa'd, VII/1, 130.
22. Ibn Ḥajar, *Tahdhīb at-Tahdhīb,* I, p. 267.
23. Ibn Ḥajar, *Tahdhīb at-Tahdhīb,* IV, p. 345.
24. See Dhahabī, *Mīzān al-I'tidāl,* III, p. 134; II, p. 7, 312.
25. Ibn Ḥajar, *Tahdhīb at-Tahdhīb,* V, p. 43.

26. In contrast to Wāqidī who belonged to the Medinan school, al-Haitham b. 'Adī was not a transmitter but a writer of works of amusement who preferred to treat historical themes, but also composed love stories (*Fihrist,* p. 306). Of low birth and because of his attempt to smuggle himself into the great tribe of Tayyi' and ridiculed by his contemporaries, he utilized his knowledge of scandalous North Arabian chronicles to unmask in his books (*al-Mathālib, Ahbār Ziyād b. Abīh, Asmā' Baghāyā Quraish,* etc.) the Arab aristocracy ('Abd al-Qādir, *Khizānat al-adab,* II, p. 511). An expert like Jāḥiẓ pointed out the artificiality of his style (*Buḥalā',* p. 243, ed. van Vloten). If Muslim authorities are unanimous in censuring him (Dhahabī, *Mīzān al-I'tidāl,* III, p. 265, and Ibn Ḥajar, *Lisān al-Mīzān,* VI, p. 209) they do take into consideration the chronological statements of his *Ṭabaqāt al-Fuqahā' wa'l-Muḥaddithīn* and his *Tārīkh.*
27. Ibn Sa'd, VII/2, pp. 185ff.
28. See *OLZ,* 38 (1935), pp. 627f.
29. On the spelling of Ma'īn, see Ibn Khallikān, *Wafayāt* (Būlāq, 1299 A.H.), III, p. 172.
30. See e.g., Dhahabī, *Tadhkirat al-Ḥuffāẓ,* II, p. 233. I have given another example in *OLZ,* 37 (1934), p. 726, n. 3.
31. This applies also to Wāqidī and Ibn Sa'd. Since the sincerity of both was recently called into question, I refer to my discussion in *Muḥammad b. Isḥaq,* p. 14, n. 10.
32. The main passage is in Muslim *Faḍā'il aṣ-Ṣaḥāba* (in the margins of Qasṭallānī, *Irshād as-Sārī* [Būlāq, 1306 A.H.], IX, pp. 423–25); Wensinck points out other passages, *Concordance et Indices de la Tradition Musulmane,* 7 vols., (Leiden, 1936), I, p. 207.
33. That is, Abū Ṭufail who was supposed to have died in the year 100 A.H. at the age of 97; Ibn Ḥajar would have him even older (*Tahdhīb at-Tahdhīb,* V, p. 82).
34. See Dhahabī, *Mīzān al-I'tidāl,* I, p. 309; Ibn Ḥajar, *Tahdhīb,* I, p. 313; Suyūṭī, *Itqān,* p. 913 (Sprenger).
35. Bukhārī, *Manāqib al-Aṣḥāb,* par. 5; Muslim, *Faḍā'il aṣ-Ṣaḥāba,* par. 221 and parallels.
36. These cases are the most abundant in *Kitāb aṣ-Ṣiyām,* next in *Qiyām al-Lail, Kitāb Taḥrīm* and *Kitāb al-Qasāma;* in addition they are found in the books of *Hiba, Nuḥl, Ruqba, 'Umra, Muzāra'a,* and *Qaṭ' as-Sāriq* as well as in a few additional passages.
37. No proof is required that the boundaries of legal, historical, and exegetical traditions merge into each other.
38. Schwally in the new edition of Nöldeke's *Geschichte des Qorans* (Leipzig, 1919), II, p. 146.
39. Nöldeke-Schwally, *Geschichte des Qorans* (Leipzig, 1919), I, 101; Tor Andrae, *Mohammed, Sein Leben und Sein Glaube* (Göttingen, 1932), 15 [English trans. *Mohammed: The Man and His Faith* (New York, 1955), 19–20.]
40. Ibn al-Kalbī, *Le livre des idoles* (Cairo, 1924), p. 19.
41. Haitham b. 'Adī in Ibn Ḥajar, *Lisān al-Mīzān,* VI, p. 210; Diyārbakrī, *Tārīkh al-Khamīs* (1302 A.H.) I, p. 308.
42. Wāqidī, p. 35 (Wellhausen).
43. Nöldeke-Schwally, *Geschichte des Qorans,* I, pp. 207, 211, 217.
44. *Kitāb al-Kharāj* (Cairo, 1347 A.H.), p. 116, no. 362.
45. *Loc. cit.* no. 363.
46. Muslim, *Faḍā'il aṣ-Ṣaḥāba,* par. 140.
47. *Loc. cit.,* no. 361. That Simāk polished his traditions rhetorically is attested by Ibn Ḥanbal (Dhahabī, *Mīzān al-I'tidāl,* I, p. 427).
48. Muslim, *loc. cit.* par. 139f.; Ibn Māja, *Ruhūn,* par. 15.
49. Zurqānī (Cairo, 1280 A.H.), IV, p. 166.
50. Ibn Sa'd, II, pp. 139ff.
51. Bukhārī, *Adab,* par. 66f.

52. Zurqānī (Cairo, 1280 A.H.), II, pp. 14f.
53. Muslim, *Janā'iz,* par. 99–101; Tirmidhī, *Janā'iz,* par. 44; Abū Dāwūd, *Janā'iz,* par. 49; Nasā'ī, *Janā'iz,* par. 70.
54. Goldziher, *Muhammedanische Studien,* I, p. 259 [English trans. *Muslim Studies,* 2 vols. (London, 1967), I, p. 233–34].
55. *Mudawwana* (Cairo, 1324 A.H.), I. p. 161.
56. *Kitāb al-Umm* (Būlāq, 1325 A.H.), VII, p. 196.
57. *Muwaṭṭa' Muḥammad* (Lucknow, 1346 A.H.), p. 131.
58. Ibn Ḥibbān in Dhahabī, *Mīzān al-Lisān,* I, p. 461.
59. See the references in Wensinck, *Concordance et Indices de la Tradtion Musulmane,* II, p. 234b.
60. Goldziher, *op. cit.,* II, p. 35 [English, trans. *Muslim Studies* (London, 1971) II, p. 44].
61. Tirmidhī, *Nikāḥ,* par. 44; Abū Dāwūd, *Nikāḥ,* par. 31; Nasā'ī, *Nikāḥ,* par. 68.
62. Ibn Qutaiba, *Ta'wīl Mukhtalif al-Ḥadīth* (Cairo, 1326, A.H.), p. 25.
63. *Kitāb al-Umm,* V, p. 61.
64. Khaṭīb, *Tārīkh Baghdād,* X, p. 418 and elsewhere.
65. Ibn Ḥajar, *Tahdhīb at-Tahdhīb,* III, p. 163.
66. Ibn Qutaiba, *Ma'ārif,* p. 270 (Wüstenfeld); Sīrāfī, *Akhbār an-Nahwīyīn al-Baṣrīyīn,* p. 60f. (Krenkow); Khaṭīb, *Tārīkh Baghdād,* X, p. 418; Ibn Khallikān, *Wafayāt* (Būlāq, 1299 A.H.), I, p. 517.
67. Mubarrad, *Kāmil,* p. 449, p. 754.
68. See the statement of Wellhausen, *Reste arab. Heidentums* (Berlin, 1887), p. 82, on Zuhair, 14, 6 (Ahlwardt), as well as Goldziher's remark in *ZDMG,* (46), p. 206 on Ḥutai'a, 7, 13, and Nābigha, 23, 6 (Ahlwardt).
69. Yāqūt, *Irshād al-Arīb* (Gibb Mem. Series, VI), I, p. 20.
70. Yāqūt, *loc. cit.;* Jāḥiẓ, *Bayān* (Cairo, 1311 A.H.), II, p. 2.
71. Ibn Ḥajar, *Tahdhīb at-Tahdhīb,* X, p. 247.
72. Marzubānī, *Muwashshaḥ,* pp. 177, 192, 208.
73. Khaṭīb, *Tārīkh Baghdād,* IX, p. 78f; Ibn Sa'd, VII/2, p. 3.
74. Yāqūt, *Irshād al-Arīb,* V, p. 64 and elsewhere.
75. *Kitāb al-Aghānī,* I, p. 408f.
76. Dhahabī, *Tadhkirat al-Ḥuffāẓ,* I, p. 212.
77. Already Aṣma'ī was reported to have been an admirer of Ibn al-Muqaffa's *Yatīma* [GAL Suppl. I, 236], Ibn Khallikān, *Wafayāt* (1299 A.H.), I, 267, line 13.
78. To the evidence given in *Muḥammad b. Isḥāq,* p. 11, n. 42, is to be added that provided by *Tārīkh Baghdād,* III, p. 415.
79. Khaṭīb, *Tārīkh Baghdād,* II, pp. 30–33.
80. Yāqūt, *Geographisches Wörterbuch,* I, pp. 616ff.

V

Catholic Tendencies and Particularism in Islam

IGNAZ GOLDZIHER

In considering the origins and historical development of early Islam, one general fact, whose proper appreciation is crucial for an understanding of the development of Islam, must not escape our attention. The fact that I have in mind is the complete absence of any dogmatic impulse. Despite the tendency toward uniformity which occasionally manifested itself, the acceptance of "legitimate particularity" *(berechtigter Eigentümlichkeiten)* always triumphed.

This particularity which stood in opposition to the tendency toward uniformity expressed itself within orthodoxy in very different spheres. From the early period on it manifested itself in characteristic features of religious development. The differences which came to the fore, even in very important areas of this development, did not, however, provide an occasion for the formation of sectarian movements. They appeared and were recognized as normal shades of Islamic catholicity.

I recently had the occasion to examine this phenomenon in connection with one particularly important development in Islam, namely the formation of the text of the Quran.[1] I shall attempt here a more comprehensive examination of this phenomenon of particularism in relation to the development of Islam.

I

Islam extended itself into the larger world by means of external power before its fundamental doctrines had crystalized and taken on definite form, before even the first lines of its practical life had been given definite shape. Those who participated in this expansion of Islam (or, more accurately, this effort to conquer the world) were Muslims who had not yet incorporated Islam into their consciousness to any substantial degree. Islam for them was a battle cry more than it was a doctrine. The Quran itself was known only to a small minority of those who fought so successfully for the victory of the Word of God in Syria, Babylon, Persia, and Egypt.[2] This ignorance is reported to have been brought under control only during the reign of the third successor of the Prophet through the redaction of the Sacred Text which stands at the very center of Islam.

It can in no way be said that the ritual institutions of Islam developed uniformly. Since the masses, who were for the most part religiously indifferent people from the various Arab tribes, shared no firmly established norms at the time of the conquest, the formal elements of Islamic practice remained without any discipline for a considerable period of time. This view of the development of Muslim ritual (established in earlier research) has gained wide acceptance through the remarkable investigations of Prince Leone Caetani and Father Henri Lammens into the origins of Islam. I will not repeat examples which I cited in an earlier study illustrating the historico-religious facts to which I here refer.[3] I might, however, cite several additional examples. In the inexhaustible documentary collection of Ibn Sa'd[4] (in a volume edited by Zetterstéen) there is a description of how the caliph 'Umar performed the evening prayer *(ṣalāt)*. The formal features of *ṣalāt* described in this account differ in detail from what we know about the forms of *ṣalāt* in later periods.

Until late in the Umayyad period very important elements of Islamic ritual were without regulation.[5] This is especially evident in the case of one particular rite. One might assume, since the rite of pilgrimage *(ḥajj)* is connected with a particular center and depends on a firm tradition which in all details requires uniform features, that these had appeared at a very early date. It is surprising, therefore, to find a report which shows that during the reign of the caliph 'Abd al-Malik (684–705)[6]—according to another version, as late as the reign of the caliph Sulaimān (715–717)[7]—the details of the *ḥajj* liturgy had still not been fixed.

Is there anything more symbolic of Islamic life than the text of the sacred Book? In the first chapter of my *Die Richtungen der islamischen Koranauslegung* I tried to show that even in the case of this text (despite the fact that an official edition had been established) homogeneity and uniformity could not be achieved.[8]

The characteristic features of Islam were not established in the beginning at a particular center, with these then radiating out to surrounding areas. Indeed, just the reverse took place. Islamic ritual and law developed initially in the provinces. Even after the establishment of regulations in these areas had become a matter of scholastic concern, the claims of local variations played an active role alongside the concern for standardization. Even the documents on which the legitimacy of the variations was formally based played a part in this provincial coloring. An effort was made to trace the basis for these back to normative statements from the Prophet. The champions of the various customary laws which diverged from each other were always able to produce sayings from the Prophet in support of these differences. The sayings of the Prophet, which we call *ḥadīth,* have thus a provincial origin and can be classified according to the area of their origin, that is, whether they were Kufan, Basran, Medinan, etc. These statements, though dealing with the same subject, were cited to prove mutually contradictory theses.[9] Accordingly, the tendencies toward the fixing of ritual and legal practices differed from each other in many details, both in their forms and stipulations.

I state nothing new when I assert that already as early as the second century A.H. several tendencies in the application of Islamic law appeared as a result of the codification of these differences and achieved recognition in different areas and that, in accordance with "the law of the survival of the fittest," four of these tendencies or schools came to play an ongoing role in determining the outward expression of Islam down to the modern period. The scholars of these schools have never ceased debating these differences in the most ingenious ways so that sober Muslim critics could describe *ijmāʻ* (consensus), the fundamental root of Islamic law, as a phantom not corresponding to reality.[10] Moreover, these four schools did not by any means exhaust the diversity of Islamic law. In the early period there were other tendencies or schools which were not able to hold their own ground. Thus for example, the great historian and theologian Ṭabarī, known to us more through his contribution to the science of history, had established his own school called the Jarīrīya after his father (Ṭabarī's name was Muḥammad b. Jarīr), but which was soon forgotten. The Jarīrīya came to this end (an end it shared with others) not because it lacked the approval of the religious authorities, but because it did not succeed in winning popular acceptance over a large area and was thus displaced by movements that had won more popular favor. The four competing schools which thrived in different areas of the Muslim world were recognized as orthodox despite their differences. Members of these schools were not allowed to question each others' orthodoxy even though theoretical criticism of their differing regulations and norms was permitted.

II

Speculative theologians (a class that strongly favored a more comprehensive uniformity in matters of religion) had to give in to these conditions in the development of religious law. A prominent feature of Islamic theology was its recognition of the *fait accompli* through which (as the result of continuous development over a long period of time) elements that were actually opposed to Islam were taken over and re-branded as "religious practice," that is, as *sunna* or normative tradition. The fact of dissent came to be one such irreversible *fait accompli.* Its legitimacy, accordingly, had to be established; the acceptance of *ikhtilāf* (dissent) had to be sanctioned. The highest form of religious authority in Islam is an attested statement from Muhammad. Since the Prophet must have expressed approval of dissent, the following statement was placed in his mouth: "Diversity in my community is a mercy [from God]." Dissent in religious matters thus was not only something that was not contrary to Islam; it was rather thought to be a privilege granted through God's mercy.[11] Each tree could not grow the same bark.

In this prophetic statement we encounter a fact of special interest for the source-analysis of Islamic history. What is represented here as an utterance from the Prophet was in other sources attributed to various caliphs even as late as 'Umar II. The earliest caliph to whom this view was attributed was Abū Bakr in the following statement: "Differences of opinion among the Companions of Muhammad are a mercy for mankind." This saying was ascribed to later caliphs as well, the latest of them being 'Umar II. And it was done without any reference to the Prophet whatsoever.[12] Critical investigation compels us to assume that the doctrine of *ikhtilāf* was formed as a reflection of actual developments as these occurred (perhaps originally as the opinion of the caliph 'Umar II and his circle who were interested in religious matters) and that it was subsequently antedated until finally it was attributed to the Prophet himself. It thereby received the highest, irreproachable sanction as a view based upon a *ḥadīth* statement. This was certainly not an exceptional case. In investigating the origins of materials which are preserved as prophetic utterances, we encounter, at every turn, examples of the fact that such statements in their earliest forms were connected with the names of later authorities.

To that group of sayings which prepared the way for the prophetic statement cited above (and perhaps even indicating that the latter was already in use) belongs an account of a conversation between the caliph Ma'mūn and a Christian convert to Islam who later apostatized. Questioned as to the motive for his apostasy, the Christian explained that his displeasure with Islam was due to the absence of uniformity in religious matters. There followed an exposition by the caliph regarding the differences in legal practice and the interpretation of the Quran. This state of affairs, he states, is a gift from God, a freedom permitted to believers, and an easing of the burden in order that they not be forced by fixed regulations into the temptation of breaking the law *(takhayyur wa tawsi'a wa takhfīf min al-miḥna)*. The ambiguity of religious texts, it was argued, was inherent in the nature of human speech and was not peculiar to Islam. Such ambiguity was manifested in a similar way and for the same reasons in the interpretations of the Torah and the Gospels. It could not, therefore, according to the caliph, be a cause for favoring another religion at the expense of Islam.[13]

III

In the sphere of law we can follow the phenomenon of dissent a step further. In addition to the dissent which was canonically recognized by the religious authorities on the basis of the prophetic statement cited above, there existed in many areas of Islam a body of customary law *('āda)* which ran counter to the canonical law of the schools but which was eventually tolerated. This customary law as a rule was identical with pre-Islamic institutions and legal practices in the various provinces. Alongside the *pia desideria* of the religious law of the schools, the *'āda* was regarded as the effective law for life. Recently a great number of such popular legal traditions, which forced the canonical law (despite the powerful influence of its representatives) to retreat as a religious *desiderium* into the dead world of book knowledge, have been collected and published, especially in North Africa and the East Indies. They were thereby elevated, as it were, to the level of *jus scriptum,* of *leges scriptae.* In North Africa it was the old customary law of the Berber substratum. In the East Indies it was that of the Indonesian population politically subjugated by Islam, with which the representatives of Islamic law had to reckon.[14] These customary laws (with some Islamic adaptations to be sure) represent a glaring contradiction to Islamic legal norms, particularly in such important areas of jurisprudence as family, inheritance, and criminal law.[15] Already from a very early period, this state of affairs led to a dualism in the administration of justice, that is, to a secular court of justice on the one hand, and a religious one on the other. The spheres of competence of these two juridical authorities were clearly marked off from each other. They cannot, therefore, be considered as antagonistic elements in the administration of justice.

One must place into the same class the bipartite adminstration of justice found in Ottoman territories, for example, where, under different influences, secular legal codes *(kānūn)* were recognized alongside the religious law or the *sharī'a* as it was called. These were secular codes whose authors tried (not too successfully) to harmonize with the *sharī'a* or, at least, to minimize the more glaring contradictions.

This dualism is not found only in the modern period. If that were the case, it might be explained through the influence and requirements of European legal views. There is literary attestation for this phenomenon going back some centuries and involving very different parts of the Muslim world such as Syria, Egypt, and Central Asia.[16] Theological book-learning naturally ignored the existing conditions or took cognizance of them only in its protest against them. Such protest, however, had little significance beyond that of easing the conscience in the sense of *dixi et salvavi animam meam.* From the beginning, Muslim practice, however, had to come to terms with the facts and to look beyond the dogmatism of canonical law. Moreover, it had to do so without disruptive results. This was not in conflict with the general tendency of the development of Islamic institutions which, even in this area, manifested very little concern for a strict, uniform discipline.

IV

When the historian of religion turns his attention to the sphere of dogmatics in Islam, he discovers the same set of conditions that prevailed in the areas of ritual and law. Just how much freedom was given for dissent in this area is shown by another statement attributed to Muhammad, a statement which also throws light on the development of *ḥadīth* interpretation. According to this statement, Muhammad is reported to have said that Judaism split up into seventy-one sects, Christianity into seventy-two, and Islam into seventy-three. The statement concludes with the remark that all of the sects in Islam are destined for hell except one. The one whose members will enter paradise has a monopoly on salvation *(al-firqa an-nājiya)*.

The significance of this statement as evidence that dissent in theological matters was regarded as a normal phenomenon is evident in the history of its interpretation, the end result of which was the definitive use of the *ḥadīth* in the form in which we have quoted it. As I attempted to show as early as 1874, the statement originally had nothing to do with doctrinal parties or sectarian groupings. After all, what sort of honor could it be for Islam to have one or two parties more than Judaism or Christianity? The original term, *shu'ba* (branch), which was eventually changed to *firqa* (party), referred not to parties or sects but to ethical branches. Of these it was said that Islam had one or two more than the earlier religions, and in this resided the superiority of Islam over its predecessors. In the original setting of the statement, the final clause which was added to the enumeration of Islamic virtues, expressed the following sentiment: The most important of these branches is the confession of faith in one God and in his Prophet; the least important is the removal of obstructions which cause people to stumble along the way. Thus the most important and the least important ethical duties take a place among those duties encumbent upon men as they are listed and discussed in the literature of *shu'ab al-īmān* (branches of faith).

However, once the seventy-three branches of duties were changed to seventy-three parties (whose origin the Prophet had foreseen), the final clause, unsuited for this new context, was changed to the one cited above concerning those who will be saved. We shall see that this altered form of the final clause did not remain unchallenged, for the view expressed therein (and not present in the original form) contradicted the actual doctrine of orthodox Islam. According to this latter, no Muslim would enter hell if he declared his membership in the orthodox community, that is, if he (as they put it) belonged to the *ahl aṣ-ṣalāt* or the *ahl al-qibla;* in short, if he invoked the name God and turned toward the same *qibla* as did those believers who were doctrinally sound.[17] Differences in doctrinal minutiae did not come into the picture in the evaluation of the individual's qualification for salvation. Only a fanatic minority held to a different position; and the final clause regarding the party to be saved *(firqa)* derived from these exclusivist circles.

In order to verify the number of seventy-three dogmatic parties concretely, the prophetic statement in its corrupted form served as a point of departure and a basis for the doctrinal history of Islam whose systematicians (in works from which we draw most of our knowledge of the branches of Islamic dogma) constructed their various schemes[18] in accordance with the numbers given in the *ḥadīth.* The seventy-three parties had to make their appearance. And this was proof of the freedom and openness of early Islam in dealing with questions of dogma, without ever leading to an authoritative fixing of doctrine. Given the complete absence of a rigid ecclesiastical organization, orthodox Islam never produced an institutional organ or forum for the fixing of dogma, nor an infalliable personal authority (except in Shī'ite Islam) such as a council or synod of doctrinal authorities recognized as competent in such matters. There were only the individual *'aqīdas* or confessions of faith which the great theologians produced as a personal testimony. It is clear then that the external conditions for uniformity in matters of doctrine were lacking. Quite to the contrary, signs of doctrinal tolerance were everywhere evident from the beginning. Indeed, the conception of diversity as a divine favor was not limited to the *ikhtilāf al-fuqahā'* (dissent among legal experts) but was extended even to doctrinal difference.[19]

V

Belief in the legitimacy of legal and theological dissent, which found widespread acceptance in Islam, was expressed in a very remarkable literary phenomenon. I do not have in mind here the mass of works in which instances of dissent were systematically enumerated,[20] but rather those writings in which the question was treated philosophicaly. The Andalusian scholar 'Abd Allāh b. as-Sīd (d. 521/1127) from Baṭalyaws (Badajos) who was known particularly for his work in the field of philology deserves special mention. After stating the principle that differences in viewpoint are grounded in the natural state of men and therefore justified[21] and that differences of approach to truth do not call into question the exclusive character of truth, he takes up a discussion of such differences in a very interesting little work entitled: *The Reasonableness of the Factors Which Call Forth Differences of Opinion Among Men.*[22] Those factors which he identifies and explains (with appropriate examples from secular literature such as ancient poetry) are mainly philological and hermeneutical.

Though al-Baṭalyawsī discusses the phenomenon of dissent from a philological point of view, another renowned orthodox authority, Faḍā'il

Aḥmad b. Muḥammad ar-Rāzī (who taught in Aqsarā), based the justification for dissent in legal and doctrinal matters on theological considerations. Around 630/1232[23] he wrote a book with the title, *Ḥujaj al-Qur'ān* (Arguments of Proof from the Quran) in which he objectively compiled those proof-texts that were quoted by the various theological schools from the Quran and, in part, even from *ḥadīth* sources. Without examining critically their value as proofs, he collected those Quranic texts which the Murji'ites, Mut'tazilites, etc., cited as arguments against the orthodox in support of their doctrines of free will, the createdness of the Quran, the definition of faith and its relation to works, the conditions of salvation, the divine attributes, the rejection of anthropomorphism, and other doctrinal issues over which the theological parties diverged substantially from the orthodox point of view. Though the author himself belonged to Ash'arite orthodoxy, he showed no interest in refuting the arguments adduced by the various parties. Indeed, he states his purpose in the preface as follows: "Our aim in this work is to arrange exhaustively the arguments which each party presents in support of its views so that no one will accept them in haste or condemn them in a presumptuous fashion, and so that every one may know that these arguments stand juxtaposed to each other in accordance with the preordained plan of God for the division of his community into seventy-three parties." He similarly emphasized in his conclusion the hope that his book "might serve as a refutation of those people who accuse persons who differ from them of error, sinfulness and unbelief . . . , and who refuse to grant 'the people of the *qibla*' membership in the orthodox community."[24]

Though it may run counter to many widely held assumptions, it can be maintained that in Islam (with the exception of a fanatic minority) heresy-hunting and the prosecution of erroneous views appeared less frequently than they do in communities concerned with doctrinal formulae. Though branded in some cases as heretics, the Mu'tazilites were not outwardly disturbed. Restive thinkers such as Naẓẓām and Jāḥiẓ were not abused by their opponents except in writing. Undisturbed in their safety, they were allowed to cultivate doctrines that were unorthodox in most respects. Aristotelian philosophers such as al-Fārābī and Ibn Sīnā who did not confine themselves to formal logic, but followed Aristotle even in matters which involved the virtual negation of the fundamental principles of Islam, were given free rein in the presentation of their views. Ibn Rushd (Averröes), the most extreme representative of Artistotelianism, who rejected the attempt by al-Fārābī and Ibn Sīnā to effect a reconciliation

NB

between philosophy and the teachings of Islam, and who considered the restoration of the teachings of Aristotle (whom he called the most perfect man) as his philosophical mission—this Ibn Rushd was able to set up his study in the court of the Almohades. The ruler of this dynasty (notorious for its religious zeal) withdrew his favor not because of the heterodoxy of Ibn Rushd's thought but because one of his writings offended the ruler's vanity. As a concrete example of this indifference to doctrinal heterodoxy, it is worth mentioning that the Mu'tazilite Zamakhsharī who not only presented his own views on doctrine in his commentary but inveighed passionately against the orthodox whom he referred to as anthropomorphists and determinists, was honored by a highly orthodox historian with the title of *imām ad-dunyā,* that is, the doctrinal authority of the world, or universal doctor.[25]

All of this is evidence of the fact that over the centuries little attention was given to the doctrinal views of people, even though a vigorous polemic was carried on in writing. It is noteworthy indeed and confirms what we know of the outward religious life of Muslims, that it was just those circles most deeply religious that rejected dogmatic subtleties and refused to coerce the subjective content of the religious sense into a doctrinal mold. This was precisely the reaction of pious individuals in early Islam to the controversies over dogmatic issues. These controversies occurred precisely among the skeptics and the intellectual fanatics. The childlike, religiously sensitive believer (even those who supported orthodoxy) had a horror of dogmatic definitions. This religious outlook shared by individuals in the eighth century was revived by al-Ghazzālī, the classical representatiave of the anti-dogmatic, religious consciousness of the eleventh century. He elevated the rejection of doctrinal exclusivism to the level of a theological principle and was more sympathetic to mystical piety than to rigid dogmatism, which the religiously sensitive soul could never subject itself to. In his mind the exclusivism of the final clause of the *ḥadīth* on the seventy-three sects or parties had been changed to the opposite of its original form by fanatics. In the wording recommended by al-Ghazzālī, it read not that seventy-two of seventy-three doctrinal parties were awaiting hell and that only one would be saved, but rather that seventy-two would enter paradise and that only one would go to hell. And this was the one that regarded religion as the creation of men, as a conventional matter devised by virtuous and clever men in response to the demands of communal well-being *(maṣlaḥa)* and for the purpose of restraining immature persons—an arrangement set up under the pretense of divine authority. This is a point of view that was widespread already in Greek rationalism and one which Plato had discussed in the tenth book of *Laws*.[26]

Evidence for the absence of a dogmatic impulse in Islam can also be found in the sphere of constitutional law (the theory of the caliphate) where uniformity was not the result of theorizing but for the most part arose in response to external pressures and secular constraints, in the face of which the theologians (following the law of the *fait accompli* referred to above) were obliged to construct their theories *post facto*, making, as it were, the best of existing conditions. I will not, at this point, go beyond this brief reference to constitutional theory since the religous ramifications of our subject lie essentially in the fields of law and dogma, which already have been treated sufficiently.

VI

It will be necessary, however, to give an account of the reaction against the acceptance of dissent which we have described in the foregoing. Not everywhere was it regarded as self-evident that Islam was a religion whose inner unity resided solely in a general symbol, or that a high level of freedom of thought was permissible in the application of external obligations or in the interpretation of fundamental doctrines of belief such as the divine attributes, freedom of the will, the conditions of salvation, etc. In such an atmosphere of openness, it was feared that schismatic developments might occur, leading perhaps to the very destruction of Islam. This concern became a matter of growing anxiety as the political unity of Islam was placed in increasing jeopardy through the rise of provincial potentates aspiring to autonomy.

The tolerant view which accepted dissent had developed among those movements of Islamic theology that permitted a subjective, speculative method in the construction of a system of principles. They wanted to reject as it were the demand made on them for an unconditional infallibility, and to grant a relative justification of their conflicting, speculative conclusions. There was, however, a substantial number of Muslims who in matters of doctrine and practice adhered to an absolute authority. They naturally could not keep up with the latitudinarianism of the toleration of dissent. There were, in the first place, the Shīʿites whose principles categorically excluded the admissibility of differences in doctrine and practice because they measured the correctness of every opinion entirely by the authoritative teachings of the infallible *imām*. In the face of this highest authority there could, as a matter of course, be no discussion regarding the acceptance of legitimate differences of opinion.[27] We shall also see that prominent Mu'tazilites, whose rationalism was linked to an extreme intolerance, were among those opposed to the principle of dissent.[28]

A strong condemnation of dissent was expressed in a letter attributed to 'Abd Allāh b. al-Muqaffā (d. 140/757),[29] the trailblazer of Arabic prose literature in early Abbasid times, and sent to the caliph—a letter in which he gave advice regarding the art of governing. Even though the authorship of this work cannot be ascribed to 'Abd Allāh b. al-Muqaffā with certainty, it gives one the impression of having come from the period to which he belonged. Among the matters recommended for special consideration by the caliph were, above all, the administration of justice, legal management, and juridical deduction. He especially objected to the fact that in the most important spheres of legal practice no uniform procedures prevailed in adjoining regions or even in one and the same region. He pointed out that in criminal cases, as well as in cases having to do with marriage and property law, what was forbidden in Hira was judged permissible in Kufa. Indeed, in Kufa itself, different legal authorities came to legal decisions that were mutually contradictory. Traditions and precedents were fabricated from the period of the Orthodox Caliphs on to justify legal practices that were mutually contradictory and based upon the most arbitrary use of the principle of analogy. The author of the letter advised the caliph to create uniform procedures in the administration of justice and jurisprudence.[30] In any case, these statements reflect the conditions of the time in which the first tentative attempts were made in Iraq to provide a juridical basis for the varieties of legal practice. The results of these efforts did not have the approval of the author who, if he in fact was the Persian Ibn al-Muqaffā, did not agree with the viewpoint of orthodoxy.

Moreover, it was not only groups which dissented from orthodoxy that shared in this disapproval. Among orthodox theological tendencies one would expect to find the principle of dissent rejected by those who recognized the scriptures (the Quran and Tradition) as sole doctrinal authority and who rejected speculative methods wherever possible. The Ẓāhirite school was the most decisive in its rejection.[31] However, even the Hanbalites are to be put in the same camp. In a special treatise on the foundation of religious law *(uṣūl)*, Najm ad-Dīn aṭ-Ṭawfī (d. 716/1316) again raised objection to the authenticity of the *ikhtilāf*-statement attributed to the Prophet.[32] We have seen how justified he was in rejecting the soundness of this tradition.

A casual report from a Hanbalite circle in South Arabia[33] during the same period is characteristic. Abū Bakr b. Yūsuf al-Makkī (d. 677/1278), a jurist belonging to the Hanafite school, is said to have reported the following shortly before his death: "I saw in a dream as though it were the day of judgment; the *imāms* (that is, the founders of the different schools) stood before God, and the Creator spoke to them: 'I have sent to you one prophet with one law, and you have made of it four.' " This charge was repeated three times and none of them could answer until Aḥmad b. Ḥanbal came forward and through his apology (which, to be sure, did not refute the charge) effected a pardon from the Almighty.[34]

We see in all of this evidence of an aversion to the otherwise highly lauded theory of dissent, an aversion which became evident especially in those tendencies oriented toward tradition.

One could naturally appeal to a tradition since there was a *ḥadīth* for everybody, but even Quranic proof was not lacking. When the Prophet warned of schism in his community (the original reference, to be sure, was not exactly to religious factions), the warning was seen as a reference to the later factions. Already in the Meccan revelations the Prophet warned of division in the community: "Be not among those who split up their religion and become partisans (the word used here is *shiya'*, pl. or *shī'a*), each group exulting in its own tenets" (30:31). Here division in the former religions was cited as a warning example, just as in surah 42:13 where uniformity in faith ("Establish the religion and be not divided therein") is mentioned as a teaching revealed to Noah, Abraham, Moses, and Jesus: "And they were not divided until the knowledge came unto them, through rivalry among themselves" (42:14). Also in the later surahs, the reprehensible character of divisions is referred to in the examples of the earlier religions (2:209): "Hold fast to the rope of God, all of you together, and do not separate. Remember God's favor to you: how you were enemies and he made friendship between your hearts so that you became brothers by his grace. . . ." "And be not as those who separated and disputed after clear proofs had come to them. For such there is an awful doom" (3:101). And pronouncing severe judgment on conditions existing in his community, he said: "Truly as for those who sunder their religion *(dīnahum)* and become schismatics *(shiya')*—with these have nothing to do. Their case will go to God. He will tell them what they used to do" (6:160). One should not understand the term *dīn* here merely in the sense of religious belief, as though doctrinal differences were prominent in the early Islamic community, but rather as a reference to the cause of Islam in general, the discipline of the community in all of its inner relations, led by Muhammad. As we know from the Quran itself, the unanimity desired by the Prophet did not always prevail; he had to defend himself against many disruptive elements (the *munāfiqūn,* e.g.).

The theologians who rejected *ikhtilāf* in matters of religion made good use of these verses as a support for their point of view. And they have been used in our own time by modernist theologians (concerned with the removal of all differences in Islam) as evidence in support of their views.[35] They naturally rejected the tradition on the divinely approved character of dissent, and generally related this not to religion but to society. What is recognized in this tradition as a sign of divine mercy is not (they say) difference in matters of religion but the fact that not all men are alike in their social actions and professional activities *(al-ḥiraf wa'ṣ-ṣanā'i').*[36]

However, in early as well as more recent times these were considerations of a theoretical nature. The actual development of Islam, as we have already seen above, produced variations; to oppose the legitimacy of these latter by arguments from the Quran, from tradition, and from dreams was nothing less than the manifestation of a pious concern which was offended by practice.

VII

The more dissent came to be accepted in actual life, the more another idea (closely associated with it and following more or less logically from it) demanded consideration. As differences came to be accepted, judgments of truth more and more had to be based on those things on which the entire community was agreed. From this consideration the doctrine of consensus (*ijmā'*) emerged as the criterion of correctness in religious matters. Dissent (so it was thought) was admissible: the decision as to which side was right was unclear and not even important. However, it had to be recognized as entirely certain that where all agreed, fault-finding had to be abolished. It was accordingly inadmissible to adopt an individual viewpoint in opposition to consensus. This was to constitute a corrective to the freedom which was granted in the permitting of dissent. It is a symbol of the catholicity of Islam and finds its expression in doctrine as well as in law and constitutional theory. Consensus eventually came to be accepted as the central pillar of orthodoxy and of loyalty to Islam. Before this principle came to be based on the agreement of the great authorities of the past (an agreement that was discoverable only by examining the written sources), it was based on the community of believers, and the possibility of its realization was subject to many a doubt. The value of the principle as such was thus very easily placed in jeopardy. It was again the most rigorous wing of orthodoxy that manifested a somewhat skeptical attitude toward this theological principle—a fact that is itself noteworthy. No less a figure than Aḥmad b. Ḥanbal, the authority of the most intransigent party of Sunni Islam, took the position that it was false to speak of doctrine as having its basis in consensus. Such a condition, he argued, could never be met given the great geographical expanse of Islam. At most one could maintain negatively and with some reservation that on this or that issue dissent is not known to exist.[37] From this same camp we hear the Hanbalite scholar, Najm ad-Dīn aṭ-Ṭawfī, from the thirteenth century, expressing the remarkable principle that considerations of well-being (*maṣlaḥa*) were to be preferred over consensus, and even over textual proof.[38]

While Ibn Ḥanbal, in emphasizing the impossibility of verifying consensus, did not dispute the value of it insofar as it could be proven with certainty the Mu'tazilite Naẓẓām attacked the principle at its roots. It was not true, he maintained, that the whole of the community always followed the truth and never submitted to error.[39] There were enough examples to prove the contrary. Such a view is entirely understandable coming as it did from a philosopher who was conscious of the fact that his ideas were in open opposition to what was regarded in his time as the consensus of the community.

Finally, it was inevitable that this principle would suffer severely in a community whose mainspring was the exclusive recognition of a personal authority and infallibility (to which the whole had to submit), and over against which no other could make any claim. The whole of the Shī'ite sect, with its belief in the infallible doctrinal authority of the *imām,* falls into this class.[40]

Even the Khārijites who dissented from the Shī'ite position rejected the authority of consensus.[41] Because of their protest against the historical development of the caliphate they formulated their position outside of it.

As a central pillar of orthodox Islam, the principle of consensus, even within this latter, had a very fluctuating historical development. Only in its latest formulation did it succeed in conquering the skepticism which it initially produced. In its definition, the essential character of consensus was located not in contemporary conditions but rather in a dead past. Certainly the vital reform of Islam theologically is not in the least dependent upon a reformulation of this conception.

NOTES

(See page xi for list of abbreviations of journal titles)

1. [Goldziher, *Die Richtungen der islamischen Koranauslegung* (Leiden, 1920).]
2. Cf. Caetani, *Annali dell'Islam,* I, p. 46. How few knew even the *Fātiḥa* [surah 1] can be seen in *Usd al-Ghāba,* IV, p. 307.
3. *Muhammedanische Studien,* II (Halle, 1890), pp. 29ff. [English trans. by Barber and Stern, *Muslim Studies,* II (London, 1971), p. 28ff.]
4. Ibn Sa'd, *Ṭabaqāt al-Kubrā,* V, p. 47.
5. Cf. pseudo-Ibn Qutaiba, *Kitāb al-Imāma wa'l-Siyāsa,* II, p. 173.
6. Ibn Sa'd, *Ṭabaqāt al-Kubrā,* V, pp. 170–71.
7. Ya'qūbī, *Historiae* (ed. Houtsma), II, p. 358. On the development of the *ḥajj*-ritual, see especially C. Snouck Hurgronje, *Het Mekkaansche Feest* (Leiden, 1880).
8. [*Die Richtungen,* pp. 1–54.]
9. *Muhammedanische Studien,* II, p. 175 [English trans., *Muslim Studies,* II, p. 164]. On the provincial *ḥadīth,* cf. Ibn Taymīya, *Raf' al-Malām,* p. 28, where he refers to a treatise of one of the six great authorities on *ḥadīth,* Abū Dāwūd as-Sijistānī (d. 275/888), on this subject entitled: *Fī Mafārīd Ahl al-Amṣār min as-Sunna* (On the Individual Sunnas of the People of the Provinces).
10. *Manār,* IV, pp. 458ff.
11. Goldziher, *Vorlesungen über den Islam* (Heidelberg, 1910), p. 52 [English trans. by Seelye, *Mohammed and Islam* (New Haven and London, 1917), pp. 54–55; French trans. by Arin, *Le Dogme et le loi de l'Islam* (Paris, 1920), pp. 42–43].
12. Ibn Sa'd, *Ṭabaqāt al-Kubrā,* V, p. 140, p. 281, p. 282. Dārimī, *Sunan,* p. 79; Ibn al-Jawzī, *Manāqib 'Umar b. 'Abd al-'Azīz* (ed. C. H. Becker, Leipzig, 1899), p. 137.
13. Ṭayfūr, *Kitāb Baghdād* (ed. Keller), p. 61. The conversation was communicated by the Mu'tazalite, Thumāma (b. al-Ashras).
14. The Koninklijke Instituut voor de Taal-, Land- en Volkenkunde van Nederl. Indie established a special commission for the collection and study of *'āda* law. Six volumes of *'ādāt* laws from various Dutch colonies have appeared to date, and as seen from the annual report of the Institute for 1912, additional volumes are already in the press.
15. Cf. [Goldziher, "Materialien zur Kenntniss der Almohadenbewegung in Nordafrika"], *ZDMG,* 41 (1887), pp. 38f. [Goldziher, "Recueil de mémoires et de textes publié en l'honneur du XIVe Congrès des Orientalistes . . . "] *RHR,* 52 (1905), p. 236. Also see the article " 'Āda" in *EI* [also *EI*^{2}].
16. See my article "Fiḳh" in the *Encyclopaedia of Islam,* II [the same article appears in the *Shorter Encyclopaedia of Islam,* pp. 102–7].
17. Goldziher, *Vorlesungen,* p. 181, [English trans. p. 194].
18. [Goldziher, "Die dogmatische Partei der Sālimijja"], *ZDMG,* 61 (1907), p. 73. [A. Christensen, "Remarques critiques sur le *Kitāb bayāni-l-adyān d'Abū-l-Ma'ālī*"], *Le Monde oriental,* V (1911), p. 209.

19. Ṭabarī, II, p. 19. 'Alī al-Qārī, commentary on *Fiqh al-Akbar* (Cairo, 1323), p. 99. Sufis emphasized that the absolute form of monotheistic dogma ought to be excepted from the large sphere of admissible dissent; no difference of opinion is permissible regarding it (Qushayrī, *Risāla fī't-Taṣawuuf,* 17; also Hujwirī, *Kashf al-Mahjūb* [trans. by Nicholson], pp. 106, 176).
20. *Vorlesungen,* p. 76, n. 7:6 [English trans., p. 80, n. 7:6].
21. In support of his view he cites a number of verses from the Quran.
22. Published by Aḥmad 'Umar al-Maḥmasānī, Cairo, 1319/1901. Cf. Shāh Walī ad-Dīn (d. 1180/1766), *al-Intiṣāl fī Bayān Sabab al-Ikhtilāf* (Bombay, n.d.).
23. Not determined precisely by Brockelmann. *GAL,* I, p. 414.
24. This work was published by Aḥmad 'Umar al-Maḥmaṣānī (Cairo, 1320/1902) on the basis of a single copy from the Khedivial Library in Cairo.
25. Abulmaḥāsin, *Annales* II, p. 2, ed. Popper, p. 380.
26. Cf. Wendland, *Die hellenistisch-römische Kultur in ihren Beziehungen zu Judentum und Christentum* (Tübingen, 1912), p. 102.
27. Goldziher, *Vorlesungen,* pp. 224ff. [English trans., p. 238.]
28. Goldziher, *Die Ẓāhiriten, ihre Lehrsystem und ihre Geschichte* (Leipzig, 1884), pp. 101ff. [English trans. by W. Behn, *The Ẓāhirīs, Their Doctrine and Their History* (Leiden, 1971), pp. 95ff.]
29. [Cf. Goitein, "A Turning-Point in the History of the Muslim State," *Studies in Islamic History and Institutions* (Leiden, 1966), p. 149ff.]
30. *Rasā'il al-Bulaghā'* (Cairo, 1908), p. 54.
31. *Die Ẓāhiriten,* pp. 99ff. [English trans. *The Ẓāhirīs,* pp. 93ff.]
32. In the collection of *uṣūl*-works published in Cairo in 1324/1906 (cf. *Manār,* X, p. 763).
33. Al-Khazrajiyy, *The Pearl-Strings: A History of the Resūliyy Dynasty of Yemen,* ed. by Muhammad Asal (*Gibb Memorial Series,* III), IV, p. 56. From this work the spread of the Hanbalite school in South Arabia in the 6th cen. A. H. is evident.
34. *Ibid.,* p. 206.
35. This effort I treated thoroughly in my Olaus Petri lectures [*Die Richtungen der islamischen Koranauslegung* (Leiden, 1920)].
36. *Manār,* XIV, p. 343.
37. Ibn Qayyim al-Jawzīya, *I'lām al-Muwaqqa'īn* (Cairo, 1325), I, 32; II, p. 335.
38. Cited. in *Manār,* XIV, p. 26; cf. X, pp. 745–70.
39. Cf. *Muhammedanische Studien,* II, p. 87 [English trans. *Muslim Studies,* p. 88].
40. *Vorlesungen,* p. 225 [English trans., p. 239].
41. Baghdādī, *Farq,* p. 129.

VI

The Juridical Consequences of the Doctrines of Al-Ḥallaj

LOUIS MASSIGNON
(translated by Herbert Mason)

I. The Consequences in Canon Law (*Furū' Al-Fiqh*)

a. The Subordination of the Prescribed Rites to a Rule of Life; the Guiding Principles of this Rule

It has been customary in recent times to reduce the cultic life of Islam to a merely external observance of rites, to the strict fulfillment of certain social rules, the five *farā'id* or "required duties": profession of faith, canonical prayer, fasting, pilgrimage, statutory alms-giving.

At the outset Islamic worship, generally speaking, did not appear to be that strictly limited to a ritual literalism, and the early Sunnis in particular required above all the practice of a minimum of moral virtues, thus outlining a kind of "rule of life" intended for the entire community.[1] Along with certain rules which were practical and material, temporary and external (the five required duties), they explicitly decreed various permanent restrictions (*wara'*) designed to discipline both the body (rules of dress, silence) and the mind (prohibited subjects of thought and conversation), and, in addition, certain expiatory works of charity (*manāsik*).[2] For these Sunnis, Islam was primarily *adab,*[3] "sociability" or "courtesy" in the broadest sense, hence a "rule of life."

For a long time this early character of the cult remained quite pronounced among the Hanbalites. These *hashwīya* who as late as the sixth/twelfth century were being criticized by the formal intellectualism of the

Hanafites for "giving equal weight to *fard, sunna* and *nafal,*"[4] in other words, for maintaining the interdependence of the external rites, the manner in which they were to be practiced, and the supererogatory intention.

Such was the distinctive feature common to the Bakrīya school[5] as well as to other disciples of Ḥasan Baṣrī, to Ibn 'Ukkāsha,[6] to Tustarī, to Ghulām Khalīl, and to the first Hanbalites,[7] up to the fourth/tenth century. Since the third/ninth century,[8] however, Shāfi'ī[9] and Bukhārī had given the ascendancy to the five required duties as being characteristic, necessary, and sufficient[10] signs of the Muslim profession.

The attitude of Ḥasan and of Ibn Ḥanbal is that of the early mystics, and also of Ḥallāj. The main thing for them is not to debate the external form of the rites,[11] although they adhere to certain details (enumerated below),[12] nor to dwell on their original meaning, even though they study the symbolism of the rites,[13] but to examine their effect upon the conscience of the practicing believer.

The rites are not the essential element of religion, but constitute its means (*wasā'il*); they are the instruments provided by God for attaining realities (*ḥaqā'iq*). This is the doctrine set forth so perfectly by Ḥallāj.[14] The observance of the rites, the manner in which one performs them, is more important than their literal substance; the intention, the spirit one puts into them, takes precedence over their textual apparatus. And [this doctrine] calls for catechetical elaboration; it involves a moral method, *ri'āya,*[15] a "way," *ṭarīqa.*

Thus the mystics do not become involved in the on-going debate among legal experts over the criterion for choosing[16] to adopt this or that rite: the *istiṣḥāb,*[17] which is the permanence of authority, the total acceptance of the traditional material without question or experimentation, the acceptance of a rite which one must practice and uphold because it has been received as is by an arbitrary fiat (Shāfi'ī, Ibn Ḥanbal, Dāwūd); or the Hanfites' *istiḥsān,*[18] *the appreciation through divine* and human reason (*taḥsīn al-'aql*) of the superior causes and rightness of the divine commandment; or Mālik's *istiṣlāḥ,*[19] the *divine* and human appreciation of the practical motives and positive social benefits[20] which may be attributed to this Quranic recommendation. To be sure, through traditionalism and tutiorism,[21] mystics tend to prefer the first criterion, but they also resort, *a posteriori,* both to symbolism, in order to make all the forms of the rites acceptable to reason, and to asceticism, so that their will may benefit from all the requirements of the rites.

The ultimate realities to be attained are the "fruits" which zealous observance of the religious acts produces in the soul, by training it in certain virtues (*mu'āmalāt*) and by guiding it by certain signs (*ishārāt*). But not for these virtues and signs in themselves, but for God, toward Whom they lead the soul.

The broad lines of this method, sketched out by Muḥāsibī, clearly developed by Ḥallāj, are underscored in the following list of superiorities:

a) for the observance of the rites themselves: *ri'aya* = *khidma* > *'ibāda.*[22] Obedience is superior to observance (all of the mystics; contra the *'ulamā'*).[23]

sunan > *farā'id.*[24] The practice of the rites is more important than the letter of the rite (Ḥasan and most of the early mystics; contra the Hanbalites).

nīya > *'amal.*[25] The intention is greater than the action itself (Ḥasan Baṣri, Tustarī; contra the Ẓāhirites).

b) for intellectual reflection on the cult: *ibāḥa* > *taḥrīm.*[26] Permission precedes interdiction (Hanafites, Qarmathians, Ibn Mu'ādh, Ibn 'Aṭā'; contra Anṭākī,[27] Ibn Ḥanbal, Junayd, 'Izz Maqdisī).

'ilm > *'aql.*[28] Knowledge (revealed) is superior to intellect (human) (Hanafites, Hanbalites, and mystics; contra the Ibādites, Mu'tazilites, Imāmites, and philosophers).

rajā' > *khawf.*[29] Hope is superior to fear (Yazīd Raqāshī, Thawrī, Ibn Ḥanbal, Ibn Mu'ādh, Tustarī and the "Murji'ites"; contra Ḥasan and the "Wa'īdites").

khulla > *'ubūdīya.*[30] The friend is greater than the servant (Rabāh, Kulayb, Qarmathians; contra a majority of the Sunnis).

c) for the ultimate realities (*ḥaqā'iq*) of the virtues to be acquired:

shukr > *sabr.* Giving thanks is better than being resigned[31] (Muḥāsibī, Tirmidhī, Ibn 'Aṭā', Ruwaym; contra Junayd and Ibrāhīm Khawwāṣ).

ma'rifa > *'ilm.* To understand is greater than to know[32] (Murji'ites, Ibn Kharrām, Muḥāsibī, extremist Imāmites; contra Junayd and Ibn Rushd).

maḥabba > *imān.* Loving is greater than believing. (Ḥallāj, *Riw.* VII; contra the *ḥadīth* adopted by Bukhārī).[33]

b. Ritual Practices Peculiar to the Mystics

Without moving in a parallel direction with the four orthodox *madhāhib* and giving birth to a legal "school" in the true sense of the term as the 'Alid[34] tradition did, the tradition of the Sufi teachers vigilantly preserved the observance of certain distinctive details in the external fulfillment of the required duties. Mentioned in the *Farīdāt* attributed to Ḥasan and in the *Ta'arruf* of Kalābādhī and the *Waṣāya* of Ibn Khafīf, they have been formulated as a body of doctrine in the *Ṣafwat al-taṣawwuf* of Ibn Ṭāhir Maqdisī.[35] The following list of these practices invites comparison with certain episodes in the life of Ḥallāj:

(*dress*): *ṣūf*[36]—dyed and patched clothing[37]—Turkish slippers. How to gird one's head and loins[38]—the wearing of beard and moustache.[39]

(*ablutions*): *ghusl,* out of tutioristic[40] precaution: beforehand.

(*contrition*): the complete act[41]—formula "*yā Rabb.*"[42]

(*pilgrimage*): go on foot, without provisions (*zād*) or mount (*rāḥila*);[43] otherwise *kaffāra;* obligatory *'umra;*[44] the fast of the day of 'Arafāt is practicable at other times also.[45]

(*fasting*): supplementary.[46]

(*retreat*): *i'tikāf* (evolved into *khalwa*). At Mecca Ḥallāj practiced this during the *'umra*[47] (a vow of the type of Abū Isrā'īl Mula'ī, criticized ap. Mālik, *Muwaṭṭa'* II, p. 377; Bukhārī, no. 29, Abū Dāwūd, *Sunan* II, p. 195—Goldziher).

(*ordinary prayer*): the two previous *rak'a,* out of tutioristic precaution. Always preceded by *ghusl* and *wuḍū'.*

(a program of *optional* prayers): *wird,* pl. *awrād:*[48] two *rak'as* (of one verse each), then *salām,*[49] *rukhṣa,*[50] and *du'ā* (in the form of *qunūt*[51] + *tashahhud*[52]), with no mention of the Prophet or *ṣalāt 'ala'n-nabī.*[53] In rhymed prose.[54]

In the "common life" (*mu'āshara*), the mystics claimed, in addition, certain traditional "dispensations" (*rukhaṣ*) of very ancient origin.[55] Here is a brief list of them, based on the lists of Sulamī and Maqdisī[56] and with references to corresponding features in the life of Ḥallāj:

tark al-kasb,[57] the right to renounce all trades,[58] to live in perpetual pilgrimage (*siyāḥa*) and as a beggar (*su'āl*).

taqsīm, distribution among the "comrades" of the gifts and offerings; this was called "*qawama Tarṣūṣ.*"[59]

(*the common meal*); the meal was blessed beforehand, and a thanksgiving was said at the end.[60] Especially to be honored was the bread, which is "consecrated" food,[61] and also salt.[62] The oldest person at the meal is the one who begins.[63] There is a meal called *'urs,* "marriage feast," eaten on the anniversary of the deaths of the most revered members of the community.[64]

samā', a spiritual concert, a session of recitation (*dhikr*), in which the chanting inspires ecstasy (*faqd al-iḥsās*)[65] and dancing (*raqs*) among the listeners.[66] Two other "dispensations," definitely suspect, the rending of clothes (*tamzīq*)[67] and the *naẓar ilā' l-murd,*[68] do not appear in Ḥallāj's biography.

da'wa, the public preaching of the mystic's doctrine.[69]

mizāḥ, the right to jest,[70] to make plays on words.

Ḥallāj sums up the qualities of the mystic as follows:[71]

> He whose heart is of a piety tested by God; who for his coat of arms has the Quran; for a cloak, faith; for a torch, meditation; for perfume, piety; for canonical ablution, contrition; for bodily hygiene, only the use of the lawful acts; and for ornament, continence; he lives only for the life to come; he cares for nothing but God; he keeps himself constantly in the presence of God; he fasts until death, breaking the fast only in Paradise; he espouses only good deeds; his only treasure is virtue; his silence is contemplation; his gaze is vision.

c. The Symbolism of the Rites

Various texts by Ḥallāj dealing with the symbolism of the legal "pilgrimage" have been translated above; they may be compared to two long and rather curious passages by Shiblī and Ḥuṣrī.[72]

In a Persian translation from before the fourteenth century there is a short text, given as being by Ḥallāj, on the symbolism of the fifteen attitudes called for during the canonical prayer: "to rinse out the mouth is to acquire sincerity; to sniff up water is to renounce pride . . . to create the intention (*nīya*) is to perceive God; to stand up straight (*qiyām*) is to take part in the divine permanence, within the hangings of His tent; to prostrate oneself (*rukū'*) is to isolate oneself in the divine aloneness; when we raise ourselves up again (*i'tidāl*), eternity turns towards us. . . . "[73]

In addition to the fairly limited symbolism of the canonical rites, mystics prior to Ḥallāj had introduced an extremely complex symbolism. A list of these symbols, provided by Tirmidhī, gave me the opportunity to trace their historical development in a previous study.[74] The following are known to be Ḥallāj's favorite allegorical themes: the wine and the cup (intoxicating with mystical joy),[75] the virgin (the inner consciousness),[76] the bird (the soul which rises from the dead),[77] the butterfly and the candle,[78] the sea and the pearl,[79] the crescent moon.[80]

d. The Ultimate Reality of the Rites

The degree of reflectiveness with which the rites are performed is more important than a mechanical subservience to every detail of the acts. This discipline of intention gradually trains the soul, familiarizing it with the virtues; and these virtues, by means of certain indications, guide it to

God. In the final analysis then, the five rites result in leading the soul into God's presence. The mystics, who voluntarily add supererogatory observances (*nawāfil*) and prayers to their obligatory duties, tend to view even their obligatory duties as pure acts of thanksgiving in which the totally free and thankful heart offers itself to God by its own *vow,*[81] following the established means and appointed hours.

Their position is therefore similar to that of the Qarmathians, who teach[82] that "all of the obligatory duties are actually supererogatory (*nāfila*) and not obligatory, for they are an expression of gratitude addressed to a Benefactor. God does not need the servitude of His creatures; therefore, worship is a thanksgiving, and he who wishes to, offers it; he who does not so wish, does not offer it; we are free to choose." But the main intent of the mystics is very different from that of the Qarmathians, as has already been stated.[83] Thus, the formalistic criticism of Ibn Bābūyā, Ibn Ḥāzm,[84] and Ibn al-Jawzī,[85] which accuses the mystics of preaching the suppression of the five obligatory duties, is tendentious. It was an appeal to the secular arm, because the orthodox legal schools had advocated sanctions against the omission of these social duties.[86] In his own life Ḥallāj had always been exceptionally strict[87] in the fulfillment of his obligatory duties. What one must remember, and what his adversaries used against him, is that his teaching presented the canonical rites of Islamic worship as external signs of a rule of communal life, as temporary tokens of a legal discipline. They were to be observed as ordinary collective procedures of asceticism, having no sacramental character of themselves, not conferring grace *ipso facto,* and destined to end[88] at the time of mystical union and in Paradise.

Ḥallāj's understanding of the shahāda: Ḥallāj's position on pilgrimage,[89] fasting,[90] alms,[91] and prayer[92] has already been examined; it remains to set forth in detail his attitude toward one of the basic features of Islamic worship, the *shahāda.*[93]

It has been pointed out above that the *shahāda,* "There is no divinity[94]—except God,"[95] should not be thought of as a complete and homogeneous judgment, but as an "exception," *istithnā',* in other words, a condensed parable; and that, as such, this heterogeneous sentence could have a useful purpose and a meaning, without having, *a priori,* either an intrinsic convincing force (logic) or an intrinsic (real) sacramental efficacy.[96]

Various Khārijites, disciples of Abū Bayhas,[97] had ascertained that reciting this formula earnestly and attentively was not enough to make a true believer. After the veto of Shāfi'ī, in opposition to certain traditionists,[98] a devout Mu'tazilite, Murdār, declared the *shahāda* of certain heretics[99] to be unacceptable and worthless. And Ghazzālī found a ḥadīth in which Jesus, called upon by Satan to recite the *shahāda,* answers, "This sentence is true, but I shall not repeat it for you, because under the guise of a pious work it tries to trick me with ambiguities (on your behalf)."[100]

The early Muslim grammarians had maintained, out of a fideistic positivism, that the sentence was homogenous[101] and had claimed that what the negation of the first member aimed at is the real existence (*wujūd*) of the divinity, not the pure idea (essence, *māhiya*) of divinity in itself.[102] This gave the *shahāda* an immediate ritual efficacy, sanctioned by various *ḥadīth* cited in Muslim and Bukharī.[103]

After the Mu'tazilites became aware of the process of elaboration of the *concept* in the thought,[104] some of them recognized that the negation of the first member could not relate either to the real existence *ad extra* or to the virtual essence *in se* of divinity outside of us, but to its representation (*mawṣūfīya*),[105] its conceivability in our minds; they recognized that this was a particular *acceptation,*[106] a *ḥāl* of the pure idea, a judgment *hic et nunc.*

Wishing to reconcile this result with the popular trend, Zamakhsharī[107] maintained that the sentence was a homogeneous proposition[108] of which the two members presented "divinity" from one and the same point of view, virtuality (*imkān*). The affirmation of the second member did not establish that God actually existed but proved that our minds represented Him as existing.[109]

He could have concluded[110] from this that, if the works of a practical faith are required for Paradise and if theoretical knowledge of the divine attributes is not sufficient, then *a fortiori* the *shahāda,* a formula which defines the existing God only by denying Him all virtual evidence of existence, would not *ipso facto* save the believer who recited it.

Reasonable theologians finally admitted, along with 'Aḍud Ījī (d. 756/1355),[111] that the *shahāda* is not a grammatically conclusive proposition. In actual fact, it is heterogeneous, shifting, in a condensed parable, like all *istithnā',*[112] from virtual divinity (of hypothetical gods) to actual and real Divinity (of God).[113]

Ḥallāj agreed with this, and he forbade his disciples to waste their time reciting or meditating on the *shahāda,*[114] because it gave them neither a logical proof for the intelligence[115] nor a real grace for the heart.[116] Only God is capable of making us articulate and decompose the *shahāda* with the intention of transference which renders it legitimate,[117] by helping us to become conscious of the mystery of His unity in the very operation of His act.[118] He makes us first deny, in our heart, our self, in order that He may then affirm Himself there by his presence.[119] Ecstasy shows us, furthermore, that the *shahāda* is only a preliminary veil;[120] it is a kind of secular interdict which, "by preoccupying the crowd, prevents it from joining with those who are united with God," in conformity with the (prohibitive) Law declared by Quranic revelation, and it will fall along with the Law at the arrival of the Grace which will consummate the union. Ḥallāj censures the criminal illusion of those[121] who imagine that by reciting the *shahāda* they prove in a real way that God is unique; they thereby dare "to associate themselves with God" (*mushrik*). Because to imagine that one "unifies" God is to affirm one's own self,[122] and to affirm one's self is implicitly to become an associate. The truth is that God alone proclaims Himself to be One (by Himself), by the tongue of those of His creatures whom He chooses; God alone can make Himself *unique*.

Such was the forceful criticism recalled by Harawī[123] in his tercet.[124]

> *No one says truly of God that He is "unique,"*
> *For he who imagines he does this denies Him.*
> *The monotheistic profession of faith of one who pronounces such an epithet*[125]
> *Is only a useless sentence, nullified by the Unique.*
> *God alone makes the Unique! It is He Himself Who unifies His Unity!*
> *And the man who tries to do this deserves the epithet of atheist.*

Ḥallāj's solution, the only correct one, could not prevail in the face of an all too human laxity, of the growing latitudinarianism (*irjā'*) which gradually lulled Islam to sleep in the reassuring illusion that divine mercy is not so demanding about giving itself to men, that it makes itself available, at their pleasure, in a simple formula.

The orientation of the evolution, parallel to that of post-Ḥallājian mysticism toward monism, stems from a desire to discover at all costs a "short cut" to finding God, and to find Him in the *shahāda* by trying to justify its grammatical construction. Abandoning conceptualism and returning, under Hellenistic[126] gnostic influences, to the realistic positivism of the early grammarians, the mystical theologians of the school of Ibn 'Arabī rigorously accepted its final logical consequences. For them, as Jāmī has shown, the *shahāda* is a regular and homogeneous proposition[127] with a single subject.[128] It is a universal negative linked to a particular affirmative, *EI:* "there are no gods, excepting from them God"; this complete proposition, according to the rules of logic, by simple conversion (*dalīl al-khilāf*) becomes this, *AO:* "there are gods, without excepting God from them."[129] For these *ittiḥādīyūn,* the error of idolators is to have singled out from among the things of the earth, which are all "places where the divine appears" (*maẓāhir*), just some of them to make into idols, to the exclusion of others. All forms may be adored, for each one manifests a design of the Unique.[130] Ibn Kamālpāshā, Kawrānī, and Nābulusī even wrote that the great mass of believers must be made to see that this monism is the only acceptable interpretation of the canonical *shahāda.*[131]

Ḥallāj, on the other hand, exclaimed in his prayers: "O my God! I know that You transcend (are transcendent, *tanzīh*) all that Your friends and Your enemies together say of You![132] Glorious Sovereign, I know and proclaim that You transcend all the *tasbīh* of those who have said "Glory to You!," transcend all the *taḥlīl* of those who have said "no divinity, except God!," transcend all the concepts of those who have conceived of You! O my God! You know I am powerless to offer You a fitting thanksgiving.[133] Then come into me and give Yourself thanks! This is the true prayer of thanksgiving! there is no other!"[134]

II. The Criticisms Aimed at This Doctrine

a. Accusations of Heresy Made Against Ḥallāj

1. By the Dogmatic Theologians (Mu'tazilites).

The text by Balkhī,[135] translated above, read together with the allusions contained in Sulamī's *Ghalatāt,* permits us to list these accusations in the order in which they were summarized by Amīr Ḥusayn Maybudhī:[136]

(1) "To say that one has lost human nature (*nāsūtīya*)" means that having arrived at sainthood, the mystic becomes "he whom everything obeys" (*muṭā'*),[137] "he who says to the object: Be! and it becomes."[138] Doctrine of the "extinction" of "carnal nature" (*fanā' al-basharīya*), or of the "human attributes" (*awṣāf*);

(2) "To say that we see God in this world, with our own eyes, and that He speaks to us"—this is the doctrine of *ru'ya* (vision), *muḥādatha* (con-

versation), by means of "infusion" (*ḥulūl*) of lights (*anwār*), attestations (*shawāhid*) and inspirations (*arwāḥ*);[139]

(3) "To say that the spirit (*rūḥ*) proceeds from the divine Light and that, if this light rejoins the Light, they become as One." A distortion of the theses concerning the "uncreated Spirit," conformation (*ittiṣāf*), and essential union.[140]

Add to these the accusations of charlatanism and pride, examined earlier.[141]

2. By the Imāmites.

Their accusations, developed by Ibn Bābūyā and Mufīd,[142] are presented here in concordance with the list drawn up by Ibn al-Dā'ī:[143]

(1) Doctrinal apostolate (*da'wa*) in public, criminal usurpation of a role reserved only to the 'Alid imām;

(2) The use of diabolical magic[144] which he learned[145] from 'Abdallāh Ibn Hilāl Kūfī,[146] who had been taught by Abū Khālid 'AA -b-Ghālib Kābilī,[147] a disciple of Zurqā, herself a pupil of the false prophetess Sajāḥ;[148]

(3) Various false propositions, the first two of which are taken from the *Bustān al-Ma'rifa:*

a) that man cannot be content with indirect knowledge of God through His works (§ 8);

b) that perfect knowledge of God, in us, is a divine substance (§ 15),[149]

(4) that the prophets are not transformed by grace like the saints (superiority of saints to prophets, according to Ibn Bābūyā);[150]

(5) that the human nature of the saint loses all individuation[151] (God imprints Himself upon it, according to Ibn Bābūyā);

(6) that all of the saint's words are God's: he becomes only an intervening hand [acting for God];

(7) that God describes Himself to Himself *ab aeterno;* this suggests the idea of the world being co-eternal with God;[152]

(8) that God actually descends to earth every night to speak with His saints.[153]

3. By Later Sunnite Mystics.

The school of Ibn 'Arabī criticized Ḥallāj on the following grounds:

a) He ought not have taught publicly the "primacy of the saints over the prophets"; Ghazzālī denied it, Ibn 'Arabī was evasive;[154]

b) He diminished the eminent dignity of the Prophet Muhammad;[155]

(c) In his descriptions of the essential mystical union, he wrongly affirmed that there would always be a distinction[156] between the saintly soul and God[157] (cf. the criticism of *Anā'l-Ḥaqq* and of *Anā man ahwā,* and the changes made by this school in the line "*A anta* . . . " and "*Juhūdī* . . . ").[158]

In all of this Ibn 'Arabī is merely establishing for us the fact that Hallāj was not a monist like himself.

Sha'rāwī clearly indicated the difference between Ḥallāj, Kīlānī, and Ibn 'Arabī when he compared their definitions of the "mystical conversation" between the soul and God:[159] "Ibn 'Arabī says, 'My heart conversed with me (*ḥaddathanī*) about my Lord';[160] Kīlānī says, "My Lord conversed with me about my Lord'; and Ḥallāj says, "My Lord conversed with me about myself';[161] this is the highest degree."[162]

Ibn Kamalpāshā also underscored this difference in his *firaq dālla:*

> [the last two are] the *ḥulūlīya* and the *ittiḥādīya* whose theses conflict but whose positions are difficult to elucidate. The *ḥulūlīya* claim that the Holy Spirit "informs" (*ḥulūl*) their hearts when they arrive at the apogee of divine knowledge (*'irfān*) and of mental purification (*tajarrud*); and this thesis is attributed to al-Hụsayn Ibn Manṣūr Ḥallāj. And it is said that the *ittiḥādīya* claim that the inward consciousness [the subconscious] of the believer becomes identified with God when it reaches the apogee of its worship of God. . . .

b. General Criticisms of His Life and Rule

1. Total Abandonment and the Single Act.[163]

To seek a state of complete passivity, to put oneself in a state of pure receptivity in order to abandon oneself blindly to grace, means, for the individual, to fall into an absurd indecisiveness; from the social point of view, it gives the appearance of idleness. Shāfi'ī had already stated, at the time of Abū'l-'Atāhīya, "Ṣūfism is based on laziness."[164] This was also Ghazzālī's objection in the beginning.[165] Ibn al-Jawzī, repeating this same accusation after Abū Yūsuf al-Qazwīnī, accused Ḥallāj of having taught that a single act of renunciation freed one definitively from every religious and social obligation.[166]

2. Anarchical Individualism.

Ḥallāj was criticized for having gradually subordinated the outward and social structure of worship to inner criteria of an individual devotion proceeding by irregular and uncontrollable intuitions, even to the point of explicitly rejecting all natural and revealed laws, of inveterate disobedience, and of the total negation of all rules.[167] This was the objection of Ibn Bābūyā, Ibn Ḥazm, and Ibn al-Jawzī.[168] It was repeated frequently against the Sufis with regard to two particular points which should be dealt with separately.

3. Mental Stability.

The objection concerning mental stability is aimed at the "spiritual concert" sessions, *samā'*, oratorios at which the recitation either of Quranic texts or of secular poems induces an abnormal state of excitement, a more or less dubious ecstasy, in those present. Ḥallāj was very explicit:[169] "externally the *samā'* is a turbulence; internally it is an intimation (*'ibra*).[170] Whoever is able to grasp the allusion (divine, *ishāra*) has the right to seek the intimation in the *samā'*. But if one tries to imitate it without understanding, one brings the turbulence upon himself, one exposes himself to the test, one slackens the reins to a suggestion of delectation, one is like a man who kills himself by his own hand."

We have few testimonies concerning Ḥallāj's own ecstasies;[171] here is one account:[172] "I saw Shaykh Ḥusayn Ḥallāj go into an ecstasy listening to a *qāri'*. He was dancing, with his feet lifted from the ground, and reciting:

> *Whoever has been told a secret in confidence, and then tells it . . .*"

4. Chastity of the Eyes.

Ḥallāj was very strict about this;[173] he was flatly opposed to the penitential laxity of the Sufi Abū Hamza,[174] who advocated a morose delectation of the forbidden beauty of limpid faces (of novices) as a means of attrition, and to the profane platonism of the Ẓāhirite school.[175] His disciple, Wāsiṭī, following the example of Fatḥ Mawṣilī, that one must shun this kind of impure attraction, said: "he whom God seeks to debase, He leads toward this stench, this decay."[176]

It is unfortunately true that in Islamic[177] community life, among the Imāmis, because of an esoteric exegesis,[178] as well as among the Sunnis, due to their aesthetic idealism,[179] the chastity of the eyes was insufficiently safeguarded. This was true in particular in the Nuṣayrī and Druze[180] initiatory circles, and in the mystical circles of certain Sunnite orders.[181] Though Ḥallāj's poems are free of any carnal element,[182] there are some mystical poets who, although claiming spiritual kinship with him, developed the conventional symbolism of *tashbīb*,[183] evoking some provocative idol to inspire thoughts of divine love, celebrating first a carnal presence in the beauty of a young, appealing face.[184] This theme was developed in an unexpected setting, the Christian convent, *dayr,* symbol of divine holiness, of union with the divine Spirit. In chapter XV of his *Gulshan-i-Rāz,* the Persian Maḥmūd Shabistarī gives a detailed explanation of the *tersābetcheh.*[185] And it is exactly the same dangerous symbolism of the *shammās,* which was so dear to Abū'l-Ḥasan al-Shushtarī, the Andalusian Shādhilite:

Awake! See, the winey sun is risen,[186] *and its*
rays conquer the light of day.
This juice of the grape, racked and decanted from all
eternity,—ah! pass it to all, both young and old!
It has not submitted to the wine-press or the cask,—and
the glass of its goblet was not formed in the fire.
We have drunk of it in a Convent where only Ḥallāj did not
blush (to enter).[187]
Primordial and glorious is the covenant by which we were
chosen for this rapture,—from which one cannot fall.
But look! adorned with a collar of pearls, a gracious Deacon,—
trailing his robes with modest decorum.
His glance spirits them out of themselves: transported,—
captivated, divested of their freedom.
Already, once entering the convent, they had thrown down—
their staffs, resolved to remain there.
In the same way Moses threw down his staff[188]*—then drew*
back, fearful, considering flight.
They have thrown away their riches,—far away, and chosen poverty.
They were obliged to give up their wealth,—as Moses was to
ask to be compelled.[189]
Shustarī's words, full of fire in their mouths,—far
removed from them, express only bitterness.

The deacon is God, the *"shābb muwaqqar"* of the *ḥadīth* about Muḥammad's nocturnal ascent, as related by Ḥammād ibn Salama Na'īm ibn Ḥammād,[190] and not a silhouette drawn by some adolescent. But the use of this symbol, intended for raising the soul from carnal desire to divine love, holds the possibility of arriving at the opposite result and scandalizing the laity, who are not entirely mistaken.[191]

c. General Criticisms of His Mysticism

Here we must briefly recount the theoretical and philosophical consequences attributed to mysticism in general and the Ḥallājian mysticism in particular:

(1) Concerning the notion of God: the expressions used by the mystic to

describe the real presence of God in the sanctified soul[192] result in attributing to the Uncreated Being a certain assimilatable, perceptible, and material composition *(anthropomorphism)*.[193] On the other hand, the constant mention of supernatural interventions "illuminating" the soul in order to transform it lead one to imagine symbols inaccessible to reason *(illuminism)*.[194] Between these two extremes, of inadequate, perceptible images and mysterious abstract definitions, the mystic limites himself to telling us about a material apprehension, a divine "taste," which he enjoys and which is absolutely unintelligible and ineffable to others *(agnosticism)*.[195] These three objections have alredy been examined separately.

(2) Concerning human reason: mystics like to oppose the "two aspects" of things, the outer appearance and the inner reality. This can lead to the doctrine of *two truths* which are antithetical and hostile, with *word* being the opposite of idea,[196] and *dogma* being contrary to religion.[197] It can also lead to a syncretistic universalism,[198] accepting the *identity of opposites*[199] and leading to the *annihilation* of the thought process in the impersonality of pure idea.[200]

The notes indicate passages from Ḥallāj's works which might give rise to these objections.

In closing, I must respond to a question concerning method. Why did I not attempt to explain the originality of this physiognomy by bringing to light certain incidents from his biography, by introducing, relative to the formation of his doctrine, certain civilizing influences foreign to Islam? An *Iranian* influence, for example, since Ḥallāj, as the son of a converted Mazdaean, accepted invitations from Mazdaeans;[201] or a *Hellenistic* influence, because he had studied the technical lexicon of the philosophers and gnostics;[202] or *Hindu,* since he had supposedly gone to seek instruction from Indian idolaters;[203] or *Syro-Chaldean,* because he lived near a Christian settlement in Jerusalem[204] and a Mandean community in Wāsiṭ.[205] It would undoubtedly be easy to construct lists of items like this, portraying Ḥallāj variously as a Persian nationalist conspirator, a Qarmathian hermetist,[206] a Hindu yogi,[207] or an unavowed Christian,[208] just as he was accused, at different times during his lifetime, of being a Sunni, a Mu'tazilite, or an Imāmi.[209] The thoughtful reader will realize why common sense[210] advised against such mental exercises, which, though certainly ingenious, are nevertheless sterile.

The first Muslim mystics found their personal vocations at the very heart of Islam in a fervent, experimental meditation on the scriptural material contained in the Quran; Ḥallāj was no exception to this rule.[211]

One might add at most that this meditation led him to go farther than his teachers into scriptural exegesis, which was as much at odds with the legalistic literalism of the Jewish Talmudists as it was consonant with the anagogical spiritualism of Christian mystics. Recalling in this connection Ibn 'Uyayna's maxim that "those among our legal doctors *('ulamā')* who have gone wrong have ended up resembling the Jews, and those of our ascetics *('ubbād)* who have gone wrong became like the Christians," Badr al-Dīn al-'Aynī adds,[212] "this is how Ḥallāj came to be accused of *ḥulūl* and *ittiḥād.*"

NOTES

(See page xi for list of abbreviations of journal titles)

1. Massignon, *La Passion de Husayn Ibn Mansūr Hallaj,* III, p. 44 [second French edition, Paris, 1975].
2. See collections of *sunan* enumerated by the *Fihrist,* in particular that of Ibn Abī Dhayb, 159/775 (Ibn Nadīm, *Fihrist* [1st. ed., Flügel, 1871], pp. 225–31): *"salāl lahāra, ṣawm, zakāt, manāsik."*
3. "Islam consists in being of a naturally upright character," corrected 'Ikrima, thus leaning toward mu'tazilism (Ibn al-Jawzī, Paris ms., 2030, s.v.). Cf. Bukhārī, *Riqāl,* IV, p. 72 ff.
4. Nasafī, *Bayān al-madhāhib, in fine.*
5. Ḥasan's *Farīdat* enumerate four of the *farā'id:* with nine rules for thought, thirteen for social practices, and twenty-seven for the personal virtues; Ḥasan himself enumerates eight social functions: fasting, prayer, pilgrimage, spiritual retreat, alms giving, holy war, barter, and arbitration *'adl wa ṣarf:* Ibn al-Jawzī says that it is *farīda wa nāfila;* (*Talbīs* [Cairo, 1923], p. 106), along the same lines (Ibn Baṭṭa 'Ukbarî, *Sharḥ wa Ibāna, in fine.* Cf. Ibn Qutayba, *Mukhtalif,* p. 58; al-Baghdādī, *Farq* [Cairo, 1328], p. 201).
6. Creed in seventeen articles (Malatī, *Tanbīh* [see *La Passion,* IV, p. 127], pp. 28–29).
7. Obligatory feature of the *mash 'alā'l-khuffayn,* etc. (Malatī, *Tanbīh,* pp. 368, 374, 383).
8. The Druzes, whose immediate predecessors, the Bāṭinīya, branched off from the common trunk before this period, still keep seven *farā'id:* the five classic duties, plus *ridā' taslīm.* [For the main body of the] Shî'ites: five plus *walāya, imāma.*
9. Abū Ḥanīfa has another heterogeneous list of *eleven* social duties. Shāfi'ī's system, quite formal in the choice of the five *farā'id,* nevertheless gives more emphasis to the importance of the "intentions" of the "consciences" in the study of rites than that of Abū Ḥanīfa.
10. Eliminating from the cult, in spite of Mālik, the imitation of the acts of the Prophet which were only *qurba* and *adab* (Qāsimī, *Maymū' [Damascus, n.d.], p. 58).*
11. Consequently they are apt to practice, out of tutiorism, the *talfīq,* of "mixing of the rites," which is what Ghazzālī (Māzarī) and Sha'rāwī were later reproached for.
12. *La Passion,* III, 240–42.
13. *Ibid.,* III, pp. 242–43.
14. *Ibid.,* 587; III, pp. 162–63.

15. *Ibid.,* III, p. 44.
16. It is God who designates the *aḥkām,* who in turn judges one thing good and another forbidden.
17. Cf. the search for the *afdat* (Ibn Hazm, III, 164). Cf. Baghdadī, *Farq* (Cairo, 1328), p. 285 (Abū Bakr). And *La Passion,* III, pp. 194–95.
18. Cf. the Mu'tazilite search for the *aḥsan* (*taḥsīn, La Passion,* III, p. 70).
19. Cf. the Mu'tazilite search for the *aṣlaḥ* (Ibn Ḥazm, *al-Fisal fi'l-Milal* (Cairo, 1317), III, pp. 165, 171, 181).
20. Idea of the Community: *"ṣalah al-kull"* (in Qur'ān 24:54), but without *irjā'* (cf. *La Passion,* III, p. 159). The true, invisible *jamā'a* of upright souls (*ahl al-infirād, Ibid.,* III, p. 72.
21. The mystics, and Ḥallāj in particular, are tutiorists (cf. *Ibid.,* I, p. 104); cf. *Kalābādhī:* "for the points discussed among jurists, the mystics adopt *al-ahwat:* by extension, if the lawfulness or unlawfulness of a thing is discussed, they choose the unlawful aspect" (*Ta'arruf,* Oxford ms., f. 63*b*).
22. Maqdisī explicitly draws this principle (*Ṣafwa,* 36) from a *ḥadīth,* applied in al-Hallāj, *Tawasīn* (Paris, 1913), VI. Misrī orders one of his disciples *not* to say his prayer ('Aṭṭār, *Tadhkirat,* French transl. by Pavet [Paris, 1890], p. 109). Hermits are excused from going to the mosque on Fridays.
23. Antākī, after Baqlī (see *La Passion,* IV, pp. 30, 64), I, 78; Wāsīlī, after Baqlī. I, 244, 245; entire; *'ināya azalīya* prime *tā'a* Sha'rāwī, *Ṭabaqāt* [Cairo, 1305], I. p. 98; cf. here, 784, n.2).
24. Already, "the Sunna rescinds the Qur'ān" (Shāfi'ī, against Ibn Ḥanbal).
25. Cf. *La Passion,* III, 169. The Shāfi'ite method is more favorable to this than the Ḥanafite: *intention,* in Ḥanafism, merely means "premeditation of the ritual act," and in Shāfi'ism, "moral orientation of the will." Cf. *wajh.*
26. *Ibid.,* III, 195.
27. *Dawā';* cf. Sarrāj, *Luma'* (Leiden-London, 1914), 424.
28. *La Passion,* III, 69; cf. *Tawasīn,* 187, maxim by Abū 'Alī al-Kātib (corr. according to Goldziher, *Der Islam,* IV, 167).
29. Ghazzālī, *Iḥy'* (Cairo, 1312), IV, 118; Makkī, *Qūt* (Cairo, 1310), II, 213 ff.
30. *La Passion,* III, 219.
31. Or, according to the customary formula, "The rich man who gives thanks is superior to the poor man who gives up." Cf. *Ibid.,* I, 13. This thesis was upheld by only twenty or so mystics and theologians: Karrāmīya Mutarrif, Ibn Abī'l-Huwwārī, Muḥāsibī, Ibn Karrām, Ibn Mu'ādh, Ibn Qutayba, Tirmidhī, Ibn 'Aṭā', Ruwaym, Ibn Sam'ūn, Daqqāq, Ibn Abī'l-Khayr, and more recently by Shādhilī and Mursī, whereas the opposing thesis received the support of the majority of the doctors (Abū Dharr, Ḥasan, Sa'īd-Ibn-Musayyib, Shaqīq, Ma'rūf, Bishr, Bisṭāmī, Junayd, Ibrāhīm Khawwāṣ, Ibn Sālim, Sāmarrī, Ibn Khafīf, Sulamī, Sarrāj, 'Abd al-Qāhir Baghdādī, A. N. Suhrawardī *Faḍā'il* (ms *waqf must. eff.* 463, appendix); and more recently, 'Izz Maqdisī, and Ibn Daqīq al-'Id. See *Qūt.,* 208–11; *Fihrist,* 185: Sarrāj, *Luma',* 411; Hujwīrī, *Kashf* (see *La Passion,* IV, 62), 22, 25, etc.; Suhrawardī, *'Awārif* (Cairo, 1312), IV, 257; Subkī, *Ṭabaqāt ash-Shāfi'īya* (Cairo 1323–4), III, 239; Jāmī, *Nahafat* (Calcutta, 1859), 43, 89, 478, 479; Burhānī; *zuhra, passim;* Sha'rāwī, *Ṭabaqāt* (Cairo, 1305), I, 75. In support, Ḥallāj notes that "the heart is more hardened in comfort than in adversity" (in Qur'ān 39: 22; cf. Tustarī, *Tafsīr* [Cairo, 1326], 25–26).
32. *La Passion,* III, 69; and *Tawasīn,* 156.
33. *La Passion,* III, 118; and Qushayrī, *Risāla* (ed. Anṣārī), II, 124.

34. Cf. "Imamites et rites ismaëliens" (Ibn Ḥammād, transl. Cherbonneau, *Journal Asiatique [Paris, 1855])*.
35. See also Sha'rāwī *('Uhūd wa mawāthīq),* Haskafī, and the attacks by the jurists at Constantinople in the seventeenth century (against Sīwāsī) and at Cairo in the nineteenth century (against Sanūsī).
36. *La Passion,* I, 143–45, 555.
37. *Ibid.,* I, 743–44.
38. *Ibid.,* I, 620.
39. Shiblī cut them (Sarrāj, *Luma'* (London, 1914), 148); cf., in contrast, the calenders.
40. *La Passion,* I, 104.
41. *Manār,* Vol. XXII, 63; the formula is Ibn Adham's (*Iḥyā'* [Cairo, 1312], I, 233).
42. Recommended by Ibn Abī'l-Dunyā (*Manār,* l.c.). *La Passion,* I, pp. 555–56.
43. Note that the proposition on I, 587 ff., omits, as do the Ḥanafites, the 4th *rukn (sa'ī),* and that it specifies only seven of the thirty-one specific points of the Ḥanbalites (without the 4 *arkān,* 5 *wājibāt,* and 15 *sunan*). Cf. Kilānī, *Ghunya* (Cairo, 1288), p. 11.
44. *La Passion,* I, p. 149.
45. The beginnings of Ḥallāj's theory on the transference of pilgrimage (*Ibid.,* I, p. 587 ff.).
46. *Ibid.,* I, p. 149.
47. *Ibid.,* I, p. 149.
48. *Ibid.,* I, pp. 104, 159, 329, 620, 649–50 (cf. prayer of the Prophet on *yawm al-Ahzāb,* according to Muzanī (Subkī, *Ṭabaqāt* [Cairo, 1323–24], p. 242).
49. *Radd.*
50. *Taslīm.* Ibn Abī Zayd, transl. of Fagnan, p. 38. Tirmidhī, *'Ilal;* prostration atoning for possible omisison.
51. *"Biḥaqq."* Attenuated formulas: Shiblī (Khark., f. 215a), Daqqā (Qushayrī, *Risāla* [Cairo, 1390], 173). Nusayris: *biḥaqq hādhidhi quddās al-bukhūr* . . . (incense of Mary in the Temple).
52. *"An turziqanī"* (Ghazzālī, *Iḥyā',* (Cairo, 1312), I, p. 216).
53. Cf. *La Passion,* III, 215. Contra: Shiblī *(l.c.)* and Ibn Abī Zayd (*l.c.,* 36–37).
54. A custom disapproved of apart from the Khuṭba.
55. *La passion,* III, p. 221.
56. Sulamī, *Jawāmi' Adāb al-Ṣūfiya* (see *GAL,* I, 200); Maqdisī, *Ṣafwat al-Taṣawwuf.*
57. Var.: *inkār, taḥrīm al-makāsib.*
58. Established by Shaqīq (Makkī, *Qūt* (Cairo, 1310), II, p. 295), Abū'l-'Atāhīya (according to Sūlī), the Karrāmīya and the Ṣūfīs of Baghdad; rejected by Muḥāsibī, the Sālimīya and Malāmatīya. Cf. *La Passion,* III, p. 122.
59. The allusion here (I, p. 202) is so clear that Maqdisī's etymology, attributing it to a *shaykh* from Jerusalem, a native of Tarsus, seems false. In reality, the matter of the Tarsus lands, which, having been conquered without capitulation, had been allotted as fiefs instead of being given to the Community (under al-Mahdī: see Antākī, *Shubuhāt*), is possibly the source of this name. Mention could be made here of the mystical transference of an illness, from Junayd to certain of Nūrī's disciples ('Aṭṭār, *Tadhkirat,* French transl. by Pavet [Paris, 1890], p. 205); cf. 'Ulwān, *Jawhar Mahbūk* (Damascus, 1329), p. 76.
60. Maqdisī, *Taflīs* (Cairo, 1324), pp. 59, 70.
61. *La Passion,* I, p. 564, and Maqdisī, *Taflīs* (Cairo, 1324), p. 68.
62. *Ibid.,* p. 72; *La Passion,* I, p. 563.
63. Maqdisī, *Taflīs,* p. 50.

64. Arnold, *India*. Ibn al-Jawzī, *Nāmūs*.
65. *La Passion,* I, p. 332.
66. Paris, 1st ed., p. 313.
67. *La Passion,* I, p. 650.
68. *La Passion,* III, p. 177. Special *risāla* by Ibn Ṭāhir Maqdisī, and text by Sulamī (quoted ap.Ibn al-Jawzī, *Nāmūs,* XI).
69. *La Passion,* I, p. 342. Begun, very informally, by Ibn Mu'ādh, Miṣrī, and Abū Ḥamza, then Junayd (Makkī, *Qūt* (Cairo, 1310), I, p. 166).
70. *La Passion,* I, p. 337. To twist the true meanings of words.
71. After Sulamī on Qur'ān, 49:3. It is a direct imitation of the *ḥadīth* of Jesus (Asin Palacios, *Logiae agrapha Domini Jesu* [Paris, 1919–1926], no. 44), reproduced in the *risāla* said to be by Ḥasan Baṣrī: "My patience is hunger, my sign, fear [of God]; my garment, the *ṣūf;* my mount, my leg; my candle at night is the moon; in winter my fire-lighter is the sunrise; my fruit and my perfume are what the earth sends forth for the wild beasts and the tamed animals. Born with nothing to call my own, my wealth exceeds all riches" (Isfahanī, *Hilya* [Cairo, 1932–8], s.v.). Cf. Ibn Karrām's rule (in my *Essai sur les origines du lexique technique de la mystique musulmane* [Paris, 1954], p. 260, no. 5) and that of Tustarī (*Tafsīr* [Cairo, 1326], p. 61). Y. Hamadhānī, P. ms. sp. 1851, f. 44a.
72. Baqlī, *Tafsīr* (Cawnpore, 1883), I, pp. 105–6 (of Qur'ān, 3:89) and II, p. 57 (of 22:27); Ibn 'Arabī, *Musāmarāt* (Cairo, 1282), I, pp. 186–87, 358; Hujwīrī, *Kashf* (see *La Passion,* IV, p. 62), 326, 329; 'Ulwān (died 936/1531), *Jawhar Mahbūk* (Damascus, 1329), p. 58.
73. *1261 = ms. Köpr. 1589 §XXIX.*
74. Cf. my *Essai* (Paris, 1954), p. 88, and Shabistarī, *Gulshan-i-rāz*.
75. Origin: Miṣrī, *La Passion,* III, p. 49.
76. *Ibid.,* III, p. 26.
77. *Tawasīn* (Paris, 1913), IV, p. 5.
78. *La Passion,* III, p. 59. Cf. *ḥadīth al-farāsh* by Ghazzālī (*Iḥyā'* [Cairo, 1312], ap. Murtadā, *Ithāf* (Cairo, n.d.), IX, p. 94; cf. Asin, *Tehafut,* pp. 191–94).
79. *La Passion,* III, p. 79.
80. *Ibid.,* III, pp. 102–3.
81. Ḥallāj, on Qur'ān 36: 61; Wāsiṭī, in Baqlī, *Tafsīr* (Cawnpore, 1883), II, P. 173.
82. Malatī *Tanbīh* (see *La Passion,* IV, p. 127), p. 35.
83. *La Passion,* III, pp. 207–8.
84. 160 -*a.* 241-*a.*
85. *La Passion,* I, p. 594 ff.
86. Especially Hanbalites (al-Baghdadī, *Farq,* [Cairo, 1328], p. 133) and Ẓāhirites (Ibn Ḥazm, *al-Fisal* [Cairo, 1317], III, pp. 229, 236, 247).
87. *La Passion,* I, p. 104; II, p. 50; III, pp. 182, 201.
88. Or to be transformed. Wāsiṭī, for his part, exaggerates and leans toward Qarmathianism: *al-tā'āt fawāhish: al-wasā'īl 'ilal al-du'f* (Baqlī, *Tafsīr* [Cawnpore, 1883] I, p. 114; II, p. 127).
89. *La Passion,* I, p. 587 ff.; which becomes a vow of immolation.
90. *Ibid.,* I, pp. 556, 562; which becomes a vow of abstinence.
91. *Ibid.,* I, p. 594 ff.; which becomes a vow of poverty (*faqr*).
92. *Ibid.,* III, p. 201; which becomes a vow of obedience (*khidma*).
93. Which becomes a thanksgiving.
94. "*Lā ilāha*" is the vocalization preferred by Sibawayh (semi-Mu'tazilite school of Baṣra); "lā ilāhu" by the school of Kūfa.

95. Syn. *kalimat al-tawḥīd.* The first member is called "negation" (*nafy*) and the second "affirmation" (*ithbāt*). *La Passion,* III, pp. 99–100.
96. Qur'ān 48:21—Cf. Maritain, *Sept leçons sur l'être* (Paris, 1933), p. 107. The *shahāda* applies the principle of identity to God.
97. Shahrastānī, *Kitab al-Milal* (Cairo, 1317), I, p. 171.
98. *La Passion,* III, pp. 207–8; cf. Ibn 'Asākir, *Sabab al-zuhāda fī'l-shahāda,* ap. Shiblī, *Akām,* 21.
99. Shahrastānī, *Kitab al-Milal* (Cairo, 1317), I, p. 88.
100. Asin Palacios, *Logiae agrapha Domini Jesu* (Paris, 1919–1926), no. 17.
101. With an ellipsis; they construct: *lā ilāha fī'l-wujūd, ghayr Allāh,* "there is no divinity *in reality other than God*" (Rāzī, § I, II, III). In this way one deduces the existence of God from the non-existence of the idols (*mughāyara*). In Greek: οὐκ ἔστιν θεὸς, εἰ μη ὁ θεὸς μόνος. In Turkish: *yuqdur labajak, lehëlëpder anjeq.*
102. A virtual hypothesis is not deniable *a priori:* one can only deny an actual thesis.
103. IV, p. 73 (*riqāq*).
104. *La Passion,* III, p. 65. I cite the X paragraphs by Fakhr Rāzī (*asrār al-tanzīl*) and the study by Jāmī after Rāghib pāshā (*Safīna* [Cairo, 1282], 7–13, 653–56).
105. Fakhr Rāzī's response to the first grammarians (*l.c.,* § 1).
106. Cf. *La Passion,* III, pp. 99–100; the *ḥukm* is contemplated before the *maḥkūm bihi.*
107. Jāmī, after Rāghib, *l.c.,* p. 654.
108. And complete: where the first member (*ilāha*) was *khabar* (attribute), and the second (*allāhu*) was *mubtadā* (subject).
109. The Mu'tazilite tendency is to consider things only insofar as they are thinkable, virtually, not realizable in actual fact: theoretical according to the intellect, but not according to the heart (*La Passion,* III, pp. 189–90).
110. Rāzī (§ VII) cites this opinion.
111. Rāghib, *l.c.,* p. 656.
112. Contrary to the early grammarians; ex.: *lā nikāḥ, illā bi walī: lā 'izz, illā bi'l-mat,* etc. Cf. Bergsträsser, *Die Negationen im Kur'ān* (1911), p. 56.
113. "*lā ilāha mumkin, illā' llāh mawjūd*" (rejected by Jāmī, *l.c.,* p. 653). Cf. Ibn al-Layth's argument against the *Surayjīya* (*La Passion,* III, p. 101, n. 2); the categorical takes precedence over the conditional (*mu'allaq*). Contra *La Passion,* III, p. 195, n.9.
114. *Ibid.,* III, pp. 143, 155.
115. Cf. the Cartesian quasi-proof of the existence of God. Contrary to Bukhārī and Muslim, and especially to the Ḥanbalites, for whom any recitation of the *shahāda* is uncreated, because it is a Qur'ānic verse.
116. Contrary to the Ja'far and to the Sālimiya (*La Passion,* III, pp. 45–46, 47).
117. Abd al-Wāḥid Ibn Zayd's thesis (Ibn 'Arabī, *Musāmarāt* (Cairo, 1282), II, 354), disregarded by Dārānī (Baqlī, *Tafsīr,* I, 74), introduced by Miṣrī (add to *Allāh,* in the ordinary shāhada, *al-ḥaqq al-mubīn:* according to Dhahabī, *I'tidāl*), strictly upheld by Bisṭāmī, Nūrī, Shiblī (Ibn al-Jawzī, *Nāmūs* XI: cf. *Essai* [Paris, 1954], p. 285, n. 5) and Ibn 'Aṭā' (Baqlī, I, 73, 52, and 73 comp. to 52). Cf. proverb about YS, *La Passion,* I, p. 322 (KN = YS = 70).
118. Cf. *Ibid.,* III, p. 50, line 14.
119. "Deny yourself and then affirm the existence of God, that is the meaning of the *shahāda*!" says Ibn Abī'l-Khayr, a little too succinctly (54th quatrain of the Ethé edition).
120. *Akhbār al-Hallāj* (Paris, 1957), nos. 41, 57, 62; and *La Passion,* III, p. 55; cf. *Tawasīn* (Paris, 1913), XI, 18.
121. The Sālimīya; a thesis for which Ibn 'Arabī will find attenuating circumstances: al-

though "God exists in His divinity before any *shahāda* is created to testify to it, and although this continuance affirms Him sufficiently and although the testimony of His creatures certifies Him very imperfectly, since they can also deny Him, it is still good to repeat this formula, simply, as a kind of recitation, to obtain the promised recompense from God." (Sha'rāwī, *Yawāgīt* [Cairo, 1889], p. 12).

122. Texts cited in *La Passion,* III, pp. 155–56. Cf. Tustarī and Naṣr Kharrāt (Qushayrī, *Risāla* [Cairo, 1290], IV, 183–84).
123. *Manāzil al-sā'irīn, in fine.*
124. Which Ibn Khaldūn does not dare to judge (transl. of Slane [Paris, 1843], III, p. 106; cf. Rāghib pāshā, *Safīna* [Cairo, 1282], p. 403). Wāsiṭī outlines the question thus: "He who worships God for his own ends, worships himself; he who worships Him to obtain the reward which is his goal (*ajal*) has not understood Who his Lord is; but he who worships Him knowing that [true] worship is an immaterial substance, in which the divine omnipotence radiates, has found the right way" (Baqlī, *Tafsīr* [Cawnpore, 1883], II, 173; on Qur'an 37:11). "To say the *shahāda* routinely is the way of an idiot; to say it obligingly separates one from God; to say it out of conviction in one's own intellectual purity is the act of a participator, for one relies on oneself for a fact [which is beyond our powers]; but to say it *really,* is to have renounced [by a vow] all individually created attestation" (*Ibid.,* II, p. 256; on 47:21), *shawāhid* (cf. *La Passion,* III, p. 34).
125. "*Unique* God."
126. Hermetists.
127. Where the first member (*ilāha*) is the subject (*mubtadā*), and the second (*Allāha*) is the attribute (*khabar*).
128. *Wahdat al-wujūd,* "monism of existence"; from the virtual being of the possible (*thubūt*) to the existence of conceptual meaning (*wujūd mutlaq*) and to the existence of individual realities (*wujūd mu'īn*), the gradation becomes less and less perceptible, from Ibn 'Arabī to Sadr Rūmī and to Balabānī; the monist tendency is to view things only in so far as they are realizable, in actual fact: according to the heart (Alūsī, *Jalā* [Cairo, 1298], p. 57 ff.).
129. A conversion which Rāzī had already judged impious (*l.c.,* p. 9, 1. 5). Cf. Eckhart, ap. Denzinger, p. 555).
130. *La Passion,* III, p. 47.
131. Alūsī, *Jalā* (Cairo, 1298), 48. Cf. the polemic begun in the sixteenth century by the monist mystic Kharrūbī (died 963/1556; a pupil of Zarrūq and commentator of Sulamī), author of the *risāla dhī'l-iflās ilā Khawāṣṣ madīnat Fās:* against Yastitni, who took up the thesis of the first grammarians (*La Passion,* III, p. 245), and Flabtī, author of the *Kitāb al-ishāda bi ma'rifa madlūl kalimat al-shahāda* (ms. Paris 5296, f. 60b, ff.) (Ibn 'Askar, *Dawhat,* transl. Graulle, ap. *Arch. Maroc,* XIX, 25, 31; Bencheneb, ap. *Actes XIVe Congrès Orient.,* Algiers, 1905, nos. 21, 23, 314; Salāwī, *Istiqsā',* III, 12–13).
132. *La Passion,* III, p. 212, n. 6.
133. No man has *really* prayed (Sulamī [see *La Passion,* IV, p. 19], 79).
134. Already quoted in *La Passion,* III, p. 116. Cf. Muḥāsibī, *maḥabba;* Tirmidhī, ap. Jāmī, *Nahafāt* (Calcutta, 1859), 132.
135. *La Passion,* III, p. 18.
136. *fawātih,* ms. *As'ad,* 1611, f. 74 *a.*
137. *La Passion,* III, p. 15. Miskawayh, *fawz asghar,* 106–107 (= *'aql*): Ghazzālī, *Mishkāt* (Cairo, 1322), 55; Ibn al-Qayīm, *Madārij* (Cairo, 1332), II, p. 170 (= *nabī*); Gairdner, ap. *Der Islam.*
138. Sentence preserved by al-'Aynī (*'Iqd*). Cf. *La Passion,* III, p. 52.

139. *Ibid.*, III, p. 34.
140. *Ibid.*, III, pp. 157–58.
141. *Ibid.*, I, p. 374.
142. *160, 179.*
143. *Tabsīrat al-'awāmm* (Tehran, 1895), pp. 400–402.
144. Ibn Bābūya adds: alchemy.
145. Ibn Hajar, *Lisān al-Mīzān* (Hayderabad, 1329–1331), 373; "rope trick"; escape boat.
146. See *Fihrist,* 310. Ibn Mundhir Harawī, summoned and consulted at Wāsiṭ in the year 83/702 by Ḥajjāj (Sérrier, *Ḥajjāj,* pp. 210–11; Yāqūt, *Irshād* (ed. Margoliouth), IV, p. 885), *'ajā'ib,* ap. Shiblī, *Akām,* 101–102; and Aghānī, s.v. "*Sāhib Iblīs*"; cf. *ZDMG,* XX, p. 487.
147. A Kaysānite (one of the five first partisans according to Fadhl-b-Shadhān, according to Jazaīrī, *hâw. al-aqwāl, London ms. 8688,* f. 224*a*) won over to Zayn al-'Abidīn (Shūshtarī, *Majālis, Paris ms., Pers. supp 190,* f. 102 *b*); under name of Kankar (= Wardān) he became the third Bāb of the Nusayrīs (Bākūra, 13). In fact, a *zujāra* by Kābilī (Tabarānī, *Majmū 'al-A'yād,* f. 134 *a*) is drafted like a prayer by Ḥallāj.
148. Cf. the Sādiqūja, Hindu Satanists of the sixteenth century, who invoked Musaylima (Fānī, *Dābistān* (London, 1894), III, p. 8; cf. *Fihrist,* 311).
149. *ma'rifa asmā' Allāh al-'uzmā, tajallī bi'l-'ibāda* (Ibn Bābūya).
150. *La Passion,* III, pp. 220–21.
151. *Ibid.*, III, p. 54.
152. *Ibid.*, III, p. 144.
153. A *ḥadīth* whose supporters were excommunicated by the *imām* 'Alī Ridā (Tabarsī, *Ihtijāj* [Tehran, 1302], 208). *Riw.* XXII (see *La Passion,* IV, p. 140).
154. *La Passion,* III, p. 221, Ghazzālī, *ladunīya,* p. 29. Shā'rāwī, *Yawāqīt* (Cairo, 1889), p. 237.
155. *La Passion,* II, pp. 347, 418. He calls it ṣāḥibuka-*ṣāḥibukum.* Cf. Qur'ān, as did Kindī.
156. *La Passion,* III, p. 55. Cf. Shams Tabrīzī ('Aflākī, transl. by Huart [*Les saints des derviches tourneurs,* Paris, 1918], II, p. 67).
157. Without either *Krypsis* or *Kenosis,* as one would say in Christian parlance. *"Anā sirr al-Ḥaqq, mā al-Ḥaqq anā"—"Ra'ayter Rabbī bi 'ayn Rabbī"; La Passion,* III, p. 318, n. 7).
158. *Tawasīn,* 140, 183–84; Jāmī, *Nafahāt* (Calcutta, 1859), 568; *ms. As'ad, 3559;* ms. Wien, III, p. 508, no. 4, f. 11 *b*, 13 *a*. Janadī: "*man Adam fi'l-kawn wa man Iblīs?*" *La Passion,* III, p. 327, "*huwiyatī 'anka fī lāhūtiyatī abdā*" (*Ibid.*, III, p. 55, n. 4). Quatrain by Rūmī criticizing "*Anā man ahwā,*" Transl. ap. Goldziher, *Vorlesungen,* French transl. (Paris, 1920), p. 127; Rūmī criticizing "*rūḥān*" (Nicholson, *Studies in Islamic Mysticism* [Cambridge, 1921]).
159. Cf. Ibn Ṣab'īn.
160. Formula already criticized by Ibn 'Aqīl (Ibn al-Jawzī, *Talbīs* [Cairo, 1923], p. 401). Comment by Shiblī (*Manṭiq*) criticizing the *isnād* of the *muḥaddithūn.*
161. Cf. *La Passion,* III, p. 50, the last line: How could I have called upon Thee "it is Thou" (Qur'ān 1:4), if Thou had not said to me "it is I"? And II, pp. 55, 184, n. 3.
162. Sha'rāwī, *jawāhir wa durar (wustā),* ms. *Watī al-Dīn, majm. 1684,* f. 357 *b*. Note that Ibn 'Arabī, contrary to Ibn Mu'ādh, Ibn Sīnā, and Ghazzālī, declares that the expression "*man 'arafa nafsahu . . .*" (Cf. *La Passion,* III, p. 46, n. 5) is true only after perception and permanent knowledge of the external world (Ibn 'Arabī, *Fuṣūṣ [Istanbul, 1309], 106, 264; cf. in contrast Ḥallāj, Tawasīn,* XI, pp. 4, 8, 18).
163. Cf. Hügel, *The Mystical Element of Religion* (London, 1908), II, pp. 141–46, 166. *Contra, La Passion,* III, pp. 126, 131, 167.

164. Ibn al-Jawzī, *Nāmūs* (Cairo, 1923), XI.
165. *La Passion,* II, p. 180.
166. *Ibid.,* I, p. 592 ff. In reality, Ḥallāj (on Qur'ān 12:67) follows Hasan's doctrine "cessation of the motive of the act (as an end in itself), and not cessation of the act" (ap. *Dīwān* in Turkish, *ms. Zah., tas.* 161): "Renounce choosing, but use the middle term [offered by God]."
167. This is the accusation by Khuldī against Ḥallāj (*La Passion,* II, p. 107) cited by Qushayrī (*La Passion,* I, p. 155; cf. II, p. 362): the reason for his break with Tustarī is not known; he did not break off completely with Junayd (his *tawaqquf;* cf. *Ibid.,* I, p. 110), but only with 'Amr Makkī (*Ibid.,* I, pp. 155–57). Wāsiṭī is more open to criticism (*Ibid.,* III, p. 244, n. 6).
168. Such is, in effect, the monist interpretation given to a maxim of Ḥallāj (*Ibid.,* III, p. 89, 1. 17–18) by Sa'īd Kāzarūnī in his commentary on a letter from Ibn Abī'l-Khayr to Ibn Sīnā. But, in fact, Ḥallāj had said "when the heart reflects on God, God preserves the body from all sin" (Kirmānī, n. 7).
169. Ibn Yazdānyār; text taken up by Shiblī (Hujwīrī, *Kashf,* transl. by Nicholson [London, 1911], p. 404). 'Amr Makkī had indicated, less plainly: that licitness depended on the anteriority of the *ishāra* (Amedroz, "Notes," *JRAS* [1912], p. 562, n. 1).
170. *La Passion,* III, p. 28.
171. *Ibid.,* I, p. 332.
172. Taken from Ibn al-Sā'ī.
173. *La Passion,* I, p. 97; cf. Thawrī: "the ordinary glance is sin" (ap. Dūrī, *l.c., infra*).
174. Which resulted in the hostility of Ghulām Khalīl (*La Passion,* I, p. 432), whose sermons were a frontal attack against sodomy.
175. *Ibid.,* I, p. 408 ff. Cf. Mudrik Shaybānī (Sarrāj, *Masāri'* [Istanbul, 1301], p. 159, 341, 400).
176. Qushayrī, *Risāla* (Cairo, 1290), p. 217.
177. It must be noted here, concerning this indelicate subject whose seriousness for society is evident, a.) that the vice of Sodom, in spite of what Burton and Nabhānī have said, is not characteristic of either a climatic zone or a race; the Iranians and the Greeks, who have embellished it with philosophical rationalizations, are not the inventors of it; it exists in its crudest form among all peoples where the rulers have resorted to sexual coercion or ruse (*dabb*) in order to subdue their slaves, like animals, whether male or female, and have been punished in return with an extreme enslavement to the instruments of their vice; b.) that this vice has ancient roots in Arabia (satirical proverbs concerning various tribes, in Mas'ūdī, *murūj*), in particular at Hīra, masculine *tiwāb* (Labīd and Rabī) and feminine *sihāqa* (Hind and Zurqâ); some of the great poets like Ibn Burd, Abū Nuwās, and Ibn al-Rūmī complacently celebrated these shameful things without even taking pleasure in them (cf. a remark by Mubarrad concerning the character of Abū Nuwās; the inimitable, entirely Voltairian transparency of his style frequently becomes stained, in his unbiased descriptions of non-physical love, with a Satanism which is more than literary); c.) that faced with the growth of this vice in the third century of the Hijra some legists, feeling defenseless, thought to contain evil through illicit concessions: absolution, without legal sanction, of the *liwāt* of slaves and non-Muslims (*'iyāl,* mālik, according to *1070 a.,* p. 154 [Qathātī, *Kashf, London ms. Supp. 202,* p. 164 ff., accuses him only of abolishing the *kaffāra* (not the *qadā'*) for the culprit if the transgression occurs in Ramadan]; Abīwardī, in Subkī, *Tabaqāt* [Cairo, 1323], III, p. 18), and of *tafkhīdn* between Muslims (Thumāma, Abū Ghaffār, Ibn Karrām: according to Ibn Dā'ī, *Tabsirat* [Tehran, 1312], p. 381; Ibn Ḥazm, *al-Fisal* [Cairo, 1317], IV, p. 197); d.) and that it is to the credit of the Sunnite traditionists,

especially the mystics, that they led a frontal attack against this crime, making a direct appeal to people's consciences (Ḥasan Baṣrī, Thawrī, Ibn Ḥanbal, and Ghulām Khalīl, according to Haytham Dūrī, *dhamm al-luvāt, ms. Zah. Majm.* 9; Ibn al-Jawzī, *Mawdū'āt,* s.v.). Cf. *La Passion,* I, p. 404; III, p. 167.

178. *La Passion,* III, p. 177, n. 5; p. 209, n. 5.
179. The theory of Platonic love (criticized from its inception by Jāḥiẓ, *Mukhtārāt* [Cairo, 1323], II, p. 31) taught, as we have seen, by the Ẓāhirite juridical school, from Ibn Dāwūd to Ibn Ḥazm and to Ibn Ṭāhir Maqdisī, under the thesis of the *jawāz al-naẓar ilā'l-murd* (cf. *La Passion,* I, pp. 404–5), was upheld by several other theologians, mostly Ḥanafites, listed by Nābulusī in chapter IV of his *Ghāyat al-Matlūb* (alias: *makhraj al-mutlaqī*), which deals with the question *ex professo.*
180. Cf. *La Passion,* III, p. 177. Accusations against Zakarī by Bahrayn and Shalmaghānī.
181. Accusation formulated in the thirteenth to fifteenth centuries against the Rifā'īya-Ḥarīrīya, and Qalandarīya-Haydarīya (Jawbarī; Turkumānī, *Luma',* ms. Cairo, tas. 701; Bisṭāmī, *fawā'iḥ,* ms. 'Umūmī, tas. 416, XXVIII; cf. Leon the African, *Descrittione,* I, p. 43); and in the nineteenth century against the 'Ammārūya of Cairo; against the Rifā'īya Mutāwi'a by Sanūsī (*salsabīl*).
182. Only two, *Dalāl, yā ḥabībī* . . . (trans. *La Passion,* I, p. 525) and Qālū': *Jafayta* (*Ibid.,* III, p. 362) could be considered suspect; the first, for its style, and the second, because of an anecdote (not aimed at Ḥallāj) to which it is linked (Ibn 'Arabī, *Muhādarāt* [Cairo, 1282], II, p. 338).
183. Cf. Massignon, *Quatre Textes* (Paris, 1914), p. 27, n. 6.
184. Cf. *Revue du Monde Musulmane,* XXXVI, p. 41.
185. *Tersá-betché:* the "son of a Christian," the offered idol (cf. the analagous term, current among Western Satanists, alluded to in Huysmans, *Sainte Lydwine de Schicdam* [Paris, 1901], p. 369, bottom); for, according to the *ḥadīth,* the *atfāl al-mushrikīn* will be the servants of the believers in Paradise (Tabarāsī, *Awsāṭ,* ap. Muttaqī, *Kanz [Cairo, 1893], VI, p. 119).* From this there developed the controversy, in Ḥanbalite law, concerning the licitness of the *tiwāl* in Paradise (Abū 'Alī Ibn al-Walīd affirms it against Abū Yūsuf Qazwīnī, cf. Suyūṭī, *Nawādir,* f. 21 *a.* Paris ms. 3068). A classic question, which makes the Shāfi'ites indignant (Sharaf Anṣārī, *Munabidhat aimmat al-sunna* against the Sāsānīya corporations (Thorning, pp. 43, 51; cf. Snouck Hurgronje).
186. *Tanabbah, qad badal shamsu'l-*'uqār . . . Cf. also his *Ta'addab bi bāb al-Dayr* . . . , commented on by Nābulūsī.
187. Expression commented by Jīlī in his *Manāẓir.*
188. Qur'ān 20:67.
189. Qur'ān 20:69.
190. Dhahabī, *I'tidāl* (Cairo, 1324), s.v., no. 2079; Ibn Qutayba, *Mukhtalif* (Cairo, 1326), p. 8.
191. The theme of Shī'ite irony aimed at the Ḥanbalites, among whom this thesis is traditional (*ẓahr al-rabī'*).
192. *La Passion,* III, p. 58.
193. *Ibid.,* III, pp. 57, 147.
194. *Tajallī, Ibid.,* III, p. 142.
195. Cf. Kierkegaard "God is different from everything, radically." Cf. *Ibid.,* III, pp. 141, 147.
196. Thesis of the Nuṣayrīs and the Druzes. Cf. *La Passion,* III, p. 88, n. 3; p. 89, n. 8; p. 94, n. 6.
197. Ritschl. Cf. the dualism "*sharī'a ḥaqīqa,*" *Ibid.,* III, pp. 162–63, 201. Mazdaeans, Manichaeans.

198. Cf. two of Ḥallāj's maxims: "Every truth has its reality (*tikulli ḥaqq ḥaqīqa*), every creature his path, every contract its pledge" (*London ms. 888,* f. 325*a;* Baqlī, *Shathīyāt* [see *La Passion,* IV, 64–5], p. 123) which is taken from a *ḥadīth* (Tirmidhī, *riyāda;* Sarrāj, *Luma'* [London, 1914], 337) and from one of Thawrī's maxims: *likull 'abd sharita* . . . ; ap. Makkī, *Qūt* (Cairo, 1310), II, 57; "Every [prophetic] warning has a foundation, every [apostolic] vocation implies an illumination."
199. A Druze thesis, identifying *tawḥīd* and *talḥīd, wujūd* and 'adam (*Kitāb al-Nuqaṭ,* ed. Seybold [see *GAL,* I, 400], 43). A thesis of Ibn 'Arabī: the only mistake of the idolators is to have been selective about their idols; for since everything is the manifestation of God, everything is an idol for the perfect Monist.

> As regards the divinity, creatures have
> acknowledged various creeds,
> But the creed which I acknowledge is the total
> of all their creeds.

(Nābulūsī, *Sharḥ al-Tarīqat al-Muḥammadīya,* I, 169–70). Cf. *Essai* (Paris, 1954): Ibn Taymīya, *Radd . . . Ḥarīrīya.*

We have shown above (*La Passion,* III, p. 89) the true meaning of the propositions which could be interpreted, wrongly, in a Hegelian sense.

200. Druze thesis (*Ibid.,* III, pp. 89–90), acceptable to students of Hellenism (*Ibid.,* III, p. 86) and Junayd (*Ibid.,* I, p. 117), which Ḥallāj rejected in particular (*Ibid.,* III, p. 89).
201. *Ibid.,* I, pp. 48, 164, 333–34.
202. *Ibid.,* I, p. 188; III, pp. 14–15; cf. *Essai* (Paris, 1954), pp. 70–73, for the neo-Platonic hypothesis so much in favor at this time.
203. *La Passion,* I, p. 222 ff.
204. *Ibid.,* I, p. 162.
205. *Ibid.,* I, pp. 99, 159.
206. *Ibid.,* III, p. 266.
207. *Ibid.,* I, 222 ff.
208. *Ibid.,* I, p. 635 ff.; and *Essai* (Paris, 1954). He perhaps knew Stephanos (died 324), secretary to Muqtadîr (Sūlī, *Awrāq, Parks ms.* f. 96) and Bishr, secretary to Mufliḥ Aswad (*'Arīb* [see *GAL,* I, 540], 112).
209. *La Passion,* I, p. 188.
210. *Ibid.,* III, pp. 51, 207–8.
211. Cf. *Essai,* p. 104 ff; and *La Passion,* III, p. 43 ff.
212. *'iqd al-jumān* (see *La Passion,* IV, 46), vol. XIV, anno 309, *maqtal al-Ḥallāj,* § 4.

VII

Muslim Mysticism: Tendencies in Recent Research

R. CASPAR

For a number of decades now Muslim mysticism[1] has received considerable attention from Orientalists. The abundance and quality of works produced by these scholars stand out by comparison with studies on Muslim theology (apart from one or two exceptions). There are numerous reasons for this fact, ranging from a widespread interest in mysticism generally to the discovery of the intellectual and spiritual wealth of Sufism in particular.

It is widely recognized that the names which still dominate the study of Sufism are those of R. A. Nicholson and Louis Massignon. The research of these two men from the very beginning achieved a level of erudition, technical precision, and spiritual depth that was rarely to be achieved after them. For half a century, most of the studies on Sufism made use of their works either popularizing them or expanding them in various directions. As a result, a vast literature comprised of translations, anthologies, theoretical essays, monographs, etc., came into existence.

The influence of these pioneers, however, was not limited to the world of Orientalists or to the European public. Islam itself was awakened, or reawakened, to an interest in Sufism. This is not an insignificant phenomenon and could well be of considerable consequence. There was first of all the search for and editing of Sufi texts in Arabic, the majority of which were still in manuscript form. As the years passed the publication of such works gradually increased.[2] There came into being consequently a body of texts which were easily accessible, often well printed, and sometimes edited critically. We may measure the great contribution of the early pioneers by observing that the two major works of L. Massignon, *La Passion d'al-Ḥallāj* (1921) and *Essai sur les origines du lexique technique de la mystique musulmane* (1922), veritable compendia of Sufism, were based almost entirely on texts that were in manuscript form and often accessible only with difficulty.

The edition and publication of these texts aroused the interest of Muslim intellectuals in the content of Sufism, seen as an integral element in the cultural heritage of Muslim civilization. Now the relations of Sufism (as those of Muslim philosophy) with Muslim orthodoxy had not been without their difficulties. Indeed, there occasionally had been rather bloody clashes. Ḥallāj and a number of others had to pay for it with their lives. And if Sunnī Islam after al-Qushairī and al-Ghazzālī had assimilated much from a Sufism that had become wiser and more acceptable, it is also true that Sufism never played more than a minor role in the curriculum of Muslim universities. Represented concretely by the religious brotherhoods, it was very much suspect among the various reform movements, from the Wahhābīs to the "orthodox reformism" of the Salafīya and the Muslim Brotherhood. Indeed it appears that it was the interest of Orientalists in the great Sufis that revealed their value to Muslim intellectuals. As a result, the writings of these once-censured Sufis were integrated into the program of university studies where they came to occupy an important place.[3] Studies and dissertations of varying degrees of merit were written on Sufism and on particular Sufis.[4]

Our purpose here, however, is not to assess the impact of this study on contemporary Islam but to attempt to highlight, among the modern works on Sufism, some of the more important studies which appear to represent, either because of their magnitude or their method, the principal tendencies in the study of Muslim mysticism. We shall leave to the side, therefore, simple translations, anthologies, and popular works as well as studies that are clearly superficial and which therefore belong to the literature of embellishment more than to scientific study.[5] These works, without doubt, are the best known and the most widely read. However, they add little to our knowledge of Sufism. By their inaccuracies, vague formulations, and superficial comparisons they may even be misleading.

Too often in fact the taste for, or rather the infatuation with, mystical phenomenon in general has led certain authors to take up and continue the works of the specialists without evidencing that depth-understanding that is so essential in matters as difficult and delicate as these. Nothing is easier than to juxtapose selected Muslim, Jewish, Hindu, or Christian texts on love, for example. It is quite another matter to place these apparently similar texts in the respective contexts from which they acquire their real meaning. It is equally easy to expatiate on union with God, grace, charity, etc., on the basis of proximate translations. It is quite another thing to isolate the precise meaning of the expressions used by the mystics of each religion by taking into consideration the essential nature of the language, the personal synthesis of each mystic and his own living experience.

Following the work of the early orientalists and the subsequent proliferation of writings, it has become necessary to define more precisely the data of Muslim mysticism and to indicate its significance. This, it would appear, is the stage that scholarly research is at today. To be sure, the task of discovering the lesser Sufis and editing their texts is far from being completed. In certain areas it has scarcely begun. However, we can no longer be satisfied with the deciphering of texts. We must go on to elucidate their philosophical and religious content, and situate them within a general conception of mysticism. Since each thinker naturally has his own vision and his own method, it might be useful to describe those tendencies which seem to us to be the most characteristic among the approaches used in the study of Muslim mysticism.[6]

I. The Esoteric Gnosis of Eastern Islam: Henry Corbin

The most extensive work on Muslim mysticism has without question been done by Henry Corbin, director of the École des Hautes Études in Paris and also of the Institute Franco-Iranien in Tehran. Corbin began his work on Sufism with a study of the writings of Shihāb ad-Dīn Suhrawardī (put to death in 587/1191), posthumously given the title *"master of ishrāq"* (illumination), and described by L. Massignon as the last of the nonmonistic Sufis. In Suhrawardī a number of different mystical traditions intersect, and Corbin devoted important studies to each of them. Out of this there came a series of works, ostensibly disparate, but unified by a common theme which one might call "the wisdom of eastern Islam."

The oldest element of this wisdom is constituted by the pre-Islamic substratum of Zoroastrianism, the religion of ancient Iran. Suhrawardī explicitly refers to it[7] and Corbin demonstrates the continuity (or the resurgence) of the principal Zoroastrian themes in Suhrawardī and in

Persian Shī'ism right down to our own time.[8] Next is the Ismā'īlī (Sevener Shi'īte) stratum or, more precisely, Iranian Ismā'īlism as it found expression in Persian texts. The latter also took over Zoroastrian themes, transposed and through symbolic interpretation or *ta'wīl* harmonized them with Shī'ite doctrines and even with Hellenistic philosophy. The principal representative of this tendency was Nāsir-i Khosraw whose work Corbin has edited along with other Ismā'īlī texts.[9] There is, finally, the important work of Ibn 'Arabī. Although born in the Muslim West (at Murcia in Spain) in the year 560/1165, he found his vocation and experienced his intellectual flowering in the East, in particular at Mecca and at Damascus where his tomb is found. His influence on Eastern Islam, especially on Shī'ite and Iranian mysticism, was particularly rich.[10] We must also mention Corbin's study on Ibn Sīnā (Avicenna) and the visionary recital of Ḥayy b. Yaqẓān, whose example Suhrawardī was determined to follow in his journey to the "orient of lights,"[11] as well as numerous articles on particularly important themes, published in specialized journals.[12]

It is obvious that from the quantitative point of view we encounter here a considerable effort. However, the lines of investigation embarked upon by Corbin are far from having been exhausted. They require the editing of numerous texts and the publication of analytical studies. This vast undertaking is to be climaxed by a definitive work on the life and work of Suhrawardī. Let us hope that this industrious scholar will bring this immense task to a successful conclusion.

These seemingly very different studies focus on Suhrawardī, his sources, and his influence. But beyond a simple critical analysis of sources and historical connections, Corbin is interested in the homologies of structure and the recurrence of certain themes in various religions or systems of thought as different as Zoroastrianism, Oriental Hellenistic philosophy, and the Shī'ite and Sunnī Islam of Suhrawardī and Ibn 'Arabī respectively. Indeed, if one follows the analyses of Corbin, one finds oneself in the presence of a spiritual world or a mode of religious thought strangely coherent and permanent, transcending the boundaries of religious doctrine. One might describe it in a very summary fashion as the world of light, of theophanies and angels, a world to which esoteric gnosis, symbolic exegesis *(ta'wīl)*, and the creative imagination provide access.

In the world of light, the source of all being is the light (the *xvarnah* or light of glory in Zoroastrianism, taken over by Suhrawardī). The successive emanations of this primordial light, its irradiations, constitute so many degrees of being, or manifestations of the supreme light. The first emanating lights are hypostasized in archangels (the governing lights, *qāhira*); next come the lights which regulate *(mudabbira)* every human being, indeed every creature. Every being therefore has a double aspect: an interior *(bāṭin)* which is its essential reality, its angel. The earth, for example, has its angel (the Spenta Armaiti of Zoroastrianism) or better, "is an angel." The other aspect, the external *(ẓāhir),* visible world, is accessible only to the senses and to the outward doctrinal formulations of religions. In order to gain access to the deeper reality of things *(bāṭin)* it is necessary to go beyond the literal, "to accompany" the world of visible things back to that of archetypal images *(mithāl).* This is the role of nonallegorical, symbolic interpretation *(ta'wīl).* But what is the instrument or organ of this knowledge? The type of reason used by philosophers and theologians is inadequate, for it can analyze, but it cannot "see." Faith in the letter of revelation provides access merely to the exterior *(ẓāhir).* Only the imagination or knowledge of the heart can reveal the depth-meaning *(bāṭin)* of things, in short, penetrate into the world of archetypal images *('ālam al-mithāl).* It is the world of imagination, to be sure, but it is for all that a world that is very real, not imagined or imaginary. It is only there that "spirits become corporeal and bodies are spiritualized." To penetrate into this intermundane sphere of the imagination by *ta'wīl* presupposes an initiation into the secret of the gnostic *('ārif)* or mystic.

To this general scheme, each school and each thinker added his own (often specific) modifications, working out his own synthesis. Suhrawardī insisted on successive planes of irradiated lights. Ibn 'Arabī distinguished between the unknowable God and the Lord *(Rabb)* of each believer *('abd).* Each of the two terms of the *Rabb-'abd* relationship is a "creator" of the other: the Lord renders the believer existent by manifesting him in the universe; however, in doing this, He (the Lord) is made manifest or is revealed to Himself; thus the creature, who is the locus of an epiphany *(maẓhar)* of the divine, is also His "creator." In effect, the notion of creation is nothing other than that of an epiphany of the divine.

Each time Corbin takes up the study of a new author of whom very little is known, he projects us into the mental universe of this latter with a precision equalled only by his ability to illuminate the underlying inspiration and lines of power common to the whole of the spirituality of eastern Islam. It is quite impossible here to go into the characteristic features of each Sufi studied by Corbin. In order to do this it would be necessary to examine almost every line of the writings of Corbin—writings whose detail and technical vocabulary can only be grasped with difficulty. It is more important to focus attention on the new perspectives which his work opens up, as well as the problems which his method and some of his conclusions pose.

In the first place, a whole dimension of the Muslim heritage is revealed to us under a new light. It is a question, as we have said, of the spirituality of Eastern Islam or, more particularly, of Shī'ite mysticism which represents the influences of Iranian spirituality derived from Zoroastrianism, Hellenistic philosophy in its Oriental forms (Neo-Pythagorism and Platonism transmitted by Ibn Sīnā and his school), the illumiative mysticism of Suhrawardī and the later disciples of Ibn 'Arabī. It needs to be emphasized that certain modern scholars had already drawn attention to some of these currents, and that Corbin was influenced by their works.[13] However, none of these presented a synthesis as vast or as detailed as that offered by Corbin. It should also be pointed out here that his synthesis rests on a documentary base of the first order, composed of texts which in large measure were unedited. Corbin undertook the considerable task of editing them. It is, therefore, under the double title of scholar and thinker that Corbin deserves the recognition of all those who are interested in the study of Islam and, in a more general sense, in the history and problems of mysticism.

I would like to make an observation which is not without consequence for the questions that we shall consider a little later. It is useful to situate the spiritual world that Corbin has uncovered for us within the larger context of Islam, for it is clear that Shī'ite mysticism, regardless of its importance, is marginal in character from an Islamic vantage point. I will not appeal here to the categories of orthodoxy or heterodoxy; they are always relative for the historian of religion. However, it is a fact that the great majority of Muslims, in the past as well as in the modern period, were scarcely aware of those currents of thought studied by Corbin. This is already true of Sufism in general. It is even more so with respect to Shī'ite Sufism, even though there still exist today in Iran certain centers or groups of persons who are nourished by it and who perpetuate it.[14] I understand very well the objections that can be raised against considerations based upon a quantitative point of view, *viz.*, that one ought rather to deal with meaning in the name of quality. On the other hand, does not this quantitative point of view mean that one ought to focus attention on living persons, on real and living Islam in preference to beautiful, seductive, speculative systems? Or at least, if the analyses of Corbin (insofar as one accepts them) are of value for the history of ideas, we must be more restrained when we speak of the possibility of dialogue between human communities on the basis of these ideas.

This remark might well serve as an introduction to the method which Corbin used. A philosopher well acquainted with the currents of modern thought, and a translator of Heidegger, he frequently states that it is his intention to penetrate his subject matter by means of the phenomenological method. We do not question the value of phenomenology as a method. By assuming the role of subjectivity inherent in all human knowledge (in the relation of intersubjectivity), it not only allows one to show respect to the thought of others, but enables one to enter into their intentions by understanding them from within. The method, however, does have its dangers, not the least of which is that in the relation of intersubjectivity it allows the adding of two subjectivities instead of reducing them, and relaxes the attempt to be objective which other methods cultivate.

One sometimes gets the impression that the thought and prejudices of Corbin tend to distort the ideas of the thinker whom he wishes to present to us. He transmits to his readers the things that attract him to his subject: a certain intellectual affinity and spiritual affection. These are conditions favorable to an intuitive understanding. However, "sympathy" goes so far that one has to ask if it is the philosopher, the historian of ideas, who speaks, or if it is a disciple of the esoteric gnosis of Shī'ite Sufism or the mysticism of Ibn 'Arabī. The tone becomes impassioned, but always polite, when it defends these gnostic masters against what he regards as a lack of understanding and erroneous judgments.

In the light of the above, we must make certain distinctions and be precise in our formulations, especially with respect to the "existential monism" of Ibn 'Arabī and the other monistic Sufis. A number of times Corbin contests the validity of this designation. For him, theophany, on the one hand, and dialogue and duality on the mystical level (that is, on the level of knowledge?), on the other, allow the thought of these Sufis to escape the label of existential monism. However, he recognizes elsewhere that this possibility of dialogue rests upon a commonness (and even a unity) of essence between God and the creature.[15] Neither Ibn 'Arabī nor Corbin makes use of analogy. The conclusion implicit in all of this seems to be to replace existential monism by essential monism. One cannot call this an advantage, though it is perhaps more accurate. The protests of

Corbin have at least provided an invitation to probe more deeply into this problem, which is certainly one of great significance.

Many other notions are taken up, discussed, and contested—and done so as vigorously. It would be impossible to consider them all here, even if it might be useful. In fact, the thought of Corbin, by taking up and extending that of the authors whom he studies, forms a tightly knit universe with its own categories and a vocabulary which (while being often that of a philosophy of being) is capable of embracing different concepts.[16] To cite only one example, to be sure a key one, let us consider what might be referred to as the ontological status of image or symbol. Corbin protests against those who see the world of imagination as an imaginary, unreal world. For him this world is very real indeed, and the visible world is only an appearance. The image and the intermundane sphere of imagination have an ontological reality. They belong to an intermediary realm, a place where spirits and bodies meet. This indeed is the world of symbols and archetypal images *(mithāl);* however, it is the symbol and not what is symbolized that is real. One might ask whether this does not involve (perhaps unconsciously) a transposition of planes: of the noetic and the ontological planes, of the plane of mystical expression and the plane of the metaphysical substructure. For my part, I do not see the value of this reification of symbols and images, nor even (as Corbin prefers) of their "personification." They find their appropriate status if one recognizes the hierarchy of the degrees of knowledge. To take one of the brilliant formulations of Corbin (by reversing it), is it not to waste one's time with the gesture at the expense of what it signifies?[17]

This is an area where the affection of the author for his subject leads him to embrace it to the point of taking over biases and perpetuating them. What we have here is an apology for gnosis against the religions of dogma. The problem is too important in itself and has too many consequences to pass over in silence. We realize of course that each person is free to make his own philosophic and religious choices. However, the confrontation with, or the dialogue between, various points of view presupposed that each be presented as it really is, as it sees itself. Now it seems to me that while Corbin brings out fully the value of gnosis, his representation of Muslim and Christian "orthodoxy" is scarcely recognizable and borders on caricature. One could have wished that the phenomenological approach had been employed with the same success and sympathy in both cases.

Especially since the beginning of this century personal, spiritual, gnostic religion has often been contrasted with literalistic, historical, doctrinal formulations which have a social character. Universal gnosis alone, it is said, can permit the uniting of all those believers who are separated by their religious beliefs. The contrast, though not new, is questionable.

The real issue here has to do with the role and the validity of a doctrinal authority in religious matters, whether it be a question of the *magisterium* of the Catholic Church or the role of *ijmāʿ* (consensus) in Islam. This authority is bound up with the definition and limits of the revealed text and thus stands in opposition to the esoteric, interiorized interpretation of gnosis which allegedly represents spiritual liberty and alone establishes an authentic mysticism. Thus from this latter point of view genuine Islam is that of the gnostic sort (a Shīʿite principle), and genuine Christianity is that of the Docetic gnosis of the first centuries of the Christian era, and later taken over by certain Rhineland mystics.[18]

This dichotomy is in part an artifical one. It has often been shown that Islam in its more official form did not completely reject *ta'wīl* (allegorical interpretation) and certainly not the whole of mysticism.[19] With respect to the Catholic *magisterium,* if it rejected primitive gnosis, it was not as a spiritual understanding of Scripture, but because its presuppositions and conclusions appeared to be contrary to the essential Christian message. If one understands gnosis etymologically, one might speak of an orthodox gnosis, eminently represented by the school of Alexandria. Catholic theology itself is a "knowing by faith" *(intelligence de la foi).* Nor is the *magisterium* opposed to a prophetic hermeneutic. On the contrary, it assumes the prophetic and recognizes as valid the breath of the Spirit "which blows where it wills." With respect to mysticism, we do not see how (from the point of history) one can exclude the Johns of the Cross, the Thérèses of Avila, and the multitude of Christian mystics who were authentically mystical and who were recognized as such by the Church.

It is true that this raises the important question of the very nature of the religious life, and particularly of the mystical life. For Corbin as for monists since Ibn ʿArabī, mysticism is essentially gnosis, that is, a matter of knowledge. It is a matter of recognizing and discovering through initiation, creative imagination, and *ta'wīl* the concealed meaning of the revealed text while avoiding the deceptive appearances of the literal sense. To comprehend is to free the soul; this is salvation by knowledge.[20] For us salvation consists not only in adhering to the knowledge of faith in the revealed text appropriated through Tradition, but in being united through it to God in saving love. Mysticism from its side is not only a form of knowledge in which love impregnates the understanding; it is a union of love which engages the whole of life and even death. Ḥallāj understood this very well.

Finally, it might be useful to indicate precisely on what level the choices exist. If it is on the plane of philosophy and the history of ideas, one might ideally prefer a religion without a *magisterium,*[21] although Crobin pertinently quotes Suhrawardī: "it is not sufficient to read books,"[22] thus indicating the importance of being guided. However, if the choice takes place on the strictly religious plane, the option is no longer between individual knowledge and doctrinal authority, but between various religious traditions, each having its own doctrinal authority. And that choice is beyond the compass of the philosopher; it is situated on the plane of faith.

This is not all, however. These remarks which are decisive for the religious problem are equally important if one intends to establish a dialogue between religions. This is what Corbin proposes, and it is for this reason we have thought it necessary to speak of it. Is it certain that the dialogue between Islam and Christianity would be easier and more effective if it were carried out by the proponents of gnosis on each side rather than by the two "orthodoxies"? Here we shall have to refer again to the marginal character of Shī'ite gnosis. Is it realistic to think that the gnostic Christianity of the early period (that of Basilides, Valentine, or Marcion), which disappeared so long ago and which was so unrepresentataive of Christian tradition even in the early period, could be revived? I do not believe that a useful dialogue could be validly established outside of real Islam and real Christianity, that is, by an Islam and a Christianity that are represented by their majority tradition, their actual life, which stands for the whole of their values, exoteric and esoteric. This would appear to be an esesntial condition if both sides of the balance are not simultaneously falsified.

The above points must be raised if confusion is to be avoided. Isolating the issues raised by certain positions or statements, it will be possible to make a distinction between the personal outlook of Corbin on the one hand, and his scholarly and scientific work on the other. This separation of personal outlook from scholarship is undoubtedly a delicate matter and at times stretches one to the limits of one's capacity. But it is worth the effort, given the quality and importance of Corbin's work—a point that can scarcely be overestimated. One can only subscribe to the assessment of an expert in the field who, not without reservation, compares the work of Corbin to that of L. Massignon and concludes that "the editing of these texts witnesses to a twofold achievement of an order that is difficult to find in one and the same person: a knowledge of manuscripts that is impressive, and a power of comprehension and revivification 'from within' of published works."[23]

II. "Tradition" and Syncretistic Monism: Titus Burckhardt

Henry Corbin was attracted to the study of Ibn 'Arabī because of his affinity to Iranian Sufism and its influence on him. It was also Ibn 'Arabī that inspired Titus Burckhardt, though, in this case, the inspiration was a more complete and exclusive one and led to his becoming an adherent of the same spiritual line. His thought and work are far from being as extensive as that of Corbin. The two authors, however, have certain things in common: a concern to establish a metaphysical basis for mysticism, an apology for esoteric gnosis, a belief in an opposition between the mystical East and the rational, scientific West. On all of these subjects, it is sufficient to refer to what has been said above regarding Corbin.

The originality of the tendency which Burckhardt represents consists, on the one hand, in his role as a spokesman for that current called "Tradition" and, on the other (and correlatively), in his explicit adherence to a syncretistic monism.

The school of Tradition, though not without antecedents as far as the history of ideas is concerned, originated more particularly with Rene Guénon, who died in Cairo in 1951. His position involved a rejection of the modern, materialistic, scientific world view and an attempt to recover the religious tradition of humanity, principally its mystical tradition which, according to him, was capable of rallying all believers or, at the very least, an initiated elite previously divided by religious dogmas. Under the title of "traditional studies," this school set out to rehabilitate the mystics of India (Jean Herbert), Zen Buddhism (D. T. Suzuki), and Islam (T. Burckhardt) by publishing introductory studies or texts in translation.[24]

Burckhardt thus represents the Sufism of Ibn 'Arabī and his monistic disciples. One must realize that Ibn 'Arabī offers a double advantage for him. His influence dominated the whole of Sufism after him and his doctrine corresponds rather well to the precepts of the school of Tradition: an esoteric gnosis reserved for those initiated, the primacy of symbol and image, and a syncretistic universalism transcending religious dogmas.

The various aspects of the doctrine of Ibn 'Arabī are analyzed by Burckhardt, and the essential elements of his thought are developed: microcosmic-macrocosmic correlation, universal man *(al-insān al-kāmil),* gnostic knowledge and *ta'wīl,* and the rites of *dhikr.* On the basis of this analysis an attempt is made to discover the metaphyscial basis of mysticism: inspired directly by Platonism, he represents it as a doctrine of emanation through irradiation *(tajallī)* and not by creation. Again one finds here themes in which Corbin was deeply interested.

However, while Corbin approaches the same subjects by means of phenomenology, Burckhardt does so as an adherent of the thought of Ibn 'Arabī, that is, by *believing* (if this term is appropriate for this kind of intellectual adherence). One might dwell on the similarities and differences between these two attitudes. Be that as it may, the position of Burckhardt has the advantage of being clear. He openly professes monism, conceived of as an essential unity of all beings, and the unreality of all that appears distinct from God. However, he rejects pantheism, the existential unity of beings *with* God. This monism is for him the logical outcome of the essential doctrine of Islam: the confession of the unity of God *(tawḥīd).* Here we have the sort of remark that merits reflection. However, on this point, as on that of the conformity of monistic Sufism with the revealed text of Islam, we leave the judgment to Muslims themselves.

To draw out this analysis further would be repetitious. It is sufficient to know that Burckhardt faithfully presents the doctrine and philosophy of monistic Sufism placed within the context of a religious attitude which demands a choice on the level of faith.

III. Natural and Supernatural Mysticism: Louis Gardet

With Louis Gardet we encounter a critical reflection on the data of Muslim mysticism that arises from an orientation that is clearly different from both that of Burckhardt (on the plane of religious options) and that of Corbin (on the plane of philosophy). A philosopher of penetrating and careful thought, Gardet specialized, as did his teacher, J. Maritain, in problems of a metaphysical nature and, more particularly, in the problems of knowledge. A theologian of rigorous Thomistic orthodoxy, he takes great pains to identify unwarranted comparisons and to respect the value of religious experiences in their various contexts. More generally, he has acquired a solid reputation for everything that has to do with the speculative aspects of Islam:[25] philosophy, theology, mysticism.[26] His studies on Muslim mysticism have appeared for a number of years in various theological journals. The main substance of these studies has recently been published under a general title in collaboration with Father Anawati.[27] In three clearly distinct parts, he sets forth the basic principles that govern his interpretation of Sufi experiences. He then presents representataive texts of the principal stages of the mystical path; and finally, he studies at some length a typical case of the Sufi technique known as *dhikr*.

The essential principle which Gardet takes as a key for his interpretation of Sufism as well as of mysticism in other religious traditions is the distinction between natural and supernatural mysticism. Natural mysticism is the resulting experience of the absolute which the very act of existing constitutes for the mystic. This experience is the fruit of radical detachment, not only from every creature, but form all intellectual activity. By this agnosticism, this *vide de l'esprit* vis-à-vis the counter-tendencies of the natural world of knowing, by this "somersault on the mental springboard" (Massignon), the mystic achieves a radical act of existing and finds there supreme enjoyment in the natural order. This mystical way in its pure state is within reach of the powers of the human spirit. It is obtained effectively by a very elaborate technique and leads to the proper subject of experience: the "I" of the Mystic. It is thus an intellectuality, a technique, an efficacy by and to the "Me."

Supernatural mysticism, on the other hand, is essentially the fruit of divine grace which makes it possible for us to detach ourselves from creatures and opens us up to God alone. Far from being the result of technique, it must be received passively, following the necessary preparations which are not themselves efficacious. It is a love, both the means and end of union with God. It is therefore love, gratuity, passivity by and toward God. Natural mysticism, which is appropriate in the natural order, can be either an aid or an obstacle to supernatural mysticism, depending on whether one stops with it—and the temptation to do so is great—or one goes beyond it.

Indeed, this distinction between the two forms of mysticism was not originally put forward in connection with Muslim mysticism. It arose from the studies of Olivier Lacombe on Hindu mysticism. Taken up by Maritain and utilized by him in his vast epistemological synthesis, it is applied by Gardet to the case of Muslim mysticism. And, in fact, certain Sufi experiences appear in part to derive from and be dependent on a natural mysticism. But in part only, for the monotheistic climate of Islam curbed the movement of withdrawal into the self. Bisṭāmī and the monistic Sufis following Ibn ʿArabī are, according to Gardet, examples of a more or less pure type of natural mysticism. Ḥallāj and the Sufis of the *shuhūd* line (those Sufis who understand the union with God as a union of intention or witness) represent rather a supernatural mysticism. The vocabulary employed by each Sufi ought to make possible a delineation of the line of cleavage between the two types of mysticism.

One might ask whether Sufism is thus being studied (by Gardet) for itself, within its own perspectives, or whether it serves simply as a field of application and verification for a theory developed on the basis of another mystical tradition. Does this approach not attach too much importance to differences in a vocabulary which is precise and technical to be sure, but not always uniform? To hope to find in Bisṭāmī and Ḥallāj, for example, specimens of natural and supernatural mysticism respectively is to oversimplify experiences that are complex and difficult to interpret, especially if one takes into account all of the texts. Bisṭāmī's writings in particular contain words of humility and a sense of the prevenient grace of God which do not seem to be very widely known.

One might respond that, if the distinction between natural and supernatural mysticism is only one way of approaching the study of Sufism and does not do justice to all of its aspects, it does at least illuminate the essential problem. Natural mysticism in its various manifestations—intellectuality, efficacity of technique, withdrawal into self—was surely "the constant temptation of Sufism." The most authentic experiences in Islam as well as elsewhere must constantly be separated out from the scoria that threatens to tarnish them. The decline of Sufism in the brotherhoods shows that the danger is not an imaginary one.

The method which characterizes Gardet's study of Sufism reveals good judgment on the religious level and a critical reflection on the philosophical. To be sure, his thought is thoroughly impregnated by Thomism, in both philosophy and theology. It is impossible to imagine a thinker who does not have his own frame of reference. The important thing is to respect the originality of the "object." Gardet is familiar with the problems of comparative doctrine in both theology and mysticism.[28] And in all these studies he exercises meticulous care to place all values in their religous context and underscores the differences as much as the analogies.

On the other hand, although the philosopher and the theologian in Gardet assist each other, they do not interfere with each other. In the particular case of the distinction between the two types of mysticism, one should pay special attention to the vocabulary. The distinction between the natural and the supernatural order is without question the result of theological reflection carried out within a Christian framework. However, its field of application may be extended beyond these limits if it is based on an observation and a critical examination of characteristic facts. Under these conditions discussions can take place on a plane that is properly philosophical.

The principles of reference employed by Gardet will perhaps not be accepted by everyone. One cannot, however, ignore his attempt to elucidate Sufism and its central problem on the philosophical and theological plane. The value of his endeavor resides both in the thoroughness of his analysis and the scope of the synthesis, in which the fundamental laws that govern the interpretation of all mysticism play an important role. One can only hope that all those who are interested in the problems of Muslim mysticism will benefit from the light that his thought and method have generated.

IV. A Scientific Monograph with Theological Perspectives: Serge de Beaurecueil

The preceding authors who advanced certain general theoretical interpretations of Sufism were well aware of the fact that their works were provisional in nature insofar as they were not based upon monograph-length studies of the principal figures and the central themes of Muslim mysticism. Every theoretical construction, in effect, assumes a study of sources, their critical edition, and a reconstruction of the historical milieu in which the mystical experiences took place.

It is to this sort of investigation that Serge de Laugier de Beaurecueil devoted his efforts. A member of the Institut Dominicain d'Etudes Orientales in Cairo, having the advantage of both a good theological education and daily contact with a Muslim milieu, he focused his attention for more than fifteen years on a Muslim mystic who was rather poorly known in the West even though he was a highly representative figure. 'Abd Allāh al-Anṣārī, a Sufi master from Herat (now located in Afghanistan) who died 481/1098, was in fact one of the principal representatives of nonmonistic (*shuhūd*) Sufism. A discrete adherent of the teachings of Ḥallāj, he is first of all noteworthy for his fierce attachment to the strictest kind of Hanbalism, even to the point of adopting an anthropomorphic literalism.[29] On this point he was claimed by the most rigorous line of orthodoxy. Not less worthy of note are his wisdom as a spiritual guide, his emotional balance, and sensitivity as seen in writings that are both technical and systematic. His writings or at least those that have been preserved are not numerous but they are of a high quality. His didactic writing on Sufism is completely contained in his principal work, the *Book of Stages (Kitāb Manāzil as-Sā'irīn)*. It is divided into ten sections and one hundred stages representing the various phases of the journey of the soul to God, culminating in the experience of *tawḥīd.*

The influence of this *shaikh al-Islām* was considerable, a fact to which the numerous commentaries on his writings testify. More remarkable still is the fact that these commentaries represent a wide range of tendencies extending from the monists (disciples of Ibn 'Arabī) such as Shams ad-Dīn at-Tustarī to Ibn Qayyim al-Jawzīya, the impetuous disciple of Ibn Taymīya. His influence appears still to exist in our time, for one can find in Cairo recent editions of the *Book of Stages* and the commentary of Ibn Qayyim al-Jawzīya.

S. de Beaurecueil has taken up the considerable task of editing and studying the whole of the thought of al-Anṣārī. During the first phase of his study he edited the commentaries on the *Book of Stages,* at least the two earliest ones. Then followed the critical edition of the text of the work itself. The life of al-Anṣārī was studied in its historical context. Finally, various smaller works filling in the teaching of the master are in the process of being edited.[30] All this constitutes the scholarly aspect of the work of S. de Beaurecueil. One can only admire him for the high quality of his scholarship: the investigation of manuscripts accessible only with difficulty (some of them have been found in Afghanistan in private libraries hitherto unexplored), the establishment of relationships between manuscripts and, above all, a meticulous concern for precision in the use of terms and ideas relating to the mystical experience of al-Anṣārī. It is indeed works as exacting as these that bring about progress in the study of Sufism and make the elaboration of a valid, general view of Muslim mysticism possible.

However, if S. de Beaurecueil is primarily a specialist on al-Anṣārī, he deserves special credit for having utilized his in-depth knowledge of one Sufi to extend his investigations into other important areas. A series of public lectures which he gave in Tunis on the principal Sufis and the present-day relevance of their message will long be remembered.[31] His knowledge of the texts and the sources of Sufism have made it possible for S. de Beaurecueil, like L. Gardet, to approach the very delicate problem of comparative mysticism. However, in line with his preference for monographic studies, he undertook the study of certain themes and stages in the mystical journey in order to elicit from al-Ansārī and his commentators a precise formulation of the views of Sufis on these themes. He then went on to compare these with more or less comparable themes in Christianity. It was within this context that he was led to take up the study of the following themse: "Love for the Neighbor" (L'amour du prochain), and "Hope and the Return to God" (L'espérance et la retour à Dieu).[32] One finds in these studies the same high quality as in those of Gardet: a solid knowledge of doctrinal matters, a precise use of terminology, a concern for the originality of the ideas in question, all of which rests on a solid documentary base. In an area where confusion and superficial views are so often the rule, the scrupulous investigations of S. de Beaurecueil, as well as those of Gardet, are particularly welcome.

The work of S. de Beaurecueil has not yet exhausted the subject with which it is concerned. A great amount of work still remains both in the critical editing of the works of al-Anṣārī and the analysis of these, as well as in the investigation of the problems of comparative mysticism. However, what has already been done augurs well for the future. If each Sufi could be the focus of such an investigation, decisive progress in the study of Sufism would be possible.

Muslim mysticism offers to the investigator a field of study that will not soon be exhausted. Numerous texts remain to be uncovered, edited, and studied. More theoretical and speculative investigations into Sufi thought are only just beginning. These first attempts, as we have seen, reveal serious differences, and reflect in turn the schools of thought to which their authors belong. It is the responsibility of each to form his own judgment and to examine the validity of these various positions. Our primary purpose here is to throw some additional light on certain facets of those lines of investigation which appear to be characteristic.

Finally if one may express a wish, it would be that the concern for precision and discrimination might triumph over easy, artificially contrived syntheses. Confusion and misunderstanding may thus be avoided. As a case in point, the very term "Sufism" (*taṣawwuf*) itself does not carry the same meaning or refer to the same authors among those who employ the term. Thus for Louis Massignon, Louis Gardet, and Serge de Beaurecueil it refers primarily to the great nonmonist Sufis of the first four or five centuries of the *Hijra,* whereas for H. Corbin and Titus Burckhardt, on the other hand, who reject these early figures as being Sufis, the beginning of Sufism is dated from the time of Ibn 'Arabī.[33] As for contemporary Muslims, the term evokes little more than the religious brotherhoods whom they hold to be responsible for the decadence of Islam and its congealed conservatism.[34] That alone may be sufficient to explain the diverse assessments of Muslim mysticism. It is important that this be kept in mind.

NOTES

(See page xi for list of abbreviations of journal titles)

1. In this article we shall use without distinction the terms *Muslim mysticism* and *Sufism.* The latter is an anglicized term for the Arabic word *taṣawwuf* and its adjective *ṣūfī.*
2. In Egypt alone, a score of sources for Sufism were edited in the space of six years. Cf. the list of texts published in Egypt, prepared by Anawati and published in six volumes of *Mélanges de l'Institut Dominicain d'Études Orientales du Caire (MIDEO).*
3. For its part, the University of Paris introduced into the program of Arabic studies some of the major texts of Sufism such as the *Kitāb ar-Ri'āya* of al-Muḥāsibī, the *Qūt al-Qulūb* of al-Makkī, and the *Kitāb Adab ad-Dunyā wa'd-Dīn* of al-Māwardī.
4. As significant works, let us mention, e.g., those of Abū'l-'Alā 'Afīfī on Ibn 'Arabī. Less useful are those by A. H. Maḥmūd on Muḥāsibī and Z. Mubārak on *taṣawwuf.*
5. The latest in date of the anthologies is that of R. Khawam, *Propos d'amour des mystiques musulmanes* (Paris, 1960). Texts are abundant, but not equally representative. There is nothing by Ḥallāj, but by numerous minor Sufis there is considerable. The corpus of translated material is large and does frequently make use of such Christian terms as "grace," "charity," etc. Under the heading of superficial studies, we might mention the works of E. Dermenghem; the cultivation of anecdotes and legends, the making of facile comparisons between different mystics, in a clearly syncretistic manner, detracts from the scientific value of these works. There is one exception, however: *Le Culte des saints dans l'Islam maghrébin* (Paris, 1954) where valuable ethnological and folkloristic data can be found.
6. The authors examined here have been chosen from among others who are by no means negligible. Among those who wrote in languages other than French one might mention H. Ritter, *Das Meer des Seele* (Leiden, 1955), a work devoted to Farīd ad-Dīn 'Aṭṭār; the works of Fritz Meier, even though his contribution at the Symposium de Bordeaux in *Classisme et déclin culturel dans l'histoire de l'Islam* (1956), where he discussed Sufism and cultural decline, was rather disappointing; the perceptive little work by Arberry on Sufism, etc. However, these authors and others do not seem to represent a line of investigation as characteristic as those we have chosen here.
7. "The celestrial irradiations, sources of the Light of Glory and of the sovereignty of Light of which Zarathustra was proclaimer." Quoted by Corbin in the introduction to *Oeuvres philosophiques et mystiques de Suhrawardi,* p. 34.
8. Corbin, *Terre céleste et corps de résurrection, de l'Iran Mazdéen à l'Iran Shī'ite* (Paris, 1960), 418 pages.
9. Nāṣir-i Khosraw, *Kitāb-i Jām' al-Ḥikmatain (Le Livre réunissant les deux sagesses) ou*

Harmonie de la philosophie grecque et de la théosophie Ismaélienne, edited by H. Corbin and M. Mo'in (Paris-Tehran, 1953). The following are other Ismā'īlī texts: Abū Ya'qūb Sijistānī, *Kashf al Maḥjūb* (ed. by Corbin, Paris-Tehran, 1949); and *Commentaire de la qasīda ismaélienne d'Abī'l-Haytham Jorjānī* (ed. by Corbin and M. Mo'in, Paris-Tehran, 1955). Further editions of Isma'īlī texts have been promised.

10. Corbin, *L'Imagination créatrice dans le Soufism d'Ibn 'Arabī* (Paris, 1958), 285 pages. [Translated by R. Manheim into English under the title, *Creative Imagination in the Ṣūfism of Ibn 'Arabī* (published by Princeton University Press in the Bollingen Series XCI, 1969), 390 pages.] This work is essential for an understanding of key themes in the thought of Corbin, beginning with his reflection on the work of Ibn 'Arabī.
11. Avicenna, *Le Récit de Ḥayy ibn Yaqẓān,* translated into French from the Arabic text and from that of the Persian commentary, with an introduction and notes by Corbin (Tehran, 1953). In concluding this narrative, Ibn Sīnā has Hayy b. Yaqzān saying: "And now, if you will, follow me; come with me toward Him." He thus invited his disciple to set out for the Orient of Lights. Suhrawardī followed the itinerary there and ended up where Ibn Sīna had; he described his journey in the *Récit de l'exil occidental (Qiṣṣat al-Ghurba al-Gharbīya)*, published by Corbin in *Oeuvre philosophiques, op. cit.*
12. Especially in the *Eranos-Jahrbuch,* particularly his study on cyclical time, vol. 20 (1959), pp. 165 ff.
13. Notably the remarkable works of W. Ivanow on Ismā'īlism, and those of Asin Palacios and 'Afīfī on Ibn 'Arabī.
14. See the presentation of the Shaikhī school and its texts in *Terre céleste,* pp. 183–87, and pp. 281–401. Founded in Iran at the end of the eighteenth century, heir of Shī'ite gnosis, it is represented in our day by groups of initiates in Iran.
15. See *L'Imagination créatrice,* pp. 82–93, and notes 63, 76, and 212 where the author speaks out against existential monism [English trans., pp. 106–22 and notes 65, 78, and p. 356, n. 53]. On the unity of essence, see pp. 82, 148, 185–86 [Eng. trans., pp. 106, 199–200, and 247–48].
16. The following is an example of the ambiguity of concepts even where the same terminology is used: L. Gardet has raised the problem of the "Zoroastrian motifs" in the thought of Suhrawardī: "Are they the key to his teaching or do they have, more precisely, in the context of thought that is Muslim in origin but informed by Platonism or Pythagorism, the value of privileged myths (mythes privilégiés)?" *La Pensée religieuse d'Avicenne* (Paris, 1951), p. 191, n. 2. Corbin finds the question "posed in very fortunate terms" but understands motifs as "motives" (*mobiles*), as "motivating motifs" (*motifs motivants*) *Oeuvres philosophiques,* p. 31. It is clear, however, that L. Gardet uses the term "motifs" in the sense of themes or schemes of thought.
17. Especially since the texts collected by Corbin to support this ontology of the image are not equally convincing. If it is clear that Suhrawardī, Ibn 'Arabī, Qushairī, and the Shaikhī school favor an ontological status for the image, the two Lahijis and especially Mulla Sadra explain the phenomenon of knowledge through the image, without recourse to a special ontological status. See the texts in *Terre céleste, op. cit.*
18. These themes recur repeatedly in the writings of Corbin. They are brought together and set forth clearly in an important chapter in *L'Imagination créatrice,* pp. 62–80, entitled: "Situation de l'ésotérisme" [Eng. trans., pp. 77–101, "The Situation of Esoterism"].
19. The most complete demonstration has been made by L. Massignon with regard to the decisive case of al-Ḥallāj. Cf. *La Passion d'al-Ḥallāj,* pp. 332–93, "Ḥallāj devant

l'Islam." Even here allusions are made to al-Qushairī and Ghazzālī. It is to be added that all of the brotherhoods are Sunnī with the sole exception of the Ni'matallāhīya.

20. Many texts could be cited: "Ismā'īlī gnosis is without question a gnosis, a salvation by knowledge" (Nāṣir-i Khosraw, p. 136). "For its [i.e., the veil of imagination] sole purpose is to enable the mystic to gain knowledge of being as it is, that is to say, the knowledge that delivers because it is the gnosis of salvation." *L'Imagination créatrice,* p. 139; also see p. 260, n. 221, etc. [Eng. trans. p. 197; see also pp. 358–59, n. 7.]
21. St. Thomas held that before the fall, man received divine gifts directly from God without mediation. It is sin and the atonement which made it inherently natural for man to receive divine things through human agents. Cf. *Summa, Th. III, q. 61, art. 1 and 2.*
22. Quoted by Corbin in the introduction to Nāṣir-i Khosraw, p. 142.
23. L. Gardet, *Revue des études islamiques,* XXII (1945), p. 134.
24. Burckhardt, *Introduction au doctrines ésotériques de l'Islam* (Algiers and Paris, 1951, 1969), 130 pages [translated into English under the title *An Introduction to Sūfī Doctrine* by D. M. Matheson and published in Lahore (1959), 155 pages]. The same author has published a translation of the *Fuṣūṣ al-Ḥikma* of Ibn 'Arabī, under the title: *La Sagesse des prophètes* (Paris, 1955). Another spokesman of the same tendency as far as Islam is concerned in Frithjof Schüon, *Comprendre l'Islam* (Paris, 1961), and *De l'unité transcendente des religions.*
25. [The reference here is to the publication of the Institut des Belles Lettres Arabes (Tunis).] Cf. *IBLA,* VIII (1945), 409–22, "La mesure de notre liberté"; vol. X (1947), pp. 109–34, "La propriété en Islam"; vol. XIII (1950), 37–47, "L'abandon à Dieu"; vol. XVI (1951), pp. 387–94, "La connaissance suprême de Dieu (*ma'rifat Allāh*) selon Avicenne."
26. Concerning philosophy: Gardet, *La Pensée religieuse d'Avicenne* (Paris, 1951), 235 pages; on Muslim theology (*'ilm al-kalām*), a major work written in collaboration with Father Anawati, *Introduction à la théologie musulmane* (Paris, 1948), 543 pages; Gardet, *Dieu et la destinée de l'homme* (Paris, 1967).
27. The principal articles have appeared in *Recherches de science religieuse* (1950), pp. 321 ff., and in *Revue thomiste* (1948), pp. 76–112; (1952), pp. 642–79; (1953), pp. 197–216.

    The general work is Anawati and Gardet, *Mystique musulmane, aspects et tendences—expériences et techniques* (Paris, 1961), 310 pages. The original edition was published in Italian: *Mistica islamica, Aspetti e tendenze—esperienze e technica* (Turin, 1960) as part of the general series, *Storia e scienza delle religioni,* ed. by Mgt. Castellino.

    The general thrust of this note tends to focus attention on the thought of Gardet. This in no way should be taken to imply that the contribution of Anawati is not important. He is concerned rather with the historical development of Sufism. It was not his intention to offer an original contribution; rather he makes use of the basic works such as L. Massignon's *Essai sur les origines. . . .* However, one must recognize the importance of the work of the director of the Institut Dominicain of Cairo (i.e., Anawati), his warning against the equating of terms and ideas, as well as his observations, taken from life, on the "spirit of early Islam"—the Islam of all periods, one might say—(*Mystique musulmane,* pp. 15–19), and on the current reaction of Muslims to Sufism, e.g., the favor which Ghazzālī enjoys among the common people (pp. 50–51).
28. For comparative theology, see *Introduction à la théologie musulmane, op. cit.* For comparative mysticism, see the two basic works: *Expériences mystiques en terres non-*

chrétiennes (Paris, 1953), 177 pages, and *Thèmes et textes mystiques, recherche de critères en mystique comparée* (Paris, 1958), 219 pages.

29. We possess from al-Anṣārī a collection of *Forty Traditions,* still unedited, in which it is said that God "walks rapidly" (*harwals*), has a thigh (*sāq*), etc. I recall having assisted in the decipherment of this manuscript with the director of the manuscript section of Dār al-Kutub in Cairo; he could not conceal his shock and astonishment at these anthropomorphic expressions. Moreover, the case is not without analogy, for other mystics reached the highest level of mysticism combined with the strictest kind of literalism. St. Bernard is a typical example.
30. One finds in the collection entitled *Anṣāriyyāt,* published by the Institut d'Archéologie Orientale in Cairo, the two commentaries on the *Book of Stages* by Firkāwī and by 'Abd al-Mu'ṭī al-Lakhmī al-Iskandarī. It was also in this collection that the critical edition of the *Book of Stages* appeared. The life of al-Anṣārī was studied in two lengthy articles in *Mélanges de l'Institut Dominicain d'Etudes Orientales (MIDEO),* IV (1957), pp. 95–140, and V (1958), pp. 47–114. *The Kitāb Ṣād Maydān,* an initial outline of the *Book of Stages,* was published by the *IFAO* (Institut Français d'Archéologie Orientale). The following should also be added: the texts of al-Anṣārī in the *Mélanges Louis Massignon* (Paris-Damascus, 1956), I, pp. 153–72 on the deficiencies of certain places of abode, and the *Mélanges G. Wiet* (*IFAO,* 1960), pp. 203–39 on the propriety of Sufis (Ādāb aṣ-Sūfiya); in the *Mélanges Taha Ḥusayn* (Cairo, 1962), pp. 46–47, a treatise by Abū Manṣūr Ma'mar al-Iṣfāhānī entitled *Kitāb Mahj al-Khāṣṣ.*
31. One will find in *IBLA,* XXII (1959), pp. 147–55, a résumé of the last conference of the series under the title: "*Vocation spirituelle et monde d'aujourd'hui.*"
32. See *MIDEO,* I (1954), pp. 9–38, "Les références bibliques de l'intinéraire spirituel chez 'Abdallah Anṣārī"; II (1955), pp. 5–70, "La place due prochain dans la vie spirituelle d'après 'Abdallāh Anṣārī"; VI (1959–1961), pp. 66–122, "Les retour à Dieu selon Anṣārī"; *Revue thomiste,* LIX (1959), pp. 339–68, "Autour d'un texte d'Anṣārī, la problématique musulmane de l'espérance."
33. For example, H. Corbin states the following (*L'Imagination créatrice,* 79 [Eng. trans., p. 100]): "This term *fidèli d'amour* does not apply . . . to the pious ascetics of Mesopotamia, who in the first centuries of Islam took the name Ṣūfī." Also: "By Ṣūfism we mean more precisely all those whom we, for reasons set forth above, group as *fidèli d'amour.* This group is dominated by two great figures: Ibn 'Arabī, the incomparable master of mystical theosophy; and Jalāl ad-Dīn or Rūmī, the Persian troubadour of the religion of love" (P. 85; Eng. trans., p. 110).
34. The following are two Muslim testimonies, coming from very different outlooks: that of the al-Azhar journal on the works of Massignon and Gardet: "Islam is extremely precise in the determination of what is Muslim and what is not. Now the great majority of those whom the orientalists call Muslim mystics have nothing in common with Islam (*Mujallat al-Azhar,* Rajab 1372 A.H., pp. 892–93, quoted in *MIDEO,* I, p. 189). It is important to be aware of this judgment and to interpret it correctly. The other testimony is that of President H. Bourguiba who in his speeches frequently referred to the misdeeds of Sufism. Regarding the *fatwā* which argued that the purpose of the fast of Ramaḍān is to weaken the material forces in order to cause the divine light to flourish, the president responded: "What a joke! Are we Sufis today? This is not the time for Sufism, it is the time for life and death battle" (Radio Tunis, 18 February 1960, quoted by P. Rondot in *L'Islam et les musulmanes d'aujourd'hui,* II, Paris, 1960, p. 193).

VIII

The Attitude of Orthodox Islam Toward the "Ancient Sciences"

IGNAZ GOLDZIHER

I

The terms *'ulūm al-awā'il* or *'ulūm al-qudamā'* (sciences of the ancients), or *al-'ulūm al-qadīma*[1] (ancient sciences) designate those branches of learning in the literature of Islam that found their way into the sphere of Muslim[2] culture through the direct influence or mediation of works (*kutub al-awā'il*)[3] that had been taken over from Hellenistic literature.[4] In the literature of Islam these ancient sciences or branches of learning were distinguished from the sciences of the Arabs[5] or the newer sciences,[6] and more specifically from those having to do with religious law (*sharī'a*). These ancient sciences included the entire range of propaedeutical, physical, and metaphysical sciences of the Greek encyclopedia, as well as the branches of mathematics, philsophy, natural science, medicine, astronomy, the theory of music and others. Since the cultivation of these fields of learning followed the Neoplatonic tradition, occult practices and various types of witchcraft (not to mention astrology) were included in the *'ulūm al-awā'il* and the sciences of the philosophers.[7]

Despite the extensive interest that these sciences aroused from the second century A.H. on in religious circles loyal to Islam (and encouraged also by the 'Abbāsid caliphs),[8] strict orthodoxy always looked with some mistrust on "those who would abandon the science of Shāfi'ī and Mālik, and elevate the opinion of Empedocles[9] to the level of law in

Islam."[10] People like 'Alī b. 'Ubaiḍa ar-Rayḥānī, whom the caliph Ma'mūm had kept as his closest advisor,[11] or Abū Zaid al-Balkhī were frequently suspected of heresy because of the philosophical tendency of their works.[12]

With the growing influence of a narrow orthodoxy, this distrust which the religious circles of Eastern Islam felt for the works of the *'ulūm al-awā'il* expressed itself with an increasing intensity. The difficulties experienced by the philosopher al-Kindī at the time of the restoration of orthodoxy under al-Mutawakkil were probably the earliest example of this phenomenon. Fortunately, however, these attempts to suppress philosophical impulses did not thwart the vigorous cultivation of these sciences.

This distrust was directed not only against philsophical investigation in the more restricted sense of the term. Al-Ghazzālī complained[13] that religious persons felt an ingrained sense of reserve even toward such sciences as arithmetic and logic simply because they were told that these disciplines belonged to fields of study cultivated by heretical philosophers, and that in spite of the fact that these disciplines did not in any way interfere with religious doctrine either negatively or positively.[14] The very term "philosophy" frightened them away from those disciplines connected with it like someone who discontinues courting a beautiful girl when he learns that she has an ugly Indian or Sudanese name. Al-Ghazzālī considered this tenacious opposition to be all the more misguided in view of the fact that people need geometry and logic.[15]

Though it cannot be regarded as anything more than an ingenious idea, the exegete al-Mursī[16] (a contemporary of Yāqūt) attempted to prove that the Quran contains references to various *'ulūm al-awā'il,* including logic, mathematics, medicine, astronomy, etc., as well as to the various crafts and industries. The verse on which he based his argument was the following: "Nothing has been neglected in the Book" (surah 6:38).[17]

The pious Muslim, however, was expected to avoid these sciences with great care because they were considered dangerous to his faith. The Prophet's prayer that God might protect him from "a science that is useless" was quoted frequently.[18] Al-Māwardī (d. 450) (who was, incidentally, a systematic thinker in the field of jurisprudence and a Mu'tazilite[19] in theology) points out explicitly that the many sayings of the Prophet commending the pursuit of learning should be applied only to religious disciplines and not in any way to the speculative sciences (*'aqlīyāt*).[20] The Hanbalite Ibn Taymīya understood *'ilm* [knowledge] as referring only to that knowledge which derives from the Prophet. Everything else he regarded either as useless or no science at all, even though it might be called by that name.[21]

The Spaniard Ibrāhīm b. Mūsā (d. 790) came to the conclusion that the average orthodox theologian regarded only those sciences as worthwhile that were necessary to, or useful for, religious practice (*'amal*). All others were without value and only led people from the straight path, as can be seen from experience.[22] Even within the religious disciplines, he distinguished between essential knowledge and nonessential or decorative knowledge.[23]

The *'ulūm al-awā'il* are pointedly referred to as the "repudiated sciences" (*'ulūm mahjūra*),[24] and are described as "wisdom mixed with unbelief" (*ḥikma mashūba bi-kufr*).[25] They can only lead in the end to unbelief and, in particular, to *ta'ṭīl,* that is, to the stripping away of all positive content from the conception of God.[26] This can be shown from such examples as that of the *maqāmāt* poet, 'Abd Allāh b. Nāqiyā[27] (d. 485 in Baghdad), who adopted *ta'ṭīl*[28] and developed a hostile attitude toward religious law through the influence of these sciences[29]—or by the example of the philologist and poet Aḥmad an-Nahrajūrī (he lived at the end of the fourth and the beginning of the fifth century, and is described as ugly and unclean) who had an intimate knowledge of philosophy and the *'ulūm al-awā'il,* and who made no effort to conceal his heretical views.[30] It was said that disrespect for religious law and its study went hand-in-hand with the cultivation of these sciences. Ibn Thābit b. Sābūr of Bādarāyā (d. 596) who settled in Baghdad and who was in great demand there because of his extensive learning, obtained access to the caliph an-Nāṣir and soon came to enjoy a very close relationship with him. This 'Abbāsid caliph who, like many of his predecessors and successors,[31] valued his training in the religious sciences, even wished to appear as a transmitter in the *isnāds* of traditions (*ḥadīth*). Abū'l-Faḍl al-Ardabīlī (d. 656) received an *ijāza* (authorization) from him to transmit in his turn traditions which he received from the caliph.[32] This latter lectured on the *Musnad* of Aḥmad b. Ḥanbal and gave *ijāzas* to his son and four other Hanbalite scholars whom he had allowed to attend his lectures. The *ijāza,* thus, gave them the authority to transmit the *Musand* in his name.[33] In the course of time, Ibn Thābit introduced the inquisitive caliph to the *'ulūm al-awā'il* and reportedly encouraged him to disdain the religious sciences he had previously cultivated. It is not surprising, therefore, that Ibn Thābit is described as a religiously disreputable person.[34] It is perhaps not coincidental that the Sufi, Shihāb ad-Dīn 'Umar as-Suhrawardī, dedicated his book, *The Exposure of Greek Infamies and Reception of Religious Counsel* (*Kashf al-Qubā'iḥ al-Yunānīya wa Rashf an-Naṣā'iḥ al-Aymānīya*), which was an attack on Greek philosophy, to the caliph an-Nāṣir.[35] This same Sufi author wrote another work, equally hostile to Greek philosophy, entitled: *Proofs Which Demonstrate the Refutation of the Philosophers by the Quran* (*Adillat al-'Iyān 'alā'l-Burhān fi'r-Radd 'alā'l-Falāsifa bi'l-Qur'ān*).[36]

As soon as someone displayed an interest in the *'ulūm al-awā'il* he was regarded as suspect.[37] The effort to track down heresy (always carried out actively in orthodox circles, particularly among the Hanbalites) found such persons even among the staunch guardians of traditional theology. The Hanbalite Ismā'īl b. 'Alī b. Ḥusayn al-Azjī of Baghdad (549–610), a man steeped in the religious sciences and a disciple of a Hanbalite traditionalist, was portrayed as a typical theologian tainted by Hellenistic learning and therefore a warning to others. His professor in tradition was the Hanbalite Abū'l-Fatḥ b. al-Munā (d. 583), reputed to be one of the greatest authorities of the school and an important link in the transmission of tradition.[38] His successor in the chair at the Ma'mūnīya College was Ismā'īl al-Azjī. The latter also lectured in the palace mosque (*jāmi'al-qaṣr*) where the theologians met to exchange ideas. In addition, he gave lectures in his house, which were very popular. He was held in high regard not only for his elegant diction and superior abilities as a debater, but also for his great competence in *fiqh* (law), in comparative jurisprudence, in the two *uṣūls* (*uṣūl al-fiqh* and *uṣūl al-kalām*), and in dialectics. His biographers describe him as "unexcelled during his time" in all of these areas. He had many students and wrote many books. The caliph an-Nāṣir showed him special favor and appointed him to positions of responsibility. This however, proved to be too much for him. As inspector of the private estates of the caliph, he is said to have acted unjustly (this is reported, however, by sources hostile to him and the information may, therefore, be biased). He was later employed for a brief period in the *dīwān aṭ-ṭabaq;* but even here his behavior was far from laudable. He was removed and imprisoned for a time. After his release he remained confined to his house. Ibn Najjār (d. 643)[39] describes his position on religious issues as follows:

> In matters of religion he was not to be taken seriously. His son Abū Ṭālib 'Abd Allāh mentioned to me, while trying to establish his father's reputation, that he had studied logic and philosophy with the Christian doctor, Ibn Marcus, who was the most knowledgeable man of this time in these sciences

> and that he frequently attended a Christian church with him. I have learned from a trustworthy source that he wrote a book with the title: *Laws of the Prophets* (*Nawāmis al-Anbiyā'*) in which he says, among other things, that the prophets were philosophers like Hermes and Aristotle. I asked one of his closest disciples about that and he neither confirmed it nor denied it. He merely said that Ismā'īl had been liberal in religious matters and had not taken things very seriously. He did not say more. He was incessantly critical in matters of tradition and its transmitters; those who knew nothing about the speculative sciences and who could not understand the true meaning of traditions (*ḥadīth*) and who stuck to the literal text he characterized as ignorant. He censured them and was highly critical of them.

There is a report which describes his response to an interesting legal problem. There was a Jew in Baghdad who had married a Muslim woman, and he had two children with her. Fearing lest he be punished for this illegal marriage, he converted to Islam. What should be done in a case of this sort? Ismā'īl's response was as follows: "Islam cancels what has taken place before its time."[40] In short, by converting to Islam previous violations are cancelled.[41]

The general tendency was to consider any digression from the theological mainstream as the result of contact with the *'ulūm al-awā'il.* According to Tāj ad-Dīn as-Subkī, the very limited knowledge that the caliph al-Ma'mūn had acquired of those sciences led him to demand acceptance of the doctrine of the created Quran.[42] The same author states that the general public (*al-'awāmm*) attributed to the influence of the *awā'il* the undeniable fact that al-Ghazzālī (who, in spite of all statements to the contrary, was not able to free himself from his philosophical past)[43] held views on many issues that were not to the liking of contemporary orthodoxy.[44]

It is not surprising, therefore, that a Hanbalite partisan like Dhahabī, after lauding the erudition of Qāsim b. Aḥmad b. Muwaffaq al-Lōrqī (d. 661), should add the following remark: "If only he had refrained from cultivating the *'ulūm al-awā'il!* These latter cause nothing but disease and ruination in religious matters. Very few of those who have cultivated them have avoided such a fate."[45] Such views, however, have been expressed not only by Hanbalites. It is significant that the Zaidī encyclopedist, Aḥmad b. Yahyā b. al-Murtaḍā (d. 840), whose religio-philosophical orientation was Mu'tazilite and who had written a very useful history on the development of this school, made the following statement regarding Abū'l-Ḥusayn al-Baṣrī (d. 436)[46] after enumerating his works: "The followers of the school of Abū Hāshim (al-Bahāshima) do not like him for two reasons. First of all, he has stained himself with philosophy and discussions about the *awā'il;* secondly . . . , etc."[47]

Orthodoxy naturally demanded that studious persons avoid association with such people as much as possible, and that they be aware of the danger which those who teach such things constitute, especially for the young. The biographer Abū Sa'd b. as-Sam'ānī reports that during his travels he attended the lectures of 'Alī b. 'Abd Allāh b. Abī Jarāda (d. ca. 540) of Aleppo. Once while he was coming out of this man's house he was asked by a pious individual what the reason for his visit was. Sam'ānī told him that he had gone there to attend the lectures of Ibn Abī Jarāda, whereupon the pious man became very angry, and replied: "One does not learn *ḥadīth from such a person.*" "Why not?", Sam'ānī asked. "Is it because he has Shī'ite leanings like most of the people of Aleppo?"[48] The pious man responded: "I only wish he would confine himself to such matters. What is worse, he believes in the stars and makes no secret of the fact that he believes in the ideas of the *awā'il.*" Indeed, many of the people of Aleppo regarded him as suspect on this account.[49]

Under these circumstances it is easily understandable why people who wanted to protect their reputations concealed their philsophical studies and pursued them under the guise of some discipline that had better standing. The example of Muḥammad b. 'Alī aṭ-Ṭayyib (d. 436) of Basra is very significant and probably not an isolated case. He is said to have done outstanding work in his study of tha *awā'il.* However, to protect himself against his contemporaries, he declined to declare himself openly as a philosopher, and instead presented his ideas in the form of *kalām* which, to be sure, was not in very good standing either with the orthodoxy of his time. Nevertheless, this seemed less dangerous than unadorned philosophy, for *kalām,* it was thought, had at least grown up out of Islamic soil.[50]

It was a matter of considerable satisfaction, therefore, when some philosopher, on his deathbed, renounced the errors of philosophy and turned his back on the intellectual leaders in whom he had confided throughout his life. It is thus reported with a sense of triumph that the blind scholar, Ḥasan b. Muḥammad b. Najā al-Arbilī ([d. 660]—a contemporary of Ibn Khallikān with whom he had a rather unpleasant encounter), turned his back on philosophy. He was a Shī'ite philosopher, and in his house in Damascus, Muslims, *Ahl al-Kitāb,* and philosophers met to hear his lectures. The last thing he reportedly said before his death was: "God the Most High is right, Ibn Sīnā has lied."[51]

Hand in hand with this pious distrust for the *awā'il*-sciences went, quite naturally, a distrust for those books which contained their doctrines. Persons who kept such books in their homes could easily acquire a reputation for having heretical tendencies. It was probably to such books that Jāḥiẓ referred when he mentioned prohibited drinks and suspicious books (*sharāb makrūh wa kitāb muttaham*) among those things which men are forbidden to look at.[52] In 277 A.H. professional copyists (in Baghdad) were required to promise under oath not to include in their professional activities the copying of books of philosophy.[53] The great mystic 'Abd al-Qādir al-Jīlānī, in a public lecture, once attacked a *qāḍī* whose only offense was that he allowed works by Arab philosophers in his library.[54] It may perhaps be somewhat humorous that it was the *awā'il*-books of 'Abd as-Sallām b. 'Abd al-Wahhāb (known as Rukn ad-Dīn, d. 611), a grandson of this famous Hanbalite mystic, that were committed to a total auto-da-fé on account of their heretical contents. The inquisition against him is said to have been an act of revenge by the vizier Ibn Yūnus who, before his rise to power, had been forced to submit to all sorts of insults from the 'Abd al-Qādir family. It was easy to attack 'Abd as-Salām from the religious side, for his orthodoxy was not very highly regarded. His own father joked about his attitude toward religion. And since he was rather careless about his speech, his views apparently came to light. The intrigues of his enemy, the famous Abū'l-Faraj b. al-Jawzī, appear to have contributed to the fact that, in the persecution of the family of the great mystic (several of whose members were imprisoned in Wāsiṭ), attention was focused primarily on 'Abd as-Sallām. During a search of his home, philosophical works such as the *Rasā'il* of the Ikhwān aṣ-Ṣafā were found, as well as books on witchcraft and astrology, works on the cult of stars (part of a decadent Oriental Neoplatonism), books of prayers addressed to the planets,[55] etc., all of which were written in the hand of 'Abd as-Sallām. 'Abd as-Sallām apparently offered the excuse that he did not believe in these things and that he had only copied them so he could refute them. In his presence and before the assembled *qāḍīs* and *'ulamā'* (among whom was Ibn al-Jawzī) a funeral pile was erected in the courtyard in front of the mosque of the caliph. His books were then thrown into the fire from the platform of the mosque where the learned dignitaries had taken seats. All of this occurred before a large crowd that had gathered in front of the mosque. A man read the contents of the books and then demanded (in the presence of 'Abd as-Sallām) that those who had written these books as well as those who believed in them be cursed.

The crowd complied with the request; the curses were extended to include *shaikh* 'Abd al-Qādir and even the *imām* Aḥmad b. Ḥanbal (since the heretic was regarded as one of their disciples). There was as much fury (directed against unbelief) as if it had been the battle of Badr itself! Poetry deriding the cult of stars was recited in his presence. 'Abd as-Sallām was then declared a heretic, his academic hood (*ṭaylasān*) was taken from him, he was thrown into prison, and the school of 'Abd al-Qādir (in which he taught) was turned over to Ibn al-Jawzī. Later, after he had been released from prison, he made a proper Islamic confession and renounced his earlier errors. After the fall of Ibn Yūnus, the school which had been taken from 'Abd as-Sallām was returned. Now Ibn al-Jawzī had to give way. He was exiled to Wāsiṭ where he in turn was imprisoned as a result of charges brought against him by 'Abd as-Sallām. Five years later he was freed, thanks to the intervention of the caliph's mother, and returned to Baghdad amidst popular acclaim. 'Abd as-Sallām lived out the rest of his life under the changing favors and disfavors of the court.[56]

During the first years of the reign of the caliph al-Mustanjid (who genuinely wanted to abolish abuses in the administration), the property of a judge who had fallen into disfavor on account of misdeeds that he had committed was confiscated. We are told that "many of the judge's possessions were seized. Even his books were taken, and those that treated of philosophy were burned. Among these latter were the *Kitāb ash-Shifā'* by Ibn Sīnā, the works of the Ikhwān aṣ-Ṣafā and others."[57]

II

Quite clearly it was primarily Aristotelian metaphysics (*ilāhīyāt*) that was rejected by orthodoxy. The principles and results of this metaphysical system were believed to be fundamentally opposed to the doctrines of Islam, and that despite the best efforts of Muslim philosophers to harmonize the areas of conflict. The orthodox frowned on a study even of the preliminary aspects of philosophy, for these were seen as a preparation for philsophy itself. They could never escape the feeling that things fundamentally indifferent to religion might very well tempt people to travel further along the path to philosophy.

In the first place there were the propaedeutical sciences (*riyāḍīyāt*) among which there was mathematics. Only a few objections, to be sure, were raised against arithmetic. From the vantage point of inheritance law (*'ilm al-farā'iḍ*) proficiency in arithmetic was required even for the teaching of jurisprudence. The complicated calculations which were presupposed by the application of Islamic law made arithmetic a necessary ancillary science for the specialist in inheritance law. As a qualification for competence in such a field, the combination of *al-faraḍī al-ḥāsib* (a specialist in inheritance law and arithmetic) was quite common.[58]

In the field of mathematics, on the other hand, it was primarily geometry that disturbed the orthodox, since it was a characteristic part of the *'ulūm al-awā'il.* Geometrical figures seem to have made them uneasy. To naive believers at the time of Abū Nuwās, circular figures commonly used in prosody appeared to be *zindiq*-like. The owner of a book which contained metric representations was condemned as a heretic.[59] Somewhat later a fanatic was terrified by figures in the astronomical book of Ibn Haytham. He suspected them of representing "shameful temptation, speechless calamity and blind misfortune."[60]

The orthodox opposition to geometry taken together with syllogistic logic (*al-qiyās al-burhānī*) is expressed in an interesting and humorous treatise (somewhat earlier in date) which dealt with the teaching of geometry. It was written by a *bel esprit* of Baghdad, Aḥmad b. Thawāba (d. ca. 273–277), and was addressed to a friend who had supposedly sent him first a Christian and then later a Muslim teacher for the purpose of instructing him in the rudiments of geometry. From the outset, the student ridiculed the principles of this science which he was being taught supposedly in order to make him into a heretic. He censured his friend for sending these people to him to work for the undermining of his faith.[61] The entire episode, of course, was invented and is highly humorous. The humor, however, undoubtedly reflects the attitude of a large cross-section of people whose religious naiveté this clever *bel esprit* held up to ridicule.

Only a few years later the lexicographer Abū'l-Ḥusayn b. Fāris expressed the feeling of the majority of traditional religious circles when he spoke of geometry as a threat to faith. In his book *Aṣ-Ṣāḥibī fī Fiqh al-Lugha wa Sunan al-'Arab fī Kalāmihā* which he dedicated to the learned vizier, Ṣāḥib b. 'Abbād (an enemy of the *awā'il* sciences, as we shall see later), he polemicizes (see my *Muhammedanische Studien,* II, p. 214) against people who maintain that the Arabs do not have the most developed grammar or poetic meter and who consider the Greeks more advanced in these areas. In support of their argument they mention as authors the names of philosophers[62] and titles of books[63] that have an offensive sound [to Arabs] so that they cannot be pronounced by the tongue of believers. In these matters, the Arabs (he maintains) enjoy superiority over those people "who claim to understand the essential nature of things[64] by the use of numbers, lines and points whose relevance I cannot understand; indeed, they weaken faith and cause conditions from which we ask God's protection."[65]

Al-Ghazzālī's views on these matters are naturally of interest; especially in view of the fact that he went through the school of the exact sciences and must, therefore, be regarded an authority on the issue of their relationship to religion. He maintained that those propaedeutical sciences (including mathematics) that are useful do not have any relationship to religious matters, either positively or negatively, since they are discovered by means of definitive (apodictic) proofs and their results cannot be denied. Nevertheless, they can lead to many dangers.[66] One who employs these sciences is easily filled with admiration for their subtleties and the certainty of their reasoning. The attitude of such a person toward philosophy may thus be favorably influenced so that he comes to believe that all the other sciences are equally as clear and convincing in their arguments as mathematics. When he learns that philosophers are unbelievers and that they reject religious law, he then concludes, because of his blind trust, that religion is not of very great significance if those who have delved so deeply into this science do not hold the truths of religion in high regard. Indeed, many people (al-Ghazzālī argues) have fallen into unbelief through this very process of thought. It is in vain that one points out to them that philogophy and religion are two very different branches of knowledge and that an individual may be competent in one without being competent in the other. They do not see that the argument of a mathematician cannot be compared with that of a metaphysician because (as everyone knows who has had some experience) mathematical demonstration is apodictic (*burhānī*) while that of the metaphysician is only hypothetical (*takhmīnī*). Those who have a blind faith in philosophers will not waver in their enthusiasm for them because of this consideration, but will stubbornly persist in their pro-philosophy bias. . . . Those who devote themselves to a study of mathematics should be warned of this danger. Even though this discipline is not related to religious matters, since it belongs to the presuppositions of philosophy, the dangers of it may easily have a detrimental influence on them. "It is very rare," al-Ghazzālī continues, "that someone becomes absorbed in this science without renouncing religion and letting go the reins of piety within him."[67]

In another work al-Ghazzālī excludes mathematics even more vigorously (and without reservation) from that sphere in which Muslims ought to be involved. In this work, he discusses the futility and even destructiveness of the art of debate. He rejects the notion that this practice might potentially serve as a means of intellectual inspiration or the development of one's mental powers,[68] and that the acceptance of such mental acrobatics is warranted despite the fact that it produces certain harmful consequences (vanity, boasting, etc.). To drink wine for the purpose of strengthening one's body is undoubtedly beneficial; nevertheless, it is forbidden. The games of *maisir* and chess involve intellectual exercises, and yet no one considers this to be sufficient justification for the pursuit of them.

> The same applies to the study of the sciences of Euclid, the *Almagest,* and the subtleties of arithmetic and geometry. They too render the mind more acute and strengthen the soul, and yet we refrain from them for one reason: they are among the presuppositions of the *'ulūm al-awā'il* and these latter (the *awā'il*) include those sciences, beside[69] arithmetic and geometry, that entail the acceptance of dangerous doctrines. Even if geometry and arithmetic do not contain notions that are harmful to religious belief, we nevertheless fear that one might be attracted through them to doctrines that are dangerous.[70]

Religious minded persons did, in fact, draw these conclusions. Thus, for example, it is reported that a certain Muḥammad b. Yūnus al-Bahrānī of Arbila (d. 585) who excelled as a philologist, cultivated some of the *'ulūm al-awā'il;* he solved the problems of Euclid and was partially successful with the *Almagest* of Ptolemy.[71] However, he finally realized that the fruits of his labors in this science were bitter and led to results that were reprehensible.[72]

III

While Neoplatonic philosophers won recognition for astrology in Islam because they identified *qadar* (divine determination) with the necessities caused by the constellation of the stars and explained *qaḍā'* as the corresponding eternal prescience of God,[73] scholastic theology (*kalām*), on the other hand, rejected astrology.[74] It regarded the admission of a causal connection between the stars and events on the earth as a negation of the doctrine that God is the exclusive and immediate creator of all events.[75] On this point, the Mu'tazilites and the Ash'arites agreed with each other.

An early Mu'tazalite, Abū'l-Ḥasan al-Bardhā'ī, interpreted the following prophetic saying: "If someone mentions the stars, stay away from him" as meaning that one should not attribute the course of events to the stars, as "the ignorant philosophers" (*juhhāl al-falāsifa*) do.[76] Similarly the Shī'ite-Mu'tazilite theologian, Ḥasan b. Mūsā an-Nawbakhtī (the turn of the fourth century) wrote a *Kitāb ar-Radd 'alā al-Munajjimūn* (*The Refutation of the Astrologers*) in which he took Jubbā'ī to task becasue the latter had not been sufficiently decisive in refuting the astrologers and indeed had taken a position of skepticism.[77] As far as the position of Ash'arite orthodoxy is concerned, the viewpoint of the founder was decisive. He wrote a polemical work against "The belief that there is a connection between events and the stars, and that good fortune is dependent on these latter."[78] This was to remain the viewpoint of Ash'arism.[79] In this matter they would also refer to Shāfi'ī, a highly learned man who was said to have been somewhat involved with astrology in his youth,[80] but who took a very hostile attitude toward it in his later years.[81] Astrology, it was said, was responsible for the religious indifference of Abū Ma'shar al-Balkhī (d. 272/885) who prior to his study of this science had been a very religious man. This famous astronomer who in his early years was regarded as a very pious theologian (he was even accused of having stirred up people against the philosopher, al-Kindī)[82] was on his way from Khurasan to Mecca to perform the pilgrimage when he visited the rich library of the vizier 'Alī b. Yaḥyā b. al-Munajjim. There "he became engrossed in the astrological (and certainly also astronomical) works to such an extent that he became a heretic, and that was the end of the *ḥajj* for him and also the end of religion and Islam."[83]

Laith b. al-Muẓaffar, grandson of Naṣr b. Sayyār (who lived during the period of the collapse of the eastern Umayyads) and editor of *Kitāb al-'Ayn,* said of himself that he had cultivated all of the fields of learning except the science of stars (*'ilm an-nujūm*). He refrained from this latter not because he was not capable of mastering it but because he had come to realize that it was abhorred by the *'ulamā'*.[84]

This term (the science of stars) probably did not refer only to astrology in spite of the terminological distinction between *'ilm an-nujūm* and *'ilm al-hay'a*.[85] Strict orthodoxy was not very much in favor of scientific astronomy, even though a knowledge of it was necessary for ritual obligations (the determination of the correct times for prayer [*'ilm al-mīqāt*],[86] and the precise direction of the *qibla* [*samt al-qibla*]). It has, indeed, been used in literature in this sense. Nonetheless, it belongs to the *'ilm al-*

awā'il and as a science which did not arise from the soil of the legal sciences is at least suspicious.

Even the great theologian and exegete Fakhr ad-Dīn ar-Rāzī, who in other respects was very closely associated with philosophy, did not have much confidence in astronomy in spite of his recognition of the value of astrology. He maintained that one could learn of the world of the spheres only through tradition.[87]

Some of the assumptions in astronomy, however, could not really be reconciled with the teachings of Islam. When word was brought to the orthodox sultan, Khwārizm Shāh, of a land of the midnight sun, he regarded the report as pure heresy (*ilḥād wa qarmaṭa*), for if such information were accurate it would put into question the very regulations which determine the times of the various prayers.[88] Only the great Bīrūnī, who then lived at the court of the sultan, could reassure him of the accuracy of the traveler's report.[89] How could the ascent of the sun in the west (a phenomenon associated in Islamic tradition with the day of judgment) be reconciled with the facts of astronomy? The impossibility of this phenomenon—a claim that was based on the assumption of the uniformity of the laws governing the movement of the spheres—was challenged by Muḥammad b. Yūsuf al-Kirmānī (d. 786), in his commentary on Bukhārī (*al-Kawākib ad Darārī fī Sharḥ al-Bukhārī*), on the grounds that the principles of the astronomers are refutable and their premises inadmissible, and that even if these were admitted, a change of east and west could not be excluded.[90]

And what position did orthodoxy take concerning the study of the natural sciences (*ṭabī'īyāt*)?

Even al-Ghazzālī who in his battle against philosophy rejected the assumption of an antithesis between the mathematically demonstrable facts of astronomy and religious tradition, who held fast to the irrefutability of the former and preferred to give up the authenticity of contradictory traditions or to resolve them through metaphorical interpretation (*ta'wīl*), took a less confident stance vis-à-vis the natural sciences.[91] In these sciences he believed that truth was mixed with the trivial, right with wrong, so that one could not decide between the victor and the vanquished.[92] This timid skepticism may perhaps have prepared the way for the decisive answer later given by one of the most respected authorities of the Shāfi'ite school, Shihāb ad-Dīn b. Ḥajar al-Haytamī, who treated this issue in the appendix to his book on the refutation of astrology. He came to the conclusion that if the object of such study was to exlore the nature of things by methods compatible with faith, there could be no objection, for such study cannot be compared with the cultivation of forbidden astrology. However, if the study is pursued in the manner of the philosophers, it is forbidden, for it leads to things that are detrimental, that is, to such things as the belief that the world has no beginning and to other evident abominations. In this case such study is, like astrology, forbidden, for both lead to harmful results even though they differ from each other in the nature and essence of their objectionableness.[93]

IV

In contrast to the other disciplines belonging to the *'ulūm al-awā'il,* orthodox Islam went much farther in developing a position regarding logic. While orthodoxy expressed its distrust of these other fields of Greek learning simply by showing a certain preventive concern, the battle against logic was an opposition of fundamental importance. It (orthodoxy) maintained that the recognition of Aristotle's methods of proof was a serious threat to the validity of religious doctrines. The general attitude of the uneducated was expressed in the saying: "He who practices logic becomes a heretic" (*man tamanṭaqa tazandaqa*).[94]

Al-Fārābī, whose chief contribution were his commentaries on Aristotle's work on logic, appears to have written a defense of logic (no longer extant) in order to combat this bias. In this work he collected all those sayings of the Prophet that were useful in setting forth, from a religious point of view, a more favorable judgment regarding logic.[95]

The scholastic theologians (the people of *kalām*) contributed substantially to the religious disparagement of logic. In their rationalistic efforts they ignored the syllogism of demonstrative methods of proof (for which the followers of Aristotle held them in contempt)[96] and believed that for the support of their theses they could manage with premises that were based only on popular acceptance or tendentious biases, without ever having to prove them correct or having to concede them.[97] Mu'tazilite as well as Ash'arite circles produced numerous polemical treatises against Aristotelian philosophy in general and against logic in particular.[98] The Ikhwān aṣ-Ṣafā charged (probably with some exaggeration) that the *mutakallimūn* (that is, the Mu'tazilites) regarded the science of medicine to be useless,[99] that they considered geometry as a means for comprehending the true nature of things[100] to be ineffective,[101] and that logic and the natural sciences were antireligious and heretical, and those who cultivated them unbelievers.[102] This general accusation can be illustrated by a case which was reported concerning the learned Buyhid vizier, Sāḥib Ismā'īl b. Abbād (d. 385), an ardent Mu'tazilite who expressed his theological partisanship even in his official duties.[103] Written by the philosopher Abū Ḥayyān at-Tawhīdī,[104] the tract containing this report was also directed against the *vizier's* colleague, Abū'l-Faḍl b. al-'Amīd. It was considered dangerous to have this tract in one's house, since it contained accusations leveled against highly respected men.[105] After having characterized Ṣāḥib's superficial pretension to culture and ready wit, Abū Ḥayyān went on to say:

> Quotations from the Mu'tazilite theologians are numerous in his writings; these latter are marred by the methods [of the Mu'tazilites] . . . ; he is filled with partisan fanaticism against the philosophers, and against those who study its various branches such as geometry, medicine, astronomy, music, logic and arithmetic. He knows nothing at all about metaphysics (*al-juz' al-ilāhī*).[106]

In Shī'ite literature, the following statement is attributed to the *imām* 'Abd Allāh (that is, Ja'far aṣ-Ṣādiq): "People will occupy themselves with logic until they even question belief in God. If you hear something of that kind, say: 'There is no god except the unique One; there is nothing like unto Him.' "[107] It should be emphasized that this statement comes from a circle that was oriented toward theology as understood by the Mu'tazilites.

V

Although the *manṭiqī*[108] (the specialist in logic) was not one of the favorites of orthodoxy, as we have seen, it is clear, based on studies of the early 'Abbāsid period[109] that the cultivation of logic was favored by the theological authorities and that it was even employed by them in the service of theology.

We are also in a position to say something regarding western Islam. After the death of the caliph Ḥakam who favored the *'ulūm al-awā'il,* his successor Manṣūr b. Abī'Āmir, whose power rested on the clerical class, imposed an auto-da-fé on all the "ancient sciences" and especially on books that dealt with logic and astronomy.[110] Nevertheless, soon after this manifestation of fanaticism, Ibn Ḥazm, one of the staunchest supporters of a strict traditionalism, came forward as an ardent defender of logic. Indeed, he regarded it as one of the most important ancillary sciences for theology. In general, he was not opposed to philosophy. True philosophy, as he understood it, had as its purpose the perfection of the soul and, therefore, was not opposed to the *Sharīʿa.* Only immature, pseudo-philosophers were hostile to it.[111] He assigned special value to the study of logic. "All the works which Aristotle had written concerning the rules of logic (*ḥudūd al-kalām*) are perfect and useful works," says Ibn Ḥazm.

> They set forth the uniqueness of God and His omnipotence, and are of great value for the exact study of all fields of learning. Those books on the principles of logic which we have mentioned above are most useful in relation to questions of religious norms. By utilizing these principles, one can discover the right way to arrive at (correct) conclusions, to understand words in accordance with their requirements, to distinguish between what is valid for special cases only and what has general validity, to differentiate between what is arranged in a summary fashion (*mujmal*) and what is determined more precisely through a specific explanation (*mufassar*), to draw conclusions based on the relationship of word forms to each other, to establish premises and draw conclusions from them, to see what is necessarily true, what is true under certain conditions, and what is absolutely wrong, to establish definitions in such a way that what is not joined together within them, cannot belong to the same root, to differentiate between rhetorical and inductive proof (*ḍalīl al-khiṭāb wa dalīl al-istiqrā'*). Indeed, the jurist (*faqīh*) who wishes to pursue his studies independently, either for himself or in the interest of his fellow-believers, cannot do so without logic.[112]

Ibn Ḥazm also mentions some of his own works on the principles of logic. Although he attempts to refute the arguments directed against the doctrine of creation (used by those who held to the eternity of the world) and characterizes this latter view as sophistry, he points out that already earlier he had warned against such logically untenable conclusions.[113] These works by Ibn Ḥazm, like other of his writings,[114] appear to be lost. However, we know something of their method and value through a contemporary,[115] Qāḍī Abū'l-Qāsim Sāʿid b. Ahmad (d. 462) of Toledo. "He [Ibn Ḥazm] occupied himself," says Abū'l-Qāsim,

> with the science of logic and wrote a book concerning it bearing the title, *Introduction to the Laws of Logic* (*at-Taqrīb li-Ḥudūd al-Manṭiq*), in which he deals at great length with the establishment of an epistemological method. He draws upon examples from *fiqh* and employs principles that are generally valid in jurisprudence. In some of his basic theses he contradicts Aristotle, the founder of this science, because he did not understand [Aristotle's] intentions and was not thoroughly acquainted with his works. Ibn Ḥazm's book is, therefore, full of errors and statements that are clearly untenable.[116]

From these critical remarks, one may draw the conclusion that the work by Ibn Ḥazm on logic was intended to serve his theological interests, as is also evident from his statement cited above on the use of logic. In any case his remarks show that the scientific tradition of Andalusian Islam, retarded for a short time by the episode of Manṣūr b. Abī 'Āmir, could not be erased from his consciousness. The cultivation of this spirit which was characteristic of Spain was not manifested universally among the theologians of that land, to be sure. Even at a time when there was a flowering of philosophical studies (which were allowed to develop even under the Almohad dynasty) we hear of narrow-minded Mālikite jurists who fought with undisguised fury against philosophical studies,[117] of which biographical literature provides many examples. The harsh epigrams directed against philosophy from the pen of the gifted geographer, Ibn Jubayr,[118] offer us an example of this intellectual tendency. However, his judgment on the "*sunna* of Ibn Sīnā and Abū Naṣr" was probably influenced by his contact with orthodox circles in the East.[119]

Among the orthodox authorities who were not in principle opposed to the study of logic, al-Ghazzālī occupied a position of prominence. However, the way in which he approached this subject reflects the uneasiness which he felt vis-à-vis the representatives of traditional theology. The Andalusian Aristotelian and defender of the study of logic, Abū'l-Ḥajjāj Yūsuf b. Muḥammad b. Ṭumlūs, who himself had written about logic and who called upon al-Ghazzālī in support of his view of the place of this science within Islam, pointed out in his account of existing conditions (and after listing the works of al-Ghazzālī on logic) that this latter by his own admission employed ambiguous titles for his works [on logic] in order to avoid using the unpopular term of *manṭiq*.[120]

> Abū Ḥāmid altered the titles of his books as well as the technical terms employed in them. In place of the terms ordinarily used by the representatives of that field, he used technical terms familiar to the *fuqahā'* and frequently used by the *'ulamā'* of his time. This he did to protect himself and to escape what other scholars had experienced who came forward with strange and unusual things, for which they had to submit to ordeals and suffer humiliation. A merciful God protected him from these.

This, however, does not apply to that part of the *Maqāṣid* devoted to logic. There he does not avoid the use of the term *manṭiq* and, indeed, employs it freely in his praise and treatment of the science of logic: "Insofar as the use of *manṭiq* involves the pursuit of knowledge whose achievement brings eternal happiness, logic is necessarily of great importance, provided, of course, we admit that all happiness is based on the perfection of the soul which can only be achieved by its purification and adornment."[121] Al-Ghazzālī himself believed that he had shown consideration for the sensitivities of his contemporaries not so much through the titles of his works as by his use of terminology, for it was through this latter that he hoped to render his methods acceptable to those persons who were skeptical of everything unusual. He believed that the traditional terms had been used, already before Jesus and Muhammad, by certain ancient peoples who had derived them from the *ṣuḥuf* of Ibrāhīm and Mūsā.[122]

Proceeding from the assumption that the method of speculation in jurisprudence cannot be distinguished from that of philosophy,[123] he tries, in his works on logic, to demonstrate the value of the methods of this science for theological investigation and to discipline these methods into the service of theology. In his *Qisṭās* he attempts to deduce from the Quran itself various forms of syllogism as the only "vehicle" of truth. In his *Mi'yār* he presents a complete system of logic though he concentrates primarily on those facets of it that apply to the field of law. It is significant that he illustrates the various forms of syllogism by examples taken only from jurisprudence,[124] and, wherever possible, explains logical concepts and statements having to do with the details of the system through examples drawn from the field of law.[125] It is not to be inferred from this, however, that he regards the deductions of *fiqh* to be in strict harmony with apodictic proof. Quite to the contrary, he underscores the differences between the two methods[126] and distinguishes between those deductions that are only hypothetical (*ẓann*)—though entirely acceptable for *fiqh*—and those that are of an apodictic character (*yaqīn*),[127] and in doing so constantly underscores the logical gaps that exist in the methods applied in the field of law. Already in his *Maqāṣid* which was intended as a compendium of Aristotelian philosophy, he takes the opportunity to examine the syllogisms of the *qiyās*-conclusions of the *fuqahā'* and *mutakallimūn,* and criticizes their logical defects.[128] In his *Mi'yār* he does the same, though in a more systematic way. There he repeatedly points out that the degree of the certainty of conclusions depends on the premises,[129] and he criticizes the superficiality of the *qiyās*-people who confuse the use of conclusions based on analogy in *fiqh* with undigested information from the speculative sciences.[130]

It should not be concluded, however, that al-Ghazzālī meant to diminish the value of legal statements. In his writings on logic he merely wanted to demonstrate the importance of logic as a methodological discipline for theological investigation. This becomes clear from the introduction to his last monumental work, *al-Mustaṣfā* (a summary of his lectures on *uṣūl al-fiqh*), in which he sums up the basic principles of logic from his earlier works on this subject.

In the indecisive way that is characteristic of al-Ghazzālī, he did eventually voice his reservations regarding the purpose of logic and its consequence for faith. In his *Miḥaqq an-Naẓar* (*The Touchstone of Speculation,* a concise work on logic written reluctantly at the request of a friend and of uncertain date),[131] he expresses his weariness of this subject. "Your request [he writes to this friend] brings me back to a subject that I already abandoned out of disgust and discontent. And now I return to it as one who looks back on something he has fled; such a glance is tedious indeed."[132] In a deeply religious manner he asked his friend to promise under oath (both in the introduction and in the epilogue), as a reward for having dedicated this effort to him, that he would pray to God for himself after every *ṣalāt* and that he request of his friends that they do the same. The prayer was to be as follows: "O God, let him recognize the truth as truth and permit him to obey it, and let him recognize wrong and permit him to avoid it."[133]

And now for his final judgments regarding a discipline that he had praised so highly in his earlier years. He expresses his concluding judgment in his *Confessions* where he discusses all of the sciences individually as they relate to religion. Like the science of mathematics, logic is not basically a threat to faith. Now what connection could possibly exist between the fundamental concerns of religion on the one hand, and the principles of definition and the forms of syllogisms (etc.), on the other, that would make it necessary for one to reject these latter? This (rejection) would, indeed, discredit the sound understanding of the opponents in the eyes of the logicians. The latter again, on the other hand, commit a grave wrong. That is, they establish the rules that are to be regarded as conditions of apodictic proof. They stop short, however, of the subjects of religious investigation (*al-maqāṣid ad-dīnīya*) and declare that it is impossible to apply their methods to proof in this field (religion). They generally treat these questions very lightly. This could well lead to a situation in which people who have a special affinity for logic might begin to think that the antireligious views of the experts in this discipline are based on solid proofs. They will thus very quickly become antireligious, even before they have had a chance to delve deeply into metaphysical investigations (*ilāhīyāt*) and recognize the truth.[134]

These then are the dangers that the study of logic involves, and that in spite of its religious indifference. This, however, should not mean a rejection of the study of logic. If al-Ghazzālī had taken that step he would indeed have contradicted a good portion of his own scholarly work.

VI

It was only after al-Ghazzālī that the opposition to the study of this discipline made decisive progress. From then on, this opposition was closely connected to the name of one of the most famous scholars of tradition in the seventh century, a period that witnessed the beginning of decline in literature and art.

Kamāl ad-Dīn b. Yūnus of Mawṣil is described as one of the most outstanding scholars of the sixth and seventh centuries. Ibn Khallikān who knew him personally and who met him frequently describes him as a miracle of genius and versatility.[135] In addition to the theological disciplines of Islam, which he knew according to all of the schools (*madhāhib*), he was also highly conversant with the Torah and the Gospel. Jews and Christians alike asked him to explain their Scriptures to them; they are said to have admitted that they could not receive such instruction from their own scholars. In addition, his knowledge of the propaeduetical, physical, and philosophical sciences was unequalled. He knew more about logic, physics, arithmetic, geometry, astronomy, medicine, music, and metaphysics than his contemporaries knew of any of these disciplines. He was as familiar with Euclid and Ptolemy as with the treasures of Arabic poetry and historical tradition. As a result, people came to him from great distances to study both the theological disciplines and the exact sciences. Among the young disciples to visit him was Ibn aṣ-Ṣalāḥ ash-Shahrazūrī (d. 643), who later was to become one of the leading authorities in the field of tradition (*ḥadīth*).[136] He made the journey to Mawṣil to study logic with Kamāl ad-Dīn secretly. However, in spite of long study and the best effort of the master, this science simply would not sink into the head of this young student oriented so definitely toward theology. Kamāl ad-Dīn finally had to tell him: "I think it would be best if you would stop tormenting yourself with these things. Until now people have had the most favorable opinion of you; however, you are about to get a bad reputation since people regard all those who cultivate this science (logic) as suspect in matters of religion. You could receive a bad reputation without having achieved anything in this field." Ibn aṣ-Ṣalāh took his advice. Ibn Khallikān was able to add that Kamāl ad-Dīn himself became suspect in religious matters on account of his love for the speculative sciences.[137] Because he was constantly preoccupied with the study of these sciences, his distraction from other disciplines led him now and then to become careless. It was for this reason that people were critical of him.

Not only did Ibn Ṣalāḥ give up the study of logic which proved to be too difficult for him. In the name of religion, he came forward as its archenemy in a written response (*fatwā*) to a question that was directed to him concerning whether, from the point of view of religious law, it was permissible to study or teach philosophy and logic and further, whether it was permissible to employ the terminology of logic in the elaboration of religious law, and whether political authorities ought to move against a public teacher who used his position to discourse on philosophy and write about it.

He introduced his *fatwā* with an orthodox description of philosophy. He states that it is

> the foundation of folly,[138] the cause of all confusion, all errors and all heresy. The person who occupies himself with it becomes colorblind to the beauties of religious law, supported as it is by brilliant proofs. He who studies or teaches philosophy will be abandoned by God's favor, and Satan will overpower him. What field of learning could be more despicable than one that blinds those who cultivate it and darkens their hearts against the prophetic teaching of Muhammad, and that in spite of the fact that his miracles are very numerous, so much so in fact that scholars who have counted a thousand[139] have still not exhausted their number. These miracles are not limited to those he performed during his lifetime, but include all those miracles he performed after his death through the saints—miracles performed for the benefit of those who turned to him in distress. And these cannot be numbered.
>
> As far as logic is concerned, it is a means of access to philosophy. Now the means of access to something bad is also bad. Preoccupation with the study and teaching of logic has not been permitted by the law-giver, nor has it been suggested by his Companions or the generation that followed him, nor by the learned *imāms,* the pious ancestors, nor by the leaders or pillars of the Islamic community whose example is followed. God has protected them from its danger and its filth, and has cleansed them of its uncleanness. The use of the terminology of logic in the investigation of religious law is despicable and

> one of these recently introduced follies. Thank God, the laws of religion are not in need of logic. Everything a logician says about definition and apodictic proof is complete nonsense. God has made it dispensible for those who have common sense, and it is even more dispensible for the specialists in the speculative branches of jurisprudence. Law and its disciplines are fixed; the specialists in this field immersed themselves in the ocean of truth and subtleties long before logic, philosophy and philosophers existed. Those who think that they can occupy themselves with philosophy and logic merely out of personal interest or through belief in its usefulness are betrayed and duped by Satan. It is the duty of the civil authorities to protect Muslims against the evil that such people can cause. Persons of this sort must be removed from the schools and be punished for their cultivation of these fields. All those who give evidence of pursuing the teachings of philosophy must be confronted with the following alternatives: either (execution) by the sword or (conversion to) Islam, so that the land may be protected and the traces of those people and their sciences may be eradicated. May God support and expedite it. However, the most important concern at the moment is to identify all of those who pursue philosophy, those who have written about it, have taught it, and to remove them from their positions insofar as they are employed as teachers in schools, and then to arrest them in their houses. This should also be done in those cases where an individual might claim that he does not approve of the doctrines of the philosophers, for evidence proves him to be a liar. The eradication of evil must involve the eradication of its roots. The employment of such a person as a teacher in a public school is a most abominable thing. God help and protect us, for He is the one who knows.

This *fatwā* henceforth was the document to which the enemies of logic referred. One should not overlook the fact that it was also directed against al-Ghazzālī who employed the methods of logic in the field of law. Ibn Ṣalāḥ raised numerous criticisms against al-Ghazzālī in other areas as well; however, among the charges directed against him, he did not forget to mention his preoccupation with *manṭiq*.[140]

This *fatwā* by Ibn Ṣalāḥ is only the explicit formulation of an attitude that prevailed over a large part of the Muslim world during his lifetime; it was an attitude that certainly did not originate with this renowned religious scholar. The fate of his contemporary, Saif ad-Dīn ʻAlī (d. 631) of Amida, offers us a clear example. This well-known theologian who had gone through the Hanbalite school of Ibn al-Munā (see note 38) but then later joined the Shāfiʻites was celebrated not only for his religious scholarship and his works in the field of law (especially in the area of *uṣūl*) but for his study of the *awā'il* sciences as well.[141] In Cairo, where he was widely known as a teacher in the traditional religious disciplines, he was persecuted fanatically by the *fuqahā'* because of his study of philosophy (logic in particular is mentioned), and that in spite of the fact that he pursued this discipline only marginally and did not introduce philosophical matters into his teaching.[142] He was accused of having perverted his faith, of having turned to *ta'ṭīl* and philosophy. A protocol was drawn up against him and signed by many persons, declaring his life subject to forfeiture.[143] Saif ad-Dīn 'Alī fled to Syria where he was given a teaching position in Damascus. However, he soon lost this too through similar accusations.

From this period on the study of logic was more or less decisively considered to be a part of the category of *ḥarām* (forbidden). A renowned teacher of the Shāfi'ite school, Tāj ad-Dīn as-Subkī (d. 771), took the most hostile attitude conceivable toward philosophy and even against the later proponents of *kalām* who inserted philosophical theses into their theological system. In an unrestricted prohibition against the study of philosophy he allied himself unconditionally with "the great majority of our *imāms* and *shaikhs,* and the *shaikhs* of our *shaikhs.*" However, he softened this prohibition against logic, somewhat, and did so most probably out of deference to authorities like al-Ghazzālī whom he greatly respected. He states that the cultivation of logic might be allowable on the condition that one first achieve mastery of the religious sciences and that one have a reputation as a *faqīh* or *muftī* among members of the school (*madhhab*). However, for persons with less background in the religious sciences, the study of logic must be considered as forbidden (*ḥarām*).[144] The reference to the *fatwās* of the *shaikhs* certainly included that of Ibn Ṣalāḥ.

The position of the distinguished Hanbalite, Taqī'd-Dīn Ibn Taymīya (d. 729), on the question discussed here seems to have been formulated independently of that of Ibn Ṣalāḥ. Ibn Taymīya was a bitter enemy of philosophy, and this hostility manifested itself in most of his numerous writings. He also composed a special tract under the title *ar-Radd 'alā 'Aqā'id al-Falāsifa* (*Refutation of the Doctrines of the Philosophers*), which his disciple, Shiḥab ad-Dñ, recommended to the followers of the master in a letter and remarked that it might be difficult to acquire a complete copy of this book.[145] As a "counsel for the pcople of true religion" Ibn Taymīya wrote a work entitled: *Refutation of the Logic of the Greeks* (*ar-Radd 'alā Manṭiq al-Yūnānī*). Jalāl ad-Dīn as-Suyūṭī prepared an abridgment of this work,[146] which is now in the Library of the University of Leiden (Warner, 474).

Suyūṭī displayed his distaste for logic in other ways as well. In his autobiography which abounds in self-praise, he writes: "At the beginning of my years of learning I studied some logic, but then God instilled in me a disgust for it. I heard that Ibn Ṣalāḥ in his *fatwā* took a position favoring the prohibition of this discipline; I have, therefore, renounced it and God has recompensed me in the science of tradition (*ḥadīth*), this most noble of all sciences."[147] Suyūṭī appears to have expressed his hostility toward logic on another occasion. We know of it through an exchange of letters which were composed in verse.[148] The correspondence in question took place between Suyūṭī and the Tuāt jurist, Muḥammad b. 'Abd al-Karīm al-Maghīlī. It is clear from this correspondence that a man called Kafūr spoke in favor of logic in a book entitled *al-Furqān* (both the author and the work are entirely unknown). Suyūṭī, on the other hand, who was in touch with theological circles in Africa,[149] registered a resolute protest [against this position]. The theologian of Tuāt[150] defends the accused writer in his rhymed letters, while Suyūṭī in his response justifies his approach, declaring logic to be a forbidden field of study. He was particularly outraged that someone should misuse the title *al-Furqān* (reserved exclusively for the holy Quran) for a work such as that by Kafūr.

Our literary sources show, however, that the viewpoint of those who condemned logic was not victorious in the educational system of Islamic theology. The position expressed in the commentaries, supercommentaries, and marginal glosses (to mention only the most influential sources), which was championed by the logical works of Abharī (an adaptation of the *Isagoge* of Porphyry), Kātibī (*Shamsīya*), Akhḍarī[151] and the authors of other compendia of logic in Islamic education offers us proof of the fact that the voices of opposition to logic gradually faded away without any lasting results. Even scholastic theology (*kalām*) made use of Aristotelian philosophy (especially from the time of Fakhr ad-Dīn ar-Rāzī [d. 606]) as a methodological tool in the establishment and elaboration of itself. Just how little impact the anathema of Ibn Ṣalāḥ ash-Shahrazūrī against logic had, has only recently[152] become evident in the theology of the North African Sanūsī (d. 892/1490)[153] who employed the methods of Greek philosophy and whose theology achieved a position of dominance within the orthodox schools of Islam.

Up until the modern period, logic was treated in the theological curriculum as an ancillary discipline. There were compendia (*mutūn*, textbooks) for students in this field of study; some of these works were actually written in the form of didactic poetry (*manẓūmāt*).[154] Somewhat more than a century ago, a renowned and prolific theologian, Shams Ad-Dīn ash-Shujā'ī of Cairo (d. 1197 A.H.), cast syllogistic forms into verse and wrote a commentary on them.[155]

This same phenomenon can also be observed in the other branches of the *'ulūm al-awā'il*—proof of the fact that the theoretical protests and desiderata of one-sided theologians in Islam were scarcely able to interfere with developments in the real world. The struggle described above belongs solely to the past. Orthodox Islam in its modern development offers no opposition to the study of the ancient sciences, nor does it see an antithesis between itself and them.

NOTES

(See page xi for list of abbreviations of journal titles)

1. *Fihrist* (1st. ed., Flügel, 1871), pp. 238, 243, 255, 271, 299, and others. Cf. *Anwā' at-Ta'ālīm al-Qadīma min al-Manṭiq wa'l-Falsafa,* Yāqūt, ed. Margoliouth, V, p. 92, frequently also *'ulūm al-ḥukamā'*, "the sciences of the wise men."
2. Ibn Ṭumlūs (from Alcira, Spain; d. 620 A.H.) defines them as the sciences that are common to all peoples and religious communities (they are therefore not specifically Islamic). I am grateful to Miquel Asin Palacios (Madrid) who permitted me to use his copy of the work by Ibn Ṭumlūs, the original of which is kept in the Escorial collection. For the author and his work, see the article by M. Asin Palacios in *Revue Tunisienne* (1908), pp. 474–79.
3. *Fihrist,* p. 169,3: *kāna mutafalsifan qara' kutub al-awā'il.*
4. And to some extent also in Indian literature; cf. Qifṭī, ed. Lippert, p. 367.
5. *Fihrist,* p. 261, 25; *'ulūm al-qudamā' wa'l-'arab;* cf. Qifṭī, ed. Lippert, p. 77.
6. *Ibid.*, p. 138, 6: *al-'ulūm al-qadīma wa'l-ḥadītha;* p. 303, 22: *al-'ulūm al-qadīma wa'l-muḥdath.*
7. *Fihrist,* pp. 309, 11 on various magical practices: *'ilm fāshī ẓāhir fī'l-falāsifa.* The inclusion of these among "the sciences of philosophers" applies to the whole of Muslim literature. It is the opinion of Abū Bakr ar-Rāzī (d. ca. 311–320) that nobody could be called a philosopher who was not familiar with alchemy (*Fihrist,* p. 351). The mystic 'Abd al-Wahhāb ash-Sha'rānī (d. 973) boasts of his *karāhatī li-ta'allum 'ilm al-ḥarf 'ilm ar-raml wa'l-handasa wa's-sīmiyā' wa ghair dhālik min 'ulūm al-falāsifa* (geometry is thus on the same level with witchcraft), *Latā'if al-Minan* (Cairo, 1321), II, p. 44.
8. According to later reports, the caliph Mu'taḍid (279–289) who liked to surround himself with men versed in the *'ulūm al-awā'il,* subjected the philosopher Aḥmad b. aṭ-Ṭayyib as-Sarakhsī, one of the students of al-Kindī, to severe punishment (after having included him among his closest associates for a long time) because he was said to have tried to lead the caliph into heresy (*ilḥād*). When accused of killing as-Sarakhsi, the caliph is said to have replied: "I am a descendent (son) of the uncle ('Abbās, uncle of the Prophet) of the founder of this religion; I now occupy his place, and I am supposed to be a heretic? What would I be then?" (Yāqūt, ed. Margoliouth, I, p. 159). However, a later report (*Fihrist,* p. 262; cf. Qifṭī, pp. 77, 14ff.) which

indicates that as-Sarkhsī was punished as severely as he was because he had divulged secret intentions which the caliph had entrusted to him, seems to be more trustworthy.

9. I have mended *RQLS* of the text which Margoliouth reads as Proclus to *DQLS*. Concerning the alterations of the name Empedocles in Oriental transcription, see D. Kaufmann, *Studien über Salomon ibn Gabirol* (Budapest, 1899), 4; cf. *ZDMG,* LXV, 362.
10. Yāqūt, ed. Margoliouth, II, p. 33.
11. *Fihrist,* p. 119.
12. *Ibid.*, p. 138.
13. We shall see that, in a later work, he did not regard this mistrust as completely unjustified.
14. *Mi'yār al-'Ilm* (Cairo, 1329), p. 117.
15. *Munkidh* (Cairo, 1309), p. 29.
16. Among the various bearers of this *nisba* was Muḥammad b. 'Abd Allāh b. Abī'l-Faḍl (d. 655) who wrote an important commentary on the Quran (Suyūṭī, *Ṭabaqāt al-Mufassirīn,* ed. Meursinge [Leiden, 1839], no. 104 according to the *Irshād al-Arīb* of Yāqūt). In his list of sources for the *Itqān,* Suyūṭī mentions him as the author of a work on *tafsīr* which he himself had used frequently but without giving a more precise reference. Cf. Brockelmann, I, 312, where his importance as an exegete is not mentioned.
17. See the excerpt from the *Tafsīr* of al-Mursī in Suyūṭī, *Itqān* (Cairo, Castelli, 1279), II, pp. 147–49 (chap. 65).
18. Muslim V, 307. Bukhārī does not quote the *ḥadīth* in question, but it appears with special force in the *Musnad* of Aḥmad, VI, p. 318.
19. *Der Islam,* III, p. 217.
20. *Adab ad-Dunyā* (Istanbul, 1304), p. 25; cf. further my "Buch vom Wesen der Seele" (Berlin, 1907, *Abhandlungen der Kgl. GDW. zu Göttingen,* IX, no. 1), p. 60.
21. *Majmū'at ar-Rasā'il al-Kubrā* (Cairo, Sharafiya, 1324), I, p. 238.
22. *Kitāb al-Muwāfaqāt* (Kazan, 1909), I. p. 26.
23. *Ibid.*, p. 45.
24. Dhahabī in his biography of Ibn Rushd (cited by Renan in *Averröes et l'Averroisme* [4th ed., Paris, 1882], p. 458): *wa nasaba ilaihi kathrat al-ishtighāl bi'l''ulūm al-mahjūra min 'ulūm al-awā'il.* Suyūṭī, *Bughyat al-Wa'āt* (Cairo, 1326), p. 224, from Ḥasan b. 'Alī al-Qaṭṭānī (a physician in Merw, d. 548): *wa kānā fāḍilan 'āliman bi'l-lugha wa'l-adab wa'ṭ-ṭibb wa 'ulūm al-awā'il al-mahjūra wa kāna yanṣuru madhhabahum wa yamīlu ilaihim.* Cf. *al-'ulūm ar-radiaya'a* in appendix, II.
25. Yāqūt, ed. Margoliouth, II, p. 48.
26. *Recueil de textes relatifs à l'histoire des Seldjoucides,* ed. Houtsma, I, p. 89.
27. Concerning his *Maqāmāt,* cf. Huart in *Journal Asiatique* (1908), II, pp. 435–54, espec. 439.
28. Suyūṭī, *op. cit.*, p. 292.
29. Ibn al-Athīr, *Kāmil,* ad. ann. 485 (ed. Būlāq, X, p. 81).
30. Yāqūt, *op. cit.*, II, p. 120.
31. Cf. Goldziher, *Muhammedanische Studien,* II, p. 66, n. 4 [English translation entitled, *Muslim Studies* (London, 1971), II, p. 71, n. 7].
32. Subkī, *Ṭabaqāt ash-Shāfi'īya,* V, p. 154.
33. Ibn Rajab, *Ṭabaqāt al-Ḥanābila* (ms. from the Leipzig University Library, D.C. no. 375, Voller's catalogue, no. 708), fol. 148a.
34. *Wa kāna muttahaman fī dīnihī,* Yāqūt, ed. Margoliouth, VI, p. 208, probably from a Ḥanbalite source.
35. Brockelmann, I, p. 440.

36. Cited in the work on the banners of the Prophet by Abū'l-Ikhlāṣ al-Ghunaimī (Landberg MS, Yale University), fol. 10b.
37. Yāqūt, *op. cit.*, V, p. 116 penult: *qudiha fī dīnihī.* Strangely enough, there were people who took it for granted that grammarians also were not generally "pious people" even though they cultivated an ancillary discipline that was recognized as important by theologians (*op. cit.*, V, p. 225, according to Sam'ānī). This is probably related to the fact that the pietists felt they observed pride and arrogance in the philologists. Abū Ṭālib al-Makkī (d. 386, *Qūt al-Qulūb* [Cairo, 1310], I, p. 166) refers in connection with this observation to one of his teachers and then added a quotation from an earlier authority which goes as follows: "Grammar eliminates all humility from the heart." He quotes the following from another authority: "He who wishes to look down on all other persons should learn *'arabīya* [arabic grammar]." Feelings of animosity against the pedantry of grammarians and, as it were, a polemical reflex against the self-praise which was expressed in their epigrams and verses manifests itself in the belief that too much study of grammar could drive a person crazy (*SBWA* [1872], LXXII, p. 588). The renowned Mālikite, 'Abd Allāh b. Tabbān (d. 371), is reported to have said: "Learn some grammar, but then give it up soon; learn some poetry, but then diminish it; learn some (religious) science, and increase it the more. For much grammar drives one crazy, much poetry debases one, but much (religious) science refines one (Ibn Farḥūn, *ad-Dībāj al-Mudhhab fī Ma'rifat A'yān 'Ulamā' al-Madhhab* [ed. Fes], p. 142). Another generalization characterizes the grammarians as fanatical partisans of 'Alī (Maqqarī, I, p. 829). This is probably based on the fact that the prevailing tradition on the beginnings of Arabic grammar follows a tendency friendly to 'Alī; cf. *ZDMG,* L, p. 492.
38. Cf. Ibn Rajab, *op. cit.*, fol. 80b.
39. He continues Ibn al-Khaṭīb's history of Baghdad; Brockelmann, I, p. 360; cf. E. Amar, *Journal Asiatique* (1908), I, p. 241.
40. A statement of the Prophet; cf. *ZDMG,* L. p. 151.
41. Ibn Rajab, *loc. cit.*
42. *Ṭabaqāt ash-Shāfi'īya,* I, p. 218.
43. Cf. *Vorlesungen über den Islam,* p. 198 (16:1) [English translation, *Mohammed and Islam* (New Haven, Conn.—London, 1917), p. 210].
44. *Ṭabaqāt ash-Shāfi'īya* IV, p. 110.
45. In Suyūṭī, *Bughyat al-Wu'āt,* p. 375.
46. Cf. *Der Islam,* III, p. 216.
47. *Al-Mu'tazila,* 71, 2.
48. Cf. Sobernheim, "Die Shī'a in Aleppo," *Der Islam,* VI, p. 95ff.
49. Yāqūt, ed. Margoliouth, V, p. 244.
50. Qifṭī, ed. Lippert, p. 293.
51. Suyūṭī, *Bughyat al-Wu'āt,* p. 266. Similarly, the Hanbalite adh-Dhahabī reports that Abū'l-Ma'ālī al-Juwaynī (teacher of al-Ghazzālī) repented on his deathbed of his involvement with *kalām,* and that the painful torture from his illness had been caused by these sinful studies (in Abū'l-Muḥāsin, *Annals,* ed. Popper, II, p. 2, 277.)
52. Jāḥiẓ, *Bukhalā'*, ed. van Vloten, p. 87.
53. Ibn al-Athīr, ad ann. 277 (ed. Būlāq, VII, p. 162). The prohibition also concerned *kalām* works.
54. In Margoliouth, *JRAS* (1907), p. 274.
55. Cf. de Goeje in *Actes du 6ème Congrès des Orientalistes, 1883, IIème* partie, Sect. I (Leiden, 1885), p. 292, 300ff.
56. Ibn Rajab, *op. cit.*, 116a ff.

57. Ibn al-Athīr, ad ann. 555 (ed. Būlāq, XI, p. 104).
58. *DLZ* (1896), p. 719; cf. Brockelmann, II, p. 167 (Sibṭ al-Māridīnī); *Ibid.*, p. 211 (Abū'l-'Alā al-Bihishtī).
59. *Aghānī,* XVII, p. 18, 9 from bottom.
60. Qifṭī, ed. Lippert, p. 229.
61. Yāqūt, *op. cit.*, II, p. 46.
62. The strangeness and dissonance of the names of the Greek philosophers with whom they tried to impress people and even to confuse them is frequently pointed out in an ironical manner by the opponents of philosophy, for example by al-Ghazzālī, *Tahāfut al-Falāsifa* (Cairo, 1302), p. 3. Other passages are cited in *REJ,* L, p. 33, n. 2.
63. Ibn Qutayba, *Adab al-Kātib* (ed. Grunert), censures the philosophers for their tendency to try to make a show by using the pompous titles of Aristotelian books. The opponents of the Greek sciences expressed the same dislike for the terminology used in these books. Abū Sa'īd as-Sīrāfī offers the most characteristic example in his struggle against the philosopher Matā b. Yūnus regarding the value of Aristotelian logic (in Yāqūt, *op. cit.* III/I, p. 119). Jāḥiẓ (*Ḥayawān,* II, p. 11) makes fun of the terminology of the atomists (as a student of Naẓẓām, he was not one of them; cf. *Bukhalā'*, p. 139; *Bayān,* II, p. 8). In all such instances, the expression is used, as Ibn Fāris does in this example. Regarding the Manicheans, Jāḥiẓ says that they wanted to impress people by their strange terminology (*Ḥayawān,* I, p. 29; *Ibid.*, III, p. 113).
64. Cf. Yāqūt, *op. cit.*, II, p. 45, where it is said of Euclid that he wrote a book in which there were various theses (*ashkāl*).
65. Quoted from Suyūṭī, *Muzhir,* I, p. 156. The book (see *ZDMG,* XXVIII, p. 13) was published in Cairo, 1328 (246 pages).
66. We have excerpted only what al-Ghazzālī stresses as being dangerous.
67. *Munqidh,* p. 9.
68. *Tasḥīdh al-khawāṭir* through *kalām, Iḥyā'*, I, pp. 95, 97; cf. the book title, *Shadh al-Fiṭna* in Yāqūt, *op. cit.*, II, p. 74, penult. Even Muḥyī'd-Dīn b. al-'Arabī is critical of the fact that contemporary *fuqahā'* concern themselves with *jidāl* (*Futūḥāt Makkīya* (Cairo, 1329), IV, p. 459).
69. Literally: behind.
70. *Fātiḥat al-'Ulūm* (Cairo, 1322), p. 56.
71. Yāqūt, *op. cit.* II, p. 160; cf. *Fihrist,* p. 265.
72. Suyūṭī, *Bughyat al-Wu'āt,* p. 124.
73. Ikhwān aṣ-Ṣafā', IV, p. 146; cf.: *istinbāṭ al-qaḍā' min an-nujūm* in Brockelmann, I, p. 219, 23. The horoscope is identified with divine determination (Yāqūt, ed. Margoliouth, V, p. 360).
74. Ikhwān, p. 74, 9.
75. Abū Ḥayyān at-Tawḥīdī, *Muqābasāt* (ed. Bombay), p. 5. Regarding an admissible formula for the causal influence of the stars, see my *Vorlesungen über den Islam,* p. 130 [Eng. trans. *Mohammed and Islam,* pp. 138–39].
76. *Al-Mu'tazila,* ed. T. W. Arnold (Leipzig, 1902), p. 53.
77. Najāshī, *Kitāb ar-Rijāl* (Bombay, 1317), p. 47. Cf. further *al-Mu'tazila, op. cit.* pp. 55, 58.
78. Ibn 'Asākir in Mehren, *Exposé,* p. 101. He polemicizes also against the meteorology of Aristotle (*Ibid.*, p. 102).
79. Emphatic reference is made to the work of Abū Bakr al-Khaṭīb al-Baghdādī (d. 463 [Brockelmann, I, p. 329]) *Kitāb al-Qawl fī Nujūm;* Subkī, *Ṭabaqāt ash-Shāfi'īya,* II, p. 235, 319.
80. It is reported that in praise of himself he boasted of his knowledge before Hārūn

ar-Rashīd. The more precise specification of his scholarship in this area seems to refer to astronomy (in Yāqūt, ed. Margoliouth, VI, p. 372)

81. Subkī, *op. cit.*, I, p. 243, 258; polemical epigrams against astrology in Yāqūt, *op. cit.* p. 197.
82. Qifṭī, p. 153.
83. Yāqūt, ed. Margoliouth, V, p. 467.
84. Yāqūt, *op. cit.* VI, p. 225.
85. E.g., *Fihrist,* p. 279.
86. People who had knowledge of astronomy were preferred for the office of *muwaqqit;* see, e.g., Brockelmann, II, p. 126.
87. *Mafātīḥ al-Ghayb* (Būlāq, 1289), VI, p. 149.
88. This fact forms the subject of the inquiry by Ḥasan al-'Abbāsī (in the work cited in *Abhandlungen zur arabischen Philologie,* I, p. 215).
89. Yāqūt, *op. cit.*, VI, p. 310.
90. In Qasṭallānī, IX, p. 324, in *riqāq* no. 40.
91. *Tahāfūt al-Falāsifa,* p. 4, 17ff.
92. *Maqāṣid al-Falāsifa* (ed. Ṣabrī al-Kurdī, Cairo 1331), p. 3.
93. *Fatāwā Ḥadīthīya* (Cairo, 1307), p. 35.
94. Mohammed Ben Cheneb, *Proverbes arabes de l'Algérie et du Maghreb II* (Paris, 1906), p. 283.
95. Ibn Abī Uṣaybi'a, II, p. 139.
96. Cf. *Vorlesungen über den Isalm,* 129 [Eng. trans. *Mohammed and Islam,* pp. 137–38].
97. *Book of the Nature of the Soul,* p. 13. Cf. al-Ghazzālī, *Mi'yār al-'Ilm,* p. 131; cf. *Mīzān al-'Amal* (Cairo, 1328), p. 160.
98. Merely as an example, we mention a *Kitāb ar-Radd 'alā Ahl al-Manṭiq* by Nawbakhtī (Najāshī, *op. cit.* p. 47).
99. Jāḥiẓ, e.g., declares himself to be opposed to medicine; the famous physician, Muḥammad b. Zakarīyā' ar-Rāzī, polemicized against this attitude of his (*Fihrist,* p. 300); cf. *WZKM,* XIII, p. 53, n. 3.
100. Cf. above note 64.
101. This probably refers to the Pyrrhonistic tendency of the *mutakallimūn.*
102. *Rasā'il* (ed. Bombay), IV, p. 95.
103. *Der Islam,* III, p. 214.
104. Cf. *JRAS* (1909), p. 775.
105. In Suyūṭī, *Bughyat al-Wu'āt,* p. 348. Cf. Amedroz, *Der Islam, loc. cit.* p. 345.
106. In Yāqūt, ed. Margoliouth, II, p. 276.
107. Kulīnī, *Uṣūl al-Kāfī* (Bombay, 1302), p. 52, 10: *inna an-nās lā yazālu bihim al-manṭiq ḥattā yatakallamū fī'llāh; fāidhā sami'tum dhālika qūlū: lā ilāha illā al-Wāḥid alladhī laisa kamithlī shai'un.* This sentence reminds one of the Sunnī tradition cited in *ZDMG,* LVII, p. 393.
108. It sometimes served as a life-long *laqab* (title) for such scholars, as e.g. Yaḥyā b. 'Adī al-Manṭiqī, Abū Sulaimān al-Manṭiqī; the latter was the focal point of a group of philosophers whose discussions were collected by Abū Ḥayyān at-Tawḥīdī in the *Muqābasāt* (de Boer, *Geschichte der philosophie im Islam,* p. 114 f. [Eng. trans. *The History of Philosophy In Islam* (London, 1903), p. 126f]); however, he also investigated dream-visions (*Fihrist,* p. 316). Besides the sound plural of *manṭiqī,* one also finds the broken plural, *manāṭiqa* (probably under the formal influence of *falāsifa*) in Sha'rānī, *Latā'if al-Minan,* I, p. 124.
109. However, the work whose annotation was assigned by the caliph Mu'taḍid to the court-scholar Zajjāj for which he received a generous stipend (and which was reserved

for the exclusive use of the caliph's library), was certainly not devoted to logic as one might conclude from the title of the original work, *Jāmi' al-Manṭiq,* given as such in many sources. The description of the work given in the *Fihrist,* p. 60, can only refer to a philological work and justifies the reading *Jāmi'an-Nuṭq* favored by Flügel and which was also transmitted by Yāqūt, ed. Margoliouth, I, p. 57. To be sure, a student of this Zajjāj, Muḥammad b. Isḥāq Abū'n-Naḍr al-Kindī, was praised as follows: *kāna 'āliman bi'l-handasa qayyiman bi-'ulūm al-awā'il;* Tanūkhī in Yāqūt, *loc. cit.* VI, p. 407.

110. A very detailed description of the destruction of those books can be found in Ibn Sa'īd, *Kitāb Ṭabaqāt al-Umam,* ed. Cheikho (Beirut, 1912), p. 66f.
111. *Kitāb al-Milal,* ed. Cairo, I, p. 94.
112. *Milal,* II, p. 95.
113. *Ibid.*, I, p. 20.
114. Cf. *ZDMG,* LXIX, p. 193.
115. He [Ibn Ḥazm] received his date of birth directly from him; from Abū Rāfi', son of Ibn Ḥazm, comes information concerning the works of the father.
116. *Kitāb Ṭabaqāt al-Umam,* p. 76, 5ff.; cf. Yāqūt, ed. Margoliouth, V. p. 27, where the passage is cited.
117. Cf. M. Asin Palacios, *Abenmasarra y su escuela* (Madrid, 1914), p. 19, n. 5.
118. Maqqarī, I, p. 716; cf. the introduction to the edition of the travels of Ibn Jubayr (ed. Wright—de Goeje), 14/15.
119. According to the description of Ibn al-'Arabī (*Futūḥāt Makkīya* [Cairo, 1326], I, pp. 153f.), Ibn Jubayr was present at the funeral of Averröes and behaved in a very dignified way.
120. Cf. *Tahāfat al-Falāsifa* (Cairo, I'lāmīya, 1302), pp. 6, 10.
121. *Maqāṣid al-Falāsifa,* p. 7.
122. *Qisṭās* (Cairo, 1900), p. 59.
123. *Mi'yār al-'Ilm,* p. 23.
124. *Mi'yār,* p. 86ff.
125. E.g., *Ibid.*, pp. 46, 58, 72 and throughout the entire book.
126. Pp. 73, 78, 148, and others.
127. P. 91.
128. *Maqāṣid,* p. 43.
129. *Mi'yār,* pp. 112, 69, 91, 130. Also his ethical work, *Mizān al-'Amal,* pp. 94, 159ff.
130. *Mi'yār,* p. 101.
131. In any case, it certainly belongs to his later years; in the conclusion al-Ghazzālī refers to the fact that he deals with logic in his *Mi'yār,* but that he had not published the work because it still required some final touches. This text, therefore, appears to be older than the definitive edition which was finally published, and to which al-Ghazzālī refers in *Tahāfut,* p. 52.
132. *Miḥaqq an-Naẓar* (ed. Na'asānī-Kabbānī, Cairo, n.d.).
133. Even in the small tract *Rasālat al-Wa'z wa'l I'tiqād* which he wrote for his friend Aḥmad b. Salāma ad-Dimimmī (Brockelmann, I, p. 421, n. 12, where it is incorrectly given as Damīmī) and which is printed in the appendix to the Cairo edition (Maṭb. Taraqqī, 1319/1901), he requests of his friend the same prayer. This same request is repeated literally in the introductory passage of *Mi'yār al-'Ilm* as well as in *Munqidh,* p. 30.
134. *Munqidh,* 10/11.
135. Editio Wüstenfeld no. 757 (IX, 24ff.), quoted in its entirety in Subkī, *Ṭabaqāt ash-Shāfi'īya,* V, pp. 159–62.
136. Brockelmann, I, p. 358, n. 19.

137. *Yattahamu fī dīnihi li-kawn al-'ulūm al-'aqlīya ghālibat 'alaihi.*
138. اسّ للسفه a word play with the second part of the word [فلـ[سفه. Abū'l-Fatḥ al-Bustī coined the word play الفلسفة فلّ السفه (in Tha'ālibī, *Yatīmat ad-Dahr* [Damascus, 1304], IV, p. 207, 13) which the jurist Abū 'Imrān used in an epigram on philosophy (*Kitāb Alif-Bā'* [Cairo, 1287], p. 23).
139. Cf. *Muhammedanische Studien,* II, p. 285, n. 2 [Eng. trans. *Muslim Studies,* II, p. 262, n. 2], 'Abd al-Qādir al-Jīlānī, *Ghunya* (Mecca, 1314), I, p. 66.
140. Subkī, *Ṭabaqāt ash-Shāfi'iya,* IV, pp. 129, 131.
141. In the work *Abkār al-Afkār,* listed in Brockelmann, I, p. 393, the passage on the Ṣābians was published by the Beirut monthly, *al-Mashriq,* IV, pp. 400–403.
142. Ibn Abī Uṣaybi'a, II, p. 174.
143. Ibn Khallikān, ed. Wüstenfeld, no. 443 (V, 20).
144. *Mu'id an-Ni'am wa Mubīd an-Niqam,* ed. Myhrman, p. 111. Here Subkī refers to the introduction in his *Sharḥ Mukhtaṣar Ibn Ḥājib,* where he collected the views of the older authorities on this question. He refers to it also in *Ṭabaqāt ash-Shāfi'iya,* IV, p. 129: a defense of al-Ghazzālī against Ibn aṣ-Ṣalāḥ.
145. The letter of condolence was printed in the *Manār,* X, pp. 616–21.
146. Cf. *Die Ẓāhiriten,* p. 130 [Eng. trans. *The Ẓāhirīs,* p. 122].
147. In Meursinge, *Sojūṭii Liber de Interpretibus Korani,* p. 6.
148. From the *Nayl al-Ibtihāj* of Aḥmad Bābā as Sūdānī in *Ta'rīf al- Khalaf bi Rijāl as-Salaf,* ed. Abū'l-Qāsim Muḥammad al-Hafnāwī, I (Algiers, 1906), pp. 169–70, where both poems are printed.
149. See my essay "Zur Charakteristik . . . Suyūṭīs und seiner literarischen Tätigkeit," *SBWA* (1871), *Phil. hist. Kl.,* LXIX, p. 17.
150. Cf. *REJ,* LX, pp. 34ff. *Revue de monde musulman,* XII, pp. 210–11.
151. Brockelmann, I, pp. 464, 466; II, p. 355.
152. M. Horten, "Sanūsī und die griechische Philosophie," *Der Islam* (1915), pp. 178–88.
153. Brockelmann, II, p. 250.
154. The famous philosopher and physician Muḥammad b. Zakarīyā' ar-Rāzī (d. ca. 311–320) had already written a didactic poem on logic (*Fihrist,* p. 301).
155. 'Alī Mubārak, *Khiṭaṭ Jadīda,* XII, p. 11.

IX
Hanbalite Islam

GEORGE MAKDISI

To my teacher and friend, Professor Henri Laoust
of the Collège de France

On the eve of the Second World War, Henri Laoust described the Hanbalite movement as "a methodological, dogmatic and juridical system that issued from the work of Aḥmad b. Ḥanbal," a jurist who died in the third/ninth century. This movement "through the personality of its founder and that of its principal representatives" was "one of the most specifically constitutive elements of Muslim culture."[1]

At that time anyone acquainted with the works of earlier Islamists on the Hanbalite school would have found these statements extravagant. Older scholars were far from being of the young French Islamist's point of view.

These statements, however, far from being gratuitous, are fully in accord with the historical facts. They agree with the facts for the period of Ibn Taymīya, the subject of Henri Laoust's dissertation, published in 1939. But they also accord with the facts for the period of Ibn 'Aqīl, a Hanbalite writer who lived two centuries earlier and whom I have studied. The time has come to elucidate the place of Hanbalite Islam in the larger history of Islamic thought.

The studies which follow will deal with the following: 1. Western Orientalism and Muslim Religious History, 2. Institutions of Learning and Religious Movements, 3. Sufism and Hanbalism, and 4. Muslim Orthodoxy.

1. Western Orientalism and Muslim Religious History

The dearth of editions of Arabic texts has always been one of the most serious problems in Islamic studies, especially in the area of Muslim religious history. In the past, both in the West and in the Muslim East, isolated individuals here and there have devoted themselves to the editing of texts. Unfortunately, however, the results were only a drop of water in the ocean. And although in our day the situation has improved and progress has been made, we are moving forward only very slowly. There are a number of reasons for this, among them the difficulty of the language, and the complexity of the technical terminology used in the religious sciences in Islam, not to mention the fact that editing texts is a most laborious and thankless task. In any case, as long as these unedited texts languish in the libraries of the East and West, unused except by an occasional researcher, the study of the religious history of Islam will suffer.

To get an idea of the documentary wealth which remains untapped in the libraries of the world one has only to consult the bio-bibliographies of Carl Brockelmann[1] and Fuat Sezgin.[2] It should be pointed out, however, that the libraries mentioned in these two works are only those whose catalogue can be consulted. There are many other libraries whose works have not been catalogued or whose catalogues (often little more than lists) have not yet been published and which consequently should be consulted on the spot. Then there are also private libraries, with or without lists, which were formerly the property of scholars whose descendants tended to neglect the contents for lack of interest.

The wealth of texts from the past thirteen centuries of Islam is such that one can only comprehend with difficulty the resultant loss for Islamic studies. One may, however, acquire some idea of this loss by paging through bibliographical compendia such as the *Fihrist* of Ibn an Nadīm[3] and the *Kashf aẓ-Ẓunūn* of Ḥājjī-Khalīfa[4] which cite works, the majority of which have not survived to our time. But what brings this loss to mind most effectively are the biographical works in which the writings of earlier authors are listed. These authors whose works are known only by titles are numerous indeed. Bibliographical lists have recently been established by Islamists for a number of Muslim authors, and these may now be examined.[5]

For the most part, these bibliographical lists are based on biographical sources whose authors ordinarily mention only a portion of a given author's total works. Again and again, the biographer himself tells us this explicitly.

The *Kitāb al-Funūn* of Ibn 'Aqīl, to mention an interesting example from my own experience, is a work which has been preserved for us at the Bibliothèque Nationale[6] in a manuscript of 267 folios and which comes to almost 800 printed pages in an edition that I have just completed.[7] This work was written in a period of about four months. Based upon my own calculations and the most conservative estimate of his biographers, I am reasonably certain that Ibn 'Aqīl wrote approximately two hundred works of the same type—in short, one hundred and eighty thousand pages. The larger part of this work consisted of accounts of scholarly discussions and debates which took place in Baghdad in his presence, and in which he himself took part. This was clearly a source of the greatest importance for the religious history of this period. And yet this is only one example of a single author from among so many others which remain unknown.

Editions of Arabic texts now available to us fall into two categories: 1. those which are genuinely edited, and 2. those which are really only "printed manuscripts." The editions in the first category are those which established again, as far as possible, the original text of the author by following either the autograph, or a unicum or several copies, and which attempt to reconstruct the archetype. Those of the second category have been edited, as V. Langlois says, "from the first copies, good or bad, that came to hand, combined and corrected at random."[8] The "printed manuscript" is little more than a reproduction of one or several of the existing copies of the work, merely one more copy reproducing the faults of the other copyists and adding its own errors. This state of affairs would never be tolerated, for example, in the classical studies, whereas in Islamic studies it is the usual practice. Yet one must be grateful to the editors of both categories for having made these documents available to us.

But even if we consider all of the published documents, critical editions, and "printed manuscripts," we have at our disposal only a small percentage of the existing works. Nonetheless, the state of Islamic studies today is improved compared to what it was a century ago when studies in the field of religious history were beginning to be taken up seriously. Then it was a rare scholar who went beyond the few, existing printed works. Competent scholars were equally few. The reading of manuscripts was in many cases an onerous and tiring task, and required an enormous amount of time. It required lengthy trips and long visits on the spot to find the documents, examine them, classify them and finally copy them by hand.

If the manuscript situation has improved with time through the acquisition of Western libraries, the study of sources, on the other hand, has failed methodologically to come to terms with the prejudices or intentional structure of these sources. Even today, fidelity to the canons of historical methodology leaves much to be desired, especially in this field of study. It is, however, true that the nineteenth century, which saw the birth of Islamic studies as a scientific discipline, must bear a large share of the blame.

In the European view of things, Islam in the nineteenth century was represented by Turkey. Diplomatic ties between the latter and Europe had existed for several centuries. Turkey and the Wahhābīs of Saudi Arabia were in conflict with each other, and the Turks accused the Wahhabis of heretical views. It was observed, moreover, that the Wahhābīs were linked to Ibn Taymīya and that he belonged to the Hanbalite school, with the result that both Ibn Taymīya and the Hanbalite school found themselves tainted with heresy. Leading scholars such as Goldziher and Macdonald attempted to show that these were not heretics who lacked respect for the prophetic traditions, but that on the contrary they were rather too respectful, for the Hanbalites and their Wahhābī disciples both belonged to the "old" Muslim orthodoxy.[9] These two scholars, however, were not interested in rehabilitating the partisans of the "old orthodoxy," since in their view, Hanbalites and Wahhābīs were the open enemies of the "new Muslim orthodoxy" which had come into being following the Mu'tazilite debacle. The result was that instead of aiding in the rehabilitation of the Hanbalites, the recognition of their orthodoxy only led to the unfounded accusations directed toward them. Thus the Hanbalites came to be considered as anthropomorphists who, in their ultra-conservative traditionalism, were opposed both to the theologians (*mutakallimūn*) and to the mystics of Islam.

Another factor contributed to making the nineteenth century the great enemy of Hanbalite studies: namely, the fact that the Hanbalite school was not as large as the other Sunni schools of law. In fact Brockelmann, in his history of Arabic literature, deals with only three Sunni schools of law: the Hanafite, the Shāfi'ite, and the Mālikite, characterizing the Hanbalite school as one of the "insignificant" (*unbedeutend*) schools.[10] It is only with the *qāḍī* Abū Ya'lā in the fifth/eleventh century that Goldziher recognized the existence of a Hanbalite school of law alongside the other Sunni schools.[11]

Fuat Sezgin has recently corrected this error in his bio-bibliographical work on Arabic literature in which he mentions the Hanbalite school among the four Sunni schools of law and links it to its founder, Ahmad b. Hanbal.[12] But having corrected this error, he unfortunately introduces another one even more serious than that of Brockelmann. Under the influence of Goldziher's *Vorlesungen,* he identifies the Ash'arites and the Māturīdīs with the *ahl as-sunna* as opposed to the Mu'tazilites. Given the character of their doctrine, as he saw it, the Hanbalite school was to be linked to the "old orthodoxy" of Aḥmad b. Ḥanbal, its founder.[13] Had it not been for the interest shown by the Salafī movement in Egypt and the Wahhābīs of Saudi Arabia in the Hanbalites, Hanbalism might well have remained even longer, perhaps forever, among the "insignificant" schools in the mind of Islamists.

The relatively small size of the Hanbalite school compared to the other schools has given rise to inaccurate impressions regarding the school. It has lent credence to the notion that Hanbalism occupied a position on the fringes of orthodoxy, a notion which has tended to discourage young scholars from taking up a serious study of the school and of its representatives. With rare exceptions, the false notions thus engendered continue to appear in our survey works on Islam. To document this lack of interest in the study of Hanbalism, one need only consult Gustav Pfanmüller's bibliographical work, *Handbuch der Islam-Literatur,* published in 1923 and concerned with the state of Islamic studies since its inception as a serious academic discipline.

In the fifth chapter of this work,[14] the Hanbalite school is listed among the schools of law. Among the studies on this school the author cites these by the following Islamists: the American Walter M. Patton, the Hungarian Goldziher, the Dutchman Juynboll, the Scotsman Macdonald, and the Hungarian Martin Schreiner. Among the authors mentioned, it is impossible to find one concerned with the study of the Hanbalite school as such, with perhaps one exception; a first-rate scholar who went to some lengths to discredit this school,[15] as he had already done to the (juridico-theological) Ẓāhirī school a quarter of a century earlier.[16] I am of course referring to Goldziher who was supported by Macdonald following closely on his heels. Both were passionately opposed to Hanbalism, as we shall see below.

The American scholar Walter M. Patton, who wrote a fine work on Ạhmad b. Ḥanbal,[17] was not able to free himself from the influence of Goldziher who had himself already expressed his own views on the Hanbalite school in his work on the Ẓāhirīs.[18] Thus we find Ạhmad b. Ḥanbal, the founder of the Hanbalite school, disassociated from his followers. To these latter Patton devotes only the last two lines of his work.[19] Patton's intention was to undertake a study of Ạhmad b. Ḥanbal as an *imām,* that is, as one of the great orthodox leaders of Islam. His work was published in 1897. Some years earlier, H. F. Wüstenfeld had published a study of another great *imām,* ash-Shāfiʿī, in which he had also dealt with the disciples of this leader up to the year 300 of the *Hijra* (A.D. 912–913).[20] Wüstenfeld's study probably inspired Patton to do his, which was carried out under the direction of the Dutch scholar, de Goeje, who had also written on the *imām* ash-Shāfiʿi.[21] But, in contrast with Wüstenfeld, Patton dealt only with the *imām* Ibn Ḥanbal and the famous inquisition (*miḥna*) directed against him. He attributed the importance of the role played by this *imām* to the fact that he had successfully resisted the Muʿtazilites, even though the latter had been supported by the ʿAbbāsid caliphs. According to Patton, the rigidity of Ibn Ḥanbal's methods and views as well as[22] his aversion to generalization and deduction

> . . . prevented him from leaving behind any system of opinions. . . . Hence the uninfluential character of the Hanbalite school. Their master's teaching was unsystematic, and much ground was lost ere his spirit and teaching could be put before the world in such a form as to accomplish any powerful effect. His personality in his lifetime and after his death was a great force in the Muslim world; and the personality seems yet to be as powerful in influence as the views which he enunciated, *though his following has never been great in comparison with that of the other three orthodox imāms.*[23]

Patton has properly appreciated Ạhmad b. Ḥanbal's importance in the history of his time as well as for the modern period, though he speaks of the latter with some hesitation. His hesitation derives from the fact that Ạhmad never had a large following and that his theological position, rigid and severe, could not have won the support of the rank and file.[24]

Patton tells us that the importance of the questions disputed during the *miḥna* "lies in the fact that they settled the orthodox character of Islam."[25] In order to maintain his objectivity, he says he does not wish to raise the question of whether the preservation of orthodoxy is a good thing or not, but simply states that "in the preservation of orthodoxy lies the preservation of Islam."[26] Still, says Patton, one must be grateful to rationalism for having affirmed the principle (though non-Islamic) that thought must be free in its search for truth. But elsewhere we find Patton condemning the rationalism of Aḥmad b. Ḥanbal's time as an "abuse of free thought" which had fallen prey to "a love of speculation for speculation's sake."[27] He characterized Aḥmad as "the most remarkable figure in the camp of Muslim orthodoxy" after the death of ash-Shāfi'ī.[28] The author then takes European writers to task for having too often written their accounts in a spirit hostile to the orthodox theology of Islam, and for having been excessive in their praise of Mu'tazilite rationalists.[29]

Having expressed his view on Aḥmad b. Ḥanbal and the inquisition, Patton makes his exit, and one hears nothing more from him. Goldziher and others enter the scene again. They pay their respects to Aḥmad, but they are not so kind when it comes to the school that bears his name. Their studies, especially Goldziher's, tended to discourage even more any serious study of the school. In the field of Sunni law, scholars focused their efforts on the other three schools, as they did to the edition and translation of their works. In theology, interest in Mu'tazilism subsided and instead they turned to the study of Ash'arism, to the edition and translation of Ash'arite works in theology, and also in biography and history.

As it fell to Goldziher (in his capacity as one of the greatest scholars of his time) to pave the way for others, his influence effectively eliminated the Zāhirite school as an object of scholarly research for three quarters of a century; that is, until the recent work by Mr. Roger Arnaldez.[30] In the wake of Goldziher's study of the Hanbalite school, the same fate would have awaited that school had it not been for the work of Mr. Henri Laoust.[31] Macdonald, also a leading scholar, was interested in al-Ghazzālī.[32] As it ḥappened, these two scholars to whom we owe so much in the field of Islamic studies, joined hands to influence, in a certain sense, the elaboration of Muslim religious history. Thus there came into being a history whose orientation was quasi-romantic, built up around a sacred triad: 1. al-Ghazzālī, a theologian and jurist who allegedly wanted to extricate himself from both theology and law in favor of mysticism; 2. the Niẓāmīya *madrasa,* a college which was characterized as Ash'arite and *official;* and 3. Niẓām al-Mulk, the Seljuk vizier who allegedly established Ash'arism as a new Muslim orthodoxy. Mu'tazilism and Hanbalism, as well as other religious movements, were relegated to an inferior position, victims of the influence which history, thus conceived, exerted, and apparently still exerts, on its readers.

Patton contributed to the success of this interpretation by characterizing Ibn Hanbal as an inflexible *imām* and accusing him of anthropomorphism,[33] despite his acceptance of *bila kaif* ("without comment"), a principle which was later appropriated by Ash'arism, but which Patton had little regard for. In this perspective, Aḥmad b. Ḥanbal appears as a great hero of Muslim orthodoxy, but in this case it is an obscurantist orthodoxy. And yet Patton attempted to write a truly objective work and in good faith.

After Patton, the study that Goldziher undertook concerned itself not with Ibn Hanbal but with Hanbalism. Goldziher had already shown an interest in this school in his work on Ẓāhirism.[34] This time he was to devote a special study to it.[35] Though it was a review of Patton's work, it offered him an opportunity to express his ideas on Hanbalism.[36] From the beginning of this study, one can see that Goldziher was fascinated by this school of which he was to become an antagonist. In the very first sentence, he draws the attention of the reader to the fact that of all the legal schools of Islam, the one linked to the name of Aḥmad b. Ḥanbal was the smallest. (Notice here the echo of Patton's thesis.) But this school, which Patton and others judged insignificant,[37] "displays the most pronounced individual character."[38] Goldziher then draws attention to the school's rigid opposition to rationalism, its literal interpretation of the Quran and the *ḥadīth,* and its appeal to the common people, an idea which does not accord with what Patton said.[39] Goldziher then goes on to state that the Hanbalites "delayed the success of the conciliatory theology of Ash'arism for a century and a half."[40]

Goldziher attributes this very pronounced individual character of the Hanbalites to the rigidity of their doctrine and to their critique of the customs and morals of the masses whereas the other legal schools were rather indifferent to such fine points. He claims that the Hanbalites were defeated as a movement—doubtless an allusion to the advent in the fifth/eleventh century of al-Ghazzālī, and the Niẓāmīya *madrasa,* and Niẓām al-Mulk—but that they again made themselves felt in Syria in the seventh/thirteenth century through Ibn Taymīya, "a personality," he adds, "whose importance in the history of Muslim theology and religious literature is awaiting a really serious study."[41] We may perhaps be permitted to think that Goldziher did not expect the results which his invitation called forth in Mr. Laoust's study of Ibn Taymīya.[42]

Goldziher then proceeds to argue that the Hanbalite school's historical influence was due to the writings of Ibn Taymīya and his disciples, among whom he includes the Wahhābīs. In effect, he links the founder of

Wahhābism to Ibn Taymīya on the basis of the fact that certain manuscripts preserved in the library of the University of Leiden are copies of works of Ibn Taymīya which Muḥammad b. 'Abd al-Wahhāb, the founder of Wahhābism had copied with his own hand.[43]

In his review of Patton's book, Goldziher refers to it as a "diligent piece of work" based on manuscripts previously unused in the study of this subject.[44] Among the sources which Patton used, the one by Maqrīzī (d. 845/1442) is, however, criticized by Goldziher. According to him, al-Maqrīzī shared the spirit of Hanbalism, since he was hostile to schools which employed *qiyās* (reasoning by analogy) in law and in theology.[45] On the other hand, Subkī's *Ṭabaqāt,*[46] a biographical history—also used by Patton—is praised as "an invaluable mine for the history of theological movements in Islam."[47]

One can readily understand Goldziher's high regard for the work by Subkī, a Shāfi'ite-Ash'arite author of very definite anti-Hanbalite sentiments. One is at first surprised to discover that al-Maqrīzī received this condemnation, for it was on the basis of a text from al-Maqrīzī that the German scholar, Alfred von Kremer, in his *Geschichte der herrschenden Ideen des Islams,* wrote his chapter on the "Victory of Orthodoxy," in which he discussed the triumphs of a theology which allegedly attempted to mediate between rationalist Mu'tazilism and traditionalist, ultra-conservative Hanbalism.[48] One will recall, however, that Goldziher does not, in fact, attribute this attempt at mediation to al-Ash'arī himself, but rather to the Ash'arites of a century and a half later. Goldziher criticizes al-Ash'arī for having capitulated to Aḥmad b. Ḥanbal's doctrine, and he insists that one must not credit him with something which belongs to the Ash'arites of the fifth/eleventh century if one is to remain within the real world.[49]

In his works entitled *Vorlesungen über den Islam* and *Mohammedanische Studien,*[50] Goldziher repeats his view of the *miḥna* or inquisition of Aḥmad b. Ḥanbal: "I have said elsewhere, and I can repeat it here: 'the inquisitors of liberalism were, quite possibly, even more repugnant than their slavishly literal colleagues; in any case, their fanaticism *is more odious than that of their victims* whom they imprisoned and maltreated.' " Here Goldziher scores a point against both the Mu'tazilites and the victims of the inquisition themselves to the eventual advantage of Ash'arism. He is also critical of the intolerant rationalism of some 'Abbāsid caliphs and says that the "old orthodoxy" (that is, Hanbalism) could again breathe freely under the caliphate of al-Mutawakkil, but that this Hanbalism was rapidly transformed from a "repressed church" into a "militant church." There was supposedly a return to the "dark ages," which "rapidly degenerated into a fanatical terrorism." This lasted until the fifth/eleventh century, at which time it was defeated. According to him, one would have to conclude that, all things considered, the inquisition served the interests of the old orthodoxy, for if the later subsequently gained in strength, it was only because of persecution.[51]

The Hungarian scholar, Martin Schreiner, devoted two sections of his monograph, *Contribution to the History of Religious Movements in Islam,* to Aḥmad b. Ḥanbal and Ibn Taymīya. This monograph was published toward the end of the nineteenth century in several parts, the first of which appeared in 1898, the same year as Goldziher's review of Patton's book and in the same journal.[52] Ten years after this monograph, Goldziher wrote a study on the Hanbalites, the title of which recalls that of Schreiner: "A Contribution to the History of the Hanbalite Movements." [53] Note here the use of the plural in the title: there was not one single Hanbalite movement, one single and continuous development, but rather several movements linked to the name of Aḥmad b. Ḥanbal. This suggests an intermittent Hanbalite struggle against a well-established new orthodoxy.

Goldziher begins his study by drawing the reader's attention to changes in the position of *kalām,* or rationalist theology, in public life, and he attributes these changes to two factors: first, the reaction during the time of the Caliph al-Mutawakkil, in favor of conservative Hanbalism; and second, the appearance of *kalām* into the full light of day in its attenuated, Ash'arite form, thanks to Niẓām al-Mulk.[54] It ought to be noted here that these two factors are linked to the policies of two political figures: an 'Abbāsid caliph and a Seljuk vizier.

Meanwhile, he says, the rationalists had to be on their guard against the attacks of an obscurantist clericalism. The attitude of those in power, hostile to the rationalists, gave considerable encouragement to the zealots who, over the centuries, considered it their principal aim to combat them. These zealots were the Hanbalites. They were hostile not only to the Mu'tazilites but also to the Ash'arites, contrary to the other orthodox school, he says. They had the authority and the approval of the masses on their side. Popular opinion was more often than not openly favorable to Hanbalite orthodoxy.[55]

Note here that he is speaking of a Hanbalism which, like Ash'arism, is also orthodox. In Goldziher's place I would be hard pressed to explain how "the other orthodox schools" were *for* the Ash'arites, whereas the

Hanbalites enjoyed the support and approval of the masses. What are they, these masses, if not orthodox? A little later we shall see how Goldziher came to distinguish *two* orthodoxies in Islam.

The Ash'arites were persecuted until the event of the Seljuk dynasty, he argues, though he does concede that there were difficult times under the first Seljuk, Tughril Beg, who claimed to have ties with orthodoxy. Goldziher points out that Tughril's vizier officially cursed Rāfiḍities and Ash'arites, but that the situation improved under the sultan Alp Arslān, thanks to the protection of the vizier Niẓām al-Mulk.[56]

It was in the middle of the sixth/twelfth century, according to Goldziher, that Ash'arism appeared to have carried the day, although the Hanbalites had not given up the fight. The latter continued to attack the positions of the prevailing doctrine in matters relating to dogma and ritual.[57] Goldziher states that Hanbalite fanaticism expressed itself not only toward others, but also, and with implacable severity, toward elements within Hanbalism itself. As an example, he mentions the case of Ibn 'Aqīl who later became the highest authority of the school and who had had the courage to study under certain Mu'tazilite scholars teachings that ran counter to those of his own school and on account of which he was harrassed.[58]

In the sixth/twelfth century, according to Goldziher, Ash'arite theology was accepted; he suggests that it was recognized by *ijmā'*, or consensus, and that Hanbalism was reduced to an inferior current of thought, tolerated by orthodoxy.[59] But in the seventh/thirteenth century, the Ash'arites of Syria continued to be troubled by the Hanbalites.[60] The condemnation of Ibn Taymīya did not diminish the Hanbalite influence among the masses.[61] Finally, even though the Ottoman Turks were hostile to the Hanbalites,[62] the Wahhābī movement in the eighteenth century associated itself with the doctrines of Ibn Taymiya.[63]

This, in summary, is the substance of Goldziher's article on what he calls the Hanbalite movements. But this is not all that Goldziher has to say about Hanbalism. He refers to it often in his works on Islam in terms which are usually not flattering. Goldziher accused the Hanbalites of anthropomorphism,[64] fanaticism,[65] and intolerance.[66] He also accused the Hanbalites of having delayed the supposed triumph of Ash'arism.[67]

This unflattering characterization of Hanbalism and its representatives may be attributed not only to certain scholars, but also to the sources on which they have drawn.[68] Further, the selection of the sources to be used was influenced by the orientation and interest which were brought to the study of the various schools and movements of Islam. With regard to the Hanbalites, the sources used were either indifferent or openly hostile. Hanbalite sources were ignored—not only the manuscript sources, but also the printed works which began to appear in the first half of the twentieth century—except when they were used to censure the Hanbalites, and even then it was only rarely. We may cite, for example, the case of Ibn 'Aqīl which we have just mentioned, for which Goldziher used Ibn Rajab's history of the Hanbalites in manuscript,[69] a work which only saw the light of day through the efforts of H. Laoust and S. Dahan in 1951.[70] Even in his work on Aḥmad b. Ḥanbal, Patton used the biographical history of Subkī, a Shāfi'ite-Ash'arite author who, as we have already seen, had very definite anti-Hanbalite tendencies. In the absence of other sources which would have provided a check on Subkī's information, Patton's conclusions were such that one could almost have predicted them in advance. Patton did assert the merit and dignity of the figure whom he had studied, but as we have already shown, he isolated the *imām* from his Hanbalite followers.[71] This is just what one finds in Subkī's work, for while he shows the greatest respect for Aḥmad b. Ḥanbal, he disassociates him from his partisans whom he accuses of anthropomorphism.[72]

Islamists have used Subkī's work as well as that of Ibn Rajab, the Hanbalite biographer. But Subkī has been used much more frequently and much less cautiously than Ibn Rajab or any other Hanbalite author. This has been unfortunate, for of the two writers of *ṭabaqāt* (works which are important for the socio-religious history of the time), it is Ibn Rajab who is the more straightforward. It is true that these two biographers had much in common. They were both from Damascus; they were both biographers of their respective schools; and they had an extensive knowledge of law and tradition. They also both had, as one might expect, prejudices against the rival schools.[73]

But these two authors did not have the same position within or in relation to their respective schools, for they belonged to two antagonistic religious movements, one to rationalistic Ash'arism, the other to traditionalist Hanbalism. As an Ash'arite, Subkī represented a minority in his Shāfi'ite school of law, where traditionalism predominated. As a traditionalist Hanbalite, Ibn Rajab, on the other hand, represented the majority of the Hanbalite school. As we have said elsewhere,[74] Subkī wanted to have his Ash'arite theology accepted by his colleagues, the Shāfi'ite jurists. He therefore wrote in a spirit of conciliation, except when he was obliged to defend Ash'arism against the frequently blunt attacks of his colleagues, the traditionalist Shāfi'ite jurists such as his famous teacher adh-Dhahabī, for example, who was incurably anti-Ash'arite.

But Ibn Rajab, who belonged to the traditionalist party which represented the overwhelming majority of the Hanbalite school, had a quite different objective from Subkī's. Ibn Rajab wanted to bring to the attention of his traditionalist colleagues all doctrines that deviated from the traditional principles of the school, and he rarely misses an opportunity to do this.

One must therfore be on one's guard when using these two biographers, as regards the dogmatic tendencies of their schools. Subkī inclines toward an Ash'arite rationalism against the traditionalist majority of his school, whereas Ibn Rajab favors Hanbalite traditionalism against the liberal minority of his school. Thus, for example, one must not accept without close scrutiny Subkī's information on Ash'arism or Ibn Rajab's information on the Ibn 'Aqīl affair;[75] and yet that is precisely what Goldziher did in both cases.

In our studies on Islam we cannot dispense with a critical analysis of the prejudices of our sources. This fundamental principle of historical methodology is all the more necessary when one is dealing with authors who belong not only to a religious movement but also to a particular group within this movement.

The results achieved by the Orientalists of the nineteenth and the beginning of the twentieth century, whom we have cited, were in large measure a function of the view that Hanbalism was an "insignificant" school. This presumption was in turn attributable to the fact that the Hanbalite school had fewer members than the other schools of Sunni law. No one, however, bothered to ask how this small school, in spite of its size, could have delayed the so-called victory of "official" Ash'arism. It is not enough simply to say that Hanbalism had the support of the masses.

2. Institutions of Learning and Religious Movements

In the nineteenth and early twentieth centuries, the works of Islamists on the religious history of Islam encountered a number of substantive difficulties, as we have already indicated. Their writings evidenced an inadequate critical attitude vis-à-vis the sources to such an extent that one must characterize them as works of philologists rather than historians. They relied on the ancient texts which were their sources without seriously attempting to ascertain what prejudices these texts transmitted. We have dealt elsewhere[1] with the two principal historians of the Ash'arite movement, Ibn 'Asākir (d. 551/1176) and Subkī (d. 771/1370), who had very pronounced biases not only against the traditionalist Hanbalite movement, which one must expect, but also against their Shāfi'ite colleagues who belonged to the traditionalist movement. And yet these are the two historians whom earlier scholars relied on in elaborating the history of the Ash'arites and, more specifically, the history of their relations with the Hanbalites. The conclusions which they arrived at continue to appear today in general works on Islam—conclusions which those who know the facts can no longer support.

Whatever may have been their strengths as philologists, Islamists of the last century failed to recognize the significance of certain technical terms in the sources. These terms, in my view, are fundamental for an understanding of religious movements and institutions of learning. For it was in linking a religious movement, Ash'arism, to an institution of learning, the Nizamiya *madrasa,* that they came up with what they called "official" Muslim orthodoxy.[2]

I have already spoken of the deplorable condition of Arabic manuscripts and of the difficulty, even today, in the age of computers, of assembling and examining historical data relative to medieval Islam. To this must be added another problem. It is that of understanding certain very ordinary words that have been suffused with a technical meaning of the greatest importance for the cultural history of the period. Now these terms do not appear in a special form such as in italics, for example, or in capitals, or between quotation marks, so that one can easily identify them. Indeed, these devices are nonexistent in Arabic. The technical term is written in the same form as all other words; and what is even more misleading, the terms may be construed in a quite ordinary sense which appears to be in harmony with the context and gives no hint of their technical meaning. The dictionaries presently available are a great help with the ordinary meanings, but they are of little value when technical meanings are involved. This makes it necessary to read the sources attentively and repeatedly, and to make lists of those terms that are capable of being construed in a technical sense, classifying them according to their contexts.

In biographical works and in the biographical portions of chronicles, whenever institutions of learning are involved, such as the cathedral mosque (*jāmi'*), the mosque-college (*masjid*), or the *madrasa,* the technical terms used have no connection with the so-called rationalist sciences. That is, we are not dealing either with what is called *'ilm al-awā'il,* the "foreign" sciences originating in ancient Greece such as philosophy and the natural sciences, or with *'ilm al-kalām,* rationalist theology which originated with the Mu'tazilites and was later taken up by the Ash'arites. Rather what we have here are the traditional sciences, since in these institutions one studied the Quran, prophetic tradition, law and its principles (*fiqh* and *usul al-fiqh*), grammar (*naḥw*) which included literary studies, and the academic sermon (wa'ẓ), which must not be confused with the *khuṭba,* the Friday sermon preached by the *khaṭīb* in a cathedral mosque. The same is true for the Nizamiya *madrasa.* A study of the technical vocabulary used in the subjects taught in this institution reveals only those terms pertaining to the traditional sciences which we have just mentioned.

It will not be possible here to list all the technical terms in their various contexts, for that would take us too far from our subject. It will be enough to mention some of them: the key terms having to do with the *madrasa.* These are derived from the root $\sqrt{\text{DRS}}$, from which also the noun *madrasa* itself comes. The words *darrasa* (causative verb of the 2nd form), *tadrīs* (verbal noun), and *mudarris* (the present participle or *nomen agentis*), when they are used *absolutely,* that is, without a direct object, become technical terms having to do more particularly with the teaching of law. Thus, *darrasa* means "to teach *fiqh,*" *tadrīs,* "the teaching of *fiqh,*" or the "function of teaching of *fiqh,*" and *mudarris,* "the one who teaches *fiqh,*" or "the one who performs the function of teaching *fiqh.*" The *madrasa* is the name of the place where mainly *fiqh* is taught, with the *mudarris* being the titular professor. The other religious or linguistic disciplines taught in the *madrasa* are ancillary sciences, taught by persons of lesser rank.

I must emphasize the use of these terms in the absolute sense, as I have said, for one critic, unmindful of the qualification, quotes the following sentence from Tibrīzī (d. 521/1127) in a review of my article: *waliya tadrīs al-adab bi'n-Niẓāmīya,* as evidence that the verbal noun *tadrīs* does not have the technical meaning which I suggested.[3] As soon as one uses this verb with an object (here *al-adab*), it loses its technical meaning and can only mean in this instance "to teach." In this case one may use the term to mean the teaching of other subjects. I am not able to tell you how long this term retained its technical meaning, but I am certain at least that it had this meaning in Baghdad during the medieval period.[4]

At the time when I was involved in this study of technical vocabulary used in the Middle Ages, some ten years ago, I came across a document that supported my conclusions. I am referring to the *waqf* or deed of endowment of the Nizamiya *madrasa,* which contains the stipulations relative to the personnel of the *madrasa.* This endowment is cited in Ibn al-Jawzī's history, *al-Muntaẓam,*[5] which was edited some thirty years ago but which scholars have begun to use only recently. Ibn al-Jawzī was a Hanbalite, whereas his grandson, Sibṭ, was a Hanfite. It is unfortunate that Ibn al-Athīr, a Shāfi'ite-Ash'arite historian, did not reproduce this document in his history, *al-Kāmil fī't-Tārīkh,* a universal history which has been used by all Islamists since its edition in the middle of the nineteenth century.

Niẓām al-Mulk, the founder of the *madrasa,* set down the following conditions as regards the personnel of the school: the professor of *fiqh,* the preacher, and the librarian all had to belong to the Shāfi'ite school of law (*fiqh*) and legal principles (*uṣūl al-fiqh*). In addition, the Nizamiya was to have a Quranic reader to teach the Quran and a grammarian to teach Arabic language and literature. In our text it is not stipulated that these last two teachers had to belong to the Shāfi'ite school. This perhaps explains why we find the Hanbalite grammarian, al-Jawālīqī (d. 540/1145), among the teachers of the Nizamiya. This is the extent of the stipulations concerning the personnel of Niẓām al-Mulk's *madrasa.* It appears, therefore, that there was no professor of rationalist theology (*kalām*), either of Ash'arite, Mu'tazilite, or any other *kalām,* a very important fact and one which is supported by the technical vocabulary used in connection with the Nizamiya *madrasa.*

There are several other interesting features which earlier were attributed to the Nizamiya, and these continue to be repeated even today in our general works on Islam. Niṣām al-Mulk is known to have been a Seljuk vizier. It was in his capacity as a Shāfi'ite Muslim, and not as a vizier that he found the Nizamiya *madrasa.* In other words, it was not in an official capacity that he found this institution, but as a private individual. Any private individual as a Muslim, having the necessary resources, could establish an institution of learning, provided he obtained a *waqf,* and thus endowed the legal system of his choice with a *masjid* or *madrasa,* or some other such institution. There is nothing—absolutely nothing—official in that. And the reason is very simple. A school of Sunni law (here the Shāfi'ite school) could not be considered "official" to the exclusion of the other equally orthodox schools of law. The Shāfi'ite Nizamiya was no exception.[6]

It should also be noted that the technical terms, a few of which we have mentioned, were used before as well as after the creation of the Nizamiya *madrasa.*[7] In short then, the Nizamiya introduced nothing new in the realm of education as such. It is in another area that we must look for what may have been new in regard to the Nizamiya of Baghdad. Before his nomination to the chair of law at the Nizamiya of Baghdad, the famous jurist, Abū Ishāq ash-Shīrāzī, taught at a *masjid,* or mosque-college, where the principal subject taught was Shāfi'ite law just as at the Nizamiya *madrasa.* Across from this *masjid* was a *khān* or residence for the foreign students who attended ash-Shīrāzī's course. Beginning in 459 of the *Hijra,* the year of the opening of the Nizamiya and the inauguration of ash-Shīrāzī's courses, students could live right at the Nizamiya itself. Thus the functions of the *masjid* of Abū Isḥāq ash-Shīrāzī and the neighboring *khān* were united in a single institution, the Nizamiya *madrasa.*[8] This is what we find to be original about the Nizamiya *madrasa* of Baghdad, assuming that there were no other institutions in that city that filled these functions before the Nizamiya. This is certainly possible, though hardly probable. But again there was nothing "official" either in the establishment or in the character of the Nizamiya. The label "official" which has been affixed to it owes its existence to gratuitous suppositions all having a common origin in the events of the fifth/eleventh century. These events, which have already been discussed elsewhere, we shall mention only briefly.

I have already mentioned the date of the Nizamiya's foundation and the fact that Niẓām al-Mulk, its founder, was a Seljuk vizier. This was the period of the Seljuk ruler Alp Arslan. At this time, the Fatimid caliphs ruled in Cairo, where the center of Fatimid Ismā'īlī propaganda, the al-Azhar mosque, was located. Consequently, it was assumed that the Nizamiya was the orthodox response to the heterodox propaganda of the Fatimids. Since the Nizamiya was founded by the Seljuk prime minister, so the reasoning went, it must have been a political mission. And since Niẓām al-Mulk had sent the Ash'arite theologian al-Ghazzālī there, it must follow that Ash'arite theology was the "official" choice of this prime minister to combat the heresy of the Fatimids.

But Ghazzālī was named professor at the Baghdad Nizamiya in his capacity as a specialist in Shāfi'ite law, in precisely the same fashion as the six professors who had preceded him in that chair.[9] The first professor named to the Nizamiya by Niẓām al-Mulk[10] was Abū Isḥāq ash-Shīrāzī (d. 476/1083), a renowned jurist whose work on law entitled *at-Tanbīh* has been published and translated into French.[11] Shīrāzī was a Shāfi'ite jurist whose anti-Ash'arite views were well known to his contemporarics, and which he himself brought to the attention of his Hanbalite colleague, the Sharīf Abu Ja'far (d. 470/1077). We are able to verify his anti-Ash'arite point of view for ourselves in one of his own works which has come down to us and has been published.[12] This Shāfi'ite professor of law, who was openly anti-Ash'arite, occupied the chair of the Nizamiya *madrasa* during the first seventeen years of this institution's existence. This being the case, it is difficult to see how the Nizamiya could have been an institution dedicated to the official teaching of Ash'arite theology. Al-Ghazzālī did not fill the role of professor of theology. The Nizamiya had only one chair: that of Shāfi'ite law. And if one wishes to characterize the Nizamiya as the center of anti-Fatimid propaganda, it should be pointed out that the Nizamiya was not alone in filling that function, for several institutions of learning similar to it were teaching the same religious sciences both before and after its establishment.

Indeed, it is not necessary to look as far as Fatimid Egypt to find an institution that rivaled that of the Nizamiya. There were two in Baghdad, one of them Hanafite, the other Shāfi'ite. The former dates from 459 of the *Hijra,* the year of the establishment of the Nizamiya; the latter was founded in 482, two years before the arrival of al-Ghazzālī. The former was the *madrasa*-mausoleum of Abū Ḥanīfa, an institution of learning which had begun to be built in 457 and which was inaugurated in 459, in other words, on the same date as the Nizamiya. Two Baghdad historians give us information about the beginnings of this *madrasa.* Ibn al-Jawzī tells us that Sharaf al-Mulk, himself also one of Alp Arslān's ministers (his minister of finance) had the mausoleum of Abū Ḥanīfa built, and next to it a *madrasa* where he lodged students of *fiqh* (*wa-anzalahā'l-fuqahā'*) and appointed a professor of *fiqh* to teach them, and for which he was paid a salary (*wa-rattaba lahum mudarrisan*).[13]

This means that if Niẓām al-Mulk, prime minister of Alp Arslān, provided for the needs of the students of Shāfi'ite law, then Sharaf al-Mulk, minister of finance of the same Hanafite sultan, who was also himself a Hanafite, could hardly avoid providing for the needs of students of Hanafite law. The rivalry between Alp Arslān's two ministers is seen more clearly in an account of the Hanafite *madrasa* written by the historian of Baghdad, al-Bundārī:

> Sharaf al-Mulk realized that the lieutenants of the vizier Niẓām al-Mulk had already begun to build the *madrasa* (that is, the Nizamiya); consequently, taking advantage of his power to do the same, he had a mausoleum built around the tomb of Abū Ḥanīfa in the Bāb aṭ-Ṭāq quarter, and a *madrasa* in honor of his followers (Hanafites), thus indicating the reward he would receive (from God) for having built a place of pilgrimage.[14]

In this passage the implication is as important as the explicit information. Here was a situation in which the two ministers of the Seljuk Alp Arslān had constructed, separately, each with his own private funds, and in honor of his own particular school of law, two *madrasas* of the same type, each with a titular professor of law and resident students. There was, however, one difference: Sharaf al-Mulk's Hanafite *madrasa* was built with a mausoleum around the tomb of Abū Ḥanīfa, thus creating a place of pilgrimage, whereas Niẓām al-Mulk's *madrasa* did not have this character at all. On the contrary, Abū Isḥāq ash-Shīrāzī, who was the first to teach there, refrained from praying inside the Nizamiya because of the illegitimate character of the materials from which it had been made, for these had been obtained from other buildings in the city which had been demolished.[15]

Above we suggested that the label "official," given to the Nizamiya, owes its existence to gratuitous suppositions. If we have subscribed to them, it was because of our ignorance of other institutions which flourished at the time of the Nizamiya. It was not at all its teaching function which distinguished it from the other institutions; it shared this function with all the other Shāfi'ite institutions, of which there were several. What distinguished it from the others was rather the goal or objective which its founder, Niẓām al-Mulk, assigned to it, for within the network of Nizamiyan *madrasas* which he had built in the cities of the 'Abbāsid empire, the right to appoint and dismiss the titular professors as he saw fit was reserved to Nizām al-Mulk.[16] This assured him of a good deal of influence with the *'ulamā'* who took an interest in such offices, and with the masses through the *'ulamā.*

It was a different matter with its rival, the *madrasa* of Abū Ḥanīfa's mausoleum. There it appears the titular professors were appointed by local authorities, in this case by the Hanafite grand *qāḍī,* according to the contemporary journal of Ibn al-Bannā', which I edited and translated some years ago. What is certain is that the first two professors enjoyed genuine security, for they continued to occupy the position until death. The first professor, Ilyās ad-Dailamī, died in 461/1069; and the second, Nūr al-Hudā az-Zainabī, who is mentioned several times in Ibn 'Aqīl's *Kitāb al-Funūn,* died in 512/1118. In short, he was the titular professor for a period of over half a century.[17]

It is interesting to note in this connection that in the sources one finds the Hanafite *madrasa* called not by the name of the founder, Sharaf al-Mulk, but rather by the name of Abū Ḥanīfa: "Madrasat Abī Ḥanīfa," "Masjid Abī Ḥanīfa," or "Mashhad Abī Ḥanīfa"; whereas the Nizamiya *madrasa* is always referred to after the name of its founder, Niẓām al-Mulk.[18] The same is true of the Nizamiya's other rival, the *madrasa* founded by Tāj al-Mulk and named "al-Madrasat at-Tājīya" after him. Tāj al-Mulk was the minister of finance of the Seljuk Sultan Malikshāh. The rivalry between these two institutions of learning, both Shāfi'ite, is mentioned by Sibṭ Ibn al-Jawzī in the manuscript part of his *Mir'āt az-Zamān.*[19] This rivalry eventually led to the violent death of the two ministers.[20]

The rivalry had to do with the influence which the founder enjoyed with those whom he named to or dismissed from the chair of his institution. Niẓām al-Mulk enjoyed the greatest influence, for he reserved to himself and his descendants the right to appoint the titular professors to *madrasas* which were protected from the influence of both caliph and the sultan. After him, sultans and caliphs, and their viziers, such as a Nūr ad-Dīn, Nāsir, Ibn Hubaira, and Saladin (all famous statesmen) only followed in the tracks of Niẓām al-Mulk, this political genius who was able to keep himself in power for some thirty years, manipulating the sources of power more than any other statesman in a century when power slipped through the fingers of the most astute.[21]

If the *madrasas* taught only the traditional religious sciences and the ancillary linguistic sciences, how did it happen that there was at this time an impressive flowering of works on *kalām* or rationalist theology? And, further, how did it happen that the rationalist science par excellence, Greek philosophy, as well as all the other "foreign" sciences, found their way through the lands of Islam to Europe?

One cannot deny the existence of the works of Muslim philosophers such as an Avicenna, an Algazel, or an Averroës any more than the works of theologians such as a Bāqillānī, an Abū Ya'lā, or a Fakhr ad-Dīn ar-Rāzī. However, the institutions of learning which we have mentioned were the very incarnation of the traditionalist ideal and consequently one could not expect the rationalist sciences to be taught there. From the beginning, the mosque functioned as the place where the religious sciences were taught. Other parallel institutions developed where the so-called foreign sciences were able to flourish. There were the libraries called *khizān at al-kutub, bait al-kutub,* and *dār al-kutub,* and the "houses of wisdom" or "houses of science" called *bait al-ḥikma, dār al-ḥikma,* and *dār al-'ilm.* These latter were also essentially libraries. To these institutions must be added the private houses where scholars could discuss all the sciences, without restriction. Ibn 'Aqīl speaks of these in his *Kitāb al-Funūn.*[22] In fact it was in the house of his teacher in *kalām,* the Hanafite Ibn al-Walīd, that he learned Mu'tazilite *kalām* in secret (*fi's-sirr*) as the Hanbalite biographer, Ibn Rajab, tells us.[23]

Thus there developed in Islam two categories of institutions: one was an embodiment of the traditionalist ideal; the other, the rationalist ideal. As a traditionalist institution, the *madrasa* taught neither philosophy nor theology (*kalām*). Moreover, Mu'tazilite and Ash'arite *kalām* flourished well before the founding of the *madrasa* and continued to prosper afterwards; the *madrasa* had no effect on that whatsoever.

The development of traditionalist institutions of learning began in the first centuries of Islam and continued into the modern period. The mosque played the most important role in this area. To this institution were added somewhat later *madrasas, ribāṭs,* or monasteries, the *dār al-ḥadīth,* and the *dār al-qur'ān.* On the other hand, the institutions of rationalist studies developed earlier, during the period of the Mu'tazilites in the third/ninth century, and then disappeared in the fifth/eleventh century. One finds others later on, but they had only an ephemeral existence.[24] The "foreign" sciences nevertheless continued to develop in private houses, and philosophy made its way to medieval Europe, with physicians being the most important agents in this process. It is interesting to note in this connection that in the universities of Italy all medical students were obliged to study philosophy.[25]

It was not, therefore, through institutions of learning in Islam that the "foreign science" came to Europe, but rather through the intermediary of the *book,* protected by the *waqf,* and transmitted by the *ijāza,* two very important Muslim phenomena. One must not, however, see in the *ijāza,* the prototype of the *licentia docendi,* the license to teach, of the medieval universities. For the *ijāza* was not a *license to teach,* but rather a license *to teach a certain book.* Furthermore, one must not see the *madrasa* as prototype of the European university. In reality, the *madrasa* has never been a *university,* that is, an institution which confers degrees. This function was unique to the medieval European university and owes its existence to the presence of a *faculty* which never was a part of the *madrasa* or of any other medieval Muslim institution. During the medieval period, the *ijāza,* therefore, was only a license to teach a book, and only later developed into a license to teach law (*fiqh*) and to issue legal decisions (*fatwā*). In any case, it was always conferred by a single teacher, never by a faculty.[26]

To return to our subject, the religious history of Islam was inevitably bound up with the *'ulamā',* the doctors of Islam, not with a single individual, like al-Ghazzālī, for example, but rather with those who had a substantial number of disciples and a following among the rank and file. Niẓām al-Mulk understood what could be gained by attracting the support of the largest possible number of these *'ulamā'*. During that period one could measure the extent of a statesman's influence by the number of *'ulamā'* in his camp. It is this, in my view, that explains the large number of Nizamiyan *madrasas* in the 'Abbāsid empire. They were important not so much for education as they were for politics. In return for their support, the *'ulamā'* obtained the funds necessary for the establishment of institutions of learning which reflected the Islamic ideal.

It was the *'ulamā'* who led the Sunni resurgence in the fifth/eleventh century; and this leadership was traditionalist. The institutions which appeared during this period and earlier, with the exception of the libraries which we have mentioned, embodied the ideals of the *'ulamā',* ideals which bore the marks of Muslim traditionalism. The political Maecenas cared very little about the character of the institutions of learning which they founded on behalf of the *'ulamā,* provided that their patronage rallied the support of the disciples and followers of these latter. The *'ulamā'* were the intermediaries between the holders of authority and power on the one hand, and the common people on the other. They were the guarantors of the Islamic character of these institutions. When a new institution of learning was founded (a *masjid* or a *madrasa,* for example), it had to be orthodox in character, and only the traditionalist religious sciences could be taught there, thus excluding those sciences which were rationalist or tainted with rationalism.

The fifth/eleventh century is a watershed in the history of Muslim institutions. It was in this century that traditionalism prevailed over its adversaries in the institutional domain, especially among educational institutions. The *madrasa* was merely a continuation of the *masjid,* to which a residence for students, the *khān,* had been added.[27] This century saw the destruction of Baghdad's last *dār al-'ilm,* in the year 451 A.H.[28] In the following century we see the inauguration of the *dār al-ḥadīth* (house of tradition) and after that, the *dār al-Qur'ān* (house of the Quran). These two new institutions symbolized the victory of traditionalism over rationalism, for the *dār al-ḥadīth* and the *dār al-Qur'ān* took the place of the *dār al-ḥikma* and the *dār al-'ilm.* The earlier libraries, independent institutions concerned with all the sciences, gave way to these new institutions, which assimilated them as annexed libraries. These were institutions which thenceforth bore the stamp of traditionalism.

As for the rationalist sciences, there remained two institutions, as we have said, which fostered them in Islam, and through which these sciences made their way toward Europe: the *waqf* and the *ijāza.* On their side, the traditionalist sciences did not entirely escape the influence of the rationalist sciences. Whereas *qiyās* (reasoning by analogy) had earlier gained entry into the discipline of *uṣūl al-fiqh,* this latter, taught in the traditionalist institutions of learning, began at this time to incorporate *jadal* or the science of dialectics.[29]

We are now able to appreciate the position occupied by the Hanbalites in the religious history of Islam and to see how they were able to influence the course of these events. Goldziher recognized the peculiar character of this school in spite of its modest size, relative to the other schools. However, he attributed the particular character of the Hanbalites to the rigidity of their doctrines and to their criticism of the moral laxity of the people, whereas the other schools of law, he said, were relatively unconcerned with dogmatic differences.[30] If Goldziher held this view of Hanbalites, it is because the sources from which he drew his information were more cautious in dealing with the other schools. He should have examined these sources more attentively, comparing them critically with traditionalist sources.

Whatever might have been their penchant for criticism, the Hanbalites could not have influenced the course of events had it not been for the cooperation of the other legal schools. Viewed strictly as a school of law, Hanbalism occupied a place of rather modest significance. However, if one considers its importance as a theological force, it must be accorded a very special position within the great traditionalist movement. In order to appreciate this position, we must avoid the temptation to confuse theological movements with legal schools. In the older view, the Hanafite school occupied a position on the far left among the schools of law and the Zāhirite school on the far right. Next to the Hanafites were the Mālikites; and next to the Ẓāhirites, the Hanbalites, with the Shāfi'ite school in the middle. According to this view Mu'tazilism stood at the extreme left theologically, and Hanbalism at the extreme right, thus leaving Ash'arism in the center. It seemed logical, therefore, to think that the Shāfi'ite school and Ash'arism, both of which stood in the center, were made for each other. What resulted was the identification of the Shāfi'ites with the Ash'arites.

Such a view seemed rather reasonable, though it has nothing to do with historical fact. Rationalism and traditionalism carried on their theological battles *within each of the legal schools.*[31] The Hanbalite school was alone in being at the same time both a legal and a theological school. This feature of the school goes back to its founder, Aḥmad b. Ḥanbal, who, by his resistance to the rationalism of his time, became the hero of the traditionalist movement and the symbol of this movement's victory over its adversary. In Baghdad, Mu'tazilism found its way into the Hanafite school, and Ash'arism into the Shāfi'ite school. Only the Hanbalite school could, *as a school,* combat rationalism. The traditionalists of all of the legal schools, including the Hanbalite school, fell in under the banner of the *ahl al-ḥadīth,* people of tradition, one of the titles given to the traditionalist movement. If the *ahl al-ḥadīth* have been identified exclusively with the Hanbalites, that is because of the fact that the traditionalists of this school acted *as a school,* whereas those of the other legal schools appeared in the histories only as individuals. And that also is related to the nature of the sources that are available to us.

The history of religious movements in Islam must be studied principally from the biographical sources. But these works, with rare exception, are based upon the schools of law rather than the theological movements. Thus the Hanbalite biographical histories deal with the traditioanlists of this school, not with those of the Shāfi'ite school. And if we have wrongly identified the Shāfi'ites with the Ash'arites, it is because the two principal sources[32] on the Shāfi'ite school were written by Shāfi'ite - Ash'arite authors. One must read them very carefully if one is to understand that the real theological struggle took place inside this school, between its two branches, the rationalists and the traditionalists.

Those who belonged to the same school of law were not to criticize each other. One had rather to curb his tongue in dealing with a colleague, no matter what one thought of his views in matters of dogma. But since people are human, and since it is difficult to watch continually over one's tongue, the biographers did occasionally criticize their colleagues of the same legal schools but of diverging theological tendencies. We have indicated several examples in Subkī's work. A careful reading of this work which Goldziher frequently utilized will provide one with several examples of the barely disguised hostility of its Ash'arite author toward his Shāfi'ite colleagues, in particular, his teacher, the famous adh-Dhahabī, who belonged to a very marked traditionalist theological tendency.[33] It is unfortunate that we are only able to use the first volumes of Dhahabī's monumental work, the *Tārīkh al-Islām.* Until the whole work is available, we must use the manuscript of this Shāfi'ite traditionalist not only as a check against Subkī's great work, but also (and this is not the least of the services which he can render us) in order to bring out the value of the latter's information, and to throw it into relief.

However, in contrast to Shāfi'ite biographers, Hanbalite biographers had a free hand, especially in the case of Shāfi'ite-Ash'arites, against whom they could write in complete freedom. Thus the Hanbalites, who were simply a part of the traditionalist movement, themselves became the mouthpiece of this movement, defending their views in biographical works where they did not suffer the constraints which impeded their traditionalist colleagues of the other schools of law. That was due entirely to the unique position which they occupied within their movement, and the influence of their position was out of proportion to their numerical importance as a school of law.

3. Sufism and Hanbalism

We tend to represent religious movements in Islam as monolithic entities, juxtaposed to each other like blocks of stone, and thus opposed to all other movements. We then set about looking for the characteristics of each movement based on the attitudes and views of a number of its representatives. The results are dubious at best, for they tend to violate the individuality of Muslin scholars who, like all thinkers, refuse to be reduced to a common denominator. This tendency is particularly unfortunate in the field of Islamic studies. There are no comprehensive studies of any movement based on previous monographic works which deal with the great representatives of the movement over the centuries of its evolution. Since the monographs are lacking, we tend to resort to generalizations based on evidence from sources whose authors had some particular interest to serve. And we remain content for the most part to describe this or that scholar as belonging to this or that movement, as if he were inaccessible to all other influences.

Let us take, for example, the attitude of Muslim scholars toward the study of *kalām* or rationalist theology. Some movements were opposed to it, while others approved it. However, the supporters of a particular movement were not always in agreement on this question. It is also possible for a scholar to be influenced by the very doctrines which he opposes. In a penetrating study, Ignaz Goldziher shows how the Mu'tazilite doctrines opposed by the famous Ash'arite theologian, Fakhr ad-Dīn ar-Rāzī (d. 606/1209), affected his thinking and, to a degree, even crept into his own thought.[1]

Another example of this phenomenon is the famous Hanbalite theologian and legal expert, Abu'l-Wafā' b. 'Aqīl (d. 513/1119), who between the ages of twenty-five and thirty-five was influenced in some measure by the Mu'tazilite doctrines which he studied under the direction of two teachers[2] of Mu'tazilite *kalām*. Though he was a Hanbalite, he was one of those very precocious minds, eager to learn everything that he could.

Thus there can be significant doctrinal differences not only between scholars of the same movement, but between successive views of a single scholar during different periods of his life. This fact requires careful study of a given scholar's thought, taking into consideration the chronology of his works. This is not always possible, however, and can lead to the attribution of views which a scholar might have held at the beginning of his career, but later abandoned. Furthermore, as these scholars belonged to more than one group, they were subjected to a diversity of influences. One must expect, therefore, that members of the same group or of the same school could have different views and interests.

In order to understand the hostility which existed between scholars belonging to the same school, one has only to refer to the thinly disguised criticisms and the mutual refutations, often exchanged openly between them. We have already mentioned the case of the biographer, as-Subkī, and his hostility toward his teacher, the famous traditionalist, adh-Dhahabī. Here is an instance of one Shāf'ite scholar opposing another of the same legal school, but belonging to opposing theological movements.[3] There is also the case of al-Māzarī, who severely criticizes al-Juwaynī and al-Ghazzālī for having diverged from the primitive doctrine of al-Ash'arī.[4] These antagonisms were not limited only to the Shāfi'ite school; the

Hanbalite school, which has for too long been considered a monolithic movement, also had its share of these antagonisms. Ibn Qudāma took Ibn 'Aqīl to task for what he believed to be rationalist, Ash'arite tendencies. He attacked him in a work entitled (*Taḥrīm an-Naẓar fī Kutub Ahl al-Kalām,* a work that I discovered several years ago under an erroneous title which is, however, suggestive of the content of the work, namely: *The Refutation of Ibn 'Aqīl* (*ar-Radd 'alā Ibn 'Aqīl*).[5]

Again, within the Hanbalite school, there is the example of Ibn al-Jawzī, who wrote a work refuting three of his Hanbalite predecessors:[6] Ibn Ḥāmid (d. 403/1012), the Qādī Abū Ya'lā (d. 458/1066), and Abū'l-Ḥasan b. az-Zāghūnī (d. 527/1132), the latter having been the author's very own teacher. We are also indebted to him for a refutation of the Hanbalite Sufi, 'Abd al-Qādir al-Jīlānī, contained in a work which no longer exists.[7]

Thus the Hanbalite movement cannot, any more than the Ash'arite movement, be considered to form a single monolithic phenomenon. These two movements have their leading representatives who must each be studied on the basis of his own works, after a chronology of those works has first been established. This is a difficult and often impossible undertaking, given the present state of our documentation. And we have still not reached the point even for the Ash'arite school, which has received more attention than any other movement. Our knowledge of socio-religious movements is advancing very slowly indeed. As far as the Hanbalite movement is concerned, our greatest need at the present is to rid ourselves of nineteenth-century views which still continue to encumber our general survey of works on Islam.

I would now like to turn to an examination of the relations between Hanbalism and Sufism. On this subject, received ideas are certainly not lacking. For example, there is the notion that al-Ghazzālī made Sufism orthodox by reconciling it with Muslim orthodoxy. There is also the notion that an implacable hostility existed between jurisprudence and Sufism, so that a jurist (*faqīh*) could not be a mystic (*ṣūfī*). Then there is the notion—and it is this that concerns us here—that Hanbalism was the great enemy of Sufism. In fact, if one refers to the very useful *Index Islamicus,*[8] one will find there under the heading "opposition to Sufism," the name of the famous Hanbalite Ibn al-Jawzī[9] and the title of his work *Talbīs Iblīs,*[10] (translated into English by Margoliouth)[11] in which he is supposed to have condemned Sufism.

I have repeatedly had the occasion to mention al-Ghazzālī, here and elsewhere in my studies, and often in regard to theories inherited from the past. I would not like to leave the impression that he does not deserve the greatest attention from Islamists. But to study him without having examined his period in depth and without having devoted sufficient attention to the other great scholars of this period, would be to risk attributing to al-Ghazzālī a role which does not belong to him. It would also involve the risk of producing generalizations without sufficient attention to the historical facts. This does not mean of course that al-Ghazzālī is "over-studied." I would say rather that he is "under-studied," although less so then other Muslim thinkers.

How did we arrive at the notion that it was al-Ghazzālī who effected the so-called reconciliation of Sufism and orthodox Islam? It was al-Ghazzālī, we are told, who reconciled Ash'arite *kalām* with orthodoxy, and we are even given the date when this took place. It was supposed to have occurred during the period of al-Ghazzālī's professorship at the Nizamiya, that is, between the years 484 and 488 A.H. (1091 and 1095 A.D.). We have seen, however, that according to the charter creating this institution of learning and the technical terminology contained in it, there was no chair of theology at the Nizamiya. What al-Ghazzālī occupied was rather a chair in Shāfi'ite jurisprudence. Since it was believed that he had reconciled Ash'arism and orthodox Islam, it was also believed that he had played the same role in the case of Sufism.

But if Islam had to wait five centuries before al-Ghazzālī could reconcile Sufism and orthodoxy, how are we to view the Sufis who preceded him? What about al-Junayd,[12] for example, or Abū Ṭālib al-Makkī,[13] whose work *Qūt al-Qulūb*[14] is fundamental to the conception of al-Ghazzālī's *Ihyā' 'Ulūm ad-Dīn,*[15] or again, Abū 'Abd ar-Raḥmān as-Sulamī,[16] a Sufi biographer whose work, *Ṭabaqāt as-Ṣūfīya,*[17] is filled with Sufis who lived before al-Ghazzālī (for as-Sulamī himself died some thirty-eight years before al-Ghazzālī's birth)?[18] And what are we to make of Abū'l-Qāsim al-Qushayrī, author of the famous *Risāla* on Sufism, who died in 465/1072, when Ghazzālī was only fifteen years old?[19]

The existence of Sufism before al-Ghazzālī was clearly recognized, but it was not thought to have been an integral part of orthodox Islam. Here is the way this Sufism was viewed:

> In place of the silent and ineffectual opposition to a rigid formalism and dogmatism offered by devout Sufis and their devoted disciples, who stood aloof from the main body of orthodoxy, one hears from al-Ghazzālī, a highly respected orthodox authority, a forceful protest against the corruption of

> Islam through the activities of its *kalām* and *fiqh* authorities. The respect which al-Ghazzālī enjoyed as an orthodox teacher in Muslim circles favored the success of his efforts.[20]

According to this and other similar statements from Goldziher, al-Ghazzālī effected a reconcilation between Sufism and Muslim orthodoxy. Goldziher understood how much al-Ghazzālī owed to Abū Ṭālib al-Makkī, whom he described as "an old classic of Sufism," "who was widely known as *shaikh ash-sharī'a wa'l-ḥaqīqa* (master of law and of mystical truth) to whose work al-Ghazzālī acknowledged himself to be indebted."[21]

One can see quite clearly that Goldziher himself did not consider Abū Ṭālib to be "a master of law and of mystical truth," a characterization which, according to him, was premature, since it belonged to al-Ghazzālī and should not have been applied to anyone before him. It would be anachronistic, therefore, to regard any scholar before al-Ghazzālī in this way, since, according to Goldziher and others whom we will mention later, the reconciliation of law with mystical truth had been effected by al-Ghazzālī alone.

After remarking that al-Ghazzālī had put his finger on the defects and contradictions of Aristotelian philosophy, Goldziher goes on to observe that he also denounced:[22]

> The hair-splitting of *kalām* as a tedious waste of the mind, which works against the purity and immediacy of religious thought and feeling, especially when, as the *mutakallimūn* claim, it is carried beyond the confines of the school and lodges in the minds of common people, where it can only cause confusion.

Let us examine this statement before continuing with al-Ghazzālī's career. Was it not al-Ghazzālī who had reconciled this same *kalām* with Muslim orthodoxy when he was appointed by Niẓām al-Mulk to the Nizamiya *madrasa,* where he alledgedly taught Ash'arite *kalām* which had not yet been accepted by Muslim orthodoxy? If al-Ghazzālī denounced this *kalām,* had it then lost the orthodox status that al-Ghazzālī had so recently won for it? Nowhere in Goldziher's work is one told that Ash'arite *kalām* had lost its orthodox status. Nevertheless, if we are to accept Goldziher's claim that al-Ghazzālī achieved an orthodox standing for Ash'arite *kalām* and then also for Sufism, while denouncing the *fuqahā'* and the *mutakallimūn,* we run into the difficulty of no longer knowing where in the new orthodoxy to place Ash'arite *kalām,* recently admitted into orthodoxy.

Let us cite several more statements concerning al-Ghazzālī. After his attack on *kalām,* he "took to task even more violently the people of *fiqh* and their judicial casuistry."[23] He could do this because he had himself "acquired fame and respect by his literary contribution to (this) discipline against which he now drew the sword." He criticized juridical casuistry and its intrusion into religious affairs, for according to Goldziher, the legal scholars were opposed to the tendencies and ideals of the mystics. These latter were searching for union with God; the fuqahā' were opposed to it. In his polemic against the *fugahā',* Goldziher made the most of the fact that they had not moved beyond the simple perceptions of the senses, wheras al-Ghazzālī saw in love of God the only goal worth striving for.[24] For him, love of God was the central concern of the religious life. Goldziher concludes by telling us that al-Ghazzālī's role was to draw "Sufism out of its isolation from the dominant religious conception," and to make it "an accepted part of the religious life in Islam."[25] Before al-Ghazzālī, then, Sufism was supposed to have been a stranger to the dominant spirit of Islam. Thus before al-Ghazzālī, there was supposed to have been an opposition between jurisprudence and Sufism, and between rationalist theology and Sufism.

This way of looking at Sufism was shared by other Islamists besides Goldziher. For Carl Becker, Muslim mysticism filled the void left by law and theology. It was supposedly out of reaction against these two areas of religion that mysticism attached itself to Islam as a foreign body.[26] Another Islamist, K. Vollers, in an article published in the *Encyclopedia of Religion and Ethics,* expressed surprise to find that Sha'rānī was at the same time jurist, theologian, and mystic. "The extraordinary significance of Sha'rānī," he says, "lies in the fact that he was practically and theoretically a mystic of the first order, and at the same time a prominent and original writer in the field of theology and jurisprudence."[27] Vollers was astonished because he did not see how in Islam mysticism could be reconciled with jurisprudence and theology in the person of a single scholar.

Muslim biographers, on the other hand, saw things in quite a different light. Subkī, for example, mentions several individuals in his biographical work who were both jurist and Sufi. This was the case of Abū Nu'aym al-Iṣbahānī, "a Sufi," he says, "who combined the knowledge of *fiqh* with that of *taṣauwuf."[28] It is also the case of Abū Khalaf aṭ-Ṭabarī who "was a ṣūfī-faqīh* (*wa-kāna faqīhan ṣūfīyan*)."[29]

It should be noted that these two jurist-mystics of the Shāfi'ite school lived and died before al-Ghazzālī brought about the alleged reconciliation of Sufism and orthodox Islam. Abū Nu'aym al-Iṣbahānī died in 430/1039, and Abū Khalaf aṭ-Ṭabarī, around the year 470/1078, several years before the appointment of al-Ghazzālī to the Nizamiya. This same Abū Khalaf, a contemporary of the famous Shāfi'ite mystic al-Qushayrī, had written a treatise on Sufism, comparable to the *Risāla Qushayrīya,* but which has not survived.[30]

In spite of the statements of Muslim biographers which one finds in works representing a number of different legal schools, we have persisted in following the notion of a fundamental divergence between orthodoxy on the one hand and Sufism on the other. Consequently, Hanbalism, the most conservative orthodox group, came to be thought of as Sufism's worst enemy.

Marijan Molé's recent work on Sufism[31] is interesting precisely because it diverges from this notion. In discussing the *'ulamā'* and the dervishes, he says that "they represent two distinct spiritual families whose co-existence and antagonism appear to be characteristic of Islamic civilization. But this antagonism does not imply that Sufism needed to be reconciled with Muslim orthodoxy. For this, it would have been necessary for it to have left it, for it to have developed outside of orthodoxy and against it, which was never the case. There have always been Sufis who were also jurists: the case of Junayd is well known, and it was not the only one. Their doctrines are not exclusive of the law, they add to it."[32]

Although Molé refused to believe in the necessity of a reconciliation, he nevertheless followed the accepted view that the Nizamiya had been established for the teaching of Ash'arite *kalām,* and he could not free himself from the notion of an antagonism between Hanbalism and Sufism. "Sufism," he insists, "was born in a thoroughly Quranic atmosphere. While other Islamic movements—such as Hanbalism—sprang from the same atmosphere, they did not necessarily evolve in the same direction. To the initial call of the sacred text, certain individuals responded in a particular way that conformed to their deepest yearnings."[33]

The "deepest yearnings" of Hanbalites, according to Molé, were not for Sufism. We must nevertheless be grateful to him for having rejected the theory of a reconciliation of Sufism with Muslim orthodoxy. On the other hand, the fact that he did not see the need to reject the alleged hostility of the Hanbalites toward Sufism says a great deal about the influence of this notion in our studies. It is indeed this "thoroughly Quranic atmosphere" out of which Hanbalism arose, that will, in the final analysis, enable us to show that the Hanbalites also had actually evolved in much the same direction as Sufism had. Documents which have long been available to us reveal a close relationship between Hanbalism and Sufism, as Molé has suggested, but Islamists have sought rather to prove the contrary, or to find a satisfactory explanation for the notion of an implacable antagonism between the two.

The existence of the two great sufi-Hanbalites, al-Anṣārī al-Harawī and 'Abd al-Qādir al-Jīlānī, could not, however, be denied. But scholars have been satisfied simply to note that they were repelled by the sophistry of the dogmaticians and that it was this that led them to affiliate with the Hanbalite school where they were safe from the subleties of dogmatic theology. As proof of this, they noted that al-Anṣārī al-Harawī had written a work refuting *kalām,* his *Dhamm al-Kalām.*[34] They did not really believe in the sincerity of their affiliation with the Hanbalite school, for Sufis were supposed to reject *kalām* for other reasons than those of the Hanbalites. We are not told, however, what these reasons were. They did not take seriously the public statements of those Sufis who favored Hanbalism, such as, for example, those of al-Anṣārī who sang his Hanbalism in verse, and appealed to his Sufi colleagues to become Hanbalites: *wa-waṣīyatī li-n-nāsi an yataḥanbalū.*[35]

The notion that these Sufis associated with Hanbalism to escape the subleties of Ash'arite *kalām* raises even more problems than it resolves. How could these Sufis, for example, find refuge within the Hanbalite school, if this school was really anti-Sufi? Al-Ghazzālī, we are told, was himself a Sufi who detested theological subtleties. Why did he not join the Hanbalite school, or some other school hostile to Sufism? How did it happen that the Sufi Abū Naṣr al-Qushayrī,[36] son of the Qushayrī already mentioned, aligned himself with the Ash'arites (a school of *kalām*), against the Hanbalites?

There is also the example of the Sufi-Hanbalite Ibn Qayyim al-Jawzīya.[37] Scholars have seen in his mystical ideas, especially concerning the love of God, the influence of al-Ghazzālī rather than that of his own Hanbalite school. Very little attention seems to have been paid to the fact that this Sufi-Hanbalite had written a commentary on the famous mystical work, the *Manāzil as-Sā'irīn* of the Sufi-Hanbalite al-Anṣarī al-Harawī.[38]

There is also the fact that the Sufi brotherhood, the Qādirīya, named after the Sufi-Hanbalite 'Abd al Qādir al-Jīlānī, was Hanbalite, and was the first brotherhood of its kind. Very little has been made of this important fact. Recently it has even been suggested that this Sufi brotherhood may have owed its existence to al-Ghazzālī. It was inevitable that this idea should come into somebody's mind, given the diversity of roles which has been attributed to the omnipresent al-Ghazzālī in our studies. It was impossible for scholars to believe that Hanbalism could have been the source of the Qādirīya, even though the founder himself was a Hanbalite, the author of an important Hanbalite creed.[39] He has even been spoken of as having *previously* been a Hanbalite jurisconsult, as if to insinuate that once he became a Sufi he ceased to be a Hanbalite. These instances are sufficient to indicate how tenacious the tendency to preserve at all cost the traditional notion of an antagonism between Hanbalism and Sufism *was* and still *is*.

To get to the heart of the matter, we must turn to the theories of the origins of Muslim mysticism. There are those who believe that Muslim mysticism is exogenous, that it owes its origin to external causes. These latter also believe that mysticism encountered a strong opposition in Islam, especially from more orthodox and conservative elements. Then there are those who believe that mysticism was endogenous, that it had its source in Islam itself. Those who belong to this school of thought also believe that there is no hostility between Sufism and orthodoxy, no matter how conservative. It is here that we see one of the most important contributions of Louis Massignon to Islamic studies. In maintáining the theory of an endogenous Muslim mysticism, he prepared the way for the eventual solving of the problem which concerns us. He saw quite correctly that Sunni orthodoxy had never been unanimous in its condemnation of Sufism, and that moderate Sufism had never been excommunicated by Sunni Islam. His views may be found in an important article entitled "*taṣauwuf*" in the first edition of the *Encyclopaedia of Islam*. What he has to say regarding the hostility of certain Hanbalites toward Sufism, especially Ibn al-Jawzī, Ibn Taymīya, and Ibn Qayyim al-Jawzīya, must however be modified in the light of a new interpretation of the facts available to us, thanks to certain recently discovered documents.

It seems evident that Marijan Molé was influenced both by the theory of an endogenous Sufism as developed by Louis Massignon and by the theory of Hanbalite hostility toward Sufism, as maintained by Goldziher. In my view, he was right in seeing the common origin of Hanbalism and Sufism, but wrong in believing that Hanbalism followed a different course than that taken by Sufism.

To be sure, there was in our sources material to support the notion of a Hanbalite opposition to Sufism, especially Ibn al-Jawzī's *Talbīs Iblīs,*[40] which we have already mentioned. There were also the polemics of other

Hanbalites such as Ibn Taymīya. *Talbīs Iblīs,* in fact, is not concerned with Sufism as such, certainly not only with Sufis. It is concerned rather with the abuses of several groups: philosophers, pagans, theologians, traditionists, popular preachers, philologists, poets, Sufis, the common people, and the rich. It attacks heterodox doctrines and practices, which are not based on revealed texts. If the section on Sufis is the most fully developed, it is because the author saw in them the greatest danger of his time. But we should not lose sight of the fact that Ibn al-Jawzī also in this work indicted certain groups in the Muslim community to which he himself belonged such as traditionists, popular preachers, and the jurists.

Ibn al-Jawzī wrote several works in favor of Sufism: he abridged two works regarded as foundational in this field, *viz., Ḥilyat al-Awliyā'* by Abū Nu'aym al-Iṣbahānī[41] and *Iḥya' 'Ulūm ad-Dīn* by al-Ghazzālī.[42] He also wrote biographical works of the *faḍā'il* and *manāqib* type on several early ascetics and Sufis.[43] In the biographical section of his *Muntaẓam,* he wrote several biographical accounts in praise of the Sufis.[44] It is true that he condemned 'Abd al-Qādir al-Jīlānī,[45] a Hanbalite like himself and also his contemporary, but on the other hand he wrote a work in praise of the famous mystic of Islam Rābi'al-'Adawīya.[46]

As for Ibn Taymīya, Mr. H. Laoust has already spoken of the affinities of this Hanbalite scholar for Sufism[47] and pointed out that one will look in vain to find any condemnation for Sufism in his works.[48] It is true that he did oppose the pantheistic Sufism of the *ittiḥādīya,* but he did not conceal his admiration for the works of such Sufis as al-Junayd, Sahl at-Tustarī, Abū Ṭālib al-Makkī, Abū'l-Qāsim al-Qushayrī, Abū Ḥafṣ as-Suhrawardī, and 'Abd al-Qādir al-Jīlānī.

Recently I discovered several documents which support Mr. Laoust's contention. In these documents Ibn Taymīya himself states that he belonged to the Sufi brotherhood of 'Abd al-Qādir al-Jīlānī. He writes: "I have worn the Sufi robe (*kirqa*) of 'Abd al-Qādir (al-Jīlānī), with two Sufi *shaikhs* between him and myself."[49] He also says: "I have worn the *khirqa* of several *shaikhs* belonging to different *ṭarīqas,* including that of 'Abd al-Qādir al-Jīlānī, whose *ṭarīqa* is the most important of those that are better known."[50]

Elsewhere Ibn Taymīya mentions the *nisba-s* which Muslims may use; among the *nisba-s* allowed are those which refer to founders of mystical schools and, in particular, the *nisba-s* al-Qādirī and al-'Adawī. The other admissible *nisba-s* refer to the founders of the four orthodox schools of Sunni law.[51] These are the only ones that he mentions, thus indicating that the *fuqahā'* and the Sufis occupied first place in his thoughts. There is nothing surprising in this, for he was himself a *faqīh* and *ṣūfī*.

I have already spoken of the technical terms in Arabic sources from the Middle Ages and of the importance of defining them in relation to their contexts, for one will not always find in our dictionaries all of the meanings which they may have. I have already given several examples from the history of institutions of learning. Now certain terms pertaining to Sufism found in the biographical works seem to have escaped notice. These terms, taken in their technical sense, throw light on the questions before us. One will see in reading the *Ṭabaqat* of Ibn Rajab that the term *zāhid,* for example, which ordinarily should mean "ascetic," is used here in the sense of Sufi. In a recent study, I found that among the Hanbalites whose biographies occur in this work by Ibn Rajab, there are over one hundred Hanbalite mystics, which is more than one-sixth of the Hanbalites mentioned in the work.[52]

Other sources support this interpretation. For some time I suspected Ibn Qudāma of having a sympathy for Sufism: first in his *Kitāb at-Tawwābīn,*[53] where he quotes some verses of the mystic al-Hallāj without identifying them, and the next in his *Taḥrīm an-Naẓar fī Kutub Ahl al-Kalām*[54] where he passes over Ibn 'Aqīl's Ḥallājian sympathies without mentioning them, whereas he condemns the latter's rationalism. Recently I discovered a Sufi chain of initiation, a *silsila,* in which Ibn Qudāma is mentioned as having received the Sufi robe of initiation directly from the *shaikh* 'Abd al-Qādir al-Jīlānī. This document which I found in a *majūm'a* of the Ẓāhirīya Library[55] in Damascus was later corroborated by other documents, also in manuscript, found in libraries in Istanbul, Leiden, Dublin and Princeton. In the printed bibliographical work *ad-Durar al-Kāmina,*[56] Ibn Ḥajar al-'Asqalānī mentions the chain of intitiation belonging to Dunaisirī, in which the latter traces his *khirqa* or Sufi cloak back to Ibn Quadāma, through two other Hanbalite Sufis. Several Hanbalites are mentioned in this *sisila,* Hanbalites who died between 371 and 620 of the Hijra: 'Abd al-'Azīz at-Tamīmī (d. 371/981),[57] 'Abd al-Wāhid at-Tamīmī (d. 410/1019),[58] Abū Sa'd Al-Mukharrimī (d. 513/1119),[59] 'Abd al-Qādir al-Jīlānī (d. 561/1165),[60] and Muwaffaq ad-Dīn b. Qudāma (d. 620/1223).[61] Other mystical genealogies include Hanbalite names from the dynasty of the Taymīyas, the Quadāmas, as well as the Hanbalites Ibn al-Jawzī, Ibn Qayyim al-Jawzīya, and Ibn Rajab.

One need not, therefore, see extra-Hanbalite influence in the Sufism of Ibn Qayyim al-Jawzīya, not even in his ideas on the love of God, which he could have learned from his master, Ibn Taymīya. In fact we now have a text in which Ibn Taymīya describes the worship of God as consisting of, among others, a complete love: *wa'l-ibādatu tataḍammanu kamāla 'l-ḥubbi wa-kamāla't-ta'ẓīmi wa-kamāla 'r-rajā'i wa'l-khishyati wa'l-ijlāli wa'l-ikrām.* This passage comes from his commentary on the *Kitāb Futūḥ al-Ghayb* of 'Abd al-Qādir al-Jīlānī.[62] It is in this same work that he describes al-Jīlānī and Ḥammād ad-Dabbās as orthodox Sufi *shaikhs,* even though the first had been condemned by Ibn al-Jawzī and the second by Ibn 'Aqīl.[63] He declares them to be "orthodox" while, on the other hand, condemning al-Anṣārī al-Harawī, the other great Hanbalite Sufi whose views he found to be tinged with pantheism.

It is interesting to note that both al-Ghazzālī and Ibn Taymīya criticized the excesses of Sufism, especially the doctrine of *tawakkul* or confidence in God, carried to the extreme by certain Sufi ascetics. Both declared this extremist tendency to be contrary to the Companions of the Prophet who practised *tawakkul* correctly. It is also contrary to the *law,* which forbids such a passive attitude.

Like Ibn Taymīya, al-Ghazzālī attacked Sufism in its pantheistic form, and in its devaluation of the *religious law.* In this respect, al-Ghazzālī was in agreement with the Hanbalites. But while al-Ghazzālī earned the praise of Islamists, Ibn Taymīya was condemned by them. It is clear, then, that there is need of more accurate and precise understanding of this question.

4. Muslim Orthodoxy

The use of the term "orthodoxy" implies the possibility of distinguishing between what is true and what is false. This term implies the existence of an absolute norm as well as an authority which has the power to excommunicate those whose doctrines are found to be false or heretical. Such an authority exists in Christianity, in its councils and synods.[1] It does not exist in Islam.

It was Goldziher who so effectively brought this fact to our attention:

> The dogma of Islam cannot be compared with the same constituent part of the religion of any of the Christian churches. There are no councils and synods which, after a vigorous debate, can establish the formulae that must stand henceforth as the symbol of the true faith. There is no ecclesiastical function which represents the criterion of orthodoxy; there is no exegesis exclusively authorized by the sacred texts on which the doctrinal method and

> substance of the Church rests. Consensus, the highest authority in all questions of religious theory and practice, is an expandable spring, difficult to specify and diversely defined. Particularly in dogmatic matters, it is difficult to reach agreement on what should pass unquestionably for consensus. What one party regards as such, another will reject.[2]

After describing the cruel fate of an *infidel* who was banished from society because of his heretical views, Goldziher remarks that "for all practical purposes, there were only a very few people, perhaps a tiny minority of Hanbalite fanatics, who actually considered the application of such a conception." And here Goldziher refers us to his article, published two years earlier under the title "A Contribution to the History of Hanbalite Movements" where he discussed Ibn Taymīya among others.[3]

According to Goldziher, the spirit of tolerance which had characterized the early period in Islamic history gave way to one of intolerance. "It was only after the scholastic cultivation of dogmatics," he says, "that there appears on both sides, orthodox as well as rationalist, the pernicious spirit of intolerance."[4] According to him, the period of al-Ash'arī which followed Mu'tazilism was a one of agitation and intolerance. Of two statements attributed to al-Ash'arī on his deathbed, the one tolerant, the other intolerant, Goldziher says that he "is inclined to give more credence" to the intolerant version, for "the spirit of dogmatic agitation of this period was more favorable to excommunication than to tolerance and accommodation."[5]

Goldziher adds again that Sufism alone displayed a tolerant spirit during that period. "We have seen," he says, "that it even went so far as to reject confessionalism."[6] "Ghazzālī," he states again, "did not, however, go so far,"[7] though "he did write a special work on the idea of tolerance entitled: *The Criterion for the Distinction between Islam and Heresy*.[8] In it he proclaims to the world of Islam the view that agreement on the fundamental principles of religion is the basis for recognizing persons as *believers,* and that differences on matters of dogma and ritual, even if it involves the rejection of the caliphate recognized in Sunni Islam and consequently the Shī'ite schism, does not provide grounds for excommunication: 'You must impose restraint on your tongue in regard to the people who turn toward the *qibla*.' "[9]

In the concluding part of his chapter on "Asceticism and Sufism,"[10] Goldziher says of al-Ghazzālī that "his most significant contribution to the history of Islam was the fact that he reminded his fellow Muslims of this ancient doctrine and, having himself taken it seriously, won new support for it."[11] At the end of this statement there is a footnote (number 154) referring to the expanded notes at the end of the work. From this note it appears that Goldziher found the same tolerant spirit in Ibn Taymīya that he had found in al-Ghazzālī.[12] If Goldziher relegated this fact to the notes rather than developing it in the text of the chapter itself, it is perhaps that he saw this tolerant spirit to be uncharacteristic of Ibn Taymīya whom he regarded as a fanatical Hanbalite and an anthropomorphist. The following is the text of this note:

> It is characteristic of the general orientation of orthodoxy after Ghazzālī, that even a theologian as given to fanaticism and exclusivism as the zealous Hanbalite, *Taqī al-dīn ibn Teïmiyya* (*ZDMG, LXII,* 25), comes nearer on this question to Ghazzālī whom he combats, than many of the rationalist theologians. In his commentary on the 112th sura, *Sūrat al-Ikhlāṣ* (Cairo, 1323, ed. Na'sānī, 112–13), there is a special excursus which ends with the concession that Mu'tazilites, Khārijites, Murji'ites, as well as moderate Shī'ites (*al-tashaiyu'al-mutawassiṭ*) are not to be regarded as *infidels*. They remain within the bounds of the Quran and the Sunna, and are in error only in their interpretation; they in no way threaten the principle according to which the law is regarded as binding. The Jahimyya are excluded, because they reject uncompromisingly all of the names and attributes of God (*nafy al-asmā' ma'a nafy al-ṣifāt*), and in particular the Ismā'īlīs, because they deny the value of the ritual law. In this moderate conception of the combative Hanbalite, one can see *the influence of an attitude that accords with the early, tolerant Sunna.*[12a] In two positions distinctly opposed to each other, al-Ghazzālī and his principle antagonist Ibn Teïmiyya both reject the influence of scholastic definitions of the essence of Islam.

It is clear that Goldziher attributes these views to Ibn Taymīya, somewhat reluctantly, as though it was something exceptional, or like "an attitude that accords with the early tolerant Sunna." Since then, thanks to the illuminating works of Henri Laoust, we have come to recognize the substantive character of Ibn Taymīya's tolerant spirit.

But let us now return to the question of orthodoxy in Islam. Goldziher has led us to see, and rightly so, that in Islam there are no councils or synods, nor ecclesiastical institutions to determine the criterion of orthodoxy. Even consensus, which is the highest authority—as Snouck Hurgronje so well said[13]—is according to Goldziher, an expandable spring difficult to specify and diversely defined. What one group regards as consensus, another group rejects.[14] Nonetheless, it is *ijmā'* that is the distinctive mark of Sunni Islam. Sunnism, Goldziher correctly observes, "is a church based on *ijmā',*" where as Shī'ism is "a church based on *authority.*"[15]

One sees from the works of Goldziher that he was concerned to identify that element within Islam that represented Sunni orthodoxy. Since there was no criterion even within Sunnism, it was necessary to look elsewhere. Goldziher found this criterion in the Seljuk state, in the person of the vizier, Niẓām al-Mulk, who founded the Nizamiya *madrasa* at Baghdad for the purpose of having Ash'arite *kalām* taught there, according to Goldziher. It was there that the famous al-Ghazzālī came to teach in 484 of the *Hijra.*

It was thus that Goldziher came to designate Ash'arism "official orthodoxy." It was "official" because it was taught at the Nizamiya, which itself was "official" because it was founded by Niẓām al-Mulk, an offical representative of the Seljuk Alp Arslān. This latter represented the state, because the caliph was little more than a marionette in his hands as he had been in the hands of earlier Seljuks and Buwayhids.

In fact, Goldziher's reasoning was in error. First of all, *kalām,* whether Ash'arite or any other, was not taught at the Baghdad *madrasa,* as we have already shown elsewhere.[16] Next, there was nothing "official" in the character of the Nizamiya, for like all the other *madrasas* and mosque-schools, indeed like all institutions of learning, it was instituted as a *waqf.* Any Muslim at all, with the necessary means, could found *madrasas,* or any other institution of learning, as a *waqf.*[17] Being a Shāfi'ite and wishing to attract Shāfi'ite support, Niẓām al-Mulk decided to establish a Shāfi'ite *madrasa.* His superior, Alp Arslān, was on the other hand a Hanafite, as was Abū Sa'd al-Mustawfī, his minister of finance, who founded at the same time as the Nizamiya another *madrasa,* this one Hanafite. These were then "exclusive" colleges, in the sense that only Shāfi'ite students could attend the Nizamiya, in the same way that Abū Sa'd al-Mustawfī's Hanafite *madrasa* admitted only Hanafite students. No *kalām*—whether Ash'arite or any other—was taught there. One must ask, then, how a secular power could choose a particular theological school within Sunni Islam and established it as an "official" theology. Consensus, or *ijmā',* had nothing to do with the secular power. It was dependent only on the Muslim community, over which the scholars, guardians of religion, presided.

From what source then did Goldziher derive this notion of "official orthodoxy"? I was perplexed by it for some time, particularly since it did not seem to be justified by the course of events in Islam. I have been hard pressed to explain its formation in the mind of the great Islamist. Although I do not claim to have found a full answer, this notion might well have been suggested to Goldziher by the course of events which took place in the Catholic Church and which, from the time of Leo XIII,[18] a contemporary of Goldziher, led to the establishment of Thomism as a quasi-official theology in the Church.

Pope Leo XIII sought to renew philosophical thought in the Church based upon Thomism. This latter provided him with the ideas which he wished to set against the social and political liberalism of his time. His attempt to restore Thomism is seen in a series of events which took place during the time that Goldziher was immersed in his studies on Islam. I am referring here in particular to the nomination of Cardinal Mercier to the chair of Thomism at Louvain in 1882 and to the reorganization of the Roman Academy of St. Thomas in 1886. In his encyclical entitled *Aeterni Patris,* dated August 4, 1879, Leo XIII set forth the notion that the evils of the modern period derived from a false philosophy. As an antidote, he advocated an in-depth study of the thought of St. Thomas Aquinas, whom he admired for his freedom of spirit and whom he regarded as the most representative thinker of the Christian tradition, to which the Church Fathers had assimilated Greco-Roman culture.

Goldziher may have been influenced by contemporary developments such as these. And let us remember in this connection that he also wrote an article on Catholic tendencies in Islam.[19] The parallel between the historical events of the time in which he was living and those of the time which he was studying could have appeared too attractive for him not to have been influenced by them. The reorganization of the Roman Academy of St. Thomas corresponded to the foundation of the Nizamiya, which he, in fact, called an "Academy"; the nomination of Cardinal Mercier to the chair of Thomism at Louvain corresponded to the nomination of Ghazzālī to the so-called chair of Ash'arism at Baghdad; the Thomism which Leo XIII wished to juxtapose to the social and political liberalism of his time corresponded to the Ash'arism which Niẓām al-Mulk, patron of Shāfi'ite-Ash'arite jurist-theologians, wished to oppose to the excesses of Mu'tazilism and of Hanbalism in that time; and the idea of an "official" Thomism, chosen by Leo XIII within Catholic orthodoxy, without the other orthodox schools being suppressed, corresponded to the idea of an "official" Ash'arism, chosen by Niẓām al-Mulk within Muslim orthodoxy, without the other orthodox schools being suppressed by this orthodoxy. For Goldziher it was enough to describe Ash'arism as official orthodoxy in order to distinguish it from the older orthodoxy of the traditionalist followers of the *Salaf* (pious Ancestors).

The views on Islam during the period in question still persist today, even among some of the best informed Islamists, and have contributed to the formation of this notion of an "official orthodoxy" or theology. It was believed, for example, that the caliph was only a puppet in the hands of the sultans and that Niẓām was the true holder of power in the name of the Seljuk sultans. And although in Islam there was no spiritual authority residing in a single individual equivalent to that of the Pope, the power which was believed to have fallen to the vizier Niẓām al-Mulk was deemed sufficient for him to establish Ash'arism as "official orthodoxy" in the fifth/eleventh century. But there is nothing in all of this that is based on the realities of history. Neither Niẓām al-Mulk nor his Seljuk masters had this authority. It resided alone in the person of the caliph. And furthermore, the caliph could not, in the manner of the Pope and the councils, create an "official orthodoxy" against the consensus of the community (*ijmā'*).

The fact remains that Goldziher came to see two types of orthodoxy in Islam: one which he called "official," that is, Ash'arism from the time of al-Ghazzālī onward; and the other, which he called the "old" orthodoxy, that is, Hanbalism, a school which he consistently characterized as fanatical, rigid and opposed to progressive principles. He called it "old" because it claimed as its authority the pious Ancestors, the *salaf*. This school which he desribed as "rigid and fanatical," was represented to him largely in the person of one of its most distinguished spokesmen, Taqī ad-Dīn ibn Taymīya.

Let us look now more closely at Ibn Taymīya's views on Muslim orthodoxy. Ibn Taymīya sets forth his ideas on orthodoxy in a number of his works, but the ideas which I shall outline here appear in a work which was published in 1951 under the title *Naqḍ al-Manṭiq,*[20] or "The Destruction of Logic." In the preface, Muḥammad Ḥāmid al-Fiqī, the editor of the text tells us that Ibn Taymīya had not given a title to his work, and that, after seeking the advice of another scholar, al-Fiqī chose the title *Naqḍ al-Manṭiq* on the ground that Ibn Taymīya, according to one of his biographers, had written several works on the refutation of logic.[21]

In reality, only a very small part of the work is devoted to a discussion of logic. The larger part of the work is concerned with the question of orthodoxy. From the beginning it is clearly a *fatwā* by Ibn Taymīya, that is, a response issued by him in his capacity as a religious expert in Islam to a Muslim who had asked the following questions.[22]

First question: What is your opinion on the doctrine of the pious Ancestors (*salaf*) as concerns faith, and what is the doctrine of the moderns (*al-muta'akhkhirūn*)? What is the truth of the matter, and which of the two do you follow?

Second question: What is your opinion on the traditionalists (*ahl al-ḥadīth*)? Are they more justified than others in claiming the truth? Do they represent the sect that will escape hell (*al-firqa an-nājiya*)? Did new knowledge come into being after them, of which they were ignorant but which others knew?

Third question: What is your view of logic?, etc.

These questions are given under the heading *mas'ala* or "question," and the remainder of the work under the heading *jawāb* or "response." It is clearly a *fatwā* which, like other *fatwās* given by this scholar, had no title, and where the question of logic is taken up only in the last portion of the work.

Of the series of three questions asked, it is the first two that interest us here. And our interest is limited to Ibn Taymīya's idea of the Muslim community and what might be called "orthodoxy" within this community.

Without going into certain details, Ibn Taymīya's conception of the Muslim community may be described by a series of concentric circles whose common center is marked by the Quran and tradition. Around this common center the various schools of theology are located, each of them arranged according to the degree of its "orthodoxy." The sole criterion of orthodoxy is the scripture supported by the consensus of the Muslim community.

In the first circle, inside all the others, the one which encloses the common center, we find the *salaf.* Then come the *ahl as-sunna wa'l-ḥadīth* who are followers of the Quran and of the Tradition of the Prophet. Next come the Sufis. And after them the *ahl al-kalām,* proponents of rationalist theology. These latter are divided into two groups: the *ahl al-ithbāt,* and the *ahl an-nafy,* also called *aṣ-ṣifātīya* and *an-nufāt,* respectively. The former is composed of those rationalist theologians (*mutakallimūn*) who accept the divine attributes (from whence the terms *ahl al-Ithbāt* [= *ithbāt aṣ-ṣifāt*], ṣifātīya); the latter refers to the theologians who deny (*nafy, nufāt*) the attributes of God. The former are divided into three groups: the Ash'arīya, the Kullābīya, and the Karrāmīya, while the second are represented by the Mu'tazilia. Next come the philosophers, the *Khawārij* and, finally, the *Rāfiḍa* who are farthest removed from the *salaf.* Only the *Jahmīya* are outside the community, but they must be well-informed *Jahmīya,* for there are some among the common people who are dupes of the theorists and consequently must not be condemned because of their ignorance.

Here then are the positions of the various theological schools in relation to Muslim orhtodoxy which, *in its pure state,* is found at the common center of all the concentric circles. The circles which we have just described are large circles, each one encompassing an entire school, so that one must picture as many circles as there are theological positions, locating the adherents of each school nearer to or farther from the common center. The schools are not monolithic, however, and it is possible that a theologian who is a member of the Ash'arite school might be, on a given doctrinal point, nearer to the center than another theologian who belongs to the *ahl as-sunna wa'l-ḥadīth.* The concentric circles are therefore numerous: there are as many as there are positions on theological questions. It is for this reason that Ibn Taymīya was able to censure a Hanbalite colleague while at the same time holding a high opinion of an Ash'arite. One has only to read his work *Minhāj as-Sunna* to rid oneself of the opinion that Ibn Taymīya was "fanatical and exclusivist."

In the general picture that emerges, the orthodoxy of each group or individual is measured by the distance which separates it or him from the common center, and this distance is determined by the position of the ideas professed in relation to the common center of the concentric circles, in other words, in relation to the scriptures. Ibn Taymīya clearly was a member of the *ahl as-sunna wa'l-ḥadīth.* It is therefore understandable that he should attribute the most complete orthodoxy to his own group and that he place it within the circle nearest to the center. But to keep from being accused of partiality, he states that the position occupied by the traditionalists, at the very center of orthodoxy, is supported by the consensus of the community (*ijmā'*).

In order to understand Ibn Taymīya's idea of *ijmā'* and to appreciate its true merit, one must recall another Islamic principle, the principle of *khilāf* or divergence which is the opposite of *ijmā'*. For one can hardly hold that there was, on the part of the theologians at any time of Muslim religious history, an explicit *ijmā'* of all the schools judging the traditionalists as the most orthodox theologians of the community. The reality was quite other, and Ibn Taymīya was very conscious of this. But it is no less true that this *ijmā'* existed as Ibn Taymīya tells us, and he demonstrates it by means of *khilāf.*

Divergence within the community is inevitable, he states. In this connection he recalls a tradition in which the Prophet asked God to exempt the community from it. However, God refused his request, and one must therefore expect that there will be divergence within God's community. This divergence is very pronounced among the heretics and all but absent among the orthodox. In the diagram which we have outlined of Ibn Taymīya's notion of the Muslim community, this divergence, which is minimal with the traditionalists, becomes greater and greater as one moves away from the common center.

When there are disputes, they are settled in accordance with the authority of the scriptures, even among the heretics. All are in agreement on the priority of the *salaf* in matters of faith. Following a general pattern of movement from the common center toward the outer circles, each group blames the one that follows it for opposing the doctrine of the *salaf.* The essence of the doctrine of these latter consists in affirming the existence of the divine attributes as they are presented to us in the scriptures, that is, the Quran, and Tradition.

The superiority of the *ahl as-sunna wa'l-ḥadīth* comes from the fact that they follow the *salaf.* And each group has merit only to the extent that it makes itself the defender of the faith of Islam. It is thus that Ibn Taymīya demonstrates both his tolerance of the various schools within the community and the fact that every theological position apart from that of the *salaf* derives its value from its purely defensive function. The superiority of the traditionalists is seen in several facts of which four are mentioned: 1. whenever they find themselves opposed by others, they are in the right and triumph over their adversaries; 2. their adversaries concede that they are right and return to their original faith; 3. their doctrines is attested by the believers who are the witnesses of God on earth (it is to be noted here that Ibn Taymīya states that the majority adhere to traditionalism); 4. each of the other theological schools use the traditionalists as support against its adversaries and attacks its adversaries more sharply than it attacks the traditionalists.

To appreciate the support given by the masses to the traditionalists, one has only to recall the multitudes which followed the coffin of Aḥmad b. Ḥanbal, whose reputation within the community derived from the fact that he followed the *ḥadīth* and the *sunna.* The Mu'tazilites have merit only insofar as they follow the doctrine of those who affirm the *sunna* and the *ḥadīth.* They also have merit for having refuted the *Rāfiḍa* where these latter have departed from the *sunna* and the *ḥadīth* in connection with such questions as the *imāmate* of the caliphs, the *'adāla* of the companions, tradition, and the excessive veneration of 'Alī, etc. The early Shī'ites have more merit than the Muṫazilites with whom they were at odds over the question of the divine attributes, predestination, and intercession. They also have merit for their opposition to the Khārijites who declared both 'Alī and 'Uthmān to be infidels; and also for their opposition to the Murji'ites on the matter of faith (*īmān*).

The people of *kalām,* called "people of *ithbāt,*" in other words the Kullābīya, the Karrāmīya, and the Ash'arīya were accepted, followed and appreciated by the community because of the the principles of faith which they affirmed (uṣūl al-īmān): namely, 1. the existence of God and his attributes, 2. prophecy, 3. the refutation of associationists, unbelievers, and the people of the Book, and the exposure of contradictions in their arguments.

These rationalist theologians who affirm the divine attributes are appreciated also for their refutation of the Jahmīya, the Mu'tazila, the Rāfiḍa, and the Qadarīya insofar as their doctrines diverge from the traditionalists, the *ahl as-sunna wa'l-jamā'a.* They are appreciated for two reasons 1. for their agreement with the *ahl as-sunna wa'l-ḥadīth,* and 2. for their refutation of those who oppose them. The doctrines of al-Ash'arī were followed for one or the other of these reasons. Al-Bayhaqī (d. 458/1066), Abū'l-Qaṣim al-Qushayrī (d. 465/1072), and Ibn 'Asākir (d. 571/1175) pleaded the case of al-Ash'arī by maintaining that he was part of the *ahl as-sunna wa'l-ḥadīth,* by citing his doctrines to this effect, or by affirming that he refuted the adversaries of the *ahl as-sunna wa'l-ḥadīth.* In this way they defended him before the community, its *'ulamā',* and its princes. If Ash'arī had not been close to the traditionalistists, the scholars who defended him would have put him in the same category as Abū 'Alī (al-Jubbā'ī, d. 303/915) his former teacher, and his teacher's son, Abū Hāshim (d. 331/942). But on many points the doctrines of al-Ash'arī were in agreement with the *sunna* and the *ḥadīth,* especially those dealing with the divine attributes, free will, the *imāmate* (that is to say, the status of the four first caliphs, in opposition to the doctrine of the Rāfiḍa and of the Shī'ites), intercession, the "basin," the "bridge" (*ṣirāṭ*), and the "balance." They defended him because he also refuted the Mu'tazilites, the Qadarites, the Rāfiḍa, and the Jahmīya. Those who protect the *sunna,* even if they do not believe in it, are to be commended; those who both defend it and believe in it are to be doubly appreciated and commended. The *sunna* is concerned with obedience to God and his apostle, and with belief in the revelation and the message of God.

A prohibition against cursing Ash'arites was requested by the Ash'arite *'ulamā'* on account of their defense of the *uṣūl ad-dīn,* that is, the Quran, the *sunna,* and the *ḥadīth,* as well as for their refutation of the adversaries of the Quran, the *sunna,* and the *ḥadīth.* This is why the Shāfi'ite scholar Abū Isḥāq ash-Shīrāzī said: "The Ash'arites are entirely welcome among the people [Shāfi'ites] because they trace their origin back to that of the Hanbalites"[23] (this is undoubtedly an allusion to the fact that al-Ash'arī declared himself a Hanbalite by saying in the preface of his work *al-Ibāna an Uṣūl ad-Diyāna:* "We confess what Ibn Hanbal taught us . . . and we combat everything that his doctrine combats.")[24] This affinity, Ibn Taymīya points out, could be seen in him and in the works which his disciples wrote up until the time of the uprising of al-Qushayrī's son (Abū Naṣr). This is why Ibn 'Asākir said (in his *Tabyīn*) in defense of the Ash'arites: "the Hanbalites and the Shāfi'ites continued to have a relationship of understanding until the uprising of al-Qushayrī."[25] However, even after as well as before this event, Ash'arī continued to be commended when he was in agreement with the *sunna* and the *ḥadīth,* and was censured when he opposed them.

After examining the past events of religious history, Ibn Taymīya, who had a considerable knowledge in this matter, came to the following conclusion: all of the schools agree in revering the *sunna* and the *ḥadīth* and in recognizing that the truth is to be found there. Consequently, the scholars of Islam are to be revered insofar as they are in agreement with the *sunna* and *ḥadīth.* Thus al-Ash'arī is the most revered because of the affinity of his doctrine with that of the *salaf;* after him comes al-Bāqillānī. But as for al-Juwaynī, al-Ghazzālī, and others who are in disagreement with al-Ash'arī, one will find them revered only to the degree to which they are in harmony with the *sunna* and the *ḥadīth;* and they enjoy that through their fidelity to the principles of Shāfi'ite law which takes its inspiration from the *sunna* and the *ḥadīth;* they are revered on other matters only because of their refutation of the adversaries of the *sunna,* and not for any other reason.

We will not be able here to follow Ibn Taymīya in the details of his argument. The main point is that the Muslim community is in agreement on the primacy of the *sunna* and of the *ḥadīth.* There is no question about the commitment of the community to this principle. This principle is guaranteed by the very consensus of the religious experts, in other words, their agreement at the very moment they are in disagreement on a disputed point or question; for, in order to settle the question, they all appeal to the *salaf* and to the scriptures. It has been said of Ibn Taymīya that he was a "fanatic and an exclusivist." These two epithets, like others of the same nature, are very difficult to justify on the basis of his own works. By repeating them, one echoes the opinions of his medieval adversaries.

The concepts of community and orthodoxy in Ibn Taymīya's thought remind one of the function of *kalām* in Islam, which Louis Gardet has expressed very well. In comparing Christian and Muslim theology, Gardet suggests that "The primary function of Christian theology which is, in the words of Augustine, an 'understanding of faith,' does not enter directly into the perspectives of Islam. Faithful to its origins, it (*kalām*) is less concerned with a knowledge of the mysteries of faith than with defending its formulations 'against doubters and negators.' Thus, it is the apologetic function, which Christian theology regards as secondary, that becomes the *raison d'être* of *kalām:* a defensive, not a directly illuminative function."[26] Again he says: "A true 'theology of Islam' should not limit itself to the study of *kalām* but should draw on *usūl al-fiqh* as well. I do not find it paradoxical to say that there is perhaps more 'theology' (of the sort that deepens the values of faith) in certain Hanbalite writings . . . than in that of many of the *mutakallimūn.*"[27]

It is considerations such as these that led my former teacher, the late Louis Massignon, to make the following remark in his preface to the work of Gardet and Anawati on Muslim theology: "We are here shown in a most interesting fashion that the future of theology in Islam belongs to Hanbalism."[28]

Conclusion

From the preceding studies, it is evident that the Hanbalite movement presents itself in an entirely different light from what we find in our general survey works on Islam. For a long time I myself accepted the history of this movement as it is found in these survey works. However, I eventually came to see that this account does not accord with the facts which are found in the sources, unless one reads only the Ash'arite sources without comparing them with those of Hanafite, Shāfi'ite, and Hanbalite origin. Indeed, these latter are indispensable for an understanding of the history of the Hanbalite and Ash'arite movements.

Far from an existence on the fringes of Islam, the Hanbalite movement stood at the very center of the Muslim community. From its beginning, this movement saw itself as the protector of the heritage of the Prophet, first of all within the community, and then against external foes. It conceived of itself has having been given this mission by its founder, the

Imām Aḥmad b. Ḥanbal, one of Islam's most influential personalities, and one who continued to live in the memory of the Muslim community as the hero-victim of the caliph al-Ma'mūn's Inquisition.

The Hanbalite school found itself in the vanguard of the traditionalist movement, that of the "*ahl al-ḥadīth,*" in whose ranks were to be found scholars of all the other schools. It is in the light of this fact that one must understand a statement which appears again and again in the biographical sources, that this or that scholar was a Shāfi'ite in the area of positive law, and Hanbalite as regards the principles of religion (*shāfi'īya'l-fiqh, ḥanbalīya'l-uṣūl*). Supporters of the traditionalist movement belonged to the various schools of Sunni law and were known as "people of the prophetic tradition (*ahl as-sunna*)," or as "people of the prophetic tradition and of the Muslim community (*ahl as-sunna wa'l-jamā'a*)," as well as other such names.

If one goes back to the early period of Western studies on Islam, to the second half of the nineteenth century, one sees clearly that it was inevitable (or nearly so), that the Hanbalites should appear in a false light to Islamists. At that time the West viewed Islam through Turkey, with whom it was more familiar and with whom it had diplomatic ties dating back to the reign of the sultan Sulayman the Magnificent. This perspective produced predictable results for the Hanbalites, given the hostile relations between the Turks and the Wahhābīs, and given the Hanbalite orientation of Wahhābī doctrines through the influence of Ibn Taymīya's teaching. The obscure Ibn Taymīya appeared as the adversary of al-Ghazzālī, himself known to the West since the Middle Ages under the Latinized name of Algazel.

This perspective influenced the choice of documents utilized for the study of the religious history of Islam. Moreover, these documents for many years were the only ones published, the only ones available to the majority of Islamists. They were documents in which the Hanbalites appeared in a false light, if they appeared at all. The search for what is "orthodox" in Islam was impeded by our preconceived notions. What in fact properly belonged only to the Western experience was assumed to exist in Islam. To find this "orthodoxy," scholars set out in search of a *theology,* which they translated by the word *kalām.* The only *kalām* to be found was that of the Ash'arite movement, since Mu'tazilite *kalām* had run aground already during the reign of al-Mutawakkil. And when they looked for a *kalām* which could rival Ash'arite *kalām,* they found none. They overlooked the fact that, in the Islamic order of things, traditionalist theology took care not to be called *kalām*. The preferred name of their theology was *uṣūl ad-dīn,* "the sources or foundations of religion," by analogy with the term *uṣūl al-fiqh,* "the sources or foundations of jurisprudence." In other words, this was a theology or a jurisprudence based on the sacred Scriptures: the Quran and the sunna of the Prophet. The traditionalists juxtaposed this theology, inspired by the Quran and the sunna, to *kalām* which was a theology of rationalist inspiration.

Add to this the fact that "Ash'arism" appeared to them to be a synonym for "Shāfi'ism"; and that the Hanbalite school, the only one that attracted attention as the adversary of the Ash'arite movement, was believed to be too small and consequently too insignficant to be able to represent Muslim orthodoxy. It was not realized that his school was in fact in the vanguard of the traditionalist movement. They saw only the tip of the iceberg and failed to realize that the invisible portion represented the great majority of the community.

The only matter that remained to be clarified was the date of Ash'arism's triumph over its enemies, when Ash'arite *kalām* became the "orthodoxy" of Islam. Von Kremer placed it at the beginning of the fourth/tenth century, when the founder of the movement, Ash'arī himself, was still alive. Goldziher, however, first located it in the sixth/twelfth century,[1] but then moved it back to the fifth/twelfth century, the period of the Nizamiya, and also the period of the vizier Niẓām al-Mulk and al-Ghazzālī. In other words, he ended up with a school, a founder, and a professor to whom he attributed roles which do not in fact accord with the data in the sources.

It is now time to rethink our idea of Muslim orthodoxy. For the only orthodoxy which is certified in Islam by the consensus of the community (*ijmā'*) is Sunni orthodoxy, represented since the third/ninth century by the four schools of Sunni law: Hanafite, Mālikite, Shāfi'ite, and Hanbalite. There is no other orthodoxy recognized by the majority of Muslims. There is nothing surprising in this. In the realm of religion, everything must be legitimized through the schools of law. For Islam is nomocratic and nomocentric.

NOTES

(See page xi for list of abbreviations of journal titles)

1. H. Laoust, *Essai sur les doctrines sociales et politiques de Takī-d-Dīn Ahmad b. Taimīya* (Cairo, PIFAO, 1939), p. 2.

Part 1: Western Orientalism and Muslim Religious History

1. C. Brockelmann, *Geschichte der arabischen Litteratur,* 2nd ed. (Leiden: E. J. Brill, 1943–49) Supplementband (1937–42).
2. F. Sezgin, *Geschichte des arabischen Schrifttums,* I, (Leiden: E. J. Brill, 1967).
3. Ibn an-Nadīm, *al-Fihrist* (Cairo, n.d.); recently translated into English by Bayard Dodge, *The Fihrist of al-Nadīm: A Tenth-Century Survey of Muslim Culture* (New York-London: Columbia University Press, 1970).
4. Hājjī Khalīfa, *Kashf aẓ-Ẓunūn 'an Asāmī al-Kutub wa'l-Funūn* (Istanbul, 1941–43); see also the continuation of Muḥammad Amīn al-Baghdādī, *Īḍāḥ al-Maknūn fī adh-Dhail 'alā Kashf aẓ-Ẓunūn 'an Asāmī l'Kutub wa'l-Funūn* (Istanbul, 1945–1947).
5. Like the bibliography of Ibn 'Arabī, for example, by O. Yaḥyā, *Historie et classification de l'oeuvre d'Ibn 'Arabī* (Damascus: Publications de l'Institut Français de Damas, 1964); of al-Ash'ari by Father R.J. McCarthy, *The Theology of al-Ash'arī* (Beirut, 1953), "Bibliographical Note," pp. xvii–xxii; of al-Jāhiẓ, by Ch. Pellat, *Le Milieu baṣrien et la formation de Ǧaḥiẓ* (Paris, 1953); of Ibn Qutaiba, by G. Lecomte, *Ibn Qutaiba, L'Homme, son oeuvre ses idées* (Damascus: Publications de l'Institut Français de Damas, 1965) particularly chapters IV and V, pp. 85–178; of Ibn Qudāma, by H. Laoust, *Le Précis de droit d'Ibn Qudāma* (Beirut: Publications de l'Institute Français de Damas, 1950), p. xxx, n. 2; and of Ibn-'Aqīl, by G. Makdisi, *Ibn 'Aqīl et la résurgence de l'Islam traditionaliste au XI siècle* (Damascus: Publications de l'Institut Français de Damas, 1963); "Essai bibliographique sur l'oeuvre d'Ibn 'Aqīl," pp. 509–21.
6. *Fonds arabe,* no. 787.
7. The work is now published; see G. Makdisi, *The Notebooks of Ibn 'Aqīl: Kitāb al-Funūn.* Arablic Text Edited with Introduction and Critical Notes. Recherches, ILOB, vols. 44 and 45 (Beirut, 1970–1971).
8. Ch. V. Langlois and Ch. Seignobos, *Introduction aux études historiques* (Paris, 1898) [see p. 74 of the English translation].
9. Goldziher, *Vorlesungen über den Islam.* Religionswissenschaftliche Bibliothek Bd. I (Heidelberg, 1910); translated into French by F. Arin, *Le Dogme et la loi de l'Islam. Histoire du développement dogmatique et juridique de la religion musulmane* (Paris, 1920), expressions such as "les vieux croyants théologiens," "la vieille école intransigeante," and p. 105, "la vieille école traditionnelle." Similarly one reads in D. B. Macdonald, *Development of Muslim Theology: Jurisprudence and Consitutional Theory* (New York: 1903; republished in Lahore: The Premier Book House, 1960, 1964), p. 121 ("content with nothing but the rehearsal of the old dogmas in the old forms"): cf. *passim* and other similar phrases.
10. *GAL,* vol. I, p. 181, Suppl. I, p. 308: "Die unbedeutenderen Schulen."
11. *GAL,* vol. I, p. 398, Suppl. I, p. 686 ("Die Ḥanbaliten").
12. *GAS,* vol. I, p. 502 ("Ḥanbaliten").
13. *GAS,* vol. I, pp. 598 f.: "Die Ḥanbaliten blieben bei der Lehre des Begründers ihres

madhab." But one must not lay the blame on these two authors who, given the situation, were only reflecting the orientation of accepted ideas. Arabists and Islamists are indebted to them for the indispensible bio-bibliographical aid which they have given us and especially to Mr. Sezgin who is working alone to continue Brockelmann's work with a remarkable erudition.

14. G. Pfanmüller, *Handbuch der Islam - Literatur* (Berlin-Leipzig, 1923), 235 ff.
15. Goldziher, "Zur Geschichte der ḥanbalitischen Bewegungen," in *ZDMG,* vol. 62 (1908), pp. 1–28.
16. Goldziher, *Die Ẓāhiriten, ihr Lehrsystem und ihre Geschichte. Beitrag zur Geschichte der muhammedanischen Theology* (Leipzig, 1884).
17. W. M. Patton, *Aḥmed ibn Ḥanbal and the Miḥna: A Biography of the Imām Including an Account of the Mohammedan Inquisition called the Miḥna, 218–234 A. H.* (Leiden, 1897).
18. See his *Die Ẓāhiriten,* pp. 86–89 ("Verhältniss der ẓāhiritischen Lehren zu denen dem Ḥanbaliten").
19. W. M. Patton, *op. cit.,* p. 194.
20. H. F. Wüstenfeld, *Der Imām el-Schāfi'ī, seine Schüler und Anhänger bis zum Jahre 300 d.H.,* in *Abhandlungen der Königlichen Gesellschaft der Wissenschaften,* vols. 36 and 37 (Göttingen, 1890–91).
21. M. J. de Goeje, "Einiges über den Imām aš-Šāfi'ī," in *ZDMG,* vol. 47 (1893), pp. 106–17.
22. W. M. Patton, *op. cit., loc. cit.*
23. The two lines which I have italicized are the only ones dealing with the Hanbalites.
24. *Op. cit.,* p. 125—Goldziher has always maintained that Hanbalism appealed only to the lower classes.
25. *Op. cit.,* p. 2.
26. *Op. cit., loc. cit.*
27. *Op. cit., loc. cit.*
28. *Op. cit., loc. cit.*
29. *Op. cit.,* p. 6.
30. R. Arnaldez, *Grammaire et théologie chez Ibn Ḥazm de Cordoue. Essai sur la structure et les conditions de la pensée musulmane* (Paris, 1956).
31. See his studies on the Hanbalite school beginning in 1939, in particular his *Essai* (see p. 264, note 1); *La Profession de foi d'Ibn Baṭṭa* (Damascus: PIFD, 1958); "Le hanbalisme sous le califat de Baghdad," in *REI* (1959), pp. 67–128; "Le Ḥanbalism sous les mamlouks bahrides," in *REI* (1960), pp. 1–71.
32. In particular: "The Life of al-Ghazzālī with Special Reference to His Experiences and Opinions," in *JAOS,* vol. xx (1899), pp. 71–132; *Development of Muslim Theology,* index (particularly part III, ch. IV); in the article "al-Ghazzālī" in *EI.*
33. W. M. Patton, *op. cit.,* p. 188.
34. Cf. supra, note 18.
35. Cf. supra, note 15.
36. Goldziher, "Patton's Aḥmad ibn Ḥanbal and the Miḥna (Zusammenhang zwischen Ibn Ḥanbal, Ibn Tejmijja und 'Abdul Wahhāb)," in *ZDMG,* vol 52 (1898), pp. 155–58.
37. See notes 10 and 19.
38. Goldziher, *op. cit.,* p. 155.
39. *Op. cit., loc. cit.;* cf. W. M. Patton, *op. cit.,* p. 125.
40. Goldziher, *op. cit., loc. cit.*
41. *Op. cit.* p. 156.

42. H. Laoust, *Essai.*
43. Goldziher, *op. cit.,* p. 156 and n. 4.
44. *Op. cit.,* p. 157.
45. *Op. cit., loc. cit.* Concerning al-Maqrīzī see *GAL,* vol. II, pp. 38 ff., Suppl. II, pp. 36 ff. His father and grandfather were Hanbalites. At first he was a Hanafite, like his maternal grandfather, then became a Shāfi'ite after he was twenty and remained a Shāfi'ite but with Ẓāhirite tendencies; in this regard, see the biographical notes in Sakhāwī, *ad-Dau' al-Lāmi' li-Ahl al Qarn at-Tāsi'* (Cairo, 1353–1355/1934–1936), vol. II, pp. 21–25; and Ibn al-'Imād, *Shadharāt adh-Dhahab fī Akhbār man Dahab* (Cairo, 1350/1931), vol. VII, pp. 254–55.
46. Tāj ad Dīn as-Subkī, *Ṭabaqāt ash-Shāfi'īya al-Kubrā* (Cairo, 1323–24/1905–06).
47. Goldziher, *op. cit.,* p. 157.
48. A. von Kremer, *Geschichte der herrschenden Ideen des Islam. Der Gottesbegriff, die Prophetie und Staatsidee* (Leipzig, 1868; Hildesheim: Georg Olms, 1961); see book II, ch. X, "Sieg der Orthodoxie," pp. 245–52.
49. Goldziher, *Vorlesungen,* pp. 120–21, 123 (*Le Dogma et la loi de l'Islam,* pp. 99, 101).
50. Goldziher, *Muhammedanische Studien,* 2 vols. (1888–1890; Hildesheim: Georg Olms, 1961), vol. II, p. 59.
51. Goldziher, *Patton's Aḥmad,* p. 158; Goldziher concludes his review of Patton's work with two pages of corrections; on p. 158, n. 2, Goldziher quotes three interesting lines, where the second hemistich of the first line is to be corrected: the three words are *maṣdar-s,* not verbs; it should read: *"wa-tashaiyu'in wa-tamash'urin wa-tama'zuli."*
52. M. Schreiner, "Beiträge zur Geschichte der theologischen Bewegungen im Islam," in *ZDMG,* vol. 52 (1898), pp. 486–510, and vol. 53 (1899), pp. 51–88 and 513–63.
53. Goldziher, "Zur Geschichte der ḥanbalitischen Bewegungen," in *ZDMG,* vol. 62 (1908), pp. 1–28.
54. *Op. cit.,* p. 1.
55. *Op. cit.,* p. 5.
56. *Op. cit.,* p. 9.
57. *Op. cit.,* p. 11.
58. *Op. cit.,* p. 17.
59. *Op. cit.,* p. 21.
60. *Op. cit.,* p. 24.
61. *Op. cit.,* pp. 25–26.
62. *Op. cit.,* p. 28.
63. *Op. cit., loc. cit.*
64. Goldziher, *Dogme,* pp. 86, 87, and 102.
65. *Op. cit.,* pp. 93, 152–53, 219–20.
66. *Op. cit.,* p. 258, 1, 12 *infra*—D. B. Macdonald was in agreement; cf. his *Development,* index, s.v. "Ḥanbalites," in particular pp. 191, 200, 207, 208, 212, 273, 274, 278.
67. Goldziher, *Patton's Aḥmad,* p. 155.
68. For example, the works of al-Ash'ari (d. 324/935; see *GAL,* vol. I, p. 194, Suppl. I, p. 345; *GAS,* vol. I, p. 602); of al-Baghdādī (d. 429/1037; see *GAl,* vol. I, p. 385, Suppl. I, p. 666; *GAS,* vol. I, pp. 589, 590, 594); of Ibn'Asākir (d. 571/1176; see *GAL,* vol. I, p. 331, Suppl. I, p. 566); of Ibn al-Athīr (d. 630/1233; see *GAL,* vol. I, 345, Suppl. I, p. 587); of as-Subkī (d. 771/1370; see *GAl,* vol. II, p. 89, Suppl. II, p. 105); etc. It is interesting to note that Pfanmüller realizes the fact that Goldziher's study on the Hanbalite movements is based on as-Subkī's *Ṭabaqāt* (Pfanmüller, *Handbuch,* p. 244); he makes the observation, but does not say anything more about it; farther on, however, he approves of the fact that Arnold uses a Mu'tazilite source on the Mu'tazilites,

whereas the works by Steiner, von Kremer, and Houtsma are based on authors who are hostile to Mu'tazilism (Pfanmüller, *op. cit.,* p. 259).

69. Goldziher, "Zur Geschichte der ḥanbalitischen Bewegungen," p. 19, n. 4.
70. Ibn Rajab, *Dhail 'alā Ṭabaqāt al-Ḥanābila,* ed. H. Laoust and S. Dahan (Damascus, PIFD, 1951).
71. Cf. supra, n. 19.
72. Cf. the biographical note which he devotes to Aḥmad b. Ḥanbal, *Ṭabaqāt,* vol. I, pp. 199–221.
73. Concerning Ibn Rajab, see my article in *EI*[2], s.v., and the accompanying bibliography. For information concerning Subkī and his *Ṭabaqāt,* may I refer the reader to my article "Ash'arī and the Ash'arites in Islamic Religious History" in *Studia Islamica,* XVII (1962), pp. 37–80, vol. XVIII (1963), pp. 19–39.
74. See my article mentioned below on p. 268, n. 1.
75. See my article, "Nouveaux détails sur l'affaire d'Ibn 'Aqīl," in *Mélanges Louis Massignon* (Damascus, PIFD, 1956–1957), vol. III, pp. 91–126. Concerning Ibn 'Aqīl's public retraction, see my *Ibn 'Aqil et la résurgence de l'Islam traditionaliste au XI*[e] *siècle,* pp. 426 f.

Part 2: Institutions of Learning and Religious Movements

1. G. Makdisi, "Ash'ari and the Ash'arites in Islamic Religious History," in *Studia Islamic,* XVII (1962), pp. 37–80.
2. Cf. I. Goldziher, *Vorlesungen,* p. 120 (*Dogme,* pp. 98–99).
3. See A. L. Tibawi, "Origin and Character of al-madrasah," in *Bulletin of the School of Oriental and African Studies* (*BSOAS*), XXV (1962), pp. 225–38; cf. page 231 and note 1.
4. For further details on these technical terms, see G. Makdisi, *"Muslim Institutions,"* pp. 10.
5. Ibn al-Jawzī, *al-Muntaẓam fi Tārīkh al Mulūk wa 'l-Umam,* vol. V. 2nd part -X (Haridarabad, 1357–58/1938–39), IX, p. 66; mentioned in my "Muslim Institutions," p. 37 (and in my article "Law and Traditionalism in the Institutions of Learning of Mediaeval Islam," in G. E. von Grunebaum (ed.), *Theology and Law in Islam* (Wiesbaden, 1971), pp. 75–88, see especially p. 82).
6. See G. Makdisi, "The Madrasa as a Charitable Trust and the University as a Corporation in the Middle Ages," in *Actes du V*[e] *Congrès International d'Arabisants et d'Islamisants (1970)* (Brussels, 1972), pp. 329–37; see in particular p. 335 and n. 12.
7. To realize this, one has only to read the biographical accounts of professors who taught in the *madrasas* and in the mosque-schools (*masjid*) at that time, before as well as after the establishment of the Nizamiya.
8. Concerning this, see the autobiographical note of a student of Abū Isḥāq ash-Shīrāzī, in Ibn Jawzī, *Muntaẓam,* X, p. 37, translated in G. Makdisi, "Muslim Institutions," p. 54.
9. G. Makdisi, *op. cit.,* pp. 39–39: Abū Naṣr b. aṣ-Ṣabbāgh (two different times: about twenty days, and at least two years); Abū Isḥāq ash-Shīrāzī (sixteen years); Abū Sa'd Al-Mutawallī (twice, no more than two years each time); Abū'l-Qāsim ad-Dābusī (three years); Abū 'Abd Allāh aṭ-Ṭabarī (one year and several months, concurrently with the next professor); Abū Muḥammad al-Fāmī ash-Shīrāzī (approximately a year and one month).

10. Strictly speaking, the first professor named to the Nizamiya at Baghdad was Abū Naṣr b. aṣ-Ṣabbāgh (d. 477/1084), but he was not appointed to the post by Niẓām al-Mulk, who, as the founder (*wāqif*) and sole administrator of the foundation (cf. my article "The Madrasa as a Charitable Trust," p. 335), was the only one with the authority to appoint or dismiss the titular professor. For the details of the Abū Naṣr b. aṣ-Ṣabbāgh affair, see G. Makdisi, "Muslim Institutions," pp. 31f.
11. Abū Isḥāq ash-shīrāzī, *Kitāb al-Tanbih* (Leiden: E. J. Brill, 1879), French translation by C. H. Bousquet, *Kitāb et-Tanbīh ou Le Livre de l'admonition* (Algiers, n.d.).
12. Abū Isḥāq ash-Shīrāzī, *Kitāb-al Luma' fī Uṣūl al-Fiqh* (Cairo, 1347/1928–29), p. 7 (line 13), p. 8 (line 17), p. 15 (lines 24 and 26), p. 18 (line 1), p. 46 (line 4); see also Ibn Rajab, *Dhail 'alā Ṭabaqāt al-Ḥanābila,* vol. I, ed. H. Laoust-S. Dahan (Beirut, 1957), p. 26 (ed. M. Ḥāmid al-Fīqī, Cairo, 1372/1952, v. 1., p. 20) where Shīrāzī declares his opposition to Ash'arism in *uṣūl al-fiqh: "wa-hadhihi kutubī fī uṣūli'l fiqh aqūlu fī-hā khilāfan l-Ash'arīya."*
13. Ibn al-Jawzī, *Muntaẓam,* vol. VIII, p. 245; G. Makdisi, "Muslim Institutions," p. 19 and n. 1.
14. Bundārī, *Zubdat an-Nuṣra wa-Nukhbat al-Uṣra* (*Histoire des Seljoukides de l'Iraq par al-Bondari*), vol. II, ed. M. Th. Houtsma (Leiden, 1889), p. 32; G. Makdisi, "Muslim Institutions," p. 20 and n. 1.
15. G. Makdisi, *op. cit.,* especially p. 34 (lines 13–19) and n. 3.
16. Cf. G. Makdisi, "The Madrasa as a Charitable Trust," p. 335.
17. Ibn al-Bannā', ms. of the Bibliothèque Ẓāhiriya in Damascus, an autograph diary without title; see G. Makdisi, "Autograph Diary of an Eleventh-Century Historian of Baghdad," in *BSOAS,* XVIII (1956), parts 1–2, XIX (1957), parts 1–3. For the details, see G. Makdisi, "Muslim Institutions," p. 22 and the notes.
18. The reason is, I think, that Niẓām formally reserved for himself, in the charter, the right to appoint the professors and the directors of his foundation (cf., in this regard, my "The Madrasa as a Charitable Trust," p. 335); this was in contrast with Abū Sa'd al-Mustawfī, founder of the *madrasa* of Abū Ḥanīfa; on this, see my "Madrasa and University in the Middle Ages," in *Studia Islamica,* XXXII, p. 263 and n. 2.
19. Sibṭ b. al-Jawzī, *Mir'āt az-Zamān,* Ms. Fonds arabe 1506, in the Bibliothéque Nationale (Paris), folio 198 b; cf. my *Ibn 'Aqīl et la résurgence de l'Islam traditionaliste au XIe siècle* (Damascus: PIFD, 1963), pp. 137–38.
20. *Op. cit.,* pp. 138f.
21. Concerning the plots which revolved around the statesmen, see G. Makdisi, *op. cit.,* ch. III, *passim.*
22. See this recently published work, G. Makdisi, *The Notebooks of Ibn 'Aqīl: Kitāb al-Funūn* (Beirut, 1970–71).
23. Ibn Rajab, *Dhail,* I (ed. Laoust-Dahan), p. 174 (lines 11–12).
24. As, for example, in the 6th/12th century, the *dār al-'ilm* of Ibn al-Māristānīya (d. 599/1203), a Hanbalite scholar who had become interested in the "foreign sciences"; on this, see Ibn Rajab, *Dhail,* I (ed. M. Hāmid al Fiqī), p. 443 (lines 10–11); Ibn al-'Imād, *Shadharāt adh-Dhabab fī Akhbār man Dhahab* (Cairo, 1358/1939), vol. IV, p. 340. Ibn al-Māristānīya was dismissed from his position as manager of the *waqfs* of the "al-Māristān al-'Aduḍī" hospital in Baghdad and was imprisoned in the room for the insane, and his *dār al-'ilm* was sold. He was accused of embezzlement. It would be interesting to study this affair which took place at a time when the Hanbalites had just lost their Hanbalite patron Ibn Yūnus (d. 593/1196), the vizier of the caliph an-Nāṣir.
25. Ḥ. Rashdall, *The Universities of Europe in the Middle Ages* (1895), new edition by F. M. Powicke and A. B. Emden (Oxford, 1936), vol. 1, p. 235.

26. See now G. Makdisi, "Law and Traditionalism in the Institutions of Learning of Mediaeval Islam," in *Theology and Law in Islam,* ed. G. E. von Grunebaum (Wiesbaden, 1971), pp. 79–80.
27. See G. Makdisi, "Muslim Institutions," p. 54.
28. Ibn al-Jawzi, *Muntaẓam,* vol. VIII, p. 205; Ibn al-Athīr, *al-Kāmil fi 't-Tārīkh* (Cairo, 1348/1929 seqq), vol. VIII, p. 88 (*sub anno* 451); G. Makdisi, "The Topography of Eleventh-Century Bagdad," in *Arabica,* vol. VI, pp. 195–6; *EI*[2], s.v. "Dār al-'Ilm" (by D. Sourdel).
29. Cf. Ibn 'Aqīl, *Kitāb al-Jadal* in G. Makdisi, "Le Livre de la dialectique d'Ibn 'Aqīl," *BEO,* vol. XX (1967), pp. 119–206, see especially pp. 119–20. It is the first independent work of *jadal* to be published. I hope some day to prepare a provisional bibliographical list of this science.
30. See his review of W. M. Patton's work (*Aḥmed ibn Ḥanbal and the Miḥna*) in *ZDMG,* vol. LII (1898), pp. 155–58, in particular p. 156.
31. I have already shown this in my study, "Ash'ari and the Ash'arites in Islamic Religious History," in *Studia Islamica,* vols. XVII and XVIII, see in particular vol. XVII (1962), pp. 37–80.
32. Ibn 'Asākir (Abū 'l-Qāsim), *Tabyīn Kadhib al-Muftarī fī-mā Nusiba ilā 'l-Imām Abī 'l-Ḥasan al-Ash'arī* (Damascus, 1347/1928); and Subkī (Tāj ad-Dīn), *Ṭabaqāt ash-Shāfi'īya al-Kubrā* (Cairo, 1324/1906).
33. Cf. my "Ash'ari and the Ash'arites," pp. 70ff.

Part 3: Sufism and Hanbalism

1. I. Goldziher, "Aus der Theologie des Fachr al-din al-Razi," in *Der Islam,* vol. III (1913), pp. 213–47.
2. Ibn al-Walīd and Ibn at-Tabbān; on these two Mu'tazilite teachers of the Hanbalite Ibn 'Aqīl, see G. Makdisi, *Ibn 'Aqīl,* pp. 407f.
3. Cf. my "Ash'ari and the Ash'arites," p. 70ff.
4. Cf. Subkī, *Ṭabaqāt,* vol. IV, pp. 122–31, and al-Murtaḍā az-Zabīdī, *Itḥāf as-Sāda al-Muttaqīn bi-Sharḥ Asrār Iḥya' 'Ulūm ad-Dīn* (Cairo, 1311/1893–94) vol. I, p. 28 (beginning with line 12) and p. 179 (line 21) on al-Ghazzālī, and vol. III, p. 264, on al-Juwaynī. On al-Māzarī (d. 536/1141), a Mālikite belonging to early traditionalist Ash'arism, who was born in Māzara in Sicily and lived in Mahdīya in Spain, see *GAL,* I, p. 663, where there is additional bibliographical information. On the spelling of his *nisba* (Māzarī, Māzirī) it seems that the only correct one is "Māzarī"; cf. Shams ad-Dīn adh-Dhahabī, *al-Mushtabah fī'r-Rijāl, Asmā'ihim wa-Ansābihim* (Cairo, 1962), p. 565, where there is only one spelling "Māzarī" (cf. Yāqūt, *Mu'jam al-Buldān,* ed. F. Wüstenfeld, 6 vols. [Leipzig, 1866–73], *s.v.* "Māzar"; see also the biographical account on al-Māzarī where there are two optional spellings (al-Māzarī or al-Māzirī), in Ibn Khallikān, *Wafayāt al-A'yān wa-Anbā' Abna' az-Zamān,* ed. by Mr. Muḥyī' d-Dīn 'Abd al-Ḥamīd (Cairo, 1948–49), vol. III, p. 413.
5. See G. Makdisi, *Ibn Qudāma's Censure of Speculative Theology* (London, Gibb Memorial, New Series XXIII, 1962).
6. This work by Ibn al-Jawzī is entitled *al-Bāzī'l-Ashhab al-Munqaḍḍ 'alā Mukhālifī'l-Madhhab,* cf. *GAL,* vol I, p. 504, Suppl. I, p. 918 (no. 29).
7. This work by the Hanbalite Ibn al-Jawzī against the Sufi 'Abd al-Qādir al-Jīlānī, also a

Hanbalite, is mentioned under the title *Kitāb fī Dhamm 'Abd al-Qādir* in Ibn Rajab, *Dhail* (ed. Fiqī), vol. II, p. 420 (line 17).

8. J. D. Pearson, *Index Islamicus, 1906–1955* (Cambridge, 1958); with three published supplements dealing with the years 1956–1970.
9. *Op. cit.,* p. 78; "Opponents of Sufism. Ibn al-Gawzi" (Ibn al-Jawzī is cited here as the only opponent of Sufism).
10. Ibn al-Jawzī, *Naqd al-'Ilm wa'l-'Ulamā' aw Tālbīs Iblīs* (Cairo: as-Sa'ada Publishers, 1340/1921–22; and Cairo: al-Munīrīya Publishers, 1369/1950).
11. D. S. Margoliouth, "The Devil's Delusion by Ibn al-Jawzī," in *Islamic Culture* (1935–1938 and 1945–1948); for the pagination see *Index Islamicus, 1906–1955,* p. 78 (bottom of the page).
12. On al-Junayd, see *EI²*, *s.v.* "al-Djunayd" (by A. J. Arberry) and the bibliography given there.
13. On him, see *EI²*, *s.v.* "Abū Ṭālib al-Makkī" (by L. Massignon) and the bibliography given there; add to this F. Sezgin, *Geschichte des arabischen Schrifttums,* vol. 1 (Leiden, 1967), pp. 666–67.
14. Al-Makkī, *Qūt al-Qulūb* (Cairo, 1310/1892); see *GAL,* Suppl. I, pp. 359–60, and *GAS* I, p. 667; identical to *'ilm al-qulūb,* cf. *GAS, loc. cit.,* and *GAL,* I, p. 360, where it is mentioned as an independent work.
15. Al-Ghazzālī, *Iḥyā' 'Ulūm ad-Dīn,* in several editions; for its dependence on *Qūt al-Qulūb* by Makkī, see L. Massignon, *EI²*, article mentioned above; *GAL* I, p. 359, *GAS,* vol. I, p. 667.
16. On him, see *GAL,* vol. I, pp. 361–62; *GAS,* vol. I, pp. 671–74.
17. On the editions of this work, see *GAS,* I, p. 672.
18. Sulamī died in 412/1021; Ghazzālī was born in 450/1058.
19. On al-Qushayrī and his *Risāla,* see *GAL,* I, pp. 770–72.
20. I, Goldziher, *Dogme,* pp. 150–51 (*Vorlesungen,* p. 180).
21. *Dogme,* p. 278, No. 140 (*Vorlesungen,* p. 198, no. 2 of paragraph 16).
22. *Dogme,* pp. 148–49 (*Vorlesungen,* p. 178).
23. Dogme, p. 149 (*Vorlesungen,* p. 178).
24. *Dogme, loc. cit.* (*Vorlesungen, loc. cit.*).
25. *Dogme, loc. cit.* (*Vorlesungen, loc. cit.*).
26. C. H. Becker, *Vom Werden und Wesen der islamischen Welt: Islamstudien* (Leipzig, 1924–32), vol. I, p. 49.
27. *Encyclopedia of Religion and Ethics,* ed. J. Hastings (New York, 1908–1927), XI, p. 448.
28. Subki, *Ṭabaqāt ash-Shāfi'īya,* vol. III, p. 7.
29. *Op. cit.,* vol. III, p. 76.
30. *Op. cit.,* vol. III, p. 76: the title of the work is *Salwat al-'Ārifīn wa-Uns al-Mushtāqīn,* a work written for Abū 'Alī al-Manī'ī (d. 463/1071, a great Shāfi'ite patron; see my *Ibn 'Aqīl,* p. 127, n. 3, and p. 225, n. 5) but which could not compete with al-Qushayrī's *Risāla.* All we have of this work by Abū Khalaf aṭ-Ṭabarī is an abridged edition, of which the manuscript is at Leipzig. Cf., *GAL,* Suppl. I, p. 773.
31. Marijan Molé, *Les Mystiques musulmans* (Paris, 1959).
32. *Op cit.,* pp. 87–88.
33. *Op. cit.,* pp. 35–36.
34. See I. Goldziher, *Dogme,* pp. 144–45 (*Vorlesungen,* p. 173).
35. Ibn Rajab, *Dhail,* I (ed. Laoust-Dahan), p. 68 (line 3): *Anā ḥanbalīyun mā ḥayītu wa-in amut/fa-waṣīyati li 'nāsi an yataḥanbalū.* For other poetry by him in the same

spirit, see *op. cit.*, p. 67 (lines 11–14), p. 83 (lines 13–14). On al-Anṣārī al-Harawī, see especially the article by Serge Laugier de Beaurecueil in *EI*[2], *s.v.*, and the bibliography given there. On 'Abd al-Qādir al-Jīlānī, see the article by W. Braune, *EI*[2], *s.v.*, "'Abd al-Ḳādir al-Djīlī"; for al-Jīlānī's confession of faith, see his work *al-Ghunya li-Ṭālibi Ṭarīq al-Ḥaqq* (Cairo, 1322/1904–5), vol. I, in particular pp. 61–90 (chap. entitled: "Bāb fī Ma'rifat aṣ-Ṣānī'").

36. On him, see G. Makdisi, *Ibn 'Aqīl,* index *s.v.*, and the bibliography given in the notes 1 (p. 352) and 2 (p. 380).
37. On, him, see *EI*[2], *s.v.*, "Ibn Ḳayyim al-Djawziyya" (by H. Laoust), and the bibliography.
38. On al-Anṣārī and this work, see the studies by S. de Beaurecueil, mentioned in the bibliography of his article *s.v.*, "al-Anṣārī al-Harawī" in *EI*[2].
39. Cf. Jīlānī, *al-Ghunya,* I, p. 61–90.
40. See note 10 above.
41. Abu Nu'aym al-Iṣbahānī, *Ḥilyat al-Auliyā' wa Ṭabaqāt al-Aṣfiyā'* (Cairo, 1351–1357/1932–1938); Ibn al-Jawzī's abridgment is entitled *Ṣafwat aṣ-Ṣafwa;* Ibn al-Jawzī made use of other sources there; cf. *GAL,* vol. I, p. 362, Suppl. I, p. 617.
42. Al-Ghazzālī, *Iḥyā' 'Ulūm ad-Dīn* (Cairo, 1358/1939) and other editions; Ibn al-Jawzī's abridgment, of which there is a manuscript in the Biliothèque Nationale in Paris (Fonds arabe 1295), is entitled *Minhāj al-Qāṣidīn.*
43. The *faḍā'il* works on 'Umar b. al-Khaṭṭāb, 'Umar b. 'Abd al-'Azīz, Sa'īd b. al-Musaiyab, Ḥasan al-Baṣrī; and the *manāqib* works on al-Fuḍail b. 'Iyāḍ, Bishr al-Ḥafī, Ibrāhīm b. Adham, Sufyān ath-Thawrī, Aḥmad b. Ḥanbal, Ma'rūf al-Karkhī, and Rābi'a al-'Adawīya; cf. Ibn Rajab, *Dhail* (ed. M. Ḥāmid al-Fiqī), vol. I, p. 418.
44. Ibn al-Jawzi, *Muntaẓam, passim;* one should refer to the table of contents of the biographical notices where Sufis are designated as such and often as "az-zāhid."
45. This work is mentioned in Ibn Rajab, *Dhail* (ed. Fiqī), vol. I, p. 420 (line 17), (*Kitāb fī Dhamm 'Abd al-Qādir*) right after another work against the Caliph an-Nāsir (*'Aqd al-Khanāsir fī Dhamm al-Khalīfat an-Nāṣir*).
46. This work, entitled *Manāqib Rābi'a al-'Adawīya,* is mentioned in Ibn Rajab, *op, cit.*, p. 418 (line 7).
47. H. Laoust, *Essai sur les doctrines sociales et politiques de Takī-d-Dīn Aḥmad b. Taimīya* (Cairo: *PIFAO,* 1939) p. 89 and also pp. 23–32, 89–93.
48. H. Laoust, "Le Ḥanbalisme sous les Mamlouks Bahrides," in *Revue des Études Islamiques* (1960), p. 35 (". . . on chercherait vainement, dans toute son oeuvre, la moindre condamnation du soufism . . .").
49. See Jamāl ad-Dīn aṭ-Ṭalyānī, *Targhīb al-Mutaḥabbīn fī Lubs Khirqat al-Mutamaiyizīn,* ms. preserved in the Chester Beatty Library (Dublin), No. 3296 (8), folios 49a–70b, see fol. 67a: *labistu'l-khirqata l-mubārkata li' sh-Shaikh 'Abd ad-Qādir (al-Jīlānī)wa-bainī wa-bainahū'thanān.*
50. This passage is quoted by Yūsuf b. 'Abd al-Hādī in his *Bad'al-'Ulqa bi-Lubs al-Khirqa,* uncatalogued ms. from the Yahuda Collection at Princeton University, fol. 171b.–172a. (I would like to take this occasion to thank Dr. Rudolf Mach who made the index cards of this collection and his typewritten catalogue available to me.) This passage is quoted from Ibn Nāṣir ad-Dīn (d. 842/1438) who in turn quoted it in his work which is no longer extant: *Iṭfā' Khurqat al-Ḥawba bi-Ilbās Khirqat at-Tawba.* On Ibn Nāṣir ad-Dīn, see the accounts in Sakhāwī, *ad-Daw' al-Lāmi'* (Cairo, 1353–55/1934–36), vol. VIII, pp. 103–6, and Ibn al-'Imād, *Shadharāt adh-Dhahab,* vol. VII, pp. 243–45, where the work is mentioned; it is also mentioned in Ismā'īl b.

Muḥammad al-Bābānī, *Īḍāḥ al-Maknūn fī'dh-Dhail 'alā Kashf aẓ-Ẓunūn,* 2 vols. (Istanbul: Milli Egitim Baismevi, 1945–47), vol. I, p. 95, *s.v.* "*Iṭfā'*."

51. Ibn Taymīya, *Majmū' ar-Rasā'il al-Kubrā* (Cairo, 1323/1905), vol. I, p. 304 (lines 11–13; cf. H. Laoust, *op. cit.*, p. 256, note 2): ". . . *al-asmā' al-latī yasūghu't-tasammī bi-hā . . . intisābi'n-nāsi ilā . . . shaikhin al-Qādirī wa'l-'Adawī wa nahwihim* . . ."
52. G. Makdisi, "The Ḥanbali School and Ṣūfism," *Actes du IVᵉ Congrès d'Études arabes et islamiques, 1969* (Coimbre and Lisbon; in press).
53. Ibn Qudāma, *Le Livre des pénitents, Kitāb at-Tawwābīn,* edited by G. Makdisi (Damascus, 1958), p. 275 (lines 12–13); cf. my article "L'Isnād initiatique soufi de Muwaffaq ad-Dīn Ibn Qudāma" in *Louis Massignon* (Paris, 1970), pp. 88–99.
54. G. Makdisi, *Ibn Quadāma's Censure of Speculative Theology* (London, Gibb Memorial, New Series XXIII, 1962), cf. page 3 of the English translation and p. 5 of the Arabic text; for the part on Ibn 'Aqīl's retraction of al-Ḥallāj which Ibn Qudāma neglects to mention, see G. Makdisi, *Ibn 'Aqīl,* p. 427.
55. See G. Makdisi, the article mentioned in note 53 above.
56. Ibn Ḥajar al-'Asqalānī, *ad-Durar al-Kāmina fi A'yān al-Mi'a ath-thāmina* (Hadarabad, 1348–50/1929–31), vol. IV, p. 264 (no. 728).
57. See his biographical account in Ibn Abī Ya'lā,*Ṭabaqāt al-Ḥanābila,* ed. M. Ḥāmid al-Fiqī (Cairo, 1371/1952), vol. II, p. 139.
58. See his notice in Ibn Abī Ya'lā, *op. cit.*, vol. II, p. 179.
59. See his notice in Ibn Rajab, *Dhail* (ed. Laoust-Dahan), vol. I, pp. 199–205 (ed. Fiqī), vol. I, pp. 166–71.
60. On him, see the article in *EI²*, *s.v.* "Abd al-Kādir al-Djīlī" (by W. Braune) and the bibliography; and see H. Laoust, "Le Hanbalisme sons le califat de Bagdad," in *REI* (1959), pp. 110–12.
61. On him, see my article in *EI²*, *s.v.* "Ibn Ḳudāma" and the bibliographical items, among them H. Laoust, *op. cit.*, pp. 124–25.
62. I shall publish this text in the *Bulletin d'Études Orientales* of the Institut Français de Damas.
63. On Ḥammād ad-Dabbās (d. 525/1131), see G. Makdisi, *Ibn 'Aqīl,* p. 376, note 1, and p. 383, note 1.

Part 4: Muslim Orthodoxy

1. Cf. in the *New Catholic Encyclopedia,* the article "Orthodoxy," *s.v.*
2. I. Goldziher, *Vorlesungen,* p. 182 (*Dogme,* p. 152).
3. *Vorlesungen,* p. 182 (*Dogme,* pp. 152–53).
4. *Vorlesungen,* p. 183 (*Dogme,* p. 154).
5. *Vorlesungen,* p. 183 (*Dogme,* p. 154).
6. *Op. cit., loc. cit.*
7. *Op. cit., loc. cit.*
8. Al-Ghazzālī, *Faiṣal at-Tafriqa baina 'l-Islām wa'z-Zandaqa* (Cairo, 1325/1907).
9. I. Goldziher, *Vorlesungen,* p. 184 (*Dogme,* p. 155).
10. *Vorlesungen,* pp. 137–85 (*Dogme* pp. 111–55).
11. *Vorlesungen,* p. 184 (*Dogme,* p. 155).
12. *Vorlesungen,* p. 200, note 3 (*Dogme,* p. 279, note 154 [instead of note 155 which does not exist]).

12a. The italics are mine.
13. Cf. C. Snouck Hurgronje, "Nieuwe Bijdragen tot te kennis van den Islam," in *Bijdragen tot de Taal-, Landen Volkenkunde van Nederlandsch-Indie,* vol. IV (1882) pp. 357–421; see in particular pp. 399–412 concerning *ijmā';* see also by the same author, "Le Droit musulman," in *Revue de l'Histoire des Religions,* vol. XXXVII (1898), pp. 15–22 and 174–203; see in particular pp. 15–22 and 174–85 on *ijmā';* see also the same author, *Mohammedanism* (New York, 1916), index, *s.v. ijmā'.*
14. I. Goldziher, *Vorlesungen,* p. 182 (*Dogme,* p. 152).
15. *Vorlesungen,* p. 226 (*Dogme,* p. 180).
16. See my "Muslim Institutions of Learning," p. 37, on the *waqf*-deed of the Nizamiya, in which there is no provision for a professor of *kalām;* cf. also my article "The Madrasa as a Charitable Trust," in particular p. 337.
17. See my article "The Madrasa as a Charitable Trust," in particular p. 332.
18. Pontificate: 1878–1903.
19. "Katholische Tendenz und Partikularismus im Islam," *Beiträge zur Religionswissenschaft,* I, 2 (Leipzig, 1914).
20. Ibn Taymīya, *Naqḍ al-Manṭiq,* ed. M. B. 'Abd ar-Razzāq Ḥamza, Sulaimān b. 'Abd ar-Raḥmān aṣ-Ṣanī' and M. Ḥāmid al-Fiqī, with an introduction by 'Abd ar-Raḥmān al-Wakīl (Cairo: as-Sunna al-Muhammadiya, 1370/1951). In fact, only the last quarter of this work deals with logic. Of the 210 pages of this work, only the last 55 are concerned with logic. The remainder deals with the question of orthodoxy.
21. Cf. his work on this subject entitled *ar-Radd 'alā'l-Mantiqīyīn* (Refutation of the Logicians), ed. 'Abd aṣ-Ṣamad Sharaf ad-Dīn al-Kutubī, with an introduction by an-Nadwī (Bombay, 1368/1949); cf. also his work in refutation of what he calls "false dialectic": *Tanbīh ar-Rajul al-Ghāfil 'alā Tamwīh al-Jadal al-Bāṭil;* see may article "The Tanbīh of Ibn Taymīya on Dialectic: The Pseudo-'Aqīlian *Kitāb al-Farq,*" in *Medieval and Middle Eastern Studies in Honor of Aziz Suryal Atiya,* ed. S. A. Hanna (Leiden, E. J. Brill, 1972), pp. 285–94.
22. See *Naqḍ al-Manṭiq,* p. 1 (after page 18 of the introduction by 'Abd ar-Raḥmān al-Wakīl).
23. *Naqḍ,* p. 15: *"innamā nafaqat al-Ash'arīya 'inda 'n-nāsi bi'ntisābihim ilā'l-ḥanābila."*
24. Cf. Abū'l-Ḥasan al-Ash'arī, *al-Ibāna 'an Uṣūl ad-Diyāna* (Haidarabad, 1321/1903), p. 9; English translation by W. C. Klein (New Haven, Conn.: American Oriental Series, vol. 19, 1940), p. 49; cf. I. Goldziher, *Dogme,* p. 99 (*Vorlesungen, p. 121).*
25. *Naqḍ,* pp. 15–16.
26. See L. Gardet, *L'Islam—religion et communauté* (Paris, 1967), p. 200.
27. *Op. cit.,* p. 201.
28. L. Gardet and M.M. Anawati, *Introduction à la théologie musulmane, Essai de théologie comparée* (Paris, 1948), p. vi.

Conclusion

1. Cf. I. Goldziher, *Muhammedanische Studien* 2 vols. (Halle, 1888–1890), vol. II, p. 374, where the author refers to Ash'arite *kalām* as being "the theology of the golden mean" (*Vermittelungstheologie*) and "the only valid form of orthodox belief."

Index